PRACTICAL CRIMINAL EVIDENCE

GREGORY D. LEE, M.P.A.
Supervisory Special Agent (Ret.)
U.S. Drug Enforcement Administration

PEARSON
Prentice Hall

Upper Saddle River, New Jersey 07458

Library of Congress Cataloging-in-Publication Data

Lee, Gregory D., 1953–
    Practical criminal evidence / Gregory D. Lee.—1st ed.
        p. cm.
    Includes index.
    ISBN 0-13-171441-4
    1. Evidence, Criminal—United States.   I. Title.
    KF9660.Z9L44 2007
    345.73'06—dc22

                                        2006009281

Editor-in-Chief: Vern Anthony
Executive Editor: Frank I. Mortimer, Jr.
Assistant Editor: Mayda Bosco
Director of Manufacturing and Production: Bruce Johnson
Managing Editor: Mary Carnis
Production Liasion: Brian Hyland
Manufacturing Buyer: Cathleen Petersen
Senior Design Coordinator: Mary Siener
Marketing Manager: Adam Kloza
Editorial Assistant: Jillian Allison
Cover Design: Robert Aleman
Cover Image: Getty Images

Credits and acknowledgments borrowed from other sources and reproduced, with permission, in this textbook appear on appropriate page within text (or on page XX).

Microsoft® and Windows® are registered trademarks of the Microsoft Corporation in the U.S.A. and other countries. Screen shots and icons reprinted with permission from the Microsoft Corporation. This book is not sponsored or endorsed by or affiliated with the Microsoft Corporation.

Copyright 2007, 2001, 1998, 1994, 1990, 1986 © by Pearson Education, Inc., Upper Saddle River, New Jersey 07458.
Pearson Prentice Hall. All rights reserved. Printed in the United States of America. This publication is protected by Copyright and permission should be obtained from the publisher prior to any prohibited reproduction, storage in a retrieval system, or transmission in any form or by any means, electronic, mechanical, photocopying, recording, or likewise. For information regarding permission(s), write to: Rights and Permissions Department.

Pearson Prentice Hall™ is a trademark of Pearson Education, Inc.
Pearson® is a registered trademark of Pearson plc
Prentice Hall® is a registered trademark of Pearson Education, Inc.

Pearson Education LTD.
Pearson Education Singapore, Pte. Ltd
Pearson Education, Canada, Ltd
Pearson Education—Japan
Pearson Education Australia PTY, Limited

Pearson Education North Asia Ltd
Pearson Educación de Mexico, S.A. de C.V.
Pearson Education Malaysia, Pte. Ltd
Pearson Education, Upper Saddle River, New Jersey

ISBN 0-13-171441-4

Dedication

This book is dedicated to the memory of my father, Brown A. Lee, and to my mother, Dorothy, both of whom taught me so many useful things to prepare me for life.

This book is also dedicated to the men and women of law enforcement, no matter where in the world they serve.

Table of Contents

Preface   xv
About the Author   xvii
Acknowledgements   xxi

CHAPTER 1   Fundamentals of Criminal Evidence   1

Introduction   1
Purpose of Evidence   2
Types of Evidence   2
Rules of Evidence   5
Exclusionary Rule of Evidence   8
The Adversarial System   10
Burden of Proof   10
Constitutional Protections   11
Discovery Process   13
Henthorn Issues   15
Brady Material   16
Jencks Material   17
Giglio Issues   18
Direct Examination   18
Cross-Examination   18
Summary   19
Notes   21

CHAPTER 2   The Criminal Trial Process   22

Introduction   22
The Arrest   23
Court Jurisdiction   24
Indigence Determination   25
Initial Appearance Hearing   26
Detention Hearing   26
Grand Jury   30
Preliminary Hearing   31
Arraignment   32
Discovery   32
Motions   32
Change of Plea   33
Speedy Trial Issues   33
Trial   34
Sentencing   36
Post-Conviction Appeals and Pleadings   37
Appeals   37
    Appellate Decision   37
    Review of Court of Appeals' Decision   37
Summary   38
Notes   39

CHAPTER 3   Pleadings, Motions, Sentencing and Appeals   40

Introduction   40
Pleadings   41
    Not Guilty Plea   41
    Guilty Plea   41
    Nolo Contendere   42
    Double Jeopardy   43
    Not Guilty by Reason of Insanity   43
    Present Sanity   43
Speedy Trial   44
    Statutes of Limitation   44
    Motions   45
    Change of Plea   46
Sentencing   47
    Prosecutor's Role   49
    Probation Officer's Role   50
    Sentencing Guidelines   50
    Defense Attorney's Role   55

Defendant's Role 56
The Victim's Role 56
Appeals 57

Summary 58

Notes 59

CHAPTER 4 — Defense Counsel Role and Strategies 60

Introduction 60

Entrapment 62

Consent 63

Identity 63

Alibi 64

Lack of Motive 64

Criminal Intent 64

Blind Mule 65

Legal Justification 66

Legal Insanity 67

Defendant Involved in a Different Conspiracy 71

Outrageous Government Conduct 73

Summary 75

Notes 76

CHAPTER 5 — The Prosecutor's Role 77

Introduction 77

Prosecutorial Discretion 78

Venue 80

Coordination with the Prosecutor 80

Arrest Warrant Affidavits 81

Search Warrant Affidavits 81

Material Witness Warrants 82

Grand Jury Proceedings and Subpoenas 82

Sealed Indictments and Arrest Warrants 83

Plea-Bargaining 83

Offers of Immunity 83

Pre-Trial Motions 84

Post-Trial Motions 85

Jury Selection 86

Summary 88

CHAPTER 6   Exclusionary Rule of Evidence   90

Introduction   90
Fruit of the Poisonous Tree   92
Exceptions to the Exclusionary Rule   93
  Standing   93
  Good Faith   94
  Attenuation   95
  Independent Source   96
  Inevitable Discovery   99
  Collateral Use of Evidence Seized in Violation
    of the Fourth Amendment   104
Principle of Star Decisis   105
Summary   105
Notes   106

CHAPTER 7   Search Warrants   108

Introduction   108
Reasonableness   109
  Plain View   109
  Abandoned Property   110
Probable Cause   112
  Logical Inferences   112
  Time Affects Probability   113
  Professional Inferences   114
  Probable Cause Mixture   115
Establishing Probable Cause   115
  Basis of Belief   115
  Credibility   117
  Corroboration   119
  Hearsay on Hearsay   121
Constitutional Requirements   123
  Neutral and Detached Judicial
    Officers   123
  Particularly Describing the
    Place to be Searched   123
  The Persons or Things to be Seized   124
  Supported By Sworn Affidavit   126
  Probable Cause to Search   126
  Timeliness   126
  Misstatement of Facts   126
  Telephonic Search Warrants   128
  Anticipatory Search Warrants   128

Warrantless Searches and Exigent
Circumstances   129
Execution of the Search Warrant   134
Officers Present   134
Life of a Warrant   135
Time of Day   135
Knock and Notice   136
Manner of Entry   137
Use of Force   137
Extent of the Search   137
Search Time   138
Things to be Seized   138
Receipt for Seized Property   138
Returning the Warrant to the Court   138
Summary   138
Notes   139

CHAPTER 8   The Crime Scene   141

Introduction   141
Crime Scene Safety   142
Routes of Exposure   142
Bloodborne-Patheogen Safety   144
Chemical Safety   145
Light-Source Safety   146
Confined-Space Safety   147
X-Ray Safety   148
Personal Protective Equipment   148
Hand Protection   148
Eye Protection   149
Foot Protection   149
Respiratory Protection   149
Head Protection   150
Crime Scene Search   150
The Approach   150
Preparation   151
The Initial Approach   152
Preliminary Survey   153
Evaluate Physical Evidence Possibilities   153
The Narrative   153
Photography   154
Crime Scene Sketch   155
Physical Evidence Collecting and Recording   156
Final Survey   156
Release of the Crime Scene   157

Chain of Custody   157
  The Evidence Custodian   157
Summary   158
Notes   159

CHAPTER 9   Physical Evidence   161

Introduction   161
Types of Physical Evidence   162
  Fingerprints   163
  Firearms Examinations   166
  DNA Examinations   167
  Hairs and Fibers Examinations   170
    Computer Examinations   171
    Questioned Documents Examinations   171
    Paint Examinations   175
    Ropes and Cords Examinations   176
Drug Evidence   176
  Clandestine Laboratories   179
  Non-Drug Evidence   180
  Bulk Drug Evidence   180
Summary   181
Suggested Reading   181
Notes   181

CHAPTER 10   Audio, Video, Photographic and Computer
                       Evidence   182

Introduction   182
Audio Tape Recordings   184
  Body Wires   186
  Concealed Microphones   187
  Wiretaps   188
  Videotape Evidence   190
Digital Photographs   191
Computer Evidence   192
Summary   194
Notes   195

CHAPTER 11   Confessions and Admissions   196

Introduction   196
Voluntariness   197
Right to an Attorney   198

Right to Remain Silent   199
Miranda Warnings   202
   Non-Custodial Settings   203
   Detention Settings   204
   Spontaneous Outbursts   207
   Evidence Confrontation   210
   Non-Interrogation Questions   210
   In-Custody Interrogation Settings   210
Elements of the Miranda Warning   211
   Waiver of the Miranda Rights   212
   Ambiguous Responses   214
   Trickery and Deceit   215
   Suspect's Physical Condition   216
Summary   217
Notes   218

CHAPTER 12   Lay and Police Witnesses   220

Introduction   220
Competency   221
Credibility   221
Impeachment   222
Prior Inconsistent Statements   222
Lay Witnesses   223
Child Witnesses   225
Police Witnesses   225
Defendant Witnesses   228
Character Witnesses   229
Informant Witnesses   230
Jailhouse Witnesses   232
Exclusion of Witnesses in the Courtroom   235
Summary   235
Notes   237

CHAPTER 13   Expert Witnesses   238

Introduction   238
Expert Witness Categories   240
   Alcohol and Drug Intoxication   240
   Audio Tape Examinations   240
   Bite Mark Analysis   240
   Blood Grouping and Spatter Analysis   240
   Criminal Profiling   241

DNA (Deoxyribonucleic Acid) Testing   241
Eyewitness Identification   241
Fingerprint Identification   241
Firearms Examiners   241
Forensic Anthropology   242
Forensic Biology   242
Forensic Engineering   242
Forensic Entomology   242
Forensic Odontology   242
Forensic Pathology   242
Forensic Physical Science   242
Forensic Psychiatry   243
Hair and Fiber Analysis   243
Hypnosis   243
Microtrace Analysis   243
Neutron Activation Analysis   243
Photography   243
Physical and Mental Condition   243
Polygraphers   243
Questioned Document Examination   244
Sketch Artists   244
Soil Sample Analysis   244
Speed Detection Devices   244
Tool Mark Analysis   244
Toxicology   245
Traffic Accident Reconstruction   245
Truth Serum Results   245
Typewriter Comparison   245
Voice Comparisons   246

Voir Dire   246

Hired Guns   248

Summary   253

Notes   254

CHAPTER 14   Hearsay Evidence   255

Introduction   255

Exceptions to the Hearsay Rule of Evidence   256

Written Statements   261

   Hostile Witnesses   262

Prior Statements of Witnesses   263

Spontaneous Outbursts   263

Hearsay Within Hearsay   264

Dying Declarations   264

Statements Made by Co-conspirators   265

Admissions and Confessions   266
   Miranda Warnings   267
   Voluntariness   268
Declarations Against Penal Interest   268
Public and Private Records   269
Business Records   269
Summary   269
Suggested Reading   271
Notes   271

CHAPTER 15   Testimonial Privileges   272

Introduction   272
   Self-Incrimination   273
   Immunity From Prosecution   274
   Attorney-Client   275
   Husband and Wife   276
   Physician-Patient and Psychotherapist-Patient   278
   Clergy-Confessor   279
   Official Information Privilege   279
   Confidential Informant Privilege   280
Summary   283
Notes   284

Appendix A   Federal Rules of Evidence   285

Appendix B   Sample Criminal Indictment   318

Appendix C   Sample Search Warrant Affidavit   322

Glossary   335

Index   350

Preface

Anyone engaged in law enforcement must have a working knowledge of the criminal justice system and the rules of evidence. The more knowledge gained, the more effective law enforcement officers will be in obtaining viable evidence that will lead to the truth, bring criminals to justice, and exonerate the innocent.

Practical Criminal Evidence stands out from other criminal evidence textbooks in that it is written by a former practitioner for readers already in law enforcement, or those who aspire to enter the profession. It is obviously not designed to prepare students for the bar exam, but rather is designed to give him or her a good understanding of what evidence is, how it can legally be obtained, and how it is introduced at trial.

The book is replete with *Reality Checks* in which the author uses his 30 years of law enforcement experience to give the reader a real world assessment of a topic. Not only does he discuss how in a perfect world it should be, but also the way it usually is, and the many challenges law enforcement officers will face at trial.

Included in the textbook are chapters ranging from explaining the criminal trial process, the role prosecutors and defense attorneys play, as well as physical and testimonial evidence. A comprehensive chapter on obtaining search warrants is included, because police officers rely heavily on them to gather evidence and need to understand the Constitutional requirements specified in the 4th Amendment. A summary of each chapter is included to re-emphasize important teaching points, as well as a glossary of important terms that student need to understand.

Practical Criminal Evidence serves as a reference book for law enforcement officers, when they need to refer to a particular topic concerning the admissibility of evidence. The chapter on search warrants should prove to be especially useful during one's police career, as well as the appendices that include an actual affidavit for a state search warrant, which can be used as a guide.

About the Author

Gregory D. Lee retired as a Supervisory Special Agent for the United States Department of Justice, Drug Enforcement Administration (DEA) in late 2003. He resides with his wife, Virginia, in Pebble Beach, California.

Throughout his diverse government career, he has conducted and supervised numerous international drug conspiracy investigations. At one time he was the Resident Agent-in-Charge of DEA's Karachi, Pakistan office.

While in Pakistan from 1994 to 1998, Mr Lee became personally involved in several notable terrorism investigations, and participated in the arrest of Ramzi Ahmed Yousef, the mastermind behind the 1993 World Trade Center bombings. He collected evidence in the case, and later testified at Yousef's trial. Through informants, he also assisted the FBI in locating Amil Kanzi, the terrorist responsible for the murder of two CIA employees outside their headquarters in 1993. He also supervised and conducted the initial investigation of the murder of four U.S. citizen employees of the United Texas Petroleum Company, and their Pakistani driver, in Karachi, Pakistan, and collected and preserved evidence pending the arrival of FBI Special Agents.

As a result of his terrorism experiences in Pakistan, he has lectured for, and consulted with various agencies within the U.S. Intelligence Community. He also appeared in an episode of the Discovery Channel's *The FBI Files*, concerning his actions during the Kanzi investigation.

Mr Lee taught conspiracy investigations, drug smuggling, informant management, and many other courses, as an instructor at DEA's Office of Training, located at the FBI Academy in Quantico, Virginia. He developed and taught week-long conspiracy investigation seminars for federal, state, and local law enforcement officers and members of the intelligence community around the country. He spent a year as a member of one of DEA's International Training Teams, visiting many countries to provide conspiracy and drug law enforcement training to foreign law enforcement officials.

He is the author of two other textbooks, *Global Drug Law Enforcement: Practical Investigative Techniques*, published by CRC Press, and *Conspiracy Investigations: Terrorism, Drugs and Gangs*, published by Prentice Hall.

He has written several articles on drug enforcement topics for professional publications, including the *FBI Law Enforcement Bulletin*, and *The Police Chief* magazine. Mr Lee also served as a counselor for the 160th Session of the FBI National Academy in 1990.

Prior to working for DEA, he was a police officer for the cities of Salinas and Pasadena, California.

Mr Lee has a combination of over 34 years of active duty and U.S. Army Reserve service, and is a Chief Warrant Officer 5/Special Agent with the U.S. Army Criminal Investigation Command, better known as CID. As an Army Reservist, he is an associate instructor with the U.S. Army Military Police School, as a Subject Matter Expert in counter-drug operations and terrorism.

Shortly after the attacks on America on September 11, 2002, he was called to active duty and served a year at the U.S. Army Operations Center's Anti-Terrorism Operations Intelligence Cell at the Pentagon. During this year, he routinely analyzed highly classified intelligence data and briefed the Army's top leadership on terrorism and force protection issues.

Mr Lee earned a Master of Public Administration in Justice Administration degree from Golden Gate University, San Francisco, California and a Bachelor of Science in Sociology with dual minors in Vocational Education and Criminology from the University of Maryland. While attending graduate school, he taught a criminal investigation course for Monterey Peninsula College, Monterey, California.

He is a frequent guest speaker and has lectured at national and international forums, such as the Defense Intelligence Agency, International Law Enforcement Academy, Bangkok, Thailand, California Narcotic Officers' Association, the International Narcotic Interdiction Association, and the U.S. Military Academy, West Point.

In 2005, he was selected as the Lead Instructor and Manager of the U.S. Department of State's Antiterrorism Assistance Program's *Preventing, Investigating, and Interdicting Terrorism* course held in Islamabad, Pakistan.

More information can be obtained about Mr Lee from his website: www.gregorydlee.com, where his email address is also available. He encourages students and professors to contact him with questions and comments regarding this and his other works.

Acknowledgements

Many people wittingly and unwittingly helped me in the preparation of *Practical Criminal Evidence*.

My good friend, John A. Blanchard, recounted his many years of police experience, emphasizing what he believed officers needed to understand concerning criminal evidence. Mike Terrell, Assistant U.S. Attorney (AUSA) for the Central District of California, helped by making complicated legal concepts concerning admissibility understandable. Retired Los Angeles County Superior Court Judge Enrique Romero taught me, as a young DEA Special Agent, the importance of solid evidence during the many arduous criminal trials we endured together against many high profile attorneys, when he was an aggressive AUSA in Los Angeles.

Thanks also go to California Department of Justice Special Agent supervisor Gary Edgington, who provided me with a genuine search warrant affidavit that he wrote (Appendix C) that led to the seizing of evidence and the convictions of several defendants for a fraudulent investment scheme.

I would also like to thank DEA Special Agent Attorney Edward M. Hendrie, of the Office of Training, for his contributions in authoring valuable training material I reviewed for this book.

Thanks also to all those relentless, Los Angeles, California criminal defense attorneys I faced as a DEA special agent during complicated trials. These attorneys include Howard Weitzman, Leslie Abramson, Jerry Cobb, Don Re, and Tony Brooklier. Their innovative approaches to defending their clients made me a better agent, who became keenly aware of the trial tactics used by some of the nation's top criminal defense attorneys.

Fundamentals of Criminal Evidence

In order to be effective and professional, police officers and especially criminal investigators must recognize the different categories of evidence, how to collect and preserve it, and what the rules are governing criminal evidence. They are not expected to be skilled attorneys, but they must possess a good understanding of the rules of evidence, criminal procedure, and the trial process in order to avoid mistakes that could jeopardize a successful outcome in court.

Throughout their careers, police officers will be searching for, collecting, handling, and processing evidence. As in any profession, expertise comes from study and experience. The decisions police officers make, as to whether to seize an item as evidence or not, could later have a profound impact on a criminal trial. As a rule of thumb, when in doubt, seize it. Something may appear unimportant now, but become highly significant later. Officers seldom are given a second opportunity to collect a valuable piece of evidence after abandoning it at a crime scene.

Criminal evidence is anything that is offered to prove or disprove a fact. Evidence can be testimony, writings, physical objects, circumstances, or any other credible thing. Criminal evidence is admissible information allowed in a court of law; proof is the desired effect of the evidence. Without evidence,

1

criminals cannot be identified, indicted, arrested, prosecuted, or convicted. It is what criminal investigators, police officers, and prosecutors strive to obtain to prove to a jury that a crime occurred and that the defendant is the perpetrator of the offense.

PURPOSE OF EVIDENCE

Evidence serves several purposes. It is offered in court as an item of proof; to impeach a witness; or even to rehabilitate the credibility of a witness.

Evidence is primarily offered for the purpose of proving a fact at issue. The prosecutor will offer evidence to prove the elements of the crime that the defendant is charged with, as well as other evidence to prove he committed the offense. The defendant will usually offer other evidence to establish a defense or alibi.

Evidence serves as a means to attack a witness' credibility, or to rehabilitate a witness whose credibility has been weakened or destroyed. Calling other witnesses to corroborate or dispute a witness' previous testimony does this.

Evidence is also used to assist in determining the appropriate sentence a convicted defendant will receive. Only at this time may the prosecutor introduce the defendant's previous criminal record. The defense also has the opportunity to introduce character witnesses to attest to the defendant's character and good reputation.

TYPES OF EVIDENCE

There are three basic types of evidence used in U.S. courts: direct, circumstantial, and real.

Direct evidence is positive, and directly proves the fact in dispute. For example, an eyewitness testifies that he saw the defendant commit the crime.

Circumstantial evidence relates to facts other than those in issue. For example, a prosecution witness hears three gunshots from inside a motel room. He then observes the defendant run from the room's only exit. The witness enters the room to find the victim dead on the floor. Has the prosecutor proved that the defendant killed the victim?

Not quite. Circumstantial evidence complements direct evidence. In this example, assuming the facts above, the prosecutor will elicit testimony from the witness that he did not see or hear anyone else in the room at the time of the shooting.

The prosecutor will need to prove that there are no other exits in the motel room. Testimony from the hotel manager along with photographs of the crime scene can serve this purpose.

The prosecutor will also call on the arresting police officer, who will say that a search of the defendant at the time of his arrest produced a pistol.

A crime scene investigator will testify that the defendant's fingerprints were found inside the motel room.

A medical examiner will testify that he retrieved the bullets from the body of the victim, and that it is his or her opinion that the wounds were not self-inflicted.

A firearms examiner will testify that the bullets found in the victim were scientifically proven to have been fired from the weapon the defendant possessed at the time of his arrest.

If possible, the prosecutor will attempt to establish motive to show the reasons why the defendant wished the victim harm. Proving motive, however, is not necessary to obtain a conviction.

The elements of the crime may be established by direct or circumstantial evidence, or a combination of both. In any event, the prosecutor is required to prove guilt beyond a reasonable doubt.

Given the totality of the evidence, a reasonable jury most likely would conclude that the defendant shot and killed the victim, despite the lack of a credible eyewitness to the actual event.

Criminal evidence can be found in many different forms: physical, scientific, testimonial, expert opinion, circumstantial, and documentary to name a few. Many criminal investigations produce all these forms of evidence before a suspect is developed and later arrested. Investigators need to collect all available evidence and conduct every scientific examination possible, even if redundancy takes place.

For example, a convenience store owner notified the police that his business had been burgled. A hidden video camera inside the store captures the images of a man, not wearing gloves, breaking a window to gain entry, and then stealing the cash register. The owner of the store recognizes the man as a long-time customer he has had problems with in the past.

The police locate the customer who looks exactly like the man in the videotape. The man cannot account for his whereabouts during the time of the burglary. The cash register is later recovered in a dumpster near where the man lives. Is it necessary for the police to search for the man's fingerprints on the cash register and the counter where the cash register was kept?

Yes. Not collecting available fingerprints may leave a reasonable doubt in the mind of a juror who believes there may be someone else who looks like the defendant. Even if the defendant admits to the police during an interrogation that he committed the burglary, the fingerprints should still be collected. Many issues could arise that may cause the confession to be inadmissible, and the police must then rely solely on physical evidence that may still produce a conviction.

Physical evidence, also referred to as ***real*** or ***demonstrative evidence***, is anything that speaks for itself and requires no explanation, merely its identification through testimony. It can be a firearm, a bullet fragment, a dead body, an ounce of cocaine, a photograph, a fingerprint, or a recorded telephone conversation. Physical evidence is subject to scientific analysis by the prosecutor and defense to further enhance or destroy its credibility.

Testimonial evidence is just that. A witness, who must be under oath, testifies to what he or she has seen, heard, did, or did not do.

Expert opinion may be given in sworn testimony about a scientific examination of physical evidence, or the particular investigative procedures used by the police, if the expert possesses the necessary expertise and qualifications to offer such opinions.

Documentary evidence can be a hotel registration card, rental car contract, lease agreement, credit card receipt, or anything else that tends to prove a fact. For example, a police informant says the defendant rented a storage unit to conceal a methamphetamine laboratory. The police develop probable cause to obtain a search warrant for the storage unit and find the necessary equipment and chemicals to manufacture methamphetamine. A rental agreement would document that the defendant rented the storage unit, and therefore had access to the laboratory equipment and chemicals.

Documentary evidence is subject to the *Best evidence rule* that provides that the best evidence of the content of the document is the actual document itself. Original documents must be obtained as evidence unless there is an adequate reason why they are not available. When investigators locate an original document that they feel is necessary to prove an issue later, they should take the opportunity to seize it immediately, rather than rely on its custodian to maintain it. Documents have a tendency to get destroyed, misplaced, or archived, and the opportunity to obtain the original document later may be lost forever.

There are other types of evidence, such as positive or negative evidence. *Positive evidence* is when a witness states that something did or did not happen, occur, or exist. *Negative evidence* is when a witness states that he does not know anything about the event in question.

Impeachment is when the credibility of either a prosecution or defense witness is directly challenged.

Prima Facie evidence suffices for the proof of a particular fact until contradicted or overcome by other evidence.

Cumulative evidence is additional evidence of the same character to the same point.

Corroborative evidence is additional evidence of a different character to the same point.

No matter what form evidence takes, it is needed before any jury can conclude, beyond a reasonable doubt and moral certainty, that the defendant committed the offense he is accused of. A jury should be overwhelmed with evidence of the defendant's guilt, whenever possible.

FIGURE 1.1   Having finishing deliberations, a jury takes a vote on the verdict in the jury room. *Getty Images.*

RULES OF EVIDENCE

The admissibility of criminal evidence in both criminal and civil court proceedings is governed by a set of ***rules of evidence*** that exists either at the federal or state court levels.[1] Most states utilize federal rules of evidence with few revisions. These rules are designed to shield the jurors from being misled or confused during the court proceedings, and to protect and secure a fair trial for the defendant. They were established to assist the jury to arrive at the truth, and prevent undue prejudice toward the defendant. They are used as the basis to qualify evidence to ensure that it is credible, dependable, material, and trustworthy before the judge or jury can consider it. Evidence is generally admissibility if it deals with the essential circumstances surrounding the point at issue and if it tends to be material, logical, and natural by reasonable inference.

Rules of evidence also serve well in expediting a trial. Without rules of evidence, no trial would be completed in a reasonable time. Trial judges determine the admissibility of evidence while the jury ultimately has the responsibility of determining the quality and credibility of the totality of evidence, in order to determine the defendant's guilt or innocence.

Before an item of evidence can be admitted in court, it must pass a three-prong test of relevancy, competency, and materiality.

Relevant evidence relates to the case at hand and is confided to the point at issue. The rules of evidence strive to exclude material not connected with the case. Evidence is irrelevant and not admissible when it is not supporting, relating, or applicable to the matter in issue.

For example, the police develop a witness who saw the defendant give the victim a cup of coffee that was later determined to contain poison. This would be highly relevant because the witness essentially saw the murder take place. It would be irrelevant if a murder victim drank a cup of coffee on the day he was shot by the defendant.

In another example, if a murder victim were shot with a pistol, it would be relevant that the defendant is a gun owner who is an expert marksman. It would be irrelevant that the defendant is an expert with a bow and arrow.

Evidentiary matters that are considered relevant, and therefore admissible, would include:

- Motive for the crime
- The ability of the defendant to commit the crime
- The defendant having an opportunity to commit the crime
- Threats made by the defendant toward the victim
- The defendant possessed the means to commit the offense, for example, possession of the type of weapon used in the offense
- Physical evidence located by the police at the scene of the crime that links the defendant to the crime scene
- The defendant's conduct and spontaneous comments at the time of his arrest
- Attempts made by the defendant to conceal his identify or flee prosecution
- Attempts made by the defendant to destroy evidence
- Valid confessions made by the defendant to the police.

Competent evidence is that which is adequately sufficient, reliable, and relevant to the case and is presented by a qualified and capable witness. A witness commonly fulfills the requirements of competency if he has enough intelligence to understand the nature of an oath to tell the truth. This includes the affirmation or declaration under penalty or perjury similar to: "Do you solemnly swear (or affirm) to tell the truth, the whole truth, and nothing but the truth?"

A competent witness is judged on the stand by the jurors for his ability to observe, recall, and communicate with the jury. Children and older people with mental deficiencies may not be competent as witnesses. Physical defects the witness has may also have a bearing on his competency. A myopic person who did not wear his glasses at the time of the event may not be competent to testify about what he saw on the day in question.

A witness' credibility must be established by first laying a foundation. Examples of how prosecutors and defense attorneys do this is by:

- Explaining how the witness acquired his knowledge that he is about to testify about
- Demonstrating the witness has good intentions
- Showing that the witness is honest
- Showing that the witness is dishonest
- Establishing the witness' opportunity to have knowledge concerning the things he will testify about
- The witness' conduct on the witness stand
- The witness' manner of testimony
- The witness' interest, or lack there of, in the outcome of the case.

Attacks on the witness' credibility usually come from the following areas:

- Previous inconsistent statements with the presented testimony
- Proof that a witness' statements are not true
- Showing that a witness is biased, has personal interest, or hostility toward the defendant
- Demonstrating the witness lacks character through the use of criminal records or reputation
- Proving the witness has a physical or mental defect
- Showing that the witness lacks religious or ethical beliefs that would prevent him from having the obligation to tell the truth.

Defense attorneys sometimes wage effective attacks on an informant's credibility. Investigators must divulge the informant's past criminal activity and bad acts to the prosecutor to determine if these can be overcome to establish the informant's credibility.

In a recent federal case, an informant was used to make several purchases of controlled substances from a defendant. The informant lacked any criminal record, and gave the appearance of being honest and trustworthy. He testified that he had worked as an informant for the Drug Enforcement Administration (DEA) for the past three years, and had received compensation for his services.

Prior to trial, the defense hired a private investigator to look into the informant's background. The investigator determined that the informant had recently applied for a loan to purchase a home. The lender allowed the investigator to look at the informant's loan application in which his last three federal income tax returns were attached to verify income.

The investigator noted that nowhere on the tax returns did the informant declare any income derived from payments made by DEA, and therefore did not pay personal income taxes on the money received during the entire time he received compensation.

The defense attorney asked the informant under oath on the witness stand if he had ever paid federal income taxes on any of the money he earned while an informant for DEA. Not realizing that the defense attorney had access to his previous tax returns, the informant claimed that he had.

The defense proceeded to call the lender who testified about his reviewing the informant's tax return showing that no taxes had ever been paid. During a recess, the informant was asked about this, and he admitted to lying, and that he had in fact, never paid income taxes on money he earned from DEA, despite being instructed to do so.

The fact that the informant never declared paying federal income taxes on earnings from the DEA had absolutely nothing to do with the defendant selling drugs. However, this information completely destroyed his credibility as a witness.

Investigators should ask probing questions of any potential prosecution witness to satisfy himself or herself the witness will be credible in the eyes of the judge and jury. This is especially true for informants who are generally viewed as being inherently untrustworthy and unreliable.

Evidence materiality is determined by its relevance to the case, if it can substantiate a matter in dispute, and if it has a legitimate and effective influence on the decision of the jury. Materiality and relevancy are closely related, and is a degree of relevancy.

For example, if the defendant's automobile was located in the vicinity of a recent burglary, it would be material. It would be immaterial that the defendant was out of town a week after the burglary.

Corpus Delicti, or the elements of a crime, also known as the body of the crime, governs proof of the commission of crimes. Rules of evidence typically deal with evidence that deals with proof of the commission of crimes.

The prosecutor must satisfy the court that a crime was committed, or prosecution cannot be further pursued. The amount of proof does not have to go beyond prima facie proof. The corpus delicti may be proven by means of only circumstantial evidence. Murder trials are sometimes held despite the victim never being located. Most rules of evidence do not provide for the establishment of the corpus delicti of a crime solely based upon the *confession* or *admission* of the accused. Confessions and admissions differ. A *confession* is the acknowledgement of guilt whereas an *admission* is the admitting of material facts not amounting to guilt. Proof must be established, independent of any extra-judicial statements made by the defendant.

EXCLUSIONARY RULE OF EVIDENCE

The *Exclusionary rule of evidence* provides that evidence illegally obtained by the police as a result of unlawful searches and seizures as well as some confessions.

Evidence obtained by police officers in violation of the Fourth Amendment to the Constitution was at one time admissible in federal and state courts. In a 1914 United States Supreme Court decision, *Weeks* v. *U.S.*,[2] the court ruled that all evidence obtained by searches and seizures in violation of the Federal Constitution was inadmissible in a criminal trial in *federal* court. This ruling gave birth to what has become known as the exclusionary rule.

The exclusionary rule renders evidence inadmissible when it was illegally obtained, even though the exclusion of evidence is not specifically mentioned in the constitution. The court reasoned that excluding evidence that was obtained unconstitutionally would serve to deter federal officers from violating someone's Fourth Amendment rights.

Another reason for the adoption of the exclusionary rule is to maintain the dignity and integrity of the courts by keeping tainted evidence away from the courtroom and relieving the courts from participating in the illegal conduct of police officers.

The exclusionary rule in court proceedings is applicable in other than criminal trials, including juvenile proceedings, narcotics commitment procedures, and asset forfeiture proceedings. There are some types of judicial proceedings where illegally obtained evidence may be held admissible simply because the deterrent purpose of the rule is deemed outweighed by public policy favoring the use of any relevant evidence, even if it is illegally obtained. A parole revocation proceeding is an example of such a judicial proceeding where illegally obtained evidence is sometimes allowed. The sentencing hearing of a defendant may also consider illegally obtained evidence, even though it was not considered at trial.

In another landmark U.S. Supreme Court decision, *Mapp* v. *Ohio*,[3] the court extended the Fourth Amendment exclusionary rule to state courts as well.

The court's ruling caused the states to initiate procedures for the conduct of what are known as ***suppression hearings***, sometimes called ***evidentiary hearings***, to determine if evidence seized in violation of the Fourth Amendment should be excluded at trial.

Other U.S. Supreme Court decisions followed *Mapp* in which the court extended the exclusion of evidence located beyond a Fourth Amendment violation. These cases spawned the doctrine known as ***fruits of the poisonous tree***.

For example, a police officer stops a vehicle for a traffic violation. The officer asks the driver for permission to search his vehicle for illegal drugs. The driver adamantly refuses. The officer removes the driver from the car and handcuffs him. He searches the vehicle anyway, but does not find any controlled substances. However, he does find a notebook that contains a list of addresses the writer identifies as "stash houses." The officer calls narcotics detectives who later visit these locations and find copious amounts of cocaine in several of them. The fruit of the poisonous tree doctrine would require the notebook, as well as the cocaine found at these locations, to be suppressed at trial.

To avoid undue prejudice of the accused, other items are routinely excluded as evidence at trial. A defendant's criminal record is generally not admissible, except to impeach his testimony. Allowing this record as evidence might unduly prejudice the accused in the minds of the judge and jury.

Except under certain conditions, hearsay and opinion testimony is not allowed during a trial. There are many exceptions that will be discussed later.

THE ADVERSARIAL SYSTEM

The criminal justice trial system enjoyed in the United States is known as the *adversarial system*. It is comparable to an Olympic boxing match between two well-prepared athletics. The trial judge acts as the referee, determining admissibility of evidence, and the jury serves as the judges of the match, determining which attorney scored the most points to win the contest. The system is designed to discover facts that will prove the defendant is guilty of the charges against him or determine if a reasonable doubt exists to not convict. If the prosecutor alone presented a case without the benefit of an advocate for the defendant, there would be no trial. Both sides are necessary to prove the case against the defendant.

Because the prosecutor has the burden of proving the defendant is guilty, he is afforded the opportunity to present his case first. He also is first to address the jury during opening statements, and is allowed to address the jury twice at closing arguments. The defense is not required to prove innocence.

The trial procedure is conducted in the following order:

- The prosecutor's main case is presented, in which the defense is allowed to cross-examine each witness that is produced.
- The defense then presents its case, although there is no obligation to do so. The prosecutor may cross-examine the witnesses.
- The prosecutor can than present "rebuttal" witnesses to testify in dispute of any facts raised by the defense during its presentation.
- The defense may then present "rejoinder" evidence to dispute any evidence presented during the prosecutor's rebuttal.

The judge makes sure the prosecutor and defense introduces all of their evidence when they first present their cases. The judge alone determines if an objection by either side will be sustained or overruled.

BURDEN OF PROOF

A defendant in a criminal trial is presumed to be innocent until the contrary is proved. In the case of a reasonable doubt whether the defendant is guilty or not, he is entitled to an acquittal.

Reasonable doubt is not possible doubt. It is what jurors experience in their minds after considering the totality of evidence that leaves them unable to conclude the guilt of the defendant. The law does not require the prosecutor to present proof to the degree that it eliminates any possibility of error. Only moral certainty is required. The defendant's failure to substantiate his defense does not relieve the prosecutor from his burden to prove guilt beyond a reasonable doubt.

There is a substantial difference between a defendant being found *not guilty* and being innocent. Not guilty is a legal plea entered by the defendant to the charges against him. All defendants acquitted are not legally guilty of the offense, but this does not necessary mean they are innocent of the allegations. If during trial, the prosecutor feels that the evidence presented by the defense proves the defendant to be truly innocent, as opposed to legally not guilty, he is morally obligated to dismiss the charges against the defendant. This is a rare event in deed, something seen more often in movies than in actual courtrooms.

The decision to prosecute someone is never taken lightly. Conviction can result in the deprivation of the defendant's liberty and/or property. The prosecutor must be satisfied from the police investigation that a crime occurred, and that the defendant is the one who can be proven responsible for committing it. If he had doubts about the culpability of the suspect, he should not allow criminal charges to be filed against the defendant.

In criminal cases, the defense, on the other hand, is not required to prove anything. Even if the defendant introduces evidence that he did not have the opportunity to commit the crime, or acted in self-defense, the burden of proof does not shift to the defense.

CONSTITUTIONAL PROTECTIONS

In criminal trials, the prosecutor represents the government, whether it is a federal or state criminal matter. The defense attorney represents the defendant. In multiple-defendant cases during the same trial, each defendant is entitled to his own representation in order to remove any conflict of interest. Defendants, who can afford it, can hire more than one attorney to represent him in his defense. The public defender's office consists of civil servant attorneys who represent indigent defendants at no cost to them. In military justice matters, defendants are entitled to a military attorney free of charge as part of the benefits that all service members enjoy. Military defendants can also hire their own representation to use in addition to their appointed military counsel.

The Fourth Amendment to the U.S. Constitution provides: "The right of the people to be secure in their persons, houses, papers, and effects, against unreasonable searches and seizures, shall not be violated, and no warrants shall issue, but upon probable cause, supported by oath or affirmation, and particularly describing the place to be searched, and the persons or things to be seized." This amendment has set the standards by which all search warrants are obtained by the police. A detailed discussion will take place in Chapter 13.

Under the Fifth Amendment to the U.S. Constitution, the government is precluded from placing an individual on trial twice for the same offense, whether or not the person was convicted or acquitted. The **double jeopardy** clause of the amendment established the principle in law that a person who has been accused of a crime shall not be subjected to more than one prosecution when the results of the trial action produced either an acquittal or conviction. The provision was designed to prevent the defendant from being subjected to continued expense, embarrassment, and the possibility of being found guilty when he is in fact innocent.

The constitutional provision prevents second prosecutions of both the identical offense involved in the first trial, or for any other offense based upon the criminal act. Similar provisions appear in many state laws. For example, the California Penal Code provides that "no person can be subjected to a second prosecution for a public offense for which he has once been prosecuted and convicted or acquitted."[4]

For example, O.J. Simpson was acquitted of murder, despite what many believed was overwhelming evidence to the contrary. He can never be tried for the murder of his wife and her friend again.

However, when a crime has occurred that is a violation of both state and federal law, the defendant can be tried for the same crime in both jurisdictions. Thus, if a defendant is found not guilty in state court, if applicable, he could then be tried in a federal court for essentially the same offense. This is not often done, but if warranted, a second trial may take place.

The Fifth Amendment also provides that a citizen is not compelled to be a witness against himself. Therefore a defendant does not have to appear as a witness during a criminal proceeding, and does not have to answer any questions of the police other than for the purpose of establishing his or her identity.

In yet another landmark decision, *Miranda* v. *Arizona*,[5] the U.S. Supreme Court ruled that when the police have a suspect in custody, they must advise him, prior to any interrogation, that he has the right to remain silent; that anything he tells them can be used against him at trial; that he has the right to counsel; and if he cannot afford an attorney but desires one, one will be appointed to him before any questioning.

If a suspect refuses to waive his **Miranda rights**, and the police interrogate him anyway, under the exclusionary rule, any incriminating statements he makes would also be excluded in retaliation for the police ignoring the defendant's right to legal council.

Following the *Miranda* decision, the U.S. Supreme Court has made it clear, though, that only the defendant's statements made as a result of not

FIGURE 1.2   A defense attorney gives guidance to her client while in the courtroom. *Getty Images.*

being given a Miranda warning would become inadmissible, not other evidence later developed from the confession.

Under the Sixth Amendment to the U.S. Constitution, the right to counsel is guaranteed. Defendants, however, do not have to exercise that right, and may elect to represent themselves. When a defendant waives his right to counsel and elects to represent himself, in most cases the judge will still appoint an attorney to act as his legal advisor in order to expedite the trial and offer him prudent advise. Most judges will attempt to convince a defendant to obtain an attorney because they subscribe to the old adage, "a defendant who represents himself has a fool for an attorney."

DISCOVERY PROCESS

The *discovery process* is when the prosecutor and the defense disclose to each other certain evidence they intend to introduce at trial. With such disclosure, the parties can prepare in advance to test that evidence through cross-examination or expert testimony, ensuring that the judge or jury hears all sides of the case before they decide guilt or innocence. Avoiding trial by surprise is a surer route to the truth. The discovery rules that govern all federal trials require the disclosure of statements of witnesses testifying, evidentiary items intended to be used at trial, and any exculpatory information beneficial to the defendant.[6,7] Federal courts have some of the most liberal discovery rules in the nation.

The goal of the American system of criminal justice is to allow truth to prevail. One way that courts endeavor to find the truth is through pretrial discovery.

Despite there being "no general constitutional right to discovery in a criminal case,"[8] the rules of criminal procedure dictate the type of information that must be shared by the adversaries in any criminal proceeding. Rule 16 of the Federal Rules of Criminal Procedure outlines what material the government *shall* provide to the defense and, likewise, what material the defense *shall* provide to the government.[9] These are not requests for material; both sides are compelled to furnish this information. However, neither the Federal Rules of Criminal Procedure nor the Federal Rules of Evidence address the disclosure of information pertaining to the credibility of witnesses, including police witnesses. This is where the notion due process, also known as fundamental fairness, become relevant to the issue.[10]

Reality Check!

Police officers should realize that through the rules of evidence and pretrial motions, there is a good likelihood that the defense will receive all the material he requests. The entire process can become lengthy and cumbersome. Investigators should be prepared for the eventuality that everything created during the investigative process will be seen by the defense.

The police must be open and up-front with the prosecutor on what material exists, as he will be the one to argue before the court why certain materials should not be disclosed.

Typical items that may be made available for discovery include:

- Initial police reports
- Reports of investigation
- Investigators' handwritten notes
- Crime Laboratory reports and their findings
- Memorandums and e-mails
- Photographs used in line-ups
- Medical examiner reports
- The names, address, and contact telephone numbers of prosecution witnesses
- All written and signed statements of the defendant
- True copies of all audio and videotapes made during the course of the investigation

- Transcripts of tape recorded statements of the defendant
- Any written statements of prosecution witnesses
- In many cases, the written statements of confidential informants
- Copies of audio tapes created during wire taps
- Evidentiary items intended to be used at trial.

HENTHORN ISSUES

In order to maintain the public trust, law enforcement agencies conduct background investigations of applicants and often go to extraordinary lengths to ensure that they hire officers of good moral character, with backgrounds free of negative information. Police agencies are no different from other organizations in that they strive to hire people who have demonstrated a consistent pattern of honesty, trustworthiness, and mores. Besides seeking stellar candidates, police agencies have another essential reason to screen potential officers. A single indiscretion or lie can taint an officer's credibility and permanently damage him as a prosecution witness. The most compelling reason why police officers with credibility problems lose their viability as witnesses is based on the constitutional principle that defendants are entitled to a fair trial.

For example, the recent release of several convicted defendants in an extensive drug investigation in Tulia, Texas makes the point. A State judge concluded that the lead undercover investigator involved in the case had "falsified reports, misrepresented the nature and extent of his investigative work, and misidentified various defendants during his investigation."[11] All 38 convictions in the case were eventually vacated. Such a judicial finding will render the officer incompetent to testify in any future matters.

Donald Gene Henthorn was convicted of conspiring to import and possess cocaine with the intent to distribute, and for travel in interstate and foreign commerce in aid of racketeering enterprises. During the discovery process, Henthorn's attorney requested the prosecution to produce the personnel files of all law enforcement witnesses whom it intended to call at the trial. This was for the purpose of seeking any evidence of prior perjury or other dishonesty, *In Camera*, to determine if those portions of the officers' personnel files ought to be made available to the defense counsel for impeachment purposes. In Camera hearings are held in the privacy of the judge's chambers, not in open court.

The government naturally objected, citing it had no obligation to examine the personnel files of federal agents unless the defendant could show cause that they contained information material to his defense. The trial judge denied Henthorn's request because he had not identified specific wrongdoing on the part of any of the federal agent witnesses.

After his conviction, the defendant appealed, and the Ninth Circuit Court of Appeals reversed the district court decision and remanded the case. The appellate court found the government to be "incorrect in its assertion that it is the defendant's burden to make an initial showing of materiality. The obligation to examine the files arises by virtue of the making of a demand for their production."[12] The initial request for records by the defense does not obligate the government to turn over information contained in law enforcement witness personnel files. Instead, the defense request merely obligates the government to review the files. The files, or information contained therein, do not need to be provided to the defense unless they contain information that is or may be material to the defendant's case. After being remanded back to the district court, a review of the personnel files of the federal agent witnesses revealed that the files contained nothing bearing on Henthorn's case. Instead it was discovered that the files contained numerous commendations.

In light of Henthorn, in 1996 the attorney general issued a U.S. Department of Justice (DOJ) policy, which remains in effect, regarding the disclosure of potential impeachment material for all DOJ investigative agencies. These agencies include the Federal Bureau of Investigation, the Drug Enforcement Administration, the U.S. Marshall Service, and since the realignment of investigative agencies with the creation of Homeland Security, the Bureau of Alcohol, Tobacco, Firearms and Explosives. The policy obligates these agency's employees to inform prosecutors of potential impeachment material as early as possible prior to providing a sworn statement or testimony in any criminal investigation or case. Putting this obligation on the investigative agency employee relieved government prosecutors from searching for such material. When such material is brought to the attention of a prosecutor, it is reviewed for relevancy, and provided to the presiding judge for his review or the defense if appropriate. Similar policies have been initiated with other U.S. departments as well.

Henthorn has created the need for exceptionally honest employees within federal police agencies. Federal prosecutors are reluctant to pursue prosecutions when they know a tainted federal agent was involved in the investigation, regardless of the role the individual federal agent played. If a federal agent is blackballed as a prosecution witness, his value to the agency has been greatly diminished. Essentially, everything he becomes involved in is adversely affected, and his continued employment soon becomes an issue. Even issues that were not criminal in nature, such as an internal affairs investigation, if an agent lies or covers for another, his credibility comes into question, and he stands an excellent chance of being fired since *Henthorn* issues cannot be overcome.

BRADY MATERIAL

Brady Material, as it is known, stems from a U.S. Supreme Court decision in *Brady v. Maryland*.[13] The material consists of all exculpatory evidence the government possesses including impeachment evidence and prior inconsistent statements made by government witnesses. The defense is entitled to this material no later than the conclusion of the witness' testimony, but usually obtains it prior to trial.

Brady was convicted of murder during a robbery with an accomplice. Brady's attorney conceded his client had committed the robbery, but insisted that his accomplice had actually committed the murder. The defense had asked the prosecution for all statements made by the accomplice, was shown some, but not a confession to the murder he had made to police prior to trial. Because Brady's attorney was not privy to the pre-trial statements of the accomplice, he appealed the death sentence Brady received, citing the accomplice's undisclosed confession. The defense argued that if the jury had known the accomplice had actually committed the murder, this fact would have influenced them to recommend life imprisonment instead of the death penalty Brady received.

In the Supreme Court's decision, they wrote, in part: "Suppression by the prosecution of evidence favorable to an accused who has requested it violates due process where the evidence is material either to guilt or to punishment, irrespective of the good faith or bad faith of the prosecution."

JENCKS MATERIAL

In another Supreme Court case, *Jencks v. United States*,[14] Jencks had been arrested by FBI agents for lying about being a member of the Communist Party, in violation of the National Labor Relations Act, which required him to file an affidavit as the president of a labor union.

Jencks appealed his conviction based on the involvement of two government informant witnesses who testified at his trial. The defense had requested the government to furnish all reports and statements made by the informants concerning the activities of Jencks. He wanted to prepare his cross-examinations of the witnesses, and wanted to recognize any inconsistencies in their testimony to what they had reported orally or in writing to the FBI. The trial judge denied the motion. Jencks was later convicted and appealed.

The Supreme Court, in part wrote: "Petitioner was entitled to an order directing the Government to produce for inspection all written reports of the FBI agents in its possession, and, when orally made, as recorded by the FBI, touching the events and activities as to which they testified at the trial." The court also said that the defense was entitled to inspect the reports to decide whether to use them in the defense of the accused.

The court, in essence, told the government that if the reports were so sensitive that they should not be disclosed, and the court agrees with the defense that they should be disclosed, then the government had to decide whether to pursue the prosecution of the defendant, or drop the matter entirely.

GIGLIO ISSUES

Even agreements made between the prosecutor and an unindicted coconspirator must be disclosed. In *Giglio v. United States*[15] the Supreme Court held that a previous agreement by the government, not to prosecute a coconspirator in return for his testimony against Giglio, should have been disclosed to the defense so that this information could have been used at trial to discredit the witness.

An Assistant United States Attorney (AUSA) handling the grand jury presentation to seek indictments of the conspirators had promised the witness he would not be prosecuted, but failed to tell this to the AUSA who actually handled the trail.

The Supreme Court wrote, in part: "Neither the Assistant's lack of authority nor his failure to inform his superiors and associates is controlling, and the prosecution's duty to present all material evidence to the jury was not fulfilled and constitutes a violation of due process requiring a new trial."

It's apparent that disclosure of material is vital to the defendant receiving a fair trial, and withholding it without cause can create tremendous problems for the police and prosecutor alike.

DIRECT EXAMINATION

Direct examination is the questioning of a witness by the lawyer, who called the witness, to testify concerning matters that are being introduced for the first time.

In general, leading questions are not permitted. Leading questions may be allowed, however, at the judge's discretion if they will help elicit the testimony of a witness who is having difficulty communicating, for example, due to age, disability, or limited mental capacity.

Questions requiring a narrative answer require the witness to tell his story without responding to individual questions. This line of questioning deprives the opposition attorney from objecting to what he believes that is inadmissible. Narrative testimony also risks the witness rambling on about things that are immaterial to the question at hand, and in general waste valuable court time.

CROSS-EXAMINATION

Cross-examination follows the conclusion of direct examination. It is permitted to examine subjects that were testified to during the direct examination. If the defense has not had the opportunity to cross-examine a prosecution witness, the testimony is not allowed to remain in evidence.

Cross-examination of witnesses is a thorough probing of their direct testimony, and usually has few restrictions placed on it by the court. The witness may be cross-examined about anything that he has previously testified about, but is not meant to belittle or embarrass him.

If the questions elicited during the testimony during cross-examination enter into a new area, the judge has the discretion to permit the testimony to continue. Much of any cross-examination tends to delve into areas that seemingly have nothing to do with the issue at hand.

Often, defense attorneys will ask seemingly needless questions in an attempt to probe into the conduct of the police investigation that led to the defendant being arrested. Many attorneys will search for the existence of something that was not disclosed to him during the discovery process.

Many of the defense questions are designed specifically to leave an indelible image on the minds of the jurors, that the police conducted an inadequate investigation or are in general inept. Other questions will deal with specific police procedures and conduct. These attacks are designed to divert the jury away from the facts of the case, and instead focus on questionable or controversial investigative techniques that may have been deployed during the course of the investigation.

Investigators must maintain their composure on the witness stand in the face of cross-examination that is designed to attack the police and its motives.

SUMMARY

Criminal evidence is anything that is offered to prove or disprove a fact. Evidence takes the form of a physical object, a document, tape recordings, or a set of circumstances. Police officers, and especially investigators, need to have at least a basic understanding of the rules of evidence in order to be effective and professional in their jobs. Police officers should strive to collect every available piece of evidence during a criminal investigation at the time it is available. Evidence may later be destroyed, misplaced, or unavailable if it is not collected in a timely manner.

Evidence is offered for the purpose of proving a fact at issue. It serves as a means to attack a witnesses' credibility, or to rehabilitate a witness whose credibility has been destroyed or weakened. It is also used to assist in determining the appropriate sentence that a convicted defendant will receive.

Types of evidence include direct, circumstantial, physical, testimonial, including expert opinions, and documentary.

The introduction of criminal evidence in both criminal and civil court proceedings is governed by a set of rules of evidence. These rules are designed to expedite a trial, to shield the jurors from being misled or confused during the court proceedings, and to protect and secure a fair trial for the defendant. They are used as the basis to sift through evidence to ensure that it is credible, dependable, material, and trustworthy before the judge or jury can consider it.

Before an item of evidence can be admitted in court, it must pass a three-prong test of relevancy, competency, and materiality.

The Exclusionary rule of evidence provides that certain types of evidence will not be admitted in a court of law. The rule applies to evidence illegally obtained by the police as a result of unlawful searches and seizures, as well as certain types of testimony.

The criminal justice system enjoyed in the United States is known as the adversarial system. A prosecutor represents the government, whether it is a federal or state criminal matter. A defense attorney represents the defendant. In multiple-defendant cases during the same trial, each defendant is entitled to his own representation in order to remove any conflict of interest. Defendants, who can afford it, can hire more than one attorney to represent him in his defense. Under the Sixth Amendment to the U.S. Constitution, the right to counsel is guaranteed. Defendants, however, do not have to exercise that right, and may elect to represent themselves.

Other constitutional guarantees for the defendant are found in the Fifth Amendment pertaining to double jeopardy issues and self-incrimination. The Fourth Amendment describes the requirements that the police must meet before obtaining a search warrant.

A defendant in a criminal trial is presumed to be innocent until the contrary is proved. In the case of a reasonable doubt as to whether the defendant is guilty or not, he is entitled to an acquittal.

Reasonable doubt is defined as not possible doubt. It is what jurors experience in their minds after considering the totality of evidence that leaves them unable to conclude the guilt of the defendant. The law does not require the prosecutor to present proof to the degree that it eliminates any possibility of error. Only moral certainty is required. The defendant's failure to substantiate his defense does not relieve the prosecutor from his burden to prove guilt beyond a reasonable doubt.

The discovery process is when the prosecutor provides the defense with some of the materials within his files. The discovery rules that govern all federal trials require the statements of witnesses testifying, evidentiary items intended to be used at trial, and any exculpatory information to the defendant be disclosed. Federal courts have some of the most liberal discovery rules in the nation.

Direct examination is the questioning of a witness by the lawyer, who called the witness, to testify concerning matters that are being introduced for the first time.

Cross-examination follows the conclusion of direct examination. It is permitted to examine subjects that were testified to during the direct examination.

If the defense has not had the opportunity to cross-examine a prosecution witness, the testimony is not allowed to remain in evidence.

NOTES

1. Readers should review their particular state's rules of evidence. Federal law enforcement officers should refer to the Federal Rules of Evidence.
2. *Weeks v. U.S.*, 232 U.S. 383 (1914).
3. *Mapp v. Ohio*, 367 U.S. 643 (1961).
4. California Penal Code § 687.
5. *Miranda v. Arizona*, 384 U.S. 436 (1966).
6. See Rule 16, Federal Rules of Criminal Procedure.
7. Jencks Act, 18 U.S.C. § 3500.
8. Weatherford v. Bursey, 429 U.S. 545, 559 (1977).
9. Every state has rules dictating their discovery process similar to those found in the federal system.
10. The Fifth Amendment to the U.S. Constitution pertains to the federal government, and prohibits the deprivation of life, liberty, or property without due process of law. The Fourteenth Amendment to the U.S. Constitution provides, ". . . nor shall any State deprive any person of life, liberty, or property, without due process of law."
11. Lee Hockstader, "For Tulia, 'It Feels So Good': Texas Inmates Freed After Four Years in Prison on Suspect Charges," The Washington Post, June 17, 2003, p. A1.
12. *U.S. v. Henthorn* 931 F.2d 29 (9th Circuit. 1991).
13. 373 U.S. 83 (1963).
14. 353 U.S. 657 (1957).
15. 405 U.S. 150 (1972).

2

The Criminal Trial Process

To fully appreciate the rules and nuances of criminal evidence, the criminal trial process must be understood. Any defendant entering the criminal justice system is in for a traumatic experience, in that most are not skilled lawyers, but laymen who rely on their information about the system through the media or associates who have experienced it first hand. It is not something to be taken lightly. The outcome could deprive the defendant of his liberty or even cause his premature death in capital murder cases. The process described below differs from state to state. However, most aspects of it exist in all states as well as the federal system.

The catalyst for defendants entering the criminal justice system is the police, be it a city, county, state, or federal law enforcement entity. When a crime is reported, or discovered through proactive investigation, the police take action. Their investigation and overall handling of the matter will possibly, although not probably, result in a *suspect*. A suspect is someone who is suspected of committing a crime, but who has not yet been arrested, whereas a *defendant* is someone who has been arrested or indicted and has been formally accused of a crime, and now must defend himself at trial.

Many arrests and subsequent indictments result from the police filing a *complaint* before a magistrate. A complaint is a written statement of fact, constituting a public offense, made upon an oath or affirmation, before a magistrate. When a magistrate issues a complaint, or if the defendant has been indicted by a grand jury, a warrant or a summons is issued to notify the defendant of the alleged charge against him and the date and time he is to appear at his initial appearance. In most cases, defendants are arrested and lodged into a jail facility to ensure their appearance. The summons is only used if the offense charged allows for bail, and there is reason to believe that the defendant will respond voluntarily.

A complaint can be filed for both *misdemeanor* and *felony* cases. In many states, a misdemeanor is a crime punishable by up to six months in a county jail facility. In some states, such as California, the punishment for a misdemeanor conviction is a maximum fine of $1000 and confinement in a county jail facility for up to one year. Some specific crimes, such as spousal abuse, can carry a fine up to $6000 in some states. An example of a misdemeanor crime is driving while intoxicated, simple assault, disturbing the peace, and prostitution. A felony is a crime punishable by death or imprisonment in a state prison over one year. Defendants convicted of misdemeanor crimes cannot be confined in a state prison. However, many felons can be found in county jail facilities either awaiting trial on felony charges, or serving their sentence as a result of a plea agreement.

THE ARREST

Police have the authority to arrest suspects based solely upon probable cause, without first filing a complaint. This is called a *probable cause arrest*, in that there is probable cause to believe a crime was committed, and that the suspect being arrested committed it. This normally occurs when a defendant is arrested at the crime scene, or commits a crime in the presence of a police officer, such as in driving under the influence of alcohol. In neither situation would the arresting officer have time to get a complaint filed before making the arrest without the suspect fleeing the area. Public safety would be in jeopardy if police officers were required to abandon the suspect they just captured after a hot pursuit, in order to file a formal complaint or application for an arrest warrant before taking the suspect into custody. Fortunately, all U.S. law enforcement officers have the ability to make probable cause arrests that can later be scrutinized by the prosecutor and challenged by the defense.

After being arrested, the defendant is usually taken to a police facility to be booked. The *booking process* is when the police obtain the identifying data of the defendant, including his photograph and fingerprints. The defendant has no right to refuse to cooperate in this process. The defendant's personal property is inventoried and stored for safekeeping, and returned when bail is

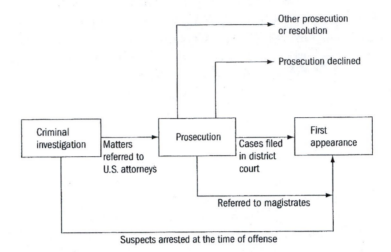

FIGURE 2.1 Prosecution.
Source: U.S. Department of Justice, *Compendium of Federal Justice Statistics, 1995* (Washington, DC, Bureau of Justice Statistics, 1998), p.10.

posted. The term "booking" originates from the days before computers, when police departments recorded arrests in a ledger.

The defendant is then lodged in a jail facility until he posts the required **bail**, or is issued a citation that documents the defendant's ***promise to appear*** in court on a particular date. Bail is the furnishing of a specified amount of money or surety bond to an officer at the jail facility that is returned upon the suspect appearing in court. Many states have bail schedules issued by judges for specific offenses, thereby eliminating the requirement for the suspect to remain in jail until his initial appearance where the amount of bail is then set. A promise to appear is similar to a traffic citation, in which the defendant signs a document promising to appear in court on a specific time and date, and is then released on his own recognizance.

If the arrestee cannot post bail, or is ineligible to be released on his own recognizance, he will remain in a jail facility until his initial appearance or arraignment. If such a defendant is booked into a jail facility on a late Friday afternoon, he will probably spend the weekend in jail until the following Monday, assuming that day is not a court holiday.

COURT JURISDICTION

Jurisdiction is the court's right to entertain a particular proceeding and to render a decision. A court must have jurisdiction over the accused and the subject matter before it can legally act in a criminal proceeding. Some state courts are limited to hearing only misdemeanor matters, and others can hear felonies. Other courts can hear both misdemeanor and felony matters. Generally, a municipal court has jurisdiction over infractions and misdemeanors, and a superior court has jurisdiction in felony matters.

Jurisdiction over the accused is a fundamental requisite in criminal proceedings. When a defendant is brought to the court, he is given the opportunity to present a defense. The court assumes jurisdiction of him and the subject matter, and will not question how the defendant came before it.

All state courts can exercise jurisdiction over a defendant accused of committing an offense within the state. Most courts can also take jurisdiction on certain offenses committed outside the state, if the offense is a crime in both states. For example, the accused steals or embezzles property in Texas, and is arrested in California for possession of the stolen property. A California court could hear the possession of stolen property matter. Also, someone from outside the state, who encourages or aids someone within the state to commit a criminal offense, can also be tried in the affected state if he is located within that state.

When a defendant is arrested outside the jurisdiction where the arrest warrant was issued, he is subjected to an ***extradition hearing***. Extradition is the return of a wanted person from a country or state where he or she is found, to the country or state where he or she is accused of, or has been convicted of, a criminal offence.

State courts cannot hear federal criminal matters and vice versa. State courts are designed for exclusive jurisdiction of state criminal matters. Federal courts have no jurisdiction over state crimes, even if there is a federal statute that parallels the offense. The defendant would have to be indicted by a federal grand jury if jurisdiction by the United States is sought.

It should be noted that double jeopardy does not apply to offenses that are both state and federal crimes. For example, a defendant who robs a bank could be first tried in federal court, and then again in state court for robbery. However, this is seldom done since federal prosecution is usually declined if a state prosecutor intends to file charges in the matter. If the defendant should be acquitted, the U.S. Attorney's Office may decide to take up federal prosecution in the matter at that time.

INDIGENCE DETERMINATION

In some state jurisdictions and in all federal courts, before the initial appearance, ***Pretrial Services***, an arm of the court, will interview the defendant and obtain his criminal history so they can advise the court regarding bail. The Pretrial Service caseworker will gather facts so the court can determine if the defendant is a potential flight risk, a danger to the community, or should be released on his own recognizance.

Pretrial Services also gather facts about the defendant's assets and income to determine if he may be eligible for free legal counsel. Under the Sixth Amendment to the U.S. Constitution, all defendants are entitled to representation by counsel in criminal proceedings. The only exception is with petty offenses, such as minor traffic infractions, where there is no prospect of the defendant being deprived of his liberty by being sent to jail if he is found guilty. The Supreme Court has determined that an indigent defendant is entitled to have an attorney appointed to represent him, at government expense, throughout the entire trial process.[1]

INITIAL APPEARANCE HEARING

Many states require that an arrestee be brought before a magistrate forthwith, or within 24 hours of his arrest, with the exception of weekends and court holidays. By this time, the defendant either has his own private attorney, or will be appointed one due to his indigent status. At the *initial appearance*, sometimes referred to *first appearance*, the judge or magistrate will:

- ascertain the defendant's true name and address.
- inform the arrestee of the specific charges again him.
- inform him of his right to counsel and right to remain silent.
- appoint counsel if the person is an indigent.
- sets a preliminary hearing date.

DETENTION HEARING

During the initial appearance, the judge will set bail for the defendant. Bail determination stems largely from the nature of the crime, the likelihood that the defendant will appear for trial at a later date, and the recommendation of the prosecutor. In federal drug crimes, there is a presumption that the defendant will not appear, and the burden is on the defense to overcome this presumption and convince the judge that bail should be granted.

Reality Check!

Defense attorneys will usually bring family members to court to testify about the defendant's ties to the local community, the fact he has a job, is a loving husband and father, etc. These family members may be willing to post a surety bond whereby they put up their homes and other property in lieu of a cash bail for the defendant. Prosecutors must be able to demonstrate that the defendant truly is a danger to the community or a flight risk, if applicable. It is not uncommon for family members and close friends to exaggerate their claims that the defendant is "a model citizen" and a "good family man."

For example, in federal court in Los Angeles, California, the Drug Enforcement Administration (DEA) arrested an Iranian immigrant for selling a kilogram of heroin to an undercover DEA agent. During the undercover negotiations, the agent found it extremely hard to understand the defendant's English because of his accent. At the detention hearing, a woman, purported to be his fiancé, testified that she would personally ensure the defendant's presence at all future proceedings. When confronted by the Assistant U.S. Attorney about whether or not she spoke and understood Farce, the official language of Iran, she admitted that she did not. Because the defendant required a Farce interpreter in the courtroom, the U.S. magistrate-judge thought her claim of being the defendant's fiancé was false, and ordered the defendant detained without bail.

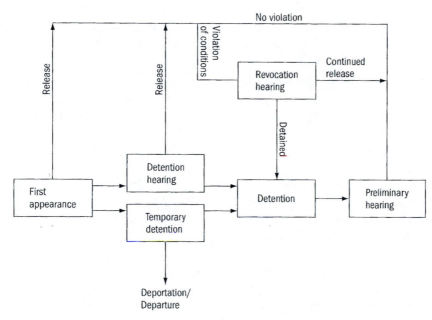

FIGURE 2.2   Pretrial release.
Source: U.S. Department of Justice, *Compendium of Federal Justice Statistics, 1995* (Washington, DC, Bureau of Justice Statistics, 1998), p. 22.

A judge will determine whether or not the defendant will be released while his case is pending trial, and the specific conditions that will be imposed if bail is granted. Judges have the following six options when determining if bail should be set or not:

1. **Own Recognizance (O.R.).** The defendant's promise to appear in court when required is sometimes sufficient for his release without posting a bond.
2. **Supervised O.R. Release.** The judge may set conditions for the defendant to avoid contact with an alleged victim, other defendants, reporting person, and other witnesses. He may require the defendant to telephonically report to a supervised release program case officer while undergoing the trial process.
3. **Third Party Custody.** This is a modification of an O.R. release with a third party, usually a relative, cosigning the release order, stating

that every effort will be made to see that the defendant appears at trail. The third party is also responsible in seeing that if any conditions of the defendant's release are violated, the court will be promptly notified.

4. **Unsecured Appearance Bond.** The defendant is released without having to post a cash bond. However, he does sign an order stating he will execute an appearance bond, binding him to pay the state a designated sum of money should he fail to appear at trial.

5. **Secured Appearance Bond.** The defendant must deposit with the court either real property or cash in the amount set forth in the order before he is released.

6. **No Bond.** A defendant can be held without bond when he is accused of a capital offense, when proof is evident or the presumption of guilt is great. This may also apply for many felony charges, especially those involving violence, where the presumption of guilt is great, or the defendant poses a continued danger to the community.

Some states require police officers to provide the court with a synopsis of their investigation leading to the defendant's arrest that will support not granting the defendant bail. The prosecutor may also present a synopsis of the state's case against the defendant as to why bail should be denied.

If bail is granted, judges will often require the defendant to surrender his passport in addition to posting bond, and may restrict the defendant's travel to the judicial district or the state without the permission of the court.

The following is an actual transcript of a federal detention hearing in which the judge, the honorable Nancy Stein Nowak, explains the proceeding to a defendant:

THE COURT: "Okay. All right. Mr Garcia,[2] my first job is to decide the matter of probable cause. Is there probable cause to believe that you committed the offense that's described in the complaint?

It's not proof beyond a reasonable doubt. I can take hearsay, third-hand hearsay. If I otherwise think that it is indeed reliability, I can rely on that in determining whether the probable cause is present.

And after hearing the evidence today, examining the complaint, I find there is probable cause to believe you've committed the violation that's alleged in the complaint.

While (your attorney) takes issue with the wording of that particular statement regarding the November 7th series of conversations, I think that the . . . when the complaint says that a person identified it, was as Jose was intercepted directing Mr Herrera, I think that it's a reasonable conclusion to be drawn from the conversations that were intercepted and in the toll records of what took place in the conversation, which itself is not recorded.

I don't think that's a misstatement. I just want to emphasize to you and members of your family that in order to be found guilty of this offense, there would have to be a much higher quality of proof and much more proof.

There is merely a probable cause hearing, and I find that there is enough evidence to continue to hold you. The other determination I have to make today is whether the government can support its request to detain you without a trial.

And if the government proves by a preponderance of the evidence that you are a flight risk or by clear and convincing evidence that you are a danger to the community, than I must hold you without bond.

Now, because of the nature of the crime that the government has charged you with, that being a serious drug crime which involves a ten-year to life imprisonment range of punishment, because of that there is a presumption that you are both a flight risk as well as a danger to the community.

And the purpose of this hearing today is to allow you to come forward to present evidence to say to me, "Judge, these presumptions might apply to other people. But they don't apply to me because look at my ties to the community. Look at my record. Look at my involvement in the particular case. Look at the weight of the evidence that the government has."

So, those are basically the things that I'm supposed to look at. And as I turn to the flight issue, of course, I am mindful that you self-surrendered.

But, sir, as I look at the rest of the information about you and I would also say that I would think that the weight of the evidence that the government has at this point is not particularly strong and that's because it's based not on eye-witnesses, not on people who have come forward and who have testified live.

It's based on informants. And lots of things can be done with your attorneys, with good attorneys at trial to try to challenge the allegations that the informants might make from the witness stand with presenting their testimony to a jury.

But acknowledging that you self-surrendered and the weight of the evidence, it may not be particularly strong at this point what I've heard. The other things that I'm supposed to consider all lead me inescapably to a conclusion that you are a risk of flight.

You don't have a stable residence. You're living with your mother but also have an apartment some place else. And there's evidence that at least in December you had an intention of leaving but for extreme financial consequences, it looks like maybe over $3,000.00 was going to be demanded of you to break the lease.

So, nevertheless, it appears that you had an intention to move to Mexico. You've got family. Your sister has testified that you've got close family in Mexico.

In several places in Mexico. So, you've got a place to go. You've got unquestionable incentive to flee, looking at ten years to life. You don't have verifiable employment, the kind of employment that would keep you here.

Employment as a musician, you can do that in lots of different places. You are not beholden to somebody for a job like the rest of the members of your family, who have had their jobs for long periods of time.

You're not in that same category. You have no assets here that would keep you here that you would risk forfeiting. So, I find for all those reasons that the government has met its burden of proof with respect to flight.

Additionally, I find the government has shown by clear and convincing evidence that you are a danger to the community, remembering again that there is a presumption of danger.

And I find that you haven't rebutted that presumption, Mr Garcia. You come to court today not as a man who's . . . this is the first time that they've been involved with law enforcement.

In fact, you have convictions for drug offenses for the very same thing that you are facing charges now here in Federal court, and these are not . . . well, at least one of them is very recent.

In addition, you were on probation for that offense at the time that this is alleged to have occurred and you were on bond on an assault charge.

I mean, we're not talking about a white collar where there's maybe not really a victim. It's an assault, assault and drug convictions and arrests. That all adds up to danger to the community.

And in addition to that, the evidence concerning past drug use and that recent arrest in Kerrville, and your refusal to submit a urine specimen at the time of your arrest, suggests that there is some active drug use going on, which heightens the danger to the community as well.

So, for all those reasons I find that the government's motion to detain you should be granted. I'll be putting together a written order either today or later this week that memorializes all the findings that I have just made on the record.

You and your attorney will get a copy of that order and you will have a chance to appeal if you feel that's appropriate.

All right. If there's nothing further then, we'll be in recess. The Defendant will be remanded to the custody of the U.S. Marshal pending further proceedings."

GRAND JURY

The next step after the initial appearance for felony matters is the presentation of the case to the grand jury. There are anywhere between nine and fifteen grand jurors, usually a minimum of nine to indict, who decide whether there is probable cause to bind the defendant over on the charges.

This proceeding is in secret, and does not allow for the defense counsel to be present. Usually within a short period of time, generally an hour or less, the prosecutor asks a knowledgeable officer to tell the grand jurors the facts underlying the charges, and the jurors decide whether to indict or not. If the grand jury indicts, this is called a **true bill**, and the foreman will sign what will become the indictment. The grand jurors can also add charges, and indict the defendant on some charges, but not all of those presented to them. If the grand jury chooses not to indict, the state can still use the preliminary hearing method, or vise versa.

In some states, such as California, prosecutors will seek the defendant's indictment instead of choosing to present evidence to a judge during a preliminary hearing. Many times this is done to speed up the trial date, and not give the defense an opportunity to preview witnesses in cases where a trial is certain.

It should be noted that in many proactive criminal investigations, such as in drug trafficking or organized crime cases, the prosecutor will call the lead, or case investigator to testify to the grand jury on a regular basis about the ongoing investigation. This is done to inform the grand jury about the existence of the investigation, and to make them knowledgeable, so that indictments can be requested later without using a single large amount of valuable grand jury time.

When indictments are requested during an ongoing investigation, the prosecutor will usually ask that the indictments remain sealed until a strategic time arrives for the police to make their arrests. Once an arrest is made, the sealed indictments and subsequent arrest warrants are broken, and the matter becomes public record. Once indictments are handed down, a judge will issue arrest warrants for the defendant(s) if they are not in custody.

PRELIMINARY HEARING

Unlike during grand jury proceedings, a preliminary hearing occurs in front of a judge who decides whether or not a crime has occurred, and if probable cause exists that the defendant committed the offense. During this hearing, the state presents witnesses and evidence. The defendant is present and his defense counsel can cross-examine prosecution witnesses and present their own defense witnesses. These proceedings are much more time consuming than a grand jury proceeding, and in some cases the preliminary hearing can last for months, depending on the complexities of the case. All preliminary hearings are open to the public.

Often, the prosecutor will choose this option rather than presenting his case to a grand jury, in order to get a preview of the witnesses he has, and to assess the quality of their testimony at trial. If a witness recants their prior statements to the police, the prosecutor can impeach them through previously provided written statements or the testimony of police officers. At trial, the preliminary hearing testimony may sometimes be used in lieu of testimony if the witness does not appear, and it provides the defense with impeachment material.

If at the conclusion of the hearing, the judge finds there is sufficient probably cause to bring the matter to trail, the defendant will be "***held to answer***" the accusation.

Preliminary hearings are also a good way for defense counsels to view the evidence against the defendant, and sometimes serve as the basis for initiating a *plea-bargain*. Many preliminary hearings that expose overwhelming evidence of the defendant's guilt will not go to a formal criminal trial.

ARRAIGNMENT

Within ten days of the defendant's indictment, or when a complaint has been filed, he must be arraigned before a judge. An *arraignment* is when the defendant appears before a judge or magistrate, and is informed of the formal criminal charges against him, and given the opportunity to make a plea of guilty, not guilty, or *nolo contendere* (no contest). Nolo contendere is the legal equivalent of pleading guilty, but there is no admission of guilt. If the defendant refuses to make a plea, the magistrate will enter a not guilty plea for him.

During the arraignment, the judge or magistrate will hear additional motions regarding the conditions of his release, set the date for a trial or pretrial conference; and advise the parties of future proceedings and important deadlines. The judge or magistrate will also advise the defendant of his right to be present at all proceedings; that the proceedings will continue even if he is voluntarily absent; and that a *bench warrant* for his arrest will be issued if applicable. A bench warrant is an arrest warrant issued by a judicial officer directing any peace officer to take a defendant into custody. Bench warrants are usually issued when a defendant has failed to appear or when someone has failed a court order. Furthermore, the defendant will be advised that he has the right to a jury trial or have the matter heard by a judge alone.

The police officer or case investigator involved in the case usually is not required to appear at these proceedings. They may, however attend at the request of the prosecutor, depending on the circumstances.

DISCOVERY

Discovery is an important area of criminal procedure. It is the procedure in which opposing parties exchange information about the case. This information may include, but not be limited to, police reports, witness lists, and the like. It is a procedure designed to ensure that there are no surprises at trial for either side. The prosecutor must disclose the names and statements of witnesses and potential exculpatory evidence that they possess usually within ten days of the arraignment.

MOTIONS

The defense may file motions asking the court to suppress certain physical evidence, suppress statements, or preclude the defendant's prior convictions or other bad acts. In most cases, motions are filed at least 20 days before trial. There is no limit to the number of motions a defense attorney may file, including filing a motion that the trial be pushed back, in order to more adequately prepare for trial.

The prosecutor may move to preclude defense evidence as being immaterial to the case. Some motions require an evidentiary hearing, after which the judge may rule from the bench, or take the issue under advisement and issue a written ruling later. If a party receives an unfavorable ruling on a motion that they feel is crucial to their case, the party may file a special action to the court of appeal prior to trial.

Some motions can be lengthy and time-consuming, causing delays in the trial. Many times, when motions concerning evidence are denied to defense attorneys, one of the parties may initiate *plea-bargaining* to dispose of the case.

CHANGE OF PLEA

In many cases, a plea agreement is offered to the defendant who might decide to take the plea rather than take their chances of going to trial. Plea-bargaining is a necessary ritual in the U.S. criminal justice system. It saves valuable court time, where judges are often limited in number. It also quickly disposes of cases that might otherwise drag on for inordinate periods of time before a disposition can be reached. Many times, victims and witnesses of crimes are anxious to have the matter finalized, so they can go on with their lives without being burdened with what might seem to be a perpetual inconvenience. Many argue that the downside to plea-bargaining is that defendants usually receive substantially less time in jail or prison, or are placed on probation for their crimes, thereby lessening the deterrent of committing future crimes. In many large metropolitan areas of the country, justice would come to a virtual halt if every criminal matter had to undergo a lengthy trial.

In court, the defendant will plead guilty to the crimes outlined in the plea agreement. The prosecutor, defense counsel, and the defendant all sign a written agreement, which is then accepted by the judge after he ascertains that the plea is knowing and voluntary, and that there is a sufficient factual basis underlying the guilty plea.

SPEEDY TRIAL ISSUES

Most defendants must be tried within a prescribed amount of time, usually 90 or 120 days.

Reality Check!

A large number of trials do not commence within the time period established by law. These cases are often delayed upon the request of the defense because more time is needed to prepare for trial. Many defense attorneys have other trial

matters that conflict, and when the schedule of the trial judge is taken into con-
sideration, it is more than likely that the trial date will be delayed until a
mutually acceptable date is established. Many cases are delayed because of the
vacation schedules of attorneys and judges, holidays, weddings, etc. Seldom, if
ever, do the personal schedules of the police witnesses matter when it comes to
scheduling a trial matter.

TRIAL

After the judge who will preside over the trial hears motions, jury selection
begins. Both the prosecutor and defense are allowed ten ***peremptory chal-***
lenges without any explanation, and as many other challenges as necessary,
based on reasons involving prejudice and bias. Motions and jury selection can
last from several hours to several weeks, depending upon the seriousness of
the case and the make-up of the jury pool.

After a jury has been selected, the prosecution always begins first by putting on its witnesses and introducing physical evidence such as guns, knives,
photographs, and laboratory results. Defense attorneys have the right to
cross-examine each prosecution witness, in an attempt to impeach them, by
showing prior inconsistent statements, bias, or a motive to lie.

FIGURE 2.3   After being subjected to voir dire, citizens selected as jurors are sworn in before
trial begins. *Getty Images.*

After the prosecution finishes its case, the defense puts on the defense case that involves defense witnesses and possibly physical evidence, photographs, laboratory evidence, and sometimes expert witnesses.

The prosecution has the right to cross-examine each defense witness in an attempt to impeach or discredit the defense case, in the same manner as the defense tried to discredit the prosecution's case.

The case concludes with closing arguments by each side. Because the burden of proof rests with the prosecutor, he or she starts with a closing argument, followed by the defense. Upon conclusion of the defense closing argument, the prosecutor is allowed to present one further argument, which might contradict the closing argument just made by the defense.

After the closing arguments are completed, the ***triers of fact***, or the jury, must unanimously decide the defendant's guilt beyond a reasonable doubt. The jury then deliberates. A jury that fails to reach a verdict is called a ***hung jury***. The judge is usually reluctant to declare a mistrial, and will order the jury to continue their deliberations. This strategy is usually successful in the jury reaching a verdict. If the jury still cannot decide, or is hung, the court will dismiss the case and the prosecution will usually ask for a new trial date if a majority of jurors voted to convict.

When the jury returns a not guilty verdict, the defendant is immediately released from custody. If a jury returns a guilty verdict, the judge will set a future

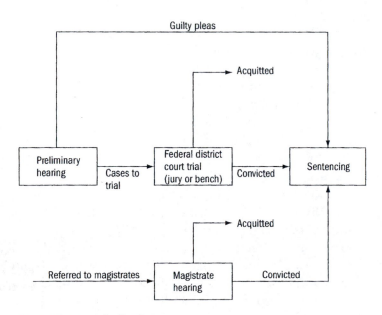

FIGURE 2.4 Adjudication.
Source: U.S. Department of Justice, *Compendium of Federal Justice Statistics, 1995* (Washington, DC, Bureau of Justice Statistics, 1998), p. 38.

date for sentencing. If convicted, the defense usually has ten days to file a motion for a new trial.

SENTENCING

Before sentencing, the probation department prepares a pre-sentence investigation report. The report includes information about the offense, as well as the defendant and victim's statements about the crime to a probation officer. Once completed, the probation officer makes recommendations regarding sentencing. The prosecutor and defense are also provided with copies of the report.

Often the judge will order restitution to the victim if he has suffered a financial loss as a result of the offense. A separate restitution hearing may take place, either prior to or after the actual sentence, when the amount of restitution is unknown or is disputed.

Some states also conduct what is called an aggravation/mitigation hearing, where the state presents aggravating evidence, and the defendant presents mitigating evidence. In the case of a capital murder, most states require such a hearing.

When a defendant is convicted of more than one offense, the judge has the option of sentencing him either to a **concurrent** or **consecutive sentence**. A concurrent sentence is when the defendant serves time for all sentences simultaneously. For example, a defendant is sentenced to five years in prison for robbery, and another five years for aggravated assault. With a concurrent sentence, after five years in prison the defendant would have completed his sentence. A consecutive sentence would require the defendant to finish his original five-year sentence before commencing the second five-year sentence, for a total of ten years.

Not all defendants are sent to jail or prison after their convictions. Many, especially those convicted of non-violent minor offenses, receive suspended sentences and are placed on **probation**. Probation is a specified period of court supervision in lieu of jail or prison time, in which the defendant may be ordered to not commit any other offenses, seek or maintain employment, not associate with known criminals, and/or perform community service, and appear before a probation offer who will track his behavior.

Probation should not be confused with **parole**. Parole is the early release from prison, usually based on the prisoner's good behavior and potential of not committing further crimes. Parolees regularly report to a parole officer who tracks the person's progress in obtaining employment, and his adjustment back into society. As a condition of parole, many parolees are required to sign a **waiver of search and seizure**, or their Fourth Amendment right, and are subject to searches by parole officers and other peace officers at any time, without probable cause, during the period of parole. Parole officers routinely make unscheduled visits to parolees to look for signs of drug abuse or any other criminality.

If the defendant is sentenced to a period of probation, and later violates its terms, the probation department may file a petition to revoke the defendant's probation. If a violation of probation is shown, and the judge revokes the defendant's probation, the court has a variety of sentencing options, including sending the person to prison for up to the original jail or prison sentence.

POST-CONVICTION APPEALS AND PLEADINGS

The right of a defendant to appeal his conviction is usually either a statutory or state constitution right. A defendant who did not plead guilty, or has not admitted to a probation violation, may be able to appeal his conviction for an offense, if allowed by statute or the state constitution. In some cases, a plea-bargain agreement may allow a defendant who pleads guilty to still appeal his case.

In order to appeal a felony conviction, the defense must file a notice of appeal, usually within 20 to 60 days after sentencing, depending on the state where the matter is heard. Appeals filed after this time period set by statute can automatically be denied. Death penalty cases are automatically sent to an appellate court for review.

Misdemeanor convictions can be appealed to the appellate section of the superior court having jurisdiction over the matter.

In many states, an appeal is initiated by filing a notice of appeal in the superior court. The notice of appeal is filed in the superior court, even though an appellate court will hear the case. This is done to notify the clerk of the court to send the trial record to the appellate court for their review.

APPEALS

Appellate Decision

The court of appeals will issue either an opinion or, in some states, a memorandum decision. Appellate court opinions are published in law journals and books, and can be used as precedents in other cases. Memorandum decisions apply to the case that the appeal was filed, and may not be cited as *precedent*. Precedent is also referred to as case law. It is a principle within the law that ensures that previously judicial decisions are incorporated into future cases. The reasoning behind the appellate court's decision is documented and distributed to the lower courts, informing them of new case law. These courts will take these decisions into consideration when deciding future cases.

Review of Court of Appeals' Decision

The losing party to an appeal may file a motion for reconsideration with the same appellate court. The state Supreme Court has discretionary powers to review and grant petitions, meaning they will only hear the petitions they so choose, and can deny those they are not interested in hearing. The state Supreme Court can also single out separate issues to review, and reject the others. If the state Supreme Court grants a review, supplemental pleadings are usually filed, and the full court hears oral arguments before their decision is made.

If the basis of the appeal deals with a U.S. constitutional issue, the defendant may appeal directly to the circuit court of appeals for the district where the matter was heard. If the appeal is heard but denied, the U.S. Supreme Court can be petitioned. However, it also has discretional powers to review appeals, and in comparison to the number of appeals the court receives each year, very few are heard. When the U.S. Supreme Court denies a petition, the matter has ended, and the decision of the next lower court stands. No other appeal process is available.

SUMMARY

The trial process can be complicated for the average citizen, whose only exposure to its complexities is usually through the media. Police officers need to have a good understanding of the process, in order to be professional and to do their jobs more effectively.

Following the commission of a felony crime, the police investigate, and when a suspect is identified, will either arrest him based upon probable cause, or complete a process that will result in the obtaining of an arrest warrant for him. Once a suspect is arrested, he is considered to be a defendant since he must now defend himself in court against the formal charges leveled against him by the government.

The defendant will than be booked into a jail facility, and if he does not post bond, or is ineligible for bail, he will be brought before a judge for an initial appearance hearing. At this hearing, the defendant is advised of the charges against him and he is appointed counsel if he cannot afford to hire an attorney.

The judge has the option of allowing the defendant to be released to his own recognizance, participate in a supervised release program, turned over to a third party, or post either a secured or unsecured appearance bond.

Usually within ten calendar days, the prosecutor will ask the grand jury for a true bill of indictment, in which the defendant is formally accused of a crime. If the defendant is not in custody, a judge then issues an arrest warrant, and any police officer may arrest the defendant when he is located.

Within the next ten days, the defendant is arraigned. The arraignment ascertains the defendant plea of guilty, not guilty, or nolo contendere. Motions are heard about conditions of release and dates are set for trial.

A preliminary hearing can take place in lieu of a grand jury indictment. This is akin to a mini trial, but the defense rarely makes serious efforts to impeach witnesses or introduce evidence. The purpose of a preliminary hearing is for a judge to determine if a crime occurred, and if there is a strong likelihood that the defendant is guilty of the offense.

The next step is the discovery process, which is the exchange of information between the prosecutor and defense attorney regarding witnesses and evidence.

Both sides then usually make motions within 20 days of trail that may include the exclusion of certain evidence. The losing party of a motion may file a petition to the court of appeals prior to trial.

Once speedy trial issues are resolved, the trial commences with the prosecutor's case, followed by the defense. At closing arguments, the prosecutor is allowed to address the jury before and after the defense presents his arguments. In the event of a conviction, the defendant is sentenced. The defense may file post conviction appeals through the state court of appeal to the state supreme court. A U.S. Circuit Court of Appeals, for the district where the trial took place, may hear U.S. Constitutional issues if applicable. The final appeal in any criminal matter rests with the U.S. Supreme Court.

NOTES

1. *Gideon* v. *Wainwright*, 372 U.S. 335 (1963).
2. The names were changed for this illustration.

3

Pleadings, Motions, Sentencing and Appeals

INTRODUCTION

Someone may be arrested based upon probable cause, or after the police file a complaint, or information, that leads a judicial officer to believe that a crime has been committed, and that the person named in the complaint committed the offense. A person who is indicted, or formally accused of committing a criminal offense, by a grand jury is subject to immediate arrest. No matter what the circumstances, once in custody and introduced into the criminal justice system, a series of events and Constitutional protections commence that will determine if a trial will take place.

Upon conviction, sentencing is pronounced, which could be anything from unsupervised probation to capital punishment, depending on the nature and severity of the crime. Many people will influence the judge in determining what the appropriate sentence should be for the individual defendant.

If convicted, the defendant may seek a remedy through an appellate court. If the appeal is based upon a U.S. Constitutional issue, relief can be sought through a federal circuit court of appeals.

PLEADINGS

Once a defendant is taken into custody, he is arraigned. The purpose of an arraignment is to inform the defendant of the exact charges again him as contained in an indictment, information, or formal complaint. He will be provided with a copy of the accusatory pleading before he is asked to make a plea, and to receive the defendant's plea to the charges. In most cases, the defendant waives the reading of the complaint, since he has an attorney who has fully explained the charges to him.

Under the federal rules, defendants have three options in pleadings: guilty; not guilty, or nolo contendere (no contest). There is no such pleading as "innocent." However, some states allow other pleadings, such as double jeopardy and not guilty by reason of insanity.

Not Guilty Plea

When a defendant pleads not guilty, he denies every single element of the crime(s) he is formally accused of.

Reality Check!

A defendant who pleads "not guilty" is not necessarily "innocent." In fact, few defendants who are found "not guilty" actually are. The prosecution has the burden of proving guilt. The defense does not have an obligation to prove anything, let alone the defendant's "innocence." The goal of the defense is to have a jury conclude that the defendant is not legally guilty, not innocent.

In the event where the defendant will not enter a plea for any reason, the court will enter the plea of not guilty for him.

A "not guilty" plea advances the matter into a criminal trial, where the burden rests with the prosecution to prove the formal charges against the defendant beyond a reasonable doubt.

Guilty Plea

With a guilty plea, the defendant admits to every element of the crime(s) formally charged, and advances the matter to sentencing. The defendant must make the plea personally. Almost without exception, during a defendant's initial appearance, he will plead not guilty, and thus begin the criminal justice trial process. Most criminal matters are settled through the process of plea-bargaining, and the defendant will reappear before the court to change his plea from not guilty to guilty. Almost all of these plea-bargain sessions will set an agreed limit on the amount of punishment the government will seek for the defendant, as an incentive for him to plead guilty so the case can be disposed of.

Before a guilty plea is made, the judge will advise the defendant that he must waive certain rights, and must do so knowingly and intelligently. These rights include his right to confront witnesses, the waiver of his right to a jury trial, and also waiver of his right against self-incrimination.

The court will also ensure that the defendant understands the nature of the charges against him, and the ramifications of pleading guilty, including being incarcerated, fined, or both as set by statute.

Nolo Contendere

Latin for *no contest*, a nolo contendere plea is the equivalent to a guilty plea, and carries the same consequences. Because of the nature of the plea, many jurisdictions require the presentation of some evidence before the plea is accepted. This satisfies the court that the defendant committed the offense if he should claim he has no memory of the event.

A nolo contendere plea is also a way for some defendants to save face. The plea relieves them from having to admit to committing a criminal

FIGURE 3.1   The judge conducts a sidebar with both attorneys during trial. *Getty Images.*

offense, even though the entering of the plea is tantamount to pleading guilty.

Double Jeopardy

The Fifth Amendment to the U.S. Constitution guarantees a defendant will not be put into jeopardy of prosecution twice for the same offense. The three elements of the double jeopardy clause of the amendment include the defendant's protection against not only a second prosecution after he's been acquitted, but also against a second prosecution if he is found guilty.

It should be noted that double jeopardy does not apply when dealing with different judicial systems. For example, a man robs a federally insured bank and is arrested by the local police. The local prosecutor indicts the defendant for the state penal code violation of robbery. The trial jury acquits the defendant. Upon learning this, the U.S. Attorney's Office federally indicts the same defendant for the same incident. However, he is now formally charged with a federal bank robbery offense. The defendant's claim of being at risk of double jeopardy does not apply.

Not Guilty by Reason of Insanity

Although this is usually an affirmative defense at trial, some states allow the pleading, and requires the defendant to prove that he was legally insane by the preponderance of the evidence. Some jurisdictions only require that the evidence presented creates a reasonable doubt that the defendant was legally sane at the time of the offense.

Present Sanity

In some states the defense may claim that the defendant is incompetent to stand trail because of his present mental condition. The condition would have to be severe enough to convince the court that the defendant is incapable of understanding the nature of the crimes and the proceedings, or from consulting with the defense counsel in preparation in his defense.

Any time prior to the verdict being returned by the jury, the claim can be made and if found to be insane, the defendant can be sent to a state mental institution to receive treatment. A trial within a trial may take place where evidence of the defendant's mental condition is presented to the judge and/or jury.

In the event that the defendant is found to be mentally incompetent to stand or continue trial, he may be confined in a mental treatment facility until his sanity is restored. This could take a substantial amount of time, sometimes exceeding the term of confinement the defendant would have received if found guilty of the criminal charges.

SPEEDY TRIAL

The accused has the Constitutional right to a fair trial and to defend himself against government accusations of criminal misconduct. Coupled with this is the right to be tried in a reasonable time, in order to avoid inflicting undue monetary expenses, loss of reputation, minimizing the anxiety of being a defendant in a criminal manner, and to lessen any possibility that the defendant will not be able to defend himself because of prolonged delays. All states also guarantee the right of a speedy trial.

The Sixth Amendment to the U.S. Constitution established: "In all criminal prosecutions, the accused shall enjoy the right to a speedy and public trial, by an impartial jury of the State and district wherein the crime shall have been committed, which district shall have been previously ascertained by law, and to be informed of the nature and cause of the accusation; to be confronted with the witnesses against him; to have compulsory process for obtaining witnesses in his favor, and to have the Assistance of Counsel for his defense."

The speedy trial right attaches, at the latest date, once formal charges are brought against the defendant, but not necessarily once he has been arrested. While the Sixth Amendment establishes the right to a speedy trial, it is not intended to limit the time period in which a defense can be established. The government is burdened with being prepared to go to trial at a set period, usually 60 to 90, or 120 days, but in almost all cases, the request to waive this right in order to further prepare an adequate defense is granted by the trial judge.

Reality Check!

In many cases, the defense will seek a waiver of a federal or state speedy trial act in order to buy more time in preparing for a defense. Most criminal defense attorneys in large districts and jurisdictions are committed to other criminal matters, or generally require more time than the statute grants to locate, interview, and vet potential witnesses. Thus, many court trials go on for months, and sometimes years, before the matter has reached a final disposition.

A defendant can also waive his right to a speedy trial if he fails to seek a prompt trial, does not present a timely claim prior to the trial by consenting to a delay, or by pleading guilty.

Statutes of Limitation

Statues of limitation limit the maximum time period in which a prosecutor can present formal charges. These limitations vary from state to state, and from crime to crime, and in some cases, such as murder, none exist.

These limitations are designed to reduce the anxiety associated with a defendant having to defend themselves against charges due to the passage of

FIGURE 3.2   The defendant and his attorney stand in front of the trial judge to make a plea. *Getty Images.*

time. The theory goes that the longer the period of time between the alleged offense and the time of trial, the more difficult it is to muster an adequate defense. Witnesses lose their memory of the event and in many cases are hard to locate or otherwise unavailable for testimony. These statutes also act as an incentive for law enforcement to conclude their investigations and seek formal charges in a timely manner.

Most federal statutes have a five-year statute of limitations.

Motions

Defense attorneys are allowed to make motions before the court to address different issues that can directly affect the prosecutor's ability to secure a defendant's conviction.

Motions are usually based on Constitutional grounds and allegations that the police or even the prosecutor acted improperly. For example, the police arrest the defendant and seize evidence from his vehicle. The defense might file a motion to suppress evidence, maintaining that one or more items of evidence the police seized was done illegally, in that the search was made without benefit of a search warrant. In this case, the prosecution will most likely counter that the seizure was made lawfully by means of a clear exception to the requirements of the Fourth Amendment.

Reality Check!

Most prosecutors are highly competent and professional. They scrutinize cases brought to them by the police before making a decision about prosecuting. When the prosecutor foresees Constitutional problems with the methods used by the police to seize evidence, in all likelihood prosecution will not be sought, and the charges will be dismissed because there is no reasonable expectancy of obtaining a conviction. Many defense attorneys go through the process of challenging evidence through suppression motions essentially to "see what sticks." When these motions are denied, the vast majority of defendants change their plea from not guilty, to guilty.

Suppression motions can also be made for confessions, admissions, and other statements against the defendant's penal interests.

Another motion may be to quash a search warrant on the grounds that it did not meet Constitutional standards, lacked details, or was based on something other than probable cause. Like other motions, this type is made early on in the proceedings, well before trial.

Motions can also be filed to suppress a warrant granting police the authority to conduct a wiretap. Recordings of the defendant discussing his criminal behavior are most damaging, and the warrant to conduct them will often be challenged. Again, defendants often change their pleas to guilty when their motion to suppress wiretap conversation is denied, because it is hard to deny involvement when the defendant says that he is in his own words.

Change of Plea

Defense attorneys often will counsel their clients to seriously consider changing their plea to guilty when the evidence against them appears to be insurmountable. Even clever defense techniques often fail to raise a reasonable doubt with the jury or sway them toward acquittal. Often a change of plea will be rewarded with a lesser sentence being sought by the prosecutor, who is relieved of the burden of proving the case and expending valuable courtroom time. The change of plea also demonstrates to the judge that the defendant is willing to take some responsibility for his actions, and the sentencing judge usually looks upon this favorably. However, when a defendant changes his plea, it is looked upon as if it was his initial plea.

When good cause is shown, a defendant is also allowed to change his plea from guilty to not guilty. Withdrawing a guilty plea must be based on a good cause, such as ignorance, inadvertence, or simple mistake. Reasons that include mistake, fraud, or duress must be demonstrated by clear and convincing evidence.[1]

When the defendant withdraws his plea, this fact generally is not admissible as evidence of guilt at trial. Furthermore, any admissions or other statements that the defendant made to a probation officer, because of his previous guilty plea, will not normally be allowed at trial either.

SENTENCING

Upon a defendant either pleading guilty or being convicted in a criminal trial, he will be subjected to the punishment prescribed by law for the committed offense. Many statutes set a range of sentencing that can be considerable, while others require a mandatory minimum sentence in every case. The sentencing range is generally commensurate with the crime as in a misdemeanor versus a felony, but extenuating circumstances will usually cause the defendant to receive the higher range of the possible sentence.

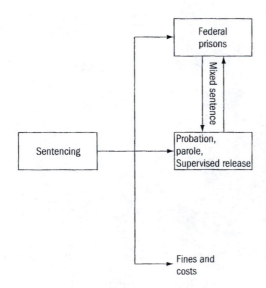

FIGURE 3.3   Sentencing.
Source: U.S. Department of Justice, *Compendium of Federal Justice Statistics, 1995* (Washington, DC, Bureau of Justice Statistics, 1998), p. 48.

Mitigating situations, however, may influence the sentencing judge to render a minor sentence, or may even produce *probation*. Probation, not to be confused with *parole*, is a specified period of court supervision in lieu of jail time, in which the defendant may be ordered to not commit any other offenses, seek or maintain employment, not associate with known criminals, and/or perform community service and appear before a probation offer, who will track his progress and behavior. Parole is when a person incarcerated in a state prison is given an early, conditional release. Parole was abolished in the federal system in 1987.

Many conditions may be set by the court for a convicted defendant to be either eligible for, or to remain on probation. For example, convicted drug users may be required to not only not commit any future criminal violations, but also submit to periodic urinalysis testing to ensure they are not reverting back to drug use. Others may be required to report to a probation officer on a regular basis to provide details about their search for gainful employment, and if they are associating with known criminals.

When a person is on probation, and is arrested and convicted again for another crime, his arrest will be promptly reported to the probation department having jurisdiction. His probation might be revoked by the sentencing

FIGURE 3.4   Businesswoman Martha Stewart (C) and lawyers Robert Morvillo (lower R) and John Tigue (third R), and son-in-law John Cuti (L) leave federal court in New York on March 5, 2004. Stewart, who built a media empire on tips for gracious living, was found guilty of lying to federal agents over a suspicious stock sale. *Corbis.*

judge, and the person will usually be required to serve the remainder of his probationary period incarcerated. This jail term will have no bearing on any future sentence he may receive for the newly-convicted offense.

Throughout the process of sentencing, many people are involved in providing input to the sentencing judge, who will ultimately determine the sentence that the defendant will receive.

Prosecutor's Role

Prosecutors have a substantial role in the sentencing of a defendant who has either pled guilty, or has been convicted of a criminal offense. In almost all jurisdictions, plea-bargaining is conducted in order to lessen the overall number of pending criminal matters, and to expedite justice. His influence on the court cannot be underestimated.

Many plea-bargaining sessions include either the acceptance of lesser charges, or the reduction of sentence that the defendant is likely to receive if he were to plead guilty in lieu of a trial. Those negotiations bring many criminal matters to a speedy close, in return for consideration in the defendant's legal dilemma.

The American Bar Association recommends that prosecutors make no recommendation in respect to sentencing, unless directly consulted by the trial judge, who ultimately approves negotiated sentences, or will set a sentence based upon a conviction. Many courts adhere to these recommendations, but of course, they are not binding.

Prosecutors will frequently argue against leniency at time of sentencing, based upon the severity of the crime, the status of the victim, or the outcry from the community. Their arguments are sometimes also designed to apply pressure on those judges who have a reputation for granting leniency, even in horrific crimes. He represents the victims in these matters, and voices the impact that the crime made upon them. He will often argue for substantial sentences for defendants who have prior criminal records and convictions, or were especially brutal towards their victims.

Prosecutors will often argue for lengthy sentencing based upon their interaction with police officials who investigated the case. These investigators can often offer insights that others cannot.

Reality Check!

Virtually all state attorney generals and county district attorneys are elected. All U.S. Attorneys are appointed by the President and confirmed by the U.S. Senate. None want to be considered "soft on crime" and will sometimes go to great lengths to ensure substantial sentences are handed out for defendants who deserve it. Perceptions by the voting public that their prosecutors are not looking out for their interests could have a direct impact on them retaining office. Many state attorney generals aspire to higher office, and will vigorously argue for substantial sentencing regardless. None want to hear about a particular case in an upcoming election, that they were less than committed to obtaining a substantial sentence for a defendant convicted of a particularly heinous crime.

Probation Officer's Role

The probation office of the court's jurisdiction will become heavily involved in sentencing by giving the judge a clear, unvarnished picture of the defendant.

Probation officer's prepare a Pre-sentence Investigation Report (PSI), which is perhaps the most important document in the criminal sentencing process, and frequently provides the basis for important sentencing decisions made by the Court. Probation Officers function as independent fact finders for the Court and provide the Court with relevant, unbiased information. Though the primary purpose of the PSI is to assist the Court in its sentencing function, the report is also a valuable resource to state and federal prison personnel, and other members of the Probation Office. The information contained in each section of the report provides these agencies with valuable intelligence, which will assist them in their respective functions. Thus, it is crucial that the Probation Officer present complete, verified information regarding the defendant's background, character, and conduct.

The comprehensive PSI report includes the defendant's criminal background, his arrest record, and the results of interviews with investigating police officers, family members, employer, and friends. Moreover, since the advent of state and federal sentencing guidelines, Probation Officers have become known as specialists in the area of guidelines sentencing.

Sentencing Guidelines

In 1984, Congress addressed the issue of fairness in sentencing by passing the Sentencing Reform Act. This Act created a new federal agency, the U.S. Sentencing Commission, and instructed it to develop uniform guidelines for sentencing in federal cases.

The guidelines were designed to be fair so that similar offenders convicted of similar crimes would receive similar sentences. The guidelines were also to be honest, in that the sentence received was to be the sentence served. Parole would be abolished. No longer would mandated parole be granted after completing only one-third of his sentence turn what appeared to be a long sentence into a short one. Inmates could still earn credits for good behavior, but this was limited to 54 days a year. And the guidelines were to be certain. A person convicted of an offense would have a clear idea of the range of sentences he or she could receive.

The guidelines became effective from November 1, 1987, and apply to all federal felonies and most serious misdemeanors. Sentencing guidelines are just that – guidelines that the court may consider when determining sentencing. The report will include the judge's sentencing options that are often based largely on sentencing guidelines.

Sentencing guidelines may include a point system, in which points are awarded for past bad acts, the defendant's failure to take responsibility for his actions, if violence was used or threatened during the crime, any injuries the victims may have sustained, the particular role he played in the crime, especially when he was involved in a conspiracy with others, and even if he used a special skill to accomplish the crime that he was convicted of. For example, a federally convicted defendant, who used his skills as the boat captain in a maritime multi-ton drug smuggling venture, is likely to receive additional points, equating to a longer sentence, since the crime could not have been accomplished without his direct involvement.

In January, 2005, the U.S. Supreme Court ruled in *U.S. v. Booker*,[2] that two provisions of the federal Sentencing Reform Act of 1984 having the effect of making the Guidelines mandatory must be invalidated in order to allow the statute to operate in a manner consistent with congressional intent. Since then, federal judges can only use the guidelines as just that, guidelines. However, many federal judges continue to impose the same sentences recommended by the guidelines, and the ruling so far appears to have little impact on the overall sentencing of federal defendants.

As stated, a Probation Officer prepares a PSI report. A typical federal PSI includes the following:

The Face Sheet

The face sheet contains significant court-related information provided for ease of reference. It also contains demographic data provided for the use of the sentencing judge, probation officer, U.S. Sentencing Commission, U.S. Parole Commission, and the Bureau of Prisons.

The Offense; Charges and Conviction(s)

This section provides a brief chronological history of the prosecution of the case, from the filing of the initial charges to the referral to the probation office for a pre-sentence report.

The Offense Conduct

This section provides all pertinent information regarding the offense, to assist the court in understanding the facts of the offense and the elements relevant to application of the sentencing guidelines, if such guidelines exist. This section may also include information indicating whether the offense of conviction was part of a larger scheme or plan that included other criminal conduct, which may be relevant to the determination of the appropriate guideline, the selection of a sentence within the guideline range, and the decision to depart from the guidelines. It further describes the role of the defendant and the conduct of codefendants and other participants during the offense, including planning, preparation for the offense, and the circumstances leading to the arrest or summons of the defendant. The objective of this section is to report what happened, as established by the probation officer's investigation, using the officer's best judgment to resolve factual discrepancies among sources.

Custody Status

This section provides relevant details of the defendant's custody status. At a minimum, the following will be included: date of arrest; by whom and where; brief history of appearances before judicial officers and decisions which have been reached; amount of bail and whether made or not; conditions of release and degree to which the defendant has complied.

Impact on the Victim

This section includes the impact on all victims of the offense, regardless of whether the information affects guideline application. An assessment of the financial, social, psychological, and medical impact upon any individual victim of the offense is presented and any financial loss caused by the defendant's conduct in the offense is reported.

Adjustment for Obstruction of Justice

This section describes any efforts made by the defendant to impede the investigation or prosecution of this case.

Adjustment for Acceptance of Responsibility

This section contains an assessment of the defendant's acceptance of responsibility for the offense of conviction.

Offense Level Computation

This section presents the application and calculation of the sentencing guidelines and includes a short synopsis of facts underlying each application, providing tentative findings for the court. For each count, it identifies the applicable guideline and shows the base offense level and any specific offense characteristics or adjustments that modify the base offense level. In cases involving multiple counts, the decision whether or not to group counts is explained. In all cases, the guideline application is displayed, resulting in the total offense level for the case.

Some guidelines contain enhancements that may override the initial guideline calculation. For example, if the defendant is a career criminal or committed the instant offense as part of a pattern of criminal conduct from which he derived a substantial portion of his income, the defendant's total offense level may be increased. Any such increase is set forth in this section, following the total offense level computation.

Offense Behavior Not Part of Relevant Conduct

This section describes criminal behavior that has not been reported in The Offense Conduct section, because it is not considered relevant conduct by the guidelines. This section may include offense behavior described in dismissed counts that is not part of relevant conduct for guideline calculations.

The Defendant's Juvenile Criminal History

This section contains a report of the defendant's record of juvenile adjudications of crime or delinquency and diversionary dispositions based on a finding or admission of guilt. Adjudications are included in chronological order, whether or not they are used in calculating the criminal history category under the guidelines. The value assigned to each sentence under Chapter 4 of the guidelines is also shown.

Criminal Convictions

This section contains a report of the defendant's adult criminal convictions and those diversions resulting from a guilty plea in a judicial proceeding. It includes a description of the defendant's prior criminal convictions and the dispositions in each case, as well as the defendant's adjustment while incarcerated or under supervision. Adult criminal convictions are included in chronological order, whether or not they are used in calculating the criminal history score under the guidelines. The value assigned to each sentence pursuant to the guidelines is also shown.

Criminal History Computation

This section displays the calculation of the criminal history category and the basis for the calculation.

Other Criminal Conduct

This section reports reliable information regarding other past criminal conduct, which may indicate that the criminal history category does not adequately reflect the seriousness of the defendant's past criminal conduct, or the defendant's likelihood to commit future crimes. The information is relevant in determining the adequacy of the defendant's criminal history category.

Other Arrests

All other arrests of the defendant are reported in this section in order to provide information to the court regarding the defendant's contact with law enforcement authorities.

Pending Charges

This section lists any pending charges against the defendant. This section is omitted if there are no charges.

Offender Characteristics

This part sets forth information relative to the defendant's personal background. Included is information concerning:

1. personal and family data
2. physical condition
3. mental and emotional health
4. substance abuse
5. education and vocational skills
6. employment, and
7. financial condition, including an assessment of the defendant's ability to make restitution or pay a fine.

Sentencing Options

This part sets forth the penalties authorized by statute along with the kinds of sentences available under the guidelines. Included are the statutory and guideline provisions for custody, impact of the plea agreement, supervised release, probation, fines, restitution and for drug offenses, and denial of benefits. By presenting the statutory and guideline provisions, the parameters of each may be compared by the court.

Impact of Plea Agreement

This part is included in PSI reports that are prepared when a plea agreement has been tendered to the court. The probation officer assesses the impact of the plea agreement on the guideline sentence by comparing the guidelines applicable under the plea agreement with the guidelines that would apply if the defendant were to plead to all counts.

Factors that may Warrant Departure from the Guidelines

This part contains the probation officer's statement of any factors that may indicate that a sentence of a different kind or of a different length from one within the applicable guideline would be more appropriate under the totality of circumstances. Inclusion of information in this section does not necessarily constitute a recommendation by the probation officer for a departure.

Addendum to the Pre-sentence Report

In some courts, the pre-sentence report is disclosed to the defendant, counsel for the defendant, and prosecutor before it is submitted to the judge. This procedure allows both counsel to communicate with the probation officer to resolve any concerns or objections regarding material information, sentencing classifications, or the sentencing guideline range contained in the pre-sentence report.

Early disclosure of the report to the attorneys allows the probation officer to conduct any further investigation and make revisions to the pre-sentence report that may be necessary. Any unresolved issues or objections are reported to the sentencing judge in the addendum to the pre-sentence report. The addendum also contains the probation officer's comments regarding the issues.

Defense Attorney's Role

A defense attorney may make representations to the court about the defendant. His role is to put a positive spin on the information gathered by the probation officer, and to challenge any information he may believe to be erroneous. If the probation officer's report is not disclosed, as is the custom in some jurisdictions, then the defense attorney will usually submit his recommendations to the court in writing. These reports will attempt to counter any derogatory information captured by the probation department, and will usually emphasis the defendant's present or future employment opportunities and plans to contribute positively to the community in the future.

The defense will also make oral pleas for leniency based on the defendant's remorse and the taking of responsibility for his actions. He may also base the need for probation or a lesser sentence on his needs and the needs of his family, their financial status, and need of maintaining the family unit. The defense attorney will surely argue that the defendant now realizes the seriousness of his crime, and the importance of learning from his past mistakes.

If no violence was conducted during the crime, the defense attorney will emphasize that fact to the court, and bring up anything that may reflect positively on the defendant, such as his having no prior criminal record, or having only been convicted of misdemeanors in the past.

If the defendant was convicted of a drug crime, or was under the influence of intoxicating substances at the time of the offense, many defense counsels will recommend that their client take steps to enroll into a treatment program to demonstrate their desire to rehabilitate themselves and become a productive, drug- and alcohol-free member of society.

The defense will also routinely ask that the defendant be given credit for time spent incarcerated since the time of his arrest and through trial, if applicable.

Defendant's Role

The defendant has the right to speak with the sentencing judge on his own behalf, whether or not he denied committing the crime he was convicted of. His defense counsel will caution him not to say anything in open court that might jeopardize his chances of appeal.

Often defendants will not speak to the court, and instead accept their fate. But those who do, will explain to the court how they intend to improve themselves by seeking additional education, securing a job, and spending quality time with their family, as well as not associating with known or suspected criminals in the future.

The Victim's Role

In many court jurisdictions, the victims, as well as the friends and family members of deceased victims, have the opportunity to address the court before sentencing.

These affected persons will emphasize their loss, either personally, or financially, by the actions of the defendant. Many of these testimonials are emotionally based, and offer powerful emphasis as to why the defendant should be incarcerated for a lengthy period of time.

In sexual abuse cases, the victims are given the opportunity to state to the court how their victimization has changed their lives and what impact it may have on their future well-being.

APPEALS

A prosecutor cannot appeal an acquittal, but he may appeal successful defense motions to suppress evidence before trial and post-conviction motions for a new trial.

Many defense appeals stem from perceived judicial errors during trial that were harmful to the defendant. If the appeal is based on the lack of sufficient evidence, the burden to prove this rests with the defense. Appellate courts will not reweigh the evidence, but instead look for evidence that supports the conviction.

Appeals must be filed within a given timeframe, after the date of judgment is made. The defense counsel may request the defendant be released on bond pending the direct appeal.

An appellate court will look for any error that may have led to a miscarriage of justice. Many of these errors are considered harmless by the appellate courts, and do not justify a reversal of the conviction. For example, the erroneous admission of a defendant's confession may be rendered moot due to otherwise overwhelming evidence of guilt. The rule of thumb used by most appellate courts is that unless the harmless error would have reasonably affected the outcome of the jury's guilty determination, the conviction will stand.

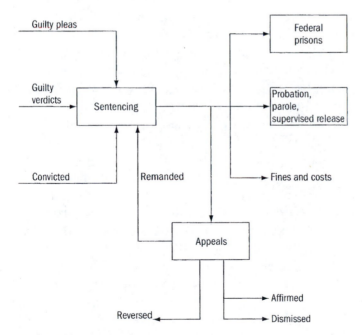

FIGURE 3.5   Appeals.
Source: U.S. Department of Justice, *Compendium of Federal Justice Statistics, 1995* (Washington, DC, Bureau of Justice Statistics, 1998), p. 60.

SUMMARY

Once arrested, a defendant has the option of pleading either guilty, not guilty, or nolo contendere, which means "no contest." This plea equates to a guilty plea, and is by and large a face-saving measure for the defendant.

Regardless of the defendant's plea, he cannot be subjected to double jeopardy. The Fifth Amendment to the U.S. Constitution guarantees a defendant will not be put into jeopardy of prosecution twice for the same offense. The three elements of the double jeopardy clause of the amendment include the defendant's protection against, not only a second prosecution after he's been acquitted, but also against a second prosecution if he is found guilty.

It should be noted that double jeopardy does not apply when dealing with different judicial systems, for example, federal, state, or military.

Some jurisdictions allow defendants to plead either not guilty by reason of insanity at the time of the offense, or present insanity. Although this is usually an affirmative defense at trial, some states allow the plea, and requires the defendant to prove that he was legally insane by the preponderance of the evidence. Some jurisdictions only require that the evidence presented creates a reasonable doubt that the defendant was legally sane at the time of the offense, or is presently insane and incapable of understanding the proceedings against him.

The Sixth Amend to the U.S. Constitution guarantees a defendant a fair trial in order to defend himself against government accusations of criminal misconduct. He also has the right to be tried in a reasonable time, in order to avoid inflicting undue monetary expenses, loss of reputation, minimizing the anxiety of being a defendant in a criminal manner, and to lessen any possibility that the defendant will not be able to defend himself because of prolonged delays. All states also guarantee the right of a speedy trial.

Statues of limitation limit the maximum time period in which a prosecutor can present formal charges. These limitations vary from state to state, and from crime to crime, and in some cases, such as murder, none exist.

Defense attorneys are allowed to make motions before the court to address different issues that can directly affect the prosecutor's ability to secure a defendant's conviction. Motions are usually based on Constitutional grounds and allegations that the police or even the prosecutor acted improperly.

Upon a defendant either pleading guilty or being convicted in a criminal trial, he will be subjected to the punishment prescribed by law for the committed offense. Many statutes set a range of sentencing that can be considerable, while others require a mandatory minimum sentence in every case. The sentencing range is generally commensurate with the crime as in a misdemeanor versus a felony, but extenuating circumstances will usually cause the defendant to receive the higher range of the possible sentence.

Prosecutors have a substantial role in the sentencing of a defendant who has either pled guilty, or has been convicted of a criminal offense. In almost all jurisdictions, plea-bargaining is conducted in order to lessen the overall number of pending criminal matters, and to expedite justice. His influence on the court cannot be underestimated.

The probation office of the court's jurisdiction will become heavily involved in sentencing, by giving the judge a clear, unvarnished picture of the defendant.

Probation officer's prepare a Pre-sentence Investigation Report (PSI), which is perhaps the most important document in the criminal sentencing process, and frequently provides the basis for important sentencing decisions made by the Court. Probation Officers function as independent fact finders for the Court and provide the Court with relevant, unbiased information.

Appeals must be filed within a given timeframe, after the date of judgment is made. A prosecutor cannot appeal an acquittal, but he may appeal successful defense motions to suppress evidence before trial and post-conviction motions for a new trial.

Many defense appeals stem from perceived judicial errors during trial that were harmful to the defendant. However, many of these errors are considered harmless by the appellate courts, and do not justify a reversal of the conviction.

NOTES

1. *People* v. *McGarvy*, 142 P. 2d 92 (Ca.1943).
2. 000 U.S. 04-104 (2005).

Defense Counsel Role and Strategies

INTRODUCTION

A defense counsel is a professionally trained and licensed attorney of law, whose job it is to represent the defendant in all phases of the criminal justice system. Whether hired by the defendant as a private criminal lawyer, working as a public defender, or appointed by the court, defense counsels are needed to ensure the defendant's civil rights are protected, and to present the best defense possible.

Private criminal lawyers either work for themselves, or are members of a firm with partners. Their fees can range in the hundreds of dollars per hour for all time spent on the criminal matter, including preparation. Well-known, or *high-powered* attorneys can earn substantially more based upon their experience and reputations.

Many of these private criminal lawyers specialize in specific areas of criminal law, such as drunk driving cases or drug offenses. Their experience in such court cases makes them formidable opponents for the prosecutor.

Public defenders are licensed attorneys and members of the state bar association where they practice. They are the representatives of poor and indigent defendants, and are government employees the same as prosecutors.

Since a significant number of defendants qualify for free legal counsel, some public defenders have a tremendous workload that sometimes brings outside criticism for the number of plea-bargains they conduct. Many feel these defense counsels do not possess the legal skills and abilities of private attorneys. This simply is not the case. Like in any profession, some professionals perform their job better than others. There are many outstanding attorneys who work for public defender offices. Many of these attorneys know the criminal justice system in their venue better than many outside private lawyers, and know the personalities and capabilities of prosecutors and judges that will most likely hear the criminal matter. Many public defenders, as prosecutors, use these public offices as stepping-stones during their career development.

Appointed or assigned counsels to defend indigent defendants are usually obtained through a roster of all members of the state bar within the venue of the court district. Many of these attorneys dread being assigned by the court to a criminal matter due to the paltry fees that come with the assignment. Critics point to the low pay as evidence that indigent defendants are not receiving adequate legal representation, as guaranteed by the Sixth and Fourteenth Amendments to the U.S. Constitution.

Typically, court-assigned counsels earn a fraction of what a "high powered" attorney makes, but earn on par or better what public defenders earn on an hourly basis. The largest complaint from court assigned counsel is that their appointments often take their valuable time away from other pressing matters they are handling at the time.

Defense attorneys have the power of subpoena to call witnesses, and can hire expert witnesses to present an alternative conclusion to scientific evidence, and render opinions about police procedures. Defense attorneys often hire private investigators to gather facts favorable to the defendant.

They negotiate plea-bargains for defendants, and attempt to secure the best deal they can for them. They are also ethically bound to not knowingly use perjured testimony or other deceptive practices in their defense. They are not obligated to disclose any information with the prosecutor or police that they receive from the defendant, without his permission. However, defense counsels are obligated to report any future crimes he may be aware of. He or she cannot use his status as an attorney as a means of disguising his aiding and abetting suspects involved in future criminal matters. Defense counsels are expected to defend their client's to the best of their ability, regardless of any personal feelings they may harbor against the defendant.

Reality Check!

Law enforcement officers should realize that defense counsels, regardless of whether they are in private practice, or work for public defenders, are not

> *your friends! They may appear polite and personable, but in the courtroom a metamorphosis occurs. They will use any tidbit of information given to them about the evidence or the officer and use it against his credibility, professionalism, or impartiality. Many good defense counsels will use every tool available to win their case, even if it means using something said in confidence to the counsel against the law enforcement officer. Officers should remain professional, polite, and courteous, but they should never discuss the trial or criminal investigation with a defense counsel without the prosecutor's permission and full knowledge. Defense attorneys sometimes exchange information about officers and detectives with other defense attorneys, to glean something they may be able to use in either the current case, or a future court proceeding.*

ENTRAPMENT

A common defense ploy used in drug and prostitution cases is called **entrapment.** The entrapment defense is when the defense counsel submits that the defendant had no predisposition to commit the criminal offense until the idea was planted in his mind by law enforcement, solely for the purpose of arresting him. Police may smooth the path for the defendant to commit his crime, but entrapment is forbidden. For example, an undercover officer may hold the ladder for a defendant to climb to the roof of a building he intends to burglarize, but the officer could not suggest he commit the crime in the first place.

In another example, drug investigators arrest someone for selling several ounces of cocaine to an undercover police officer. The defense attorney may allege the undercover officer told the defendant during several conversations prior to the purchase that he would make a lot of money, and that there was no possibility of being caught by the police.

The investigative techniques used during any drug investigation are important in defeating the entrapment defense. Making several purchases from the defendant before he is arrested is one way to disprove disposition. Recording *all* telephonic and in-person conversations between the undercover officer and the defendant is another.[1] Not recording all conversations between the police or informant in drug cases leaves the possibility of the defense claiming that the unrecorded conversations were when he or she was threatened if they did not follow through with the sale of the drugs.

Producing evidence of the defendant being arrested or convicted of other drug offenses may also help in this regard. The police, of course, should never target an individual for drug trafficking unless there is some basis to believe he is genuinely involved in drug trafficking. Relying solely on the word of an informant may be a tactical error that will often lead to this form of defense.

The quantity of drugs being negotiated between the undercover officer and defendant may also be indicative of only someone who is experienced in drug trafficking could seriously discuss.

Reality Check!

The notion that a defense attorney would allege that an undercover officer or informant actually threatened the suspect if he did not deliver drugs may seen very far fetched, but defendants will often lie to their attorneys to provide them with a ready-made defense. Other attorneys will allege such conduct to gain sympathy from members of the jury, hoping for a hung jury or outright acquittal.

CONSENT

Consent is a defense if the lack of consent is an essential element of the crime, such as rape. Other sex crimes, such as sodomy of a child, or statutory rape of a female under the age of 16, consent has no bearing since it is irrelevant.

Defense counsels will attempt to bring out the prior sexual activity of the victim, and allege she is sexually promiscuous with many men. Some states limit the discloser of a rape victim's past sexual contact, but defense attorneys may attempt to spoil the jury pool by alleging that the victim had many sexual encounters during pre-trial publicity.

Consenting to participating in a mutual affray in public also has no standing, since fighting in a public place is still a peace disturbance in most states.

IDENTITY

Defense attorneys often allege their clients are the victims of mistaken identity, or that the witnesses in the case simply do not have the capacity to see well. They will also claim that a witness to a crime was mistaken when he picked the defendant out in a line-up as the perpetrator of the offense.

Defense attorneys will also allege that the victim of violent crimes were so traumatized by the event, that the victim lost his or her ability to accurately describe the suspect to the police. This is sometimes claimed, despite an abundance of physical evidence to the contrary.

The defense may also allege that his client is simply not the person named in the criminal indictment. This simple, but often effective defense, is usually reserved for extradition hearings resulting from an out-of-jurisdiction arrest warrant. It usually serves to prolong the proceedings and requires a knowledgeable investigator to travel to the venue where the defendant was arrested, to testify that he or she can identify the person as the person named in the arrest warrant.

Alibi

Unless the defendant was caught in the act of the commission of the crime, the defense may allege it was impossible for him to commit the crime since he was elsewhere at the time.   .

The defense may produce a long list of witnesses, such as the defendant's mother, father, sister, brother, or spouse who will attempt to establish the defendant's alibi. Documents may also be produced to corroborate his claim, such as credit card receipts, car rental agreements, or airline tickets. Law enforcement officers should be cognizant that the defendant, in order to establish a false alibi, may have forged many of these forms of documentation, and more investigation will be needed to dispute these claims. Without conducting necessary follow-up investigation, sufficient doubt could develop in the minds of jurors that may result in an acquittal.

LACK OF MOTIVE

Despite the existence of physical evidence that substantiates guilt, the defendant may claim that his lack of motive should override the facts. The individual defendant's claim of lack of motive is most effective when the direct evidence against him is weak. The opposite happens when the evidence is substantial.

Motives range from personal or monetary gain, love, jealousy, greed, revenge, and hatred. Neither the prosecutor of defense is required to prove that a motive existed or not.

Claiming a lack of motive is designed to create a reasonable doubt in the minds of the jurors, who are obligated to acquit the defendant if it should be established.

CRIMINAL INTENT

As a rule, to violate the law, *criminal intent* has to be combined with the act before a crime is consummated. Not all laws require the perpetrator to have intention to do something, but many do. Theft, for instance, is commonly described as the taking of property with the intention of permanently depriving the owner of it. If someone steals a bicycle and grinds off the serial number on the frame, this would be good evidence the thief did not intend to return the bicycle to its rightful owner.

If, however, someone were to take one of two identical jackets from a coat rack in a bar after he had been drinking, and the jacket he left was in better condition than the one he took, this would serve as credible evidence he had mistaken the victim's jacket as his own.

Criminal intent can be proven through physical and circumstantial evidence. For example, in order to be charged with burglary in California, the state must show that the defendant entered a building, structure, or dwelling with the intention of committing a crime. Burglary is a felony. If a person is detained at a department store for shoplifting, and the police discover the stolen items inside a large box wrapped as a Christmas gift that has a spring loaded bottom that allows him to place smaller items inside undetected, the thief could be charged with burglary. The police could prove that the store does not sell boxes of the type the suspect had, and logic dictates that he had to have brought the box into the store with the intention of committing a theft. Even if the man had been caught before he concealed something inside the box, the police could still prove the man committed a burglary by his mere possession of what is called a "booster box" while in the store. The possession of the box shows the defentant's intention to steal from the store.

Criminal intent also has an effect on the degree of a crime. For example, two business partners engage in a heated argument over money that results in a fight, leaving one of them dead. Did one of the men murder the other? Yes, but compare that set of circumstances to one of the men hiding in the bushes across the street of his business partner's home. When the other man parks his car in his driveway and walks to the front door, the partner shoots him with a hunting rifle, killing him. The shooter, by virtue of laying in wait, armed with a rifle, is evidence that he had formed the criminal intent to murder his partner. The punishment for these two sets of murders is substantially different. Killing someone during a heated argument may bring manslaughter charges, while waiting for the man to arrive home so he could be shot most likely would qualify him for first degree murder charges, and possibly the death penalty in many states.

BLIND MULE

The *blind mule defense* is when someone denies any knowledge of being in possession of something illegal while transporting it. Most of these cases stem from drug interdiction activities at airports and other transportation nodes. It is closely related to lack of criminal intent and alibi defenses.

For example, drug investigators at an international airport have reason to suspect a passenger is transporting controlled substances in his baggage. They stop and question the man who freely gives his consent for the investigators to look in his locked suitcase. Upon opening the suitcase, they discover two kilograms of cocaine. The man immediately denies he knew the drugs were in his bag, and can offer no explanation as to how the drugs got there. He may even claim that an unknown friend of a friend asked him to take the suitcase to deliver to another friend as a favor. Either way, despite his claimed ignorance, the police must make an effort to defeat the suspect's claim that he had no knowledge of the drugs.

Investigators would be required to examine the packaging of the cocaine for the man's fingerprints. If they were found, it would tend to show he knew about the drugs since his latent fingerprints were present on the packaging. The police would also run the man's name through their databases to determine if he has ever been arrested before. If the man has prior arrests or convictions for drug possession or sales, this would be circumstantial evidence that he might not be telling the police the truth when he denies knowledge of the cocaine. Also, papers or an address book on the man may reveal where he intended to deliver the suitcase. Addresses of known drug dealers on the man's possession is further circumstantial evidence that the man knew the drugs were present in the suitcase.

Other evidence of the man being a professional drug courier could exist from the number of flights the man has taken within the last month, the locations he traveled to, the method of payment for the tickets, and how and where they were purchased. Someone who pays cash for an airline ticket from a travel agent located a considerable distance from the man's residence could be circumstantial evidence that he did not want his travels to be obvious. Paying cash for a ticket eliminates a credit card paper trail to the man and is widely used by drug couriers.

The police will often afford the suspect in these cases the opportunity to submit to a polygraph examination to substantiate his innocence. The overwhelming majority of suspects who refuse to be administered the examination do so because they are convinced their lies will be detected.

The totality of circumstantial evidence will often dilute the man's claim that he had no knowledge of the presence of drugs.

LEGAL JUSTIFICATION

Another form of defense is that there was some legal justification for the defendant's actions. Justification claims can range from self-defense, excuse, or necessity.

Self-defense or necessity are sometimes claimed in murder cases where the defendant alleges the victim was attempting to murder him, and to overcome the victim's aggression, his death was necessary. The manner in which the victim was killed, coupled with witnesses to the event, can greatly enhance the defendant's defense. For example, the town bully is in a bar harassing the defendant and initiates a fight with him. The bully produces a knife and attempts to stab the defendant who dodges the knife blade. He comes across a pool cue and strikes the victim over the head, resulting in his death. Witnesses to the fight in the bar substantiate the defendant's claims.

However, in another example, if the police arrive and they find the victim dead in an alley behind the bar with multiple gunshot wounds, the defendant's claims of self-defense may not be so credible. If there are no witnesses, and a knife cannot be found that was allegedly used by the bully, the quality of this type of defense diminishes greatly.

A legal excuse can be closely related to self-defense claims. A credible defense may be when the defendant claims that during a street fight, the victim fell backwards and hit his head on the curb, causing massive head injuries resulting in death. If police locate witnesses who state the defendant knocked the victim down and then grabbed him by his hair and flung his head into the curbing several times, the defense would most likely be defeated.

In criminal investigations, thoroughness and timeliness are the keys to discovering facts that will bring the truth to light. Missing opportunities to locate and interview witnesses to an event may open the door to this and other forms of defenses.

LEGAL INSANITY

A finding by the court that a defendant is legally insane relieves him of culpability for criminal actions. Defense counsel will sometimes assert insanity based on the particular viciousness of the crime, or the manner in which it was committed. A mother drowning her four small children is an example of a candidate for the legally insane defense.

In order to qualify for this defense, the defendant must prove that at the time of the offense:

- his mental state or defect was such that he did not appreciate or understand what he was doing was wrong.
- if he knew what he was doing was wrong, he not realize the nature of the act he was committing.

Some states allow for the defendant's intoxicated state as the source for his insanity, if he otherwise does not fully qualify as being legally insane. This doctrine of *diminished capacity* recognizes that there are other factors, including mental disorders, which fall short of legal insanity that would otherwise qualify the defendant of being relieved of criminal responsibility. This line of defense will almost always require the testimony of qualified mental health experts to substantiate that the defendant did not have the capacity to appreciate the nature of the crime or even the fact that he committed it.

Prosecutors will solicit their own experts to rebut the assertion that the defendant was "insane" at the time of the offense before trial. Because prosecutors seek justice rather than convictions, a truly insane person who commits an offense would not be charged.

> **Reality Check!**
>
> *Defendants have been known to mimic insane personality traits and physical behavior, in order to deceive the court and avoid conviction and punishment for their crimes.*

Many prosecutors feel that a claim of temporary insanity is a convenient way of avoiding responsibility for criminal actions. A 1982 multiple-murder case tested the theory of temporary insanity in the courts.

George Banks murdered 13 people with an assault rifle. Seven of the victims were infants and children, including five of his own. Banks also shot a fourteenth person, who survived to testify at trial – along with two young boys who saw Banks shoot their mother to death.

Banks lived in Wilkes-Barre, Pennsylvania. In 1982 he was 40, working as a prison guard in a state correctional institution. Over the preceding six years, Banks had acquired four different paramours, with whom he had fathered five children. The women ranged in age from 17 to 27 when Banks became involved with them. At various times, all these woman and children lived with Banks.

By the summer of 1982, however, Banks' "family" was falling apart. In July, Sharon Mazzillo, mother of Banks' son Kismayu, moved with the child to her mother's residence.

A custody battle ensued. Banks commented to friends that he would kill Sharon if he did not get his son back, and would kill her mother too, because she had put Sharon up to it.

Banks had a previous family consisting of his legal wife and their two daughters. The wife and children left the area after Banks began his new relationships.

In early September, the mother of Banks' daughter Montanzima, also moved out, to a domestic violence shelter, and made plans to relocate to another state. Several days before the murders, Susan Yuhas, mother of Banks' children Bowende and Mauritania, was seen running from the house, with Banks after her. He yelled that she was leaving just like her sister (Susan and Regina were siblings). After he punched her in the head, she returned to the house with him.

Economic pressures were also mounting, despite Banks' prison job. Regina received a monthly $1200 Social Security check that would no longer be available to Banks if she moved away. Susan's income was also lost to him when she quit her job in early September. Banks put in for a transfer to a different prison, citing financial grounds.

He also applied for a HUD loan. He voiced suspicions that his paramours were stealing money from him, and that they were unfaithful.

On the night of September 24, three of Banks' paramours were attending a party at a friend's house. Banks called the house to speak with one of them,

Dorothy Lyons, the one woman who apparently had not announced an intention to leave him. Banks instructed Dorothy to retrieve his gun from the friend's house, where he had been keeping it. Dorothy, upset and crying, did as instructed, and the three women left the party for Banks' residence. This was the last point at which they, or their children, were seen alive.

The weapon was an AR-15 assault rifle, a semi-automatic civilian version of the military's M-16. Shortly before 2:00 am, a series of gunshots were heard from Banks' house. He emerged from the house carrying the gun and ran into a group of four people standing on the street. One of them remarked, "Hey, I know you."

Banks replied, "You're not going to live to tell anybody about this." He leveled the rifle in one hand and shot the man in the chest. Then he shot the next man in the chest, while the two remaining members of the group dived to the ground.

Banks walked on down the street. He shortly came to a parking lot where two men were conversing from their cars. Banks pointed his rifle at one of the men and told him to move over or get his head blown off. Banks told the man that he had just killed his children, and it would be wise not to give him any trouble. He then drove away with the man still in the car, but soon released him.

Banks drove several miles to the trailer home where his fourth paramour, Sharon, had moved in with her mother. Also staying at the trailer that night were Sharon and Banks' son Kismayu, Sharon's nephew Scott, and the two young sons of Sharon's mother. When Banks arrived he began pounding on the door, and broke it in. He told Sharon, with whom he had had the custody fight, that she should not have come between him and the child. He said that he had attempted to procure the parts necessary to render the weapon fully automatic, but did not complete the required forms, perhaps because of a prior felony conviction for a shooting during a robbery, and that now she could watch her son die. Banks then shot Kismayu, age 5, through the forehead. As Sharon ran out the door, Banks shot her in the back.

Next Banks chased Scott, the nephew, down the hallway, until the boy tripped. Banks hit him with the gun, grabbed him by the neck, and accused him of using a racial epithet against Banks' son. The crying boy, age 7, said he did not do it. Banks shot him in the back of the head.

Meanwhile, Sharon's mother tried to telephone the police. Banks spotted her and shot her between the eyes, blowing off the top of the skull. Her two sons, ages 9 and 11, were present. Banks told them he would get them next time and left. The boys picked up the phone from their mother's body and completed the call to the police.

Authorities soon arrived at both crime scenes. All the shooting victims at the trailer were dead. At Banks' house, police discovered Banks' paramour Regina on a living room couch. She had been shot in the face. Banks' paramour Susan was in an armchair, with shots to the head and chest. In her arms was her daughter with Banks, Mauritania.

The child, age 1, had been shot behind the ear. Also in the room was Banks' paramour, Dorothy, who had been shot through the chest and neck, and Banks' son, Bowende, age 4, shot in the face. Upstairs police found the body of Banks' daughter Montanzima, age 6, shot through the chest. In another bedroom was Dorothy's 11-year-old daughter (by another man), with defensive wounds through the arms and a fatal shot to the face, and Banks' son, Foraroude, age 1, shot in the eye. All were dead at the scene.

The two victims from outside Banks' house were rushed to the hospital. The man who had recognized Banks died. The other man, although in critical condition, was evacuated by helicopter to a trauma center and survived.

Later that morning, police located Banks at the house of a friend, and surrounded the residence. Banks was still armed with the assault rifle, along with 112 rounds of ammunition. During the standoff and thereafter, Banks, the son of an interracial couple, complained that he could not get fair treatment because of racial prejudice, and that he had killed his children to spare them the same fate.

He declared that he was going to kill himself, since he would die in the electric chair anyway. Despite repeated suicide threats, however, Banks elected to surrender without harming himself.

During processing at the police station, Banks expressed remorse for one of the victims, his son Kismayu. He claimed that particularly shooting had been accidental.

Banks was brought to trial in June 1983 over a period of three weeks, before a jury selected in another portion of the state. Banks' defense team of 3 attorneys called 28 witnesses, including 3 forensic psychiatrists, to testify to Banks' love for his children and disturbed state of mind.

Through his lawyers, his experts, and his own statements and testimony, Banks presented a variety of defense themes to the jury:

1. that he had amnesia and could not remember the actual shootings.
2. that he killed his children to save them from a life of racial prejudice.
3. that he was the victim of a police conspiracy to tamper with the evidence and cast him in a more culpable light.
4. that he was under the influence of alcohol and pills, and
5. that he was legally insane.

On June 21, 1983, the jury returned guilty verdicts on twelve counts of first degree murder, one count of third degree murder, one count of attempted murder, and the remaining assault, robbery and theft charges. The next day, the court convened a sentencing hearing before the same jury. The Commonwealth of Pennsylvania sought to prove three aggravating circumstances: that Banks knowingly created a grave risk of death to other persons, that he had a significant history of felony convictions involving violence, and that he had been convicted of another offense committed at the time of the offenses at issue for which a sentence of life imprisonment or death was imposable.

Banks and his counsel, on the other hand, sought to demonstrate the presence of three mitigating circumstances:

1. that Banks was under the influence of extreme mental or emotional disturbance,
2. that he had a substantially impaired capacity to appreciate the criminality of his conduct,
3. or to conform.

The defense secured blood, CAT, and EEG examinations of Banks, and later repeated the tests a second time to evaluate potential organic problems. The results were negative.

A search of the defendant's house revealed a notebook entry written *before* the crimes, in Banks' handwriting: "Not guilty, due to temporary insanity induced by the racial abuse of my family and young children."

The jury found the presence of one aggravating circumstance, the multiple murder aggravator, and weighed this against the mitigating evidence. The jury returned twelve death sentences.

Banks filed numerous appeals to State and Federal courts citing, among many things, that the trial court's sentencing instructions violated a previous court ruling that required a jury be unanimous with respect to any mitigating circumstances.

Eleven years later, appeals were still being filed, and Banks remains on Pennsylvania's death row.

DEFENDANT INVOLVED IN A DIFFERENT CONSPIRACY

The definition of a **conspiracy** is an agreement made between two or more people to violate the law. Many state conspiracy statutes require that one member of the agreement commit at least one **overt act** to consummate the crime of conspiracy. An overt act is anything done, whether it is criminal or not, to further the goal of the conspiracy. Overt acts carried out by the conspirators demonstrate they were sincere when they entered into the agreement to commit some other crime.

Entering into a conspiracy is a crime itself. If the conspirators achieve the goal of their conspiracy, every member of the conspiracy can be charged with the substantive crime, in addition to the crime of conspiracy. Conspiracy laws have been effective tools against organized crime, drug trafficking organizations, and terrorist networks.

Since conspiracy laws have a far-reaching effect on those who enter such agreements, they are extremely hard to defend against. A defense sometimes used in trial is that the defendant was indeed a member of a conspiracy but it was an entirely different conspiracy to the one that the defendant was indicted for. This defense seeks to exploit the legal concept that a conspiracy ends when the goal of the conspiracy is either achieved, or failed.

For example, in April, an undercover investigator meets with two drug dealers to negotiate the price for the purchase of a kilogram of cocaine. They all agree on a specific price that the undercover officer will pay upon delivery of the cocaine. On the morning of the day on which the delivery is to take place, one of the conspirators telephones the officer to tell him that their cocaine supplier was arrested, and they no longer have access to the cocaine. In May, the two conspirators contact the undercover officer again and say they now have another drug supplier, and can deliver 1000 ecstasy tablets immediately. Upon delivery of the ecstasy, the two men are arrested.

At trial, the defense attorney readily agrees with the prosecution's contention that his client, one of the two men involved in the original conspiracy, is a cocaine dealer. However, he alleges that the original April conspiracy he was indicted for, ended when the cocaine could not be delivered. The agreement to deliver ecstasy to the undercover officer in May was an entirely different conspiracy, and not the one alleged in his indictment. Both were charged in one indictment that includes the conspiracy to distribution of ecstasy. Is this an entirely different drug conspiracy case from the first, or is it all one conspiracy?

It may be deemed a different conspiracy if the investigator's reports and testimony is not clear about the negotiations. This legal maneuver is designed to overturn a conviction during an appeal, or to have the indictment dismissed outright before trial. Investigators need to amass as much evidence as possible

FIGURE 4.1 A defense attorney questions a witness during trial. *Getty Images.*

about a defendant's involvement in a particular conspiracy, and be as specific as possible when writing reports of investigation and testifying about the role of each defendant in the conspiracy in order to counter such claims.

Investigators need to closely coordinate with their prosecutors to render the proper charges in the indictment, in order to avoid a situation that may generate a successful appeal. The drug traffickers may have to be charged in two different indictments if prosecution is sought for the conspiracy to deliver two different types of drugs at different locations. Each conspiracy investigation is different, and must be dealt with individually. Many legal problems can be resolved by closely examining the facts of the case before an indictment is drawn up and presented to a grand jury.

OUTRAGEOUS GOVERNMENT CONDUCT

Facts are the defense attorney's worst enemy. When the facts are undisputable, defense attorneys will often attack the conduct of the investigators and prosecutor in their quest for an arrest and conviction in the case. Good defense attorneys will attack every aspect of the investigation. Sometimes they will allege that the government engaged in conduct that was so outrageous that the jury should show sympathy toward the defendant and punish the government for its conduct by acquitting the defendant.

For example, police investigators develop a female informant who claims to have information about several men who plan to conduct a series of bank robberies in the city. She knows the men have acquired weapons and a getaway vehicle, but does not know what banks they will target. The investigators instruct the informant to engage in conversation with the men to learn further about their plans.

Several days later, the woman returns to her police handlers and reports exactly when and where the first bank robbery will take place. The police stake out the bank, and when the armed robbers enter the bank building, they are arrested. The police later learn from the informant that she gained the details of the planned bank robbery from one defendant (who is married) after she provided him with many alcoholic beverages and then orally copulated him. During his intoxicated and relaxed state, he revealed to her the location of the robbery.

A written statement is taken from the informant and through the discovery process, it is furnished to the defense.

The defense immediately attacks the "immoral" police tactic of using "illicit sex" to obtain the "tainted" information about the bank robbery. He reminds the jury that the bank robbery never took place; that the informant had such low morals that she engaged a happily married man in adulterous activity, so that she could receive a reward from the bank for information about robberies.

The fact that the defendants were armed and were found to have stolen a car for their getaway, of course, would never be mentioned by the defense

THE WIZARD OF ID PARKER & HART

FIGURE 4.2   Wizard of Id cartoon. *Creators Syndicate, Inc.*

attorney, since these facts tend to prove the men were sincere about robbing the bank. However, the tactics employed by the informant, although legal, could raise serious questions among the jurors. This tactic would be especially effective in a venue where religious beliefs are strong, and such conduct on the part of the informant is highly offensive.

Another attack from the defense may be upon the investigators themselves. The defense attorney may conduct a cursory background on one of the investigators to determine his or her level of experience, ambitions, and reputation. During cross-examination of the investigator at trial, the defense may imply that he or she only targeted the defendant in order to enhance his poor job performance, or sought headlines in the local newspapers in order to get promoted within the police department. He may also allege that the investigator was so inexperienced that to suddenly be involved in such a high-profile, complicated criminal investigation was beyond his capacity. Also, he would have to create an environment for the defendant to succumb to the temptation to commit a crime that he would not have otherwise contemplated.

Prosecutors are not immune from attack either. Defense attorneys have accused them of seeking higher office, spoiling the jury pool with lies about the defendant during news conferences, or withholding exculpatory evidence just to achieve another conviction for their record.

In other instances, the defense may hire private investigators to perform thorough background investigations of informants to determine their criminal past. If it is determined that the informant is a convicted child molester, peeping Tom, or has been arrested for other similar crimes, the use of such an informant may be sufficient to convince the jury that the government condoned such activity in order to convict the defendant. If an informant, with such a past criminal history, provided the police with information that led to an arrest in return for leniency in a pending case against him where the victim was a child, this could prove to be especially troublesome for the prosecution.

> ### *Reality Check!*
>
> *The overwhelming reason why someone agrees to become an informant for the police is to receive consideration in a pending legal matter against them. Informants provide an invaluable service, but those who have an extensive or especially horrific criminal past will always be broadly painted by the defense as lacking morals, liars, or someone eager to do anything, even setting up an innocent person, solely to receive a reduced sentence. The defense will attempt to focus the jury's attention on the informant's criminal past and make him out to be a much worse character than the defendant. Even if the information provided by the informant is proven to be completely accurate, the defense will ask the jury to acquit the defendant as a way of "sending a message" to the government that its outrageous behavior will not be tolerated.*

SUMMARY

A defense counsel is a professionally trained and licensed attorney of law, whose job it is to represent the defendant in all phases of the criminal justice system. Whether hired by the defendant as a private criminal lawyer, working as a public defender, or appointed by the court, defense counsels are needed to ensure the defendant's civil rights are protected, and to present the best defense possible.

Defense attorneys have the power of subpoena to call witnesses, can hire expert witnesses to present an alternative conclusion to scientific evidence and render opinions about police procedures, and often hire private investigators to gather facts favorable to the defendant. They negotiate plea-bargains for defendants, and attempt to secure the best deal they can for them. They are also ethically bound to not knowingly use perjured testimony or other deceptive practices in their defense.

Defense attorneys use a variety of defenses and strategies to benefit their clients. The entrapment defense is when the defense counsel submits that the defendant had no predisposition to commit the criminal offense until the idea was planted in his mind by the police, solely for the purpose of arresting him.

Consent is a defense if the lack of consent is an essential element of the crime, such as rape.

Defense attorneys often allege that their clients are the victims of mistaken identity, or that the witnesses in the case simply do not have the capacity to see well. They will also claim that a witness to a crime was mistaken when he picked the defendant out in a line-up as the perpetrator of the offense.

Unless the defendant was caught in the act of the commission of the crime, the defense may allege that it was impossible for him to commit the crime since he was elsewhere at the time. The defense may produce a long list of witnesses, such as the defendant's mother, father, sister, brother, or spouse who will attempt to establish the defendant's alibi.

Despite the existence of physical evidence that substantiates guilt, the defendant may claim that his lack of motive should override the facts. The individual defendant's claim of lack of motive is most effective when the direct evidence against him is weak. The opposite happens when the evidence is substantial.

As a rule, to violate the law, criminal intent has to be combined with the act before a crime is consummated. Not all laws require the perpetrator to have intention to do something, but many do. Theft, for instance, is commonly described as the taking of property with the intention of permanently depriving the owner of it. The defense attorney will attempt to prove that the defendant lacked any such intent.

The blind mule defense is when someone denies any knowledge of being in possession of something illegal while transporting it. Most of these cases stem from drug interdiction cases at airports and other transportation nodes. It is closely related to lack of criminal intent and alibi defenses. The totality of circumstantial evidence gathered by the police will often dilute the man's claim that he had no knowledge he was transporting drugs or other contraband.

Another form of defense is that there was some legal justification for the defendant's actions. Justification claims can range from self-defense, excuse, or necessity.

A finding by the court of a defendant being legally insane relieves him of culpability for criminal actions. Defense counsel will sometimes assert insanity based on the particular viciousness of the crime, or the manner in which it was committed.

Since conspiracy laws have a far-reaching effect on those who enter such agreements, they are extremely hard to defend against. A defense sometimes used in trial is that the defendant was indeed a member of a conspiracy. However, it was an entirely different conspiracy than the one the defendant was indicted for. This defense seeks to exploit the legal concept that a conspiracy ends when the goal of the conspiracy is either achieved, or failed.

Facts are the defense attorney's worst enemy. When the facts are undisputable, defense attorneys will often attack the conduct of the investigators and prosecutor in their quest for an arrest and conviction in the case. Good defense attorneys will attack every aspect of the investigation, and sometimes allege that the government engaged in conduct that was so outrageous that the jury should show sympathy toward the defendant and punish the government for its conduct by acquitting the defendant.

NOTES

1. Law enforcement officers should check with their local prosecutor concerning the legality of using this technique in their particular state before it is attempted.

5

The Prosecutor's Role

INTRODUCTION

Prosecutors are known by many titles, such as U.S. Attorneys, solicitors, district attorneys, state's attorneys, city attorneys or county attorneys. They represent the government in federal and state criminal matters and have tremendous discretion that has an enormous affect on the lives of every person charged with a crime.

As members of the bar, they are held to high ethical standards and are expected to seek justice, not merely convict indicted criminals.

In our system of criminal justice, the prosecutor plays an important and necessary role. His or her job is to be impartial and to seek justice. Although their job is to prosecute criminals, they must first be satisfied that the suspect was responsible for the commission of the crime. Police officers and investigators arrest suspects of crimes, but it is the prosecutor who puts convicted defendants in prison. They rely heavily on the evidence that the police gathered during the course of their investigation when deciding to prosecute, and they will present the best case they can with whatever evidence is available. Obviously the more ammunition he or she is given by way of admissible evidence, the better chance they will have in hitting the target and securing a conviction.

PROSECUTORIAL DISCRETION

Prosecutors decide who will be prosecuted for a crime, not the police. They wield considerable *prosecutorial discretion* that affects every person arrested by the police. Prosecutors are the sole decision-makers in all criminal matters, as to whether to prosecute or not. Options available to most prosecutors include referring the defendant to a variety of diversion programs: including drug courts for first-time offenders; filing some, but not all the charges a defendant was arrested for; declining to prosecute; and accepting plea-bargains.

Many prosecutors face problems of backlogged cases and numerous delays that prolong the time cases are finally adjudicated. As a result, in an effort to speed up the process, mistakes are sometimes made. Other prosecutors give the appearance of being more concerned with winning convictions, rather than striving for justice.

A prosecutor's decision to file charges usually relies on the available evidence. They also base their decisions to prosecute on the nature of the crime, the likelihood of obtaining a conviction based on the jury pool or judge who will be hearing the case, and demands of the community.

Most prosecutors work for either elected or appointed officials, and these officials dictate the direction their office will take, and set the priorities for that office.

Sometimes prosecutors are accused of abusing their powers of discretion. Criticism may stem from failing to prosecute friends and political supporters, from being over-zealous in their duties to bring criminals to justice, or selectively prosecuting only members of certain ethnic groups. Some prosecutors are accused of being too high profile in their office, and of using their office solely for their political ambitions.

Many career prosecutors seek and later receive appointments for judgeships at the state and federal levels.

Reality Check!

Voters in the communities they serve elect most district attorneys. The U.S. Attorney for the district he serves is a Presidential appointee and hires Assistant U.S. Attorneys. Convictions are the lifeblood of any prosecutor's career, and the likelihood of conviction sometimes serves as the basis for deciding whether to file criminal charges or not. The decision to prosecute someone will almost always stem from the quality of the police investigation handed to the prosecutor. Some investigations may serve to only identify a suspect, but are insufficient in the prosecutor's opinion to secure a conviction. Sometimes political factors are considered before taking on high-profile cases.

In many federal court districts, the U.S. Attorney's Office will set *thresholds* before seeking an indictment and pursuing a prosecution. For example, in federal drug cases, the threshold amount of cocaine possessed by a defendant, before the U.S. Attorney's Office will indict him for the offense, can vary dramatically from district to district. In Los Angeles, which is within the Central District of California, the threshold amount to prosecute someone in possession of cocaine for sale may be 2 kilograms (4.4 pounds). In a smaller district in the mid-west, the threshold may only be 8 ounces.

Thresholds may also apply to the value of stolen items or amount of money embezzled, or an individual having a connection with a well-established criminal organization.

The impact of the prosecution on the community is considered, as well as the availability of Assistant U.S. Attorneys (AUSAs). Many cases brought before AUSAs are also declined because of the lack of available federal judges to hear the matter, their own enormous workload, or a shift in prosecution priorities. Fortunately, many federal laws duplicate state criminal statutes and allow federal agents to approach their local district attorney or state prosecutor to seek indictments, when an otherwise good case cannot be handled by the U.S. Attorney's office.

There are many criminal statutes that are uniquely federal in nature. Counterfeiting U.S. currency, threats against the President, and violation of immigration and customs laws are several examples. There is no place other than federal court for prosecution of these violations.

Politics and the demands of the communities that these prosecutors serve have a direct influence on their decisions to prosecute. A surge of patients in hospital emergency rooms being treated for overdosing on ecstasy could be influential in the U.S. Attorney accepting more cases for sales of the drug, despite established thresholds. Demands from local politicians to have local drug dealers prosecuted in federal court, in order for them to receive sometimes significantly higher prison sentences, could also have an influence on federal prosecutions.

Local district attorneys are usually elected officials whose political survival may depend upon conviction rates. Sometimes cases, in which the likelihood of conviction is questionable, will not be pursued in order to preserve an otherwise stellar conviction rate.

A defendants reputation in the community may also have an influence on the prosecutor's decision to prosecute. Some prosecutors will either decline or accept a case to prosecute someone simply because of their community standing. Prosecutors do not want to appear to be partial or subject to influence by anyone, and prosecuting them is one way of deflecting such criticism. An example is a Hollywood star being prosecuted for shoplifting when an ordinary citizen, in the exact same circumstances, may have been referred to a diversion program in lieu of prosecution.

VENUE

Venue is defined as the locality where a crime is committed or political subdivision from which a jury is called and in which a trial is held. Where a crime occurs will dictate where it will be prosecuted. Defense attorneys have no such limitation. So long as they are licensed to practice law in a particular state, they can represent a defendant at trial there.

Venue is something experienced police and federal investigators take advantage of. Many organized criminals commit a variety of offenses in different venues. If a conspiracy is alleged, and overt acts to further the conspiracy were committed by members of the conspiracy in several venues, the investigators have the option of presenting their case to a prosecutor for their consideration in each of theses venues. An overt act is anything done, whether it is a criminal act or not, that furthers the goal of the conspiracy.

For example, two men commit a robbery. Through investigation, the police determine one of the men purchased a pistol intended to be, and actually used, in the robbery, from a gun store in a city that lies in a different venue. The police now have the option of approaching a prosecutor in either venue to seek an indictment. Police will always refer criminal investigations to their primary venue, but under certain circumstances, they may want to present their case in the other venue instead. This situation may arise from one prosecutor's office having too large a workload to handle the matter, or if a jury is more likely to return a favorable verdict against the defendants in the second venue.

COORDINATION WITH THE PROSECUTOR

Before launching a proactive criminal investigation, such as a non-reported crime like a drug case, investigators should seek the counsel of their local prosecutor. Investigations of this nature can be streamlined when a mutual understanding is reached between the investigators and the prosecutor who will be responsible for trying the case.

Strategy meetings should be conducted between the investigators and prosecutor to discuss the goal of the investigation as well as the availability of witnesses, evidence, and anticipated defense tactics that will be used at trial.

A way of "pitching" the case before a prosecutor considers prosecution, is to give him or her a realistic overview of the investigation, as well as the anticipated results. Police should strive to have a prosecutor dedicated to their case, who can be consulted with during the course of any long-term investigation. They should also seek a commitment from the prosecutor to prosecute the defendants identified during the course of the investigation, if sufficient evidence exists to prosecute.

During more traditional, after-the-fact forms of investigations, investigators should also coordinate with their prosecutors early and often to seek guidance on what evidence is likely to be located, and what other concerns he or she has about its admissibility. Prosecutors should be considered to be a member of the investigative team. They will almost always be sought for their assistance in drafting affidavits for search warrants and indictments, as their assistance is invaluable. Many prosecutors will make themselves available so that the police can immediately notify them and discuss fast-moving developments with them.

During any multiple-defendant, long-term investigation, the prosecutor will seek all information about all crimes the police have discovered that were committed by the defendants. Reports of investigation should be provided to the prosecutor as soon as they have been written and approved by a supervisor.

ARREST WARRANT AFFIDAVITS

Most uniformed police officers make arrests based upon probable cause or when a crime is committed in their presence. Investigators usually rely on arrest warrants before taking a suspect into custody.

Arrest warrants are supported by a sworn affidavit from an investigator knowledgeable about the investigation, and also the evidence that was developed to bring them to the conclusion that a particular suspect committed the crime. Investigators must coordinate with their prosecutor to draft and approve the affidavit before it is presented to a judge or magistrate for their signature.

Arrest warrants provide the police flexibility in their investigative strategy and provide civil liability for law enforcement officers who serve them.

SEARCH WARRANT AFFIDAVITS

Many criminal investigations require the execution of search warrants for evidence and fruits of the crime. Judges and magistrates only grant search warrants if sufficient probable cause exists to believe that these things are present at the location to be searched.

Prosecutors work closely with the police in drafting search warrant affidavits, and sometimes they are tailor-made to satisfy the particular judicial officer that will be approached for approval. Prosecutors know the sitting judges best, and smooth the path for investigators in doing their jobs. A detailed discussion will be made about affidavits in Chapter 7.

MATERIAL WITNESS WARRANTS

Prosecutors can seek a *material witness warrant* in some venues for a person who is essentially an unindicted coconspirator, and his testimony is necessary for future court proceedings. In most cases the witness is required to post a bond, and in some cases he may be lodged in a jail facility to guarantee his presence in court. The federal government uses material witness warrants extensively, especially during drug and terrorist investigations.

GRAND JURY PROCEEDINGS AND SUBPOENAS

In the federal system and in many jurisdictions, a suspect must be indicted by a *grand jury* within the venue of the criminal offense, within ten days of being placed into custody. Some jurisdictions will rely on a preliminary hearing before a judge, to establish probable cause that a crime occurred and that the suspect in custody is the perpetrator. In either event, a prosecutor represents the government. Defense attorneys are not allowed to attend grand jury proceedings. Once indicted, a suspect automatically becomes a defendant in a criminal matter.

Grand juries consist of a body of citizens from the venue, who are impaneled at random and serve for between 1 and 18 months. Most grand juries consist of 24 persons.

Grand juries can also indict suspects before they are in custody. Once a *true bill of indictment* is returned by the grand jury, a judge will issue an arrest warrant to have the suspect taken into custody.

Some investigators will appear before grand juries to brief them on ongoing investigations, in which there is a potential for numerous defendants. Being curious, many grand jurors will embrace taking part in the criminal justice system and learning about the progress of the investigation. By periodically briefing them on the progress of a case, investigators save themselves and the grand jury valuable time when it comes to requesting indictments of the suspects. They are already up to speed on the individual activities of the suspects, and the requirement for an extraordinary amount of grand jury time is minimized.

In many districts, grand juries only meet once or twice a week. Sometimes investigations progress more rapidly than expected, and the need to appear before a grand jury may be immediate.

A grand jury also has the power of subpoena. After coordinating with a prosecutor, an investigator can seek a subpoena from the grand jury for financial records, telephone toll information, and other documents of a suspect. Grand jury subpoenas, in many jurisdictions, are the only way for investigators to obtain financial records without having to request a search warrant for the bank's records.

SEALED INDICTMENTS AND ARREST WARRANTS

Sealing arrest warrants and criminal indictments to disguise their existence is a strategic move to not alert the suspects that they are under investigation. The prosecutor can seek the court's permission to seal these documents. Once an arrest warrant is served or a search warrant is executed, the seal is broken and it becomes a matter of public record.

PLEA-BARGAINING

An important role of the prosecutor is to negotiate through the process of *plea-bargaining* with a defendant, to accept a lesser charge or reduced sentence in return for a guilty plea. This is a necessary evil within the criminal justice system, in order to clear court calendars and speed the process to move on to other matters. It also saves large amounts of taxpayer money when a full-blown court proceeding is avoided, especially since the outcome of a trial is never certainty.

Plea-bargains are based largely on the criminal record of the defendant, the nature of the crime, and the status of the victim of the crime. The police officers and investigators involved in the matter often have input about the decision to plea-bargain with a defendant.

Plea-bargains usually include *proffers*. A proffer is a formal offer of information of facts by the defendant to the prosecutor in exchange for a reduction in charges or the sentence the defendant is likely to receive. In most cases, the defendant will be required to testify in criminal proceedings against others involved in the crime. Most proffers are conducted by means of a formal interview between police investigators, and the defendant and his attorney.

The police will evaluate the information for authenticity, and its value in expanding their instant investigation and identifying other suspects. The prosecutor will evaluate the defendant's ability to be a credible witness and the impact the information will have at trial.

OFFERS OF IMMUNITY

The prosecutor is the only person who has the authority to offer immunity to a defendant. Offers of immunity are generally based on the need of a defendant to provide testimony against the other members of a criminal conspiracy. When the prosecutor feels that the defendant's testimony will be essential to the conviction of others, or may convince other defendants in the same case to plead guilty, he or she will seriously consider granting a form of immunity.

Often there are conditions attached to the granting of immunity, such as the defendant's full and complete cooperation throughout the investigative and trial processes. Violating the agreement will subject the defendant to prosecution.

There are two forms of immunity: use and blanket. *Use immunity* only covers the crimes that the defendant is being charged with. *Blanket immunity* is seldom offered or granted, because it immunizes the defendant from all crimes he may have committed during a particular period of time. Immunity, in any form is selectively granted, and always with the promise of receiving something substantial in return.

Some criminal cases do not move on to trial, if at least one defendant in a multiple-defendant case does not testify about the words, deeds, and actions of the other codefendants.

Prosecutors will base their decision to grant immunity on the policy of the chief prosecutor, the totality of the evidence gathered during the course of the investigation, as well as other factors that may have an influence.

PRE-TRIAL MOTIONS

Prosecutors answer a variety of *pre-trial motions* presented by the defense before trial commences. A motion is an oral, but usually written, petition, requesting the court to make a specific finding or decision. Motions can be made before, during, or after trial.

Reality Check!

Many of these motions are designed to delay the start of the trial as long as possible in the hopes that prosecution witnesses will later not be available, their memories will fade, or evidence will later become unavailable or useless.

Typical pre-trial motions include:

- **Motion for Discovery.** The defense requests the court to order the prosecutor to allow him or her to view specific items of evidence, witness lists, copies of documents, photographs, police reports and other material that it intended to be introduced at trial.

- **Motion to Dismiss Charges.** The defense may petition the court to dismiss charges against the defendant, based on his own legal opinion that the indictment is not sound; a plea-bargain arrangement; violation of the speedy trial act; the death of a vital witness; the destruction of important evidence; exculpatory evidence, including the statements of a victim or witness that facts were fabricated; or lack of evidence to secure a conviction.

- **Motion to Suppress Evidence.** Motion to suppress evidence the defense believes was acquired illegally.
- **Motion for Continuance.** Defense seeks to delay the start of the trial, often based upon the inability to locate a vital witness or due to the illness of the defendant.
- **Motion for Change of Venue.** Defense alleges that pre-trial publicity has diminished the defendant's ability to receive a fair trial. Defense requests that the trial be held in a different venue, where the jury pool has not been subjected to this publicity.
- **Motion for Severance of Offenses.** Defendants, who are charged with a variety of crimes, request that they be tried separately on all, or at least some of the charges.
- **Motion for Severance of Defendants.** Defense requests that the defendant be tried separately from other defendants charged with the same offense. Defendants with a minor role in a major conspiracy often make this request.
- **Motion to Determine Present Sanity.** A tactic in delaying the trial comes when the defense requests the court to postpone trial until the sanity of the defendant can be determined. Defendants cannot be tried or punished while insane.
- **Motion for Bill of Particulars.** Defense request the court to order the prosecutor to provide specific, detailed information about the charges that the defendant will face. This motion usually arises when the defendant is charged with multiple counts of the same offense.

In many cases, once each motion presented to the court is denied, the defendant will change his plea from not guilty to guilty. The prosecutor must endure these motions and argue against them before the court. They also often offer insights into what defense strategy will be presented at trial.

POST-TRIAL MOTIONS

Post-trial motions are designed to undo the conviction that the defendant has been handed down. Although motions may be made at any time, the following are usually submitted after a defendant has been convicted:

- **Motion for a Mistrial.** Motion can be made by either the prosecutor or defense. They are usually made by the defense when they believe that highly prejudicial comments were made by the prosecutor in the presence of the jury. A dismissal of the trial does not invoke the double jeopardy clause of the constitution.
- **Motion for Arrest of Judgment.** Motion is made after a guilty verdict, but before sentencing. Defense alleges that there is a legally acceptable reason why sentence should not be pronounced. This

motion usually stems from the hospitalization of the defendant or his required presence elsewhere.

- **Motion for a New Trial.** The motion generally comes with the discovery of exculpatory evidence that will be beneficial to the defense.

JURY SELECTION

The prosecutor and defense share the responsibility for selecting the jury that will sit during a criminal trial. In most states, 12 Jurors are used in criminal matters, with two alternates to serve in the absence of an original juror because of illness or personal emergency.

Prospective jurors are selected from names gathered from voter registration roles, motor vehicle, and tax records. They are required to be English-speaking adults, not be convicted felons, be U.S. citizens, and have the capacity to understand the facts that will be presented at trial. Although possible, it is unlikely that a blind person or someone with a severe disability will be allowed to serve as a juror.

FIGURE 5.1 Prosecutor conferring with the case investigator about jury selection before the commencement of a criminal trial. *Getty Images.*

The prosecutor's job is to screen prospective jurors for open or hidden prejudices before accepting them on a criminal matter.

Reality Check!

Some jurors will disguise their prejudices in order to serve on a particular jury. Some may show undue sympathy toward the accused or disdain for the victim. Others harbor anti-government feelings, including deep-rooted dislike for the police, or have hidden agendas to receive their "fifteen minutes of fame" in high-profile cases. Others will not convict a member of their own racial group, regardless of overwhelming evidence, especially if the victim of the crime is of a different race. Prosecutors and defense attorneys both select potential jurors who will most likely side with them during deliberation.

Prosecutors and defense attorneys have three ways of challenging a juror: challenges to the array; challenges for cause; and peremptory challenges. Challenges of array usually come from defense, when he or she feels that the potential juror is either biased or does not represent the community.

Challenges for cause generally stem from the perception that the potential juror cannot or will not be impartial. The prosecutor may argue against a juror who claims he or she cannot find someone guilty if the conviction may result in him receiving the death penalty.

Peremptory challenges can be made by both the prosecutor and defense without having to give a reason. A potential jurors physical appearance, dress, or body language is sufficient reason to remove them from consideration. The number of peremptory challenges are limited to as few as 3 to as many as 20, depending upon the number in the jury pool, and if the case involves a capital offense.

An expanding new expertise in the area of **jury consultants** has emerged, in which jurors are screened for their likelihood of returning a verdict of guilty or not guilty. These experts factor the potential juror's socio-economic background, employment, ethnicity, and other considerations during the screening process. Their findings are used often during peremptory challenges in high-profile cases, where the government or defendant is willing to pay the expensive fees associated with this service.

The lead investigator involved in the case usually is invited, or required to sit at the prosecution table during the trial, in order to help the prosecutor with forming questions for witnesses and recognizing differences between a witness's testimony and what was said during the course of the investigation. Investigator's who sit as the **case agent** or **case investigator** have a tremendous opportunity to learn defense trial tactics and see the criminal justice system in action. The case investigator will also have the opportunity to give input to the prosecutor during jury selection, who he or she feels would be an acceptable juror.

FIGURE 5.2   A prosecutor addresses the jury during opening statements. *Getty Images.*

Other investigators involved in the investigation are usually sequestered from the courtroom, so they cannot form their testimony to be exactly as other witnesses who have already testified.

SUMMARY

Prosecutors are known by many titles, such as U.S. Attorneys, solicitors, district attorneys, state's attorneys, city attorneys or county attorneys. They represent the government in federal and state criminal matters and have tremendous discretion that has an enormous affect on the lives of every person charged with a crime. They play an important role in the criminal justice system.

Prosecutors wield considerable prosecutorial discretion that affects every person arrested by the police. Prosecutors are the sole decision-makers in all criminal matters, as to whether to prosecute or not. There are many other options that the prosecutor can exercise, such as a drug diversion program, in lieu of prosecuting a defendant.

A prosecutor's venue is the locality where a crime is committed or political subdivision from which a jury is called and in which a trial is held.

Before launching a proactive investigation, such as a drug case, investigators should coordinate with their local prosecutor to seek his or her counsel. Investigations of this nature can be streamlined when a mutual understanding is reached between the investigators and the prosecutor who will be responsible for trying the case.

Arrest warrants are supported by a sworn affidavit from an investigator knowledgeable about the investigation and the evidence that was developed to bring them to the conclusion that a particular suspect committed a crime. Investigators must coordinate with their prosecutor to draft and approve the affidavit before it is presented to a judge or magistrate for their signature.

Prosecutors work closely with the police in drafting search warrant affidavits, and sometimes they are tailor-made to satisfy the particular judicial officer that will be approached for approval. Prosecutors know the sitting judges best, and smooth the path for investigators in doing their jobs.

Prosecutors can seek a material witness warrant in some venues for persons who are essentially unindicted coconspirators, and their testimony is necessary for future court proceedings.

In most jurisdictions, a suspect must be indicted by a grand jury within the venue where a criminal offense occurred within ten days of being placed into custody. Some jurisdictions will rely on a preliminary hearing before a judge, to establish probable cause that a crime occurred and that the suspect in custody is the responsible perpetrator. In either event, a prosecutor represents the government in these proceedings.

Prosecutors also conduct plea-bargains, make offers of immunity in exchange for a defendant's testimony and argue for and against pre-trial motions.

The prosecutor and defense share the responsibility for selecting the jury that will sit during a criminal trial. In most states, 12 Jurors are used in criminal matters, with two alternates to serve in the absence of an original juror because of illness or personal emergency. The prosecutor's job is to screen prospective jurors for open or hidden prejudices before accepting them on a criminal matter.

6

Exclusionary Rule of Evidence

INTRODUCTION

The *Exclusionary rule* of evidence prohibits the admissibility of evidence, illegally obtained by the police. It is a judicial invention conceived to serve as both a remedy and deterrent to police misconduct, applying to both unlawfully seized evidence and confessions in violation of the U.S. Constitution.

Evidence obtained by police officers in violation of the Fourth Amendment to the Constitution was at one time admissible in federal and state courts. In a 1914 U.S. Supreme Court decision, *Weeks* v. *U.S.*,[1] the court ruled that all evidence obtained by searches and seizures in violation of the Federal Constitution was inadmissible in a criminal trial in federal court. This was even though the exclusion of evidence is not specifically mentioned in the constitution as a remedy. This ruling did not apply to state courts, but it did give birth to what has become to known as the exclusionary rule.

For example, the Fourth Amendment prohibits the government from conducting an unreasonable search or seizure, but does not expressly provide for the exclusion of evidence at trial if the government violates that prohibition. The *Weeks* decision introduced the exclusionary rule as a remedy for violations of the Fourth Amendment. Prior to the exclusionary rule, when determining the admissibility of evidence, courts would not consider the manner in which a witness gained possession of an item that was otherwise properly offered in evidence. The *Weeks* court felt that the only way to effectively enforce a defendant's Fourth Amendment right to be secure from unreasonable searches and seizures was if evidence seized by the police in violation of the amendment could not be used by the government against a defendant in trial. The Supreme Court further reasoned that a court should not sanction illegal government conduct by admitting into evidence the fruits of that illegal conduct.

The exclusionary rule announced in *Weeks* initially did not apply to the states, because at that time the Supreme Court limited the application of the Fourth Amendment to the federal government. In 1949, the Supreme Court decided *Wolf* v. *Colorado*,[2] in which the Court applied the Fourth Amendment to the states through the Fourteenth Amendment's due process clause. The Court felt that the Fourth Amendment prohibition against unreasonable searches or seizures is basic to a free society and inherent of liberty. However, the Court did not view the exclusionary rule as a necessary component of due process and refused to apply the exclusionary rule to the states as a remedy for a violation of the Fourth Amendment. The period between the *Weeks* and *Wolf* saw 47 states review the applicability of the exclusionary rule, 16 adopting the rule, and 31 rejecting it.

In 1961, the Supreme Court decided another landmark case, *Mapp* v. *Ohio*.[3]

Police officers in Ohio conducted a warrantless search of a home, looking for evidence and found illegal obscene material belonging to a woman named Mapp. She was subsequently prosecuted and convicted in state court. The court allowed the admissibility of the evidence in spite of the officers not obtaining a search warrant, because the Fourth Amendment exclusionary rule only applied in federal criminal matters.

Mapp appealed her conviction to the U.S. Supreme Court. Her attorney argued that because the exclusionary rule applied to federal court, it should be applicable to state courts. The court agreed. In their opinion, the justices said "Since the Fourth Amendment's right of privacy has been declared enforceable against the States through the Due Process Clause of the Fourteenth Amendment, it is enforceable against them by the same sanction of exclusion as is used against the Federal Government."

The Court, in part, overruled *Wolf* and applied the exclusionary rule to the states. The *Mapp* Court viewed other remedies, such as criminal sanctions, as being ineffective in ensuring compliance with the Fourth Amendment. Although the Court stated that the exclusionary rule was an essential part of both the Fourth and Fourteenth Amendments, subsequent Supreme Court decisions have abandoned that position. *Mapp* caused the states to initiate procedures for the conduct of what are known as "suppression hearings," sometimes called "evidentiary hearings," to determine if evidence seized in violation of the Fourth Amendment should be excluded at trial.

The Supreme Court now views the exclusionary rule as a judicially created remedy, which is obviously not constitutionally required. For example, in *United States* v. *Leon*,[4] the Supreme Court stated that "[t] he Fourth Amendment contains no provision expressly precluding the use of evidence obtained in violation of its commands, and an examination of its commands and purposes makes clear that the use of fruits of a past unlawful search or seizure 'works no new Fourth Amendment wrong'," quoting from *United States* v. *Calandra*.[5] The Court further stated in *Calandra* that "[t]he purpose of the exclusionary rule is not to redress the injury to the privacy of the search victim . . . Instead, the rule's prime purpose is to deter future unlawful police conduct and thereby effectuate the guarantee of the Fourth Amendment against unreasonable search and seizures . . . In sum, the rule is a judicially created remedy designed to safeguard Fourth Amendment rights generally through its deterrent effect, rather than a personal constitutional right of the party aggrieved."

Although the exclusionary rule is most often applied to violations of the Fourth Amendment, it has been applied to other constitutional violations as well.

For example, the Fifth Amendment prohibits the government from compelling someone to be a witness against himself. While the jury may wish to hear what a defendant has to say, a judge cannot compel the defendant to testify at trial. Consequently, the defendant's testimony would be excluded unless he decides to waive his constitutional right and testify. Coerced confessions made by a defendant, as well as confessions obtained by the police without first advising the defendant of his Miranda rights, are also inadmissible under the exclusionary rule doctrine.

FRUIT OF THE POISONOUS TREE

In a 1920, Supreme Court decision, *Silverthorne Lumber* v. *United States*,[6] the Court prohibited not only the introduction in evidence of those items directly seized during an illegal government search, but also *any evidence that is indirectly derived from that search*.

The Court did add, however, "of course this does not mean that the facts thus obtained become sacred and inaccessible. If knowledge of them is gained from an independent source they may be proved like any others . . . "

In a 1939 decision, *Nardone* v. *United States*,[7] the Supreme Court followed up on *Silverthorne Lumber* by adding that evidence illegally obtained will be excluded provided that the "connection between the illegal conduct and the evidence has not become so attenuated as to dissipate the taint of the illegality."

For example, the police conduct a surreptitious warrantless search of a known drug dealer's residence and discover a receipt for a storage locker in town. The police then apply for and receive a search warrant for the storage facility and discover laboratory equipment and several pounds of methamphetamine, which they seize. Because the original information about the existence of the storage facility stemmed from an unlawful search, the drugs and laboratory equipment would be considered fruits of the illegal activity, and excluded as evidence at the defendant's trial.

The same applies to information police receive as a result of an informant deliberately eliciting a statement from an already indicted defendant, because it is in violation of the defendant's Sixth Amendment right to counsel. This is even though the Sixth Amendment does not expressly provide exclusion of evidence as a remedy for a violation. In the above example, if the informant was directed by the police to find out from the defendant where he stored his methamphetamine, after he was indicted and arrested, the recovered drugs would also be excluded.

Another reason for the adoption of the exclusionary rule is to maintain the dignity and integrity of the courts, by keeping tainted evidence away from the courtroom and relieving the courts from participating in the illegal conduct of police officers.

The exclusionary rule in court proceedings is also applicable in other than criminal trials, including juvenile proceedings, narcotics commitment procedures, and forfeiture proceedings.

EXCEPTIONS TO THE EXCLUSIONARY RULE

The Supreme Court has consistently recognized that the inflexible application of the exclusionary rule would generate disrespect for the law and impede the administration of justice. Considering this, courts have carved out a number of exceptions and limitations to the rule. To otherwise apply the rule would go beyond the limited goal of a simple deterrent to illegal police conduct.

There are some other types of judicial proceedings where illegally obtained evidence may be held admissible, simply because the deterrent purpose of the rule is deemed outweighed by public policy favoring the use of any relevant evidence, even if it is illegally obtained. For example, in many states illegally obtained evidence is usually allowed in parole revocation proceedings. The sentencing hearing of a defendant may also consider illegally obtained evidence, even though it was not considered at trial.

Standing

In a 1978 Supreme Court ruling, *Rakas* v. *Illinois*,[8] the Court ruled that if the police violated the personal constitutional rights of someone other than the defendant, he lacks standing to object to the admission of the resulting evidence.

After receiving a robbery report, police stopped the suspected getaway car, which the owner was driving, with Rakas and others as passengers. Upon searching the car, the police found a box of rifle shells in the glove compartment and a sawed-off rifle under the front passenger seat. Everyone in the vehicle was arrested. Rakas and the others were convicted in an Illinois court of armed robbery, in which the rifle and shells were admitted as evidence at trial. Rakas and the other passengers of the vehicle moved to suppress the rifle and shells on Fourth Amendment grounds, but the trial court denied the motion on the grounds that they lacked standing to object to the lawfulness of the search of the car, because they concededly did not own either the car or the rifle and shells. The Illinois Appellate Court affirmed.

The U.S. Supreme Court held that "Fourth Amendment rights are personal rights which . . . may not be vicariously asserted, and a person aggrieved by an illegal search and seizure only through the introduction of damaging evidence secured by a search of a third person's premises or property has not had any of his Fourth Amendment rights infringed."

Good Faith

In *Leon*, the Court ruled that evidence, seized under the authority of an invalid warrant, would not be suppressed *if* a reasonable agent acting in good faith had relied on the warrant. This ruling severely limits defense attorneys in their attempts to invalidate otherwise valid search warrants during suppression hearings in most U.S. judicial districts.

The *Leon* decision stems from a search warrant executed by the Burbank, California Police Department, after the warrant was reviewed by a deputy district attorney and later by a state court judge who granted the warrant. The warrant allowed the police to seize a large amount of drugs at Leon's residence and within his vehicles. He was later federally indicted, and his attorney sought to suppress the warrant and thus the evidence obtained through it, based on the application lacking probable cause. The federal district court agreed, as did the 9th Circuit Court of Appeals. The U.S. Supreme Court, however, thought differently.

The Court stated "The Fourth Amendment exclusionary rule should not be applied so as to bar the use in the prosecution's case in chief of evidence obtained by officers acting in reasonable reliance on a search warrant issued by a detached and neutral magistrate but ultimately found to be invalid."

The Court went on to say "An examination of the Fourth Amendment's origin and purposes makes clear that the use of fruits of a past unlawful search or seizure works no new Fourth Amendment wrong. The question whether the exclusionary sanction is appropriately imposed in a particular case as a judicially created remedy to safeguard Fourth Amendment rights through its deterrent effect, must be resolved by weighing the costs and benefits of preventing the use in the prosecution's case in chief of inherently trustworthy tangible evidence.

FIGURE 6.1 Federal Bureau of Investigation special agents conduct a raid and remove boxes of evidence from a home in Lackawanna, New York late on September 13, 2002. Five suspects were taken into custody for having connections to the Al-Qaeda network. The five Buffalo suspects were convicted of providing material support and resources for possible attacks, and admitted they were all graduates of Osama Bin Laden's Al Qaeda terrorist training camps in Afghanistan. *REUTERS/Mark Dye/Corbis.*

Indiscriminate application of the exclusionary rule – impeding the criminal justice system's truth-finding function and allowing some guilty defendants to go free – may well generate disrespect for the law and the administration of justice.

"Application of the exclusionary rule should continue where a Fourth Amendment violation has been substantial and deliberate, but the balancing approach that has evolved in determining whether the rule should be applied in a variety of contexts – including criminal trials – suggests that the rule should be modified to permit the introduction of evidence obtained by officers reasonably relying on a warrant issued by a detached and neutral magistrate."

Until *Leon*, defense attorneys routinely challenged search warrants as lacking probable cause, despite an impartial magistrate's opinion to the contrary.

Attenuation

If the evidence is so attenuated from the illegal conduct of the police that it cannot be said that it was obtained from the exploitation by the police of that illegal conduct, then the evidence will not be suppressed.

In *Wong Sun* v. *United States*,[9] he and others were arrested by federal narcotic agents for possession of heroin based only on probable cause, and not relying on an arrest warrant issued by a magistrate. Wong was arraigned, released to his own recognizance, and several days later voluntarily submitted to an interview by the agents. During this time he made an unsigned statement admitting to possessing the heroin.

The Court ruled that even though Wong's arrest was unlawful, he had been lawfully arraigned and released on his own recognizance and had returned voluntarily several days later to be interviewed by the agents where he made his unsigned statement. The Court said, ". . . the connection between his unlawful arrest and the making of that statement was so attenuated that the unsigned statement was not the fruit of the unlawful arrest and, therefore, it was properly admitted in evidence."

Independent Source

Most courts will not suppress evidence found during an illegal search, when the evidence is also located through some independent lawful source.

In *Sugura* v. *United States*,[10] DEA Task Force Agents illegally entered the defendant's premises without a valid search warrant, and arrested one of the occupants. During a security sweep of the apartment for their own safety, DEA Task Force Agents found cocaine in plain view. They then "froze" the apartment, pending the issuance of a search warrant.

In January 1981, the New York Drug Enforcement Task Force received information indicating that Andres Segura and Luz Marina Colon probably were trafficking in cocaine from their New York apartment. Acting on this information, Task Force agents maintained continuing surveillance over them until their arrest on February 12, 1981. On February 9, agents observed a meeting between Segura and another defendant, Enrique Rivudalla-Vidal, when the two discussed the possible sale of cocaine by Segura to Rivudalla-Vidal. Three days later, February 12, Segura telephoned Rivudalla-Vidal and agreed to provide him with cocaine. The two agreed that the delivery would be made at 5 P.M. that day, at a designated fast-food restaurant in Queens, N. Y. Rivudalla-Vidal and another conspirator, Esther Parra, arrived at the restaurant as agreed. While Segura and Rivudalla-Vidal visited inside the restaurant, agents observed Colon deliver a bulky package to Parra, who had remained in Rivudalla-Vidal's car in the restaurant parking lot. A short time after the delivery of the package, Rivudalla-Vidal and Parra left the restaurant and proceeded to their apartment. Task Force agents followed. The agents stopped them as they were about to enter Rivudalla-Vidal's apartment. Parra was found to possess cocaine and both he and Rivudalla-Vidal were immediately arrested.

After Rivudalla-Vidal and Parra were advised of their constitutional rights, Rivudalla-Vidal agreed to cooperate with the agents. He admitted that he had purchased the cocaine from Segura, and he confirmed that Colon had made the delivery at the fast-food restaurant earlier that day, as the agents had observed. Rivudalla-Vidal informed the agents that Segura was to call him at approximately 10 P.M. that evening to learn if Rivudalla-Vidal had sold the cocaine, in which case Segura was to deliver additional cocaine.

Between 6:30 and 7 P.M. on the same day, Task Force agents sought and received authorization from an Assistant U.S. Attorney to arrest Segura and Colon based upon the probable cause that they had developed through their investigation. The agents were advised by the Assistant U.S. Attorney that because of the lateness of the hour, a search warrant for Segura's apartment probably could not be obtained until the following day, but that the agents should proceed to secure the premises to prevent the destruction of evidence.

At about 7:30 P.M., the agents arrived outside Segura's apartment and established surveillance. At 11:15 P.M., Segura, alone, entered the lobby of the apartment building and was immediately arrested by the agents. He first claimed that he did not reside in the building. The agents took him to his third floor apartment, and when they knocked on the apartment door, a woman later identified as Colon appeared. The agents then entered with Segura, without requesting or receiving permission. There were three persons in the living room of the apartment in addition to Colon. The agents advised those present that Segura was under arrest and that a search warrant for the apartment was being obtained.

Following this brief exchange in the living room, the agents conducted a limited security sweep of the apartment to ensure that no one else was there who might pose a threat to their safety or destroy evidence. In the process, the agents observed, in a bedroom in plain view, a triple-beam scale, jars of lactose, which is a cutting agent for cocaine, and numerous small cellophane bags, all accouterments of drug trafficking. The agents disturbed none of these items. After this limited security check, Colon was arrested. In the search incident to her arrest, agents found in her purse a loaded revolver and more than $2000 in cash. Colon, Segura, and the other occupants of the apartment were taken to Drug Enforcement Administration headquarters.

Two Task Force agents remained in Segura's apartment awaiting the warrant. Because of what is characterized as "administrative delay", the warrant application was not presented to the Magistrate until 5 P.M. the next day. The warrant was issued and the search was performed at approximately 6 P.M., some 19 hours after the agents' initial entry into the apartment. In the search pursuant to the warrant, agents discovered almost 3 pounds of cocaine, 18 rounds of .38-caliber ammunition fitting the revolver found in Colon's possession at the time of her arrest, more than $50,000 cash, and records of narcotics transactions. Agents seized these items, together with those observed earlier during the security check of the previous night.

Before trial in the U.S. District Court in the Eastern District of New York, the defendants moved to suppress all of the evidence seized from the apartment – the items discovered in plain view during the initial security check and those not in plain view discovered during the subsequent warrant search. After a full evidentiary hearing, the District Court granted the defendant's motion. The court ruled that there were no exigent circumstances justifying the initial entry into the apartment. Accordingly, it held that the entry, the arrest of Colon and search incident to her arrest, and the effective seizure of the drug paraphernalia in plain view were illegal. The District Court ordered this evidence suppressed as "fruits" of illegal searches.

The District Court held that the warrant later issued was supported by information sufficient to establish probable cause. However, it ruled that evidence seized under the valid warrant be suppressed. The District Court reasoned that this evidence would not necessarily have been discovered because, without the illegal entry and "occupation" of the apartment, Colon might have arranged to have the drugs removed or destroyed, in which event they would not have been in the apartment when the warrant search was made. Under this analysis, the District Court held that even the drugs seized under the valid warrant were "fruit of the poisonous tree."

On an appeal limited to the admissibility of the incriminating evidence, the Court of Appeals affirmed in part and reversed in part. It affirmed the District Court holding that the initial warrantless entry was not justified by exigent circumstances and that the evidence discovered in plain view during the initial entry must be suppressed. The Court of Appeals rejected the government's argument that the evidence in plain view should not be excluded, because it was not actually seized" until after the search warrant was secured.

The Court of Appeals reversed the District Court's holding requiring suppression of the evidence seized under the valid warrant executed on the day following the initial entry. The Court of Appeals described as "prudentially unsound" the District Court's decision to suppress that evidence simply because it could have been destroyed had the agents not entered.

Petitioners were convicted of conspiring to distribute cocaine and of distributing and possessing with intent to distribute cocaine. On the subsequent review of these convictions, the Second Circuit affirmed, rejecting claims by the defendants that the search warrant was procured through material misrepresentations and that the evidence at trial was insufficient as a matter of law to support their convictions.

The Supreme Court ruled that the evidence seen in plain view during the illegal entry should not have been suppressed because it was ultimately seized during the execution of a valid search warrant, which was based on information independent of the information acquired during the illegal entry.

Inevitable Discovery

In general, courts will not suppress evidence that has been illegally seized if the government can establish that the evidence would have inevitably been discovered.

The inevitable discovery exception is similar to the independent source exception. However, where the independent source exception requires that the evidence actually be obtained legally, the inevitable discovery exception only required that the evidence hypothetically could have been seized through some legal means. The inevitable discovery exception to the exclusionary rule can be thought of as a hypothetical independent source.

In 1984, the U.S. Supreme Court recognized the inevitable discovery exception in *Nix* v. *Williams*.[11] The defendant, Robert Williams, actually had two trials on the same charge, both of which were reviewed by the Court. The first decision was *Brewer* v. *Williams*,[12] and the second was *Nix*.

In the *Brewer* decision, the Supreme Court examined the follow facts. On Christmas Eve, 1968, 10-year old Pamela Powers accompanied her parents to the De Moines, Iowa YMCA to watch a wrestling match in which her brother was competing. She went to the washroom and never returned. Robert Williams, who had recently escaped from a mental institution, was a resident of the YMCA. A 14-year old boy helped Williams open his car door and saw him place inside, a blanket wrapped around a large bundle with two legs sticking out of it.

The police received an arrest warrant for Williams who self-surrendered to the Davenport police two days later. There was an agreement between Williams' attorneys and the police that Williams would not be interrogated while being transported between Davenport to Des Moines. Furthermore, Williams was advised by his attorneys not to talk to the police. During the trip to Des Moines, one of the detectives gave Williams what is not the famous "Christian burial" speech. The detective made mention that it would be nice for the child victim to have a Christian burial, rather than being left abandoned somewhere.

After traveling about 100 miles, Williams began talking and eventually led the detectives to the location of the child's body. Williams was eventually convicted of first-degree murder.

In *Brewer*, the Supreme Court ruled that the statements made by Williams should have been suppressed because they were taken in violation of his Sixth Amendment right to counsel, which attaches at the inception of adversarial judicial proceedings against a defendant. After being attached, a suspect may not be interrogated without a valid waiver or the presence of counsel. The Court ruled that the Christian burial speech was designed to elicit an incriminating response from Williams, and therefore was an interrogation. In addition, even though Williams had been warned no fewer than five times of both his right to remain silent and his right to counsel, the Court held that a valid waiver of counsel requires that the state prove not merely that a defendant comprehended that right, but also that he intended to relinquish it.

With his conviction overturned, Williams was retried and convicted a second time. This time, the prosecutor did not use the statements of Williams. His attorneys appealed the verdict, arguing that Williams' illegally-obtained statement led police to the victim's body, and additional evidence that was found on the body was used to convict him. The defense claimed that evidence was derived from the statement and should have been suppressed as fruit of the poisonous tree.

The State of Iowa argued that the body would have inevitably been discovered and therefore the evidence was properly admitted at trial. The Court of Appeals for the Eighth Circuit ruled that, in order to have the benefit of the inevitable discovery exception to the rule of evidence, the state was required to prove by a preponderance of the evidence that the officers did not act in bad faith when eliciting the statements from the defendant. Because the state failed to meet that burden, the court granted Williams petition for a writ of *habeas corpus*, and ordered that he be released, unless the State of Iowa commenced a new trial within 60 days.

The U.S. Supreme Court in *Nix* reversed the decision of the lower court of appeals and ruled that the government was not required to prove a lack of bad faith by the officers, in order to successfully invoke the inevitable discovery exception. The Court simply required that the prosecution establish by a preponderance of the evidence that the body would have inevitably been lawfully discovered. The Court did not think that a police officer would purposely engage in illegal conduct in the hope that the evidence would be admissible under the inevitable discovery doctrine, because an officer would rarely, if ever, be in a position to calculate whether the evidence sought would inevitably be discovered. Even if an officer were to foresee the lawful discovery of the evidence, he would have little to gain from taking any dubious shortcuts to obtain the evidence. The Court felt that the societal costs of a good faith requirement far outweighed any possible benefits.

The *Nix* Court viewed the exclusionary rule as a drastic and socially costly remedy, because many times it results in obviously guilty persons going unpunished for their crimes. The Court disapproved of suppressing evidence that would have inevitably been lawfully discovered, because that would undermine the adversarial justice system by putting the state in a worse position than it would have occupied, if there had been no illegal police conduct. The inevitable discovery exception ensures that the remedy of the exclusionary rule is limited to putting the prosecution in the same position that it would have been in if there had been no illegal police conduct. The *Nix* Court found that a search party would inevitably have discovered the body within a few hours had the search not been called off because Williams had led the police to

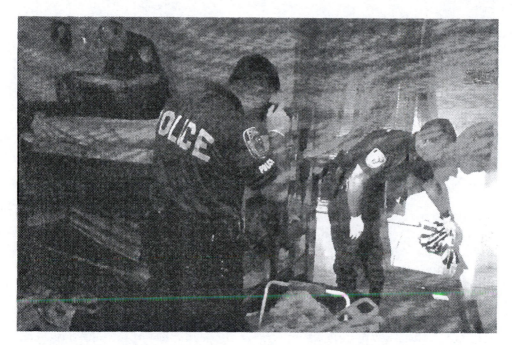

FIGURE 6.2   Police photographing evidence found in a residence as a result of a lawful search warrant. The exclusionary rule does not allow evidence illegally seized by the police to be admissible at trial, in part to deter police misconduct. *Corbis.*

the body. It is sufficient for the police to allege that under some hypothetical events the evidence *could* have been found in a lawful fashion. It must be shown that the evidence *would* have inevitably been discovered. It is not necessary to establish absolute certainty of discovery, but rather it is only required that the government establish the inevitability of discovery by a preponderance of the evidence.

Some states, such as Texas, do not recognize the inevitable discovery exception to the exclusionary rule. Texas has a statute that excludes all evidence that is obtained through a violation of the Texas or U.S. Constitutions. The statue does not expressly provide for any exceptions to that exclusionary rule. In *Garcia v. Texas*,[13] the Texas Court of Criminal Appeals stated that while courts are at liberty to adopt exceptions to a court-made exclusionary rule, they do not have the same freedom when the rule is imposed by statute. The court felt that all legislation expresses the will of the representatives of the people and that a court is limited to merely interpreting the meaning of those statutes. If the court were to establish an exception to the statutory exclusionary rule, that would be tantamount to amending the statute, and only the legislature has that authority.

In order to successfully assert the inevitable discovery exception, many courts require the prosecution demonstrate that the police were in the process of actively pursuing a lawful investigation that would have inevitably led to the discovery of the evidence at the time that it was illegally obtained.

The concern of these courts is that merely establishing what would have been the routine of the police, without establishing that alternative lawful investigative procedures were in fact being actively followed, would reduce the inevitable discovery doctrine to pure speculation.

For example, in *United States* v. *Wilson*,[14] the Court of Appeals found that evidence discovered in a hotel room wastebasket pursuant to an illegal search should have been suppressed, even though the resident gave valid written consent to search the room after the evidence was seized. The court did not apply the inevitable discovery exception because the officers did not request consent until after the illegal search. There was no indication that the police were actively pursuing a substantial alternative line of investigation at the time of the unlawful search.

Other courts do not require that the police be actively pursuing a lawful line of investigation at the time of the illegal search, in order to successfully assert the doctrine of inevitable discovery. In *United States* v. *Zapata*,[15] the court refused to adopt the active pursuit requirement. The court held that a large duffel bag containing 25 kilograms of cocaine found in the trunk of the suspect's vehicle, would have inevitably been discovered during an inventory conducted after it was impounded. The police were not actively pursuing the inventory of the vehicle at the time of the initial illegal search. The court found that whether legal means of discovery are under way at the time of the illegal search is relevant to, but is not a requisite of, the inevitable discovery doctrine.

In *United States* v. *Silvestri*,[16] the Court of Appeals found that evidence seized during an illegal search should not be suppressed, because the evidence would have inevitably been found during the execution of a subsequently obtained valid search warrant – even though the police did not begin the process of obtaining the warrant until after the illegal search.

The court felt that requiring the police to be in the process of actively pursuing a contemporaneous and lawful alternative investigation, on the facts in that case, would put the prosecution in a worse position rather than the same position it would have been, had they not conducted the illegal search. The court believed that the active pursuit requirement should not be employed when a search warrant is actually issued, that is based upon probable cause that existed prior to the illegal search. The court held that requiring active pursuit through an independent investigation is only appropriate when a search warrant is the basis of the inevitable discovery argument, and a subsequent warrant is not in fact obtained.

However, some courts do not apply the inevitable discovery doctrine, even though the police did not conduct an independent line of investigation, and a valid search warrant subsequently was not obtained. In *Martin* v. *Delaware*,[17] the

Delaware Supreme Court applied the inevitable discovery doctrine to allow the admission of evidence that was seized as a result of an illegal search of a hotel room. Although there was an ongoing murder investigation in another state at the time of the illegal search, the police were not actively seeking, and in fact, never obtained a search warrant for the hotel room. A Delaware State Police detective testified that although a search warrant was never acquired, he would have obtained a warrant before searching the hotel room, if not for the Cincinnati, Ohio police already searching the room without a warrant.

Some courts not only do not require active pursuit of an alternative legal means of discovery at the moment of the illegal search, but also do not even require that a law enforcement official be the one who would have inevitably discovered the evidence.

For example, in *Tennessee* v. *Williams*,[18] the Tennessee Court of Criminal Appeals ruled that the dead body the police discovered through the defendant's illegally obtained confession was properly admitted into evidence at trial. It would have inevitably been found by a local farmer as soon as the body decomposed because of the emitting odors. The farmer testified that he passed by the site five or six times per week.

Furthermore, in *United States* v. *Hernandez-Cano*,[19] the appeals court held that the district court should not have excluded illegally seized evidence where an airline employee would have inevitably discovered it. The court determined that limiting the application of the inevitable discovery exception to hypothetical police conduct thwarts the purpose of that exception, which is simply to avoid placing the government in a worse position than it would have been had there been no illegal search.

Some courts have limited the application of the inevitable discovery doctrine to only allow the admissibility of evidence that was obtained indirectly from unlawful police conduct. Those courts have excluded primary evidence obtained directly from illegal police conduct, regardless of where it would have inevitably been lawfully seized later.

For example, in *New York* v. *Stith*,[20] the Court of Appeals for New York reversed a lower court decision that had approved the admissibility of a gun that would have inevitably been found during a subsequent inventory search of a vehicle. The *Stith* court limited the application of the *Nix* decision to indirect evidence. In *Nix*, the dead body that would have been inevitably found was in fact indirectly located through an illegal statement. The *Stith* court felt that expanding the inevitable discovery exception, to include evidence obtained directly from an illegal search, would encourage unlawful police searches in the hopes of justifying them later claiming inevitability.

Most courts, however, do not make a distinction between direct and indirect evidence when determining whether the inevitable discovery exception should apply.

Collateral Use of Evidence Seized in Violation of the Fourth Amendment

There are eight situations where illegally seized evidence may be used inside and outside the courtroom. In these situations, the evidence is considered to be important enough to allow its admissibility in order to seek the truth of the matter:

1. The exclusionary rule of evidence does not apply at grand jury hearings. The U.S. Supreme Court held in *United States v. Calandra*,[21] that "[a], witness summoned to appear and testify before a grand jury may not refuse to answer questions on the ground that they are based on evidence obtained from an unlawful search and seizure."

2. Evidence seized in violation of the Fourth Amendment may be used at sentencing. Title 18 of the U.S. Code, Section 3661 provides that no limits shall be placed on the information concerning the background, character, or conduct of a defendant that a federal court may consider for the purpose of sentencing the defendant.

3. Evidence seized in violation of the Fourth Amendment may be used at probation revocation hearings, unless the illegal conduct was for the very purpose of obtaining evidence to be used in the probation revocation hearing or to harass the probationer.[22]

4. Evidence seized in violation of the Fourth Amendment may be used at parole revocation hearings, because the exclusionary rule is prudential rather than constitutionally mandated. Therefore, it should only be applied when the deterrence benefits of the rule outweigh the substantial costs to society and to the justice system that are incurred when a fact-finder is prevented from considering reliable probative evidence.[23]

5. The U.S. Supreme Court has ruled that illegally seized evidence may be used to impeach the credibility of the defendant.[24] However, evidence obtained from a defendant that flowed from illegal police conduct may not be used to impeach a defense witness.[25]

6. The U.S. Supreme Court has ruled that the exclusionary rule does not apply at civil deportation hearings.[26]

7. The U.S. Supreme Court has ruled that the exclusionary rule does not apply to civil tax hearings.[27]

8. The rule of thumb is that the exclusionary rule of evidence does not apply to civil proceedings. However, in a pre-*Calandra* decision, the Supreme Court ruled that the exclusionary rule does apply to civil forfeiture proceedings.[28] Subsequent to *Calandra*, courts have continued to apply the exclusionary rule to civil forfeiture cases.[29] The number of civil forfeiture cases, where money and property is seized from drug traffickers, has steadily increased since the 1980s.

PRINCIPLE OF STAR DECISIS

Stare decisis is Latin for "to stand by that which is decided" or "stand by decided matters." It is the principal that the precedent decisions of higher courts will be adhered to by lower courts. In general, when an issue has been settled by a higher court decision, it sets a precedent that should not be departed from.

According to a 9th Circuit Court of Appeals decision in a 1989 case,[30] an appeal court's panel is "bound by decisions of prior panels unless an en banc decision, Supreme Court decision, or subsequent legislation undermines those decisions." Although the stare decisis principle does not prohibit the reexamination and overruling of prior decisions, "It is . . . a fundamental jurisprudential policy that prior applicable precedent usually must be followed even though the case, if considered anew, might be decided differently by the current justices. This policy . . . 'is based on the assumption that certainty, predictability and stability in the law are the major objectives of the legal system; i.e., that parties should be able to regulate their conduct and enter into relationships with reasonable assurance of the governing rules of law.'"[31] However, this doctrine is not always relied upon, as courts through the years have found it necessary to overrule decisions that were either hastily made, or contrary to legal principles. U.S. courts have overruled hundreds of cases. For example, the U.S. Supreme Court completely reversed itself in cases dealing with the issue of segregation.

Accordingly, a party seeking the overruling of a precedent faces an arduous task. The likelihood of success would be dependant on a number of factors, including how long ago the precedent was set, the nature and extent of public and private reliance on it, and its consistency or inconsistency with other related rules of law.

In light of this, the exclusionary rule of evidence is likely to be around for many decades, barring some extraordinary event that will cause its reexamination by the courts.

SUMMARY

The Exclusionary rule of evidence prohibits the admissibility of evidence, illegally obtained by the police. It is a judicial invention conceived to serve as both a remedy and deterrent to police misconduct, and applies to both unlawfully seized evidence and confessions in violation of the U.S. Constitution.

A series of U.S. Supreme Court rulings, dating back to 1914, defined and shaped the exclusionary rule of evidence in both criminal and civil forfeiture proceedings.

There are exceptions to the exclusionary rule for both direct and indirect evidence. These exceptions deal with the defendant's standing as to him being the actual victim of a violation of his Fourth Amendment rights, good faith on the part of police officers, attenuation from the illegal conduct of the police, the receipt of evidence from independent sources, and when the evidence would have inevitably been discovered by the police. In most of these cases, the government is not required to prove a lack of bad faith by police officers, in order to successfully invoke these exceptions.

Evidence seized in violation of the Fourth Amendment can be used collaterally in grand jury hearings; probation and parole revocation hearings; the impeachment of the credibility of a defendant; civil deportation hearings; civil tax hearings; and most civil proceedings.

Stare decisis is Latin for "to stand by that which is decided." It is the principal that the precedent decisions of higher courts will be adhered to by lower courts. Accordingly, the exclusionary rule doctrine is likely to be the law of the land for the foreseeable future.

NOTES

1. *Weeks* v. *U.S.*, 232 U.S. 383 (1914).
2. 338 U.S. 25 (1949).
3. 367 U.S. 643 (1961).
4. 468 U.S. 897 (1984).
5. 414 U.S. 338, 354 (1974).
6. 251 U.S. 385 (1920).
7. 308 U.S. 338, 340–341.
8. 439 U.S. 128 (1978).
9. 371 U.S. 471 (1963).
10. 468 U.S. 796 (1984).
11. 467 U.S. 431 (1984).
12. 430 U.S. 387 (1977).
13. 829 S.W. 2d 796 (1992).
14. 36 F.2d 1298, 1304–05 (5th Cir. 1994).
15. 18 F.2d 971 (1st Cir. 1994).
16. 787 F.2d 736 (1st Cir. 1986).
17. 433 A. 2d 1025 (1981).
18. 784 S.W.2d 660, 663–64 (1989).
19. 808 F.2d 779, 782–84 (11th Cir. 1987).
20. 506 N.E.2d 911, 914 (1987).
21. 414 U.S. 338 (1974).
22. *United States* v. *Winsett*, 518 F.2d 51, 53–55 (9th Cir. 1975); *United States* v. *Brown*, 488 F.2d 94, 95 (5th Cir. 1973); *United States* v. *Rea*, 678 F.2d 382, 388–90 (2d Cir. 1982). The U.S. Supreme Court has not yet ruled on this issue.
23. 000 U.S. 97–581, (1998).
24. *Walder* v. *United States*, 347 U.S. 62 (1954).
25. *James* v. *Illinois*, 493 U.S. 307 (1990).
26. *I.N.S.* v. *Lopez-Mendoza*, 468 U.S. 1032 (1984).

27. *United States* v. *Janis,* 428 U.S. 433 (1976).
28. *One 1958 Plymouth Sedan* v. *Pennsylvania,* 380 U.S. 693 (1965).
29. *United States* v. *277,000.00 U.S. currency,* 941 F.2d 898 (9th Cir. 1991).
30. *U.S.* v. *Washington,* 872 F.2d 874, 880 (9th Cir. 1989).
31. *Moradi-Shalal* v. *Fireman's Fund Ins. Companies* 46 Cal.3d 287, 296 (1988).

7

Search Warrants

A significant source of criminal evidence originates from the execution of search warrants. The Fourth Amendment of the U.S. Constitution specifies what steps the police must take in order to obtain such warrants. The Fourth Amendment reads:

> The right of the people to be secure in their persons, houses, papers, and effects, against unreasonable searches and seizures, shall not be violated, and no warrants shall issue, but upon **probable cause,** supported by oath or affirmation, and particularly describing the place to be searched, and the persons or things to be seized" (emphasis added).

The information contained in this chapter is based largely in part upon the Fourth Amendment, as interpreted by the U.S. Supreme Court. Many states impose tougher restrictions on police conduct than the federal Constitution does, making it imperative that police officers consult with their prosecutors when contemplating requesting a search warrant.

Police officers need to have a practical knowledge of search and seizure law in order to be effective. Without it, they run the real risk of violating constitutional rights and the exclusion of any evidence they may obtain. They may also expose themselves to civil lawsuits when their actions are blatant. A way of overcoming hurdles associated with search warrants is to apply a two-step approach, for example, knowing the law, and developing a logical system to apply it. These two steps offer one of the best ways in developing a practical working knowledge of search and seizure law.

REASONABLENESS

The Fourth Amendment is intended to protect individuals from *unreasonable* search and seizures by the government, not private parties. The question then is "What's a reasonable search?" In a 1967 landmark ruling, the Supreme Court interpreted the words, "persons, houses, papers and effects" used in the Fourth Amendment in the *Katz*[1] decision. The court ruled that the Fourth Amendment not only protected a person, his houses, his papers and his effects, but also his privacy.

FBI agents had planted an electronic listening device on the outside of a public telephone booth, known to be used by Katz to convey gambling information. His conversations were captured and used at his trial where he was convicted. On appeal, Katz argued that the government had invaded his privacy since he believed his conversations would remain private. He reasoned that since his conversations were private, the government needed a warrant before they could intercept them.

The government countered that a public phone booth was not a constitutionally protected area, stressing that it was not a home, nor was it any part of his papers or other effects. Therefore, a search warrant was not required.

The Supreme Court disagreed with the government and in reversing Katz's conviction, ruled: "The Fourth Amendment protects people, not places. What a person knowingly exposes to the public, even in his own home or office, is not a subject of Fourth Amendment protection ... But what he seeks to preserve as private, even in an area accessible to the public, may be constitutionally protected."

Since Katz reasonably expected his conversations to be private, they were protected from unreasonable government intrusion. From then on, police officers needed probable cause and a search warrant under the same set of circumstances.

Plain View

Katz created what is known as "The reasonable expectation of privacy test." It is now considered a search when the government invades an individual's reasonable expectations of privacy. A two-prong test was now established to determine if a search warrant is required. Did the individual actually expect privacy *and* was his expectation of privacy reasonable? A reasonable expectation of privacy exists only if these questions are answered in the affirmative. In almost every case, the first prong must be presumed, but whether his expectations were reasonable or not is an entirely different matter.

Among the many factors to consider in applying this first prong of the test is the place, area, or context in which the government intends to intrude, such as a patio, backyard, bedroom, or public restroom. Furthermore, the second prong deals specifically with the nature of the intrusion, for example, a physical entry into a building, observation, use of eaves-dropping devices, etc.

Things that the police can see, hear, or smell without invading a reasonable expectation of privacy are considered to be in **plain view**. Things that are in plain or open view have been exposed to the public and are not protected by the Fourth Amendment. For example, police are called to a residence where the occupant informs them about his neighbor growing marijuana on his back porch. The man directs the police officer to his rear decking and instructs him to stand on a bench that will allow him to peer over the common six-foot fence separating him and his neighbor. The police officer steps on the bench and clearly sees several large pots with several three-foot marijuana stalks growing out of each of them. Does the conduct of the police officer constitute a search?

No. A search only occurs when the police officer invades an individual's reasonable expectations of privacy. Furthermore, a reasonable expectation of privacy requires that the individual actually expected privacy and that the expectation be reasonable. In this situation, the neighbor most probably expected privacy. However, his expectation that no one would ever see the plants is not reasonable. Most persons would not expect to be free from observation while in a yard surrounded only by a six-foot fence. Since the plants were in open view, the police officer's conduct in observing the plants is not a Fourth Amendment search.[2]

Using the above example, suppose the caller had recently visited his neighbor, where he saw the marijuana plants on the back porch. After calling the police, the officer steps on the bench, but cannot see over it because the fence was ten-feet high. The officer calls a police helicopter to hover over the backyard, and the pilot, with the aid of binoculars, observes the marijuana being grown. Is this police conduct now a Fourth Amendment search?

Yes. The higher fence increases the neighbor's reasonable expectation of privacy from both entry and observation. Since the helicopter invaded the neighbor's reasonable expectation of privacy, the conduct is a search under the Fourth Amendment.

Abandoned Property

Before *Katz*, the Supreme Court ruled that a person has no right to challenge the search or seizure of an area or thing that he has voluntarily abandoned.[3]

For example, drug investigators received information from an inner city shop owner who said he believes that a local drug dealer is hiding his drugs in an abandoned vehicle in a vacant lot. The investigators go to the vacant lot and observe a single vehicle resting on blocks. The windows are broken, and the doors to the vehicle are unlocked. A search of the vehicle reveals several packages of drugs, which they leave in the vehicle. The police conduct surveillance on the vehicle, and when a man arrives and goes into the vehicle as if to retrieve something, they arrest him and find the identical drugs. Does the Fourth Amendment control the search of the abandoned vehicle?

No. The Fourth Amendment would only apply if the police invade an individual's reasonable expectations of privacy. Any privacy the suspect might have expected is clearly unreasonable. Most courts would never expect any privacy in a vehicle that is left abandoned in this manner. The police conduct in finding the drugs in the vehicle is not a Fourth Amendment search. The vehicle and the drugs are, in this case, considered to be in open view.

In another example, a police officer observes the driver of a vehicle committing a traffic violation. After activating his emergency lights in an attempt to stop the vehicle and issue the driver a citation, the driver speeds up and flees. A vehicle pursuit ensues, during which time the police officer sees the driver throw a small cardboard box from the car. Another police officer retrieves the box and discovers inside four small plastic bags, each containing one ounce of methamphetamine. The driver is eventually stopped and arrested for possession of methamphetamine, as well as the traffic violations. Has there been a Fourth Amendment Search requiring a search warrant?

No. The cardboard box and its contents were abandoned and in open view.

In a third example, a police investigator assigned to an airport drug interdiction unit observes the passengers disembark. From experience, he knows that passengers on this particular flight have transported drugs. The investigator sees a passenger who he believes matches the profile of a drug courier. He stops the man and identifies himself as a police officer. He asks the passenger questions, most of which he answers satisfactory. After a few minutes, the passenger asks to leave since he will miss his ride to a hotel. The investigator refuses, and orders the man to accompany him to his office for further questioning. While on the way to the office, the passenger panics and dashes out of the terminal with the investigator in hot pursuit. During the pursuit, the passenger throws a small paper bag in a trashcan. The passenger is captured and the paper bag is retrieved. Inside the bag is a quantity of drugs. Does the opening of the paper bag require a search warrant as provided by the Fourth Amendment?

Yes. Although a person generally has no reasonable expectations of privacy in property that has been abandoned, the abandonment must not be caused by unlawful government conduct. Although the investigator has every right to stop and question a suspicious person, he lacked probable cause to arrest the man. The investigator's engagement in extended interrogation and the demand that the passenger accompany him to his office prompted the passenger to flee.

If the government is to conduct a search, it must be reasonable under the provisions of the Fourth Amendment. The courts have held that a search is presumed to be reasonable if a judge issues a valid search warrant based upon *probable cause*.

PROBABLE CAUSE

One of the most quoted definitions of probable cause is found in *Carroll* v. *United States*.[4] "This is to say that the facts and circumstances within their (the police) knowledge and of which they had reasonably trustworthy information were sufficient in themselves to warrant a man a reasonable caution in the belief that (property subject to seizure would be found in a particular place or on a particular person)." Another definition is that probable cause is more than mere suspicion, but less than absolute proof.

There are two elements of probable cause. First, there must be probable cause to believe certain property or contraband is crime connected, therefore subject to seizure. Second, there must be probable cause to believe this property or contraband can be located in a particular place. Probable cause cannot be based upon a police officer's mere suspicious or upon his educated guess. These conclusions cannot be used to establish probable cause. It must be based on specific, articulable, facts and circumstances.

For example, does the following paragraph, written by a police officer or federal agent in an affidavit, establish probable cause to search?

"Your affiant has received reliable information from a credible person and believes that drugs are being kept at 123 Elm Street, for the purpose of sale."

No. The affiant, or person who is submitting the affidavit, has left out the facts and circumstances to support his conclusions. How did the affiant conclude that the information he received came from a credible person? How does he know the information is trustworthy? What are the facts and conclusions that made the officer believe there are drugs at this address?[5]

Logical Inferences

Police officers must include as much detail as practicable when they articulate probable cause in an affidavit. Any facts and circumstances that are logically connected can be used to establish probable cause. Probable cause determination is based upon logic and common sense. The facts and circumstances must logically make it probable, not possible, that property or contraband subject to seizure is located in a particular place. Absolute certainty is not required, nor is proof beyond a reasonable doubt. Determining if probable cause exists should be measured by what a reasonable person would conclude, after hearing the facts and circumstances about a particular event.

The passage of time also affects a judge's decision as to whether or not there is probable cause to search. If the police have a reliable informant who personally saw stolen property in someone's home an hour ago, it is very likely the items are still there. However, if the informant saw the stolen property over a month ago, what likelihood is there that the property is there now?

Probable cause is based upon all the facts and circumstances available to a police officer at the time he makes application for a search warrant. It is also based upon all the logical inferences that can be drawn from these facts, and upon any professional inferences drawn by the officer, provided that he can articulate his basis for drawing them.

Police officers must be able to articulate the experiences, training, and expertise that caused him or her to draw a professional inference. These professional inferences, not available to the average citizen or judges, make it much more likely that what is being alleged is correct.

For example, on a Saturday evening, an undercover police investigator meets with a man who solicits him to murder his wife. He is willing to pay the "hit man" $10,000 to do the job. Their conversations are captured on audiotape. The man gives the investigator an envelope containing the cash, and says he has an untraceable handgun that he wants the undercover investigator to use in the murder. He says he will furnish the investigator with the gun, but will not have access to it until the following Monday morning. The police arrest the man and contact his wife who says her husband has a private safety deposit box at a local bank. Is there probable cause to search the safe deposit box?

Yes. The logical inference that a reasonable person would draw from these facts is that the defendant's handgun is located in the safety deposit box. Banks are not open on Sundays, limiting his access to the weapon until Monday. Furthermore, although he could have the weapon hidden somewhere in his home, that he shares with his wife, it would appear unlikely he would chance her finding it. The average person would conclude the handgun is probably in the safety deposit box. Therefore, there is probable cause to search the safety deposit box.

Time Affects Probability

The passage of time will always affect a judge's decision of whether there is probable cause to search. If a confidential informant tells the police he saw drugs at someone's home less than an hour ago, it is very likely the drugs are still there. If the informant saw the drugs three months ago, the likelihood the drugs still exist diminishes greatly.

Since the existence of probable cause to search is logically affected by the passage of time, police must include the times of occurrence of the facts and circumstances they rely upon. When preparing affidavits for the issuance of a search warrant, the preferred method of stating the facts and circumstances is in a chronological order.

Professional Inferences

Logical inferences drawn by police officers based upon their special expertise, training, or experience can be used to establish probable cause.

For example, an experienced police officer knows that there has been an explosion in the number of clandestine laboratories manufacturing methamphetamine in his area. During patrol, the officer stops a Sports Utility Vehicle. The officer can clearly see the rear portion of the vehicle contains chemistry glassware and plastic tubing, as well as a can of red phosphorous and many large jars marked as pseudoephedrine, a non-controlled substance used in medicine for common colds. The officer knows from his training and experience in drug law enforcement that these items are commonly used in the manufacturing of methamphetamine. The driver of the vehicle becomes visibly nervous when the officer approaches, noticeably more than someone who has only committed a traffic violation. From this set of facts, the officer draws logical inferences that a layman would not normally draw. The officer concludes that the driver is involved, or at least knowledgeable, about methamphetamine manufacturing. If the driver refuses to grant permission for the officer to search the SUV, does he have probable cause to seek a search warrant?

Yes. A layman may not make the connection between the jars of pseudoephedrine, red phosphorous, and chemistry equipment with the manufacturing of methamphetamine, but a trained, experience police officer can.

The court in *Bell* v. *U.S.* stated the rule of professional inferences concisely:[6]

"Probable cause is not a philosophical concept existing in a vacuum; it is a practical and factual matter. A fact which spells reasonable cause to a doctor may make no impression on a carpenter, and vice versa . . . An officer experienced in the narcotics traffic may find probable cause in the smell of drugs and appearance of paraphernalia, which to the lay eye is without significance. His action is not measured by what might be probable cause to an untrained civilian passerby . . . The question is what constituted probable cause in the eyes of a reasonable, cautious and prudent police officer under the circumstances of the moment."

The one important limitation on the use of professional inferences to establish probable cause is that police officers must be able to articulate their experience, training, and expertise that cause them to draw professional inferences.

Police officers are required to set forth their probable cause, either in an affidavit in support of a warrant or in a subsequent suppression hearing. A judge who is not in possession of the police officer's expertise and training will draw only the logical inferences from the facts, in the same way as an average citizen would. If the judge is to also draw professional inferences from the facts, the police officer will have to advise him of the special experiences and training that are behind his professional judgments.

Probable Cause Mixture

Probable cause is always based upon all the facts and circumstances available to the police officer, upon all the logical inferences that can be drawn from these facts, and in addition, upon any professional inferences drawn by the police officer, provided that he articulates his basis for drawing them.

In a 1966 decision,[7] Chief Justice Warren Burger gave insight in how the Court decides probable cause issues: "Probable cause is the sum total of layers of information and the synthesis of what the police have heard, what they know, and what they observe as trained officers. We weigh not individual layers but the laminated total."

ESTABLISHING PROBABLE CAUSE

Probable cause can be established either through a police officer's personal knowledge or through reports to the officer by a third party, usually a citizen witness or informant.

Facts and circumstances related to an officer, that are not within the officer's personal knowledge, are hearsay. Probable cause can be based upon hearsay, provided the hearsay is trustworthy.

As a whole, society is suspicious of rumors, gossip, or slander. Those who confidentially provide information to authorities are widely considered to be "tattletales." Confidential informants are generally considered to be unreliable or untruthful, until proven otherwise. The police can overcome this presumption of unreliability when the informant's basis of belief *and* credibility can be shown.

The Supreme Court developed this two-prong approach about relying on hearsay, when it decided *Aguilar* v. *Texas*[8] and *Spinelli* v. *U.S.*[9] Both prongs of this test must be satisfied before hearsay, standing alone, can be relied upon to establish probable cause.

Basis of Belief

This prong of the Aguilar-Spinelli test measures the reliability of the information, usually provided by an informant. Police officers need to be prepared to answer questions as to how they obtained the information. Did the informant receive the information first-hand, or through a third party? If a third party received the information, how did he receive it? Is the information merely casual rumor? Is the information based on the source's conclusions about the information that he received? What facts did the informant rely upon to reach these conclusions? What is his basis of belief?

Information will meet the basis of belief prong if the informant tells how he obtained it, either by personal observation or in some other dependable way, or it is extremely detailed so that the average person would conclude that the informant has first-hand knowledge of the facts and is not relying on rumors.

For example, a previously reliable informant informs a police investigator that within the past day he has been inside a residence where he personally saw numerous unopened boxes of stolen satellite television equipment. A "previously reliable informant" is someone who has provided information to the police resulting in arrests, seizures of stolen property or contraband, and has never been known to lie or knowing supply false or misleading information. He said that while inside the residence, he heard the occupant, John, talking on the telephone to someone about selling the equipment to him tomorrow afternoon, but he does not know exactly where or when the sale of the stolen merchandise will take place. Does this informant's tip meet the Aguilar-Spinelli test?

Yes. Hearsay is trustworthy under this test if you can show the informant's basis of belief and his credibility. Here, the informant has first-hand information concerning the whereabouts of stolen property, and he has a record of credibility.

In a second example, a previously reliable informant contacts his police investigator handler and says that a large truck is being loaded as he speaks, with hundreds of pounds of marijuana. He said the truck was backed up to a private storage facility, and that "numerous" boxes containing marijuana were being loaded on to the truck from the storage garage. The informant also says that the loaders, John and Bob, will drive the truck, a white 2006 Ford (with slight body damage to the right rear quarter panel), southbound on Interstate five, and exit at the Crown Valley Parkway where it will park at a specific restaurant nearby. They intend to depart around 4 p.m. A buyer of the marijuana will arrive to inspect the quality of the drugs. Before any more information is obtained, the informant tells the investigator that he has to go, and hangs up the phone abruptly. Does this informant's information meet the basis of belief requirement of the Aguilar-Spinelli test?

Yes. The information meets the basis of belief prong if the informant tells the investigator how he obtained it, or if it is extremely detailed. Here, we do not know how the information was obtained, but it is so detailed that it is reasonable to conclude that he has first-hand knowledge and is not relying upon rumors.

In a final example, a police investigator received a phone call from a credible informant who says he just had a drink with John and Bob at a local bar, and "just found out" that one of them has a stolen handgun in his possession. He then hangs up before they can hear him talking on the phone. Does this information meet the basis of belief prong?

Clearly no. The informant was not able to tell the investigator how he obtained this information. Nor is the information extremely detailed. The information sounds as though it is a rumor, rather than fact. A very real possibility exists that the informant is relying on overheard information as the basis for his belief. The basis of belief requirement has not been satisfied.

Credibility

The credibility prong focuses on the truthfulness of the declarant. Is the person providing the information telling the truth?

To satisfy this prong of the Anguilar-Spinelli test, a police officer must articulate facts that tend to show the declarant is inherently credible, such as a priest or nun, or that he is being truthful on this particular occasion. Credibility can be shown in many ways:

- **Past Reliability**. An informant has established a track record of previously providing reliable information to demonstrate his credibility. If he has been truthful and accurate in the past, than he is likely to be truthful now. It should be noted that credibility and reliability are not synonymous, and they should not be confused.
- **Statements Against Penal Interest**. If the informant has participated in a crime and, as part of the information he discloses, he makes statements that may subject him to prison, he will generally be considered credible. In a 1971 U.S. Supreme Court decision,[10] Chief Justice Burger explained why statements against penal interests tend to show the informant is being truthful: "Common sense in the important daily affairs of life would induce a prudent and disinterested observer to credit these statements. People do not lightly admit to a crime and place critical evidence in the hands of the police in the form of their own admissions. Admissions of crime, like admissions against proprietary interests, carry their own indicia of credibility – sufficient at least to support a finding of probable cause to search."
- **Counsel is Present**. If the informant provides statements in the presence of counsel, he will generally be considered credible.
- **Good Citizen Informant**. "Good citizen" informants, or ordinary citizens who have nothing to gain by providing information to the police, other than to assist them in the enforcement of the law, will usually be presumed credible by most courts.

- **Law Enforcement Official**. Statements made by fellow law enforcement officials are presumed to be credible.
- **Victim of the Crime**. Statements given by a victim of a crime will generally be presumed credible until proven otherwise.
- **Eyewitnesses**. Statements made by an eyewitness in reporting a crime will generally be presumed credible.

Police officers must articulate facts to support their claim that an informant is credible. Unvarnished conclusions such as, "information was received from a reliable informant," or "information was received from a citizen," are not sufficient. The officer must be able to articulate some of the underlying facts from which he or she concluded that the informant is reliable, or that he is a good citizen.

For example, in an affidavit for a search warrant, the investigator writes:

I have been a drug investigator for the city police department for approximately 10 years. A citizen-informant advised that today he personally observed John Smith, the sole occupant of 1234 5th Street, provide several baggies of what he believed to be marijuana, to a juvenile who attends a nearby school. According to the citizen, he is the next-door neighbor of Smith, and daily observes numerous vehicles park in front of Smith's residence and the drivers and occupants of the vehicle go into Smith's residence for short periods of time. Through open windows, the citizen-informant can see people inside Smith's home lighting hand rolled cigarettes he believes are marijuana. Your affiant knows that the citizen-informant is a registered voter, is employed full-time in a good paying, respectable job, has never been arrested, and is respected in the community. He has personally expressed to other police officers patrolling his community, his concerning over young people using illegal drugs. He has never previously provided confidential information to law enforcement authorities.

Is the hearsay information contained in the above paragraph trustworthy? Yes. It meets the basis of belief test since the citizen-informant personally observed the suspected criminal activity, and he has described when and how the observations were made. Furthermore, the citizen-informant is credible in that the affidavit contains facts tending to demonstrate he is a good citizen who has nothing to gain by providing the information. Since both prongs of the Aguilar-Spinelli test are met, this hearsay would most probably be considered trustworthy.

In another example, a state trooper stops a van for a minor traffic violation. The driver becomes very nervous, arousing the officer's suspicions. Upon the driver granting permission to search the vehicle, the officer searches it and discovers numerous firearms in boxes. Having knowledge of a recent burglary of a gun store, and after ascertaining that at least one firearm's serial number is listed among the weapons stolen from the store, the officer arrests the man. Investigators interview the driver who, after waiving his rights, tells them that he was hired to transport the stolen weapons to another city and was instructed to offload them at a rented storage facility where other firearms and stolen property from other burglaries are being stored. The defendant provides the investigators with the exact address and number of the storage garage, as well as the name of the person who hired him to transport the stolen property. Does this hearsay meet the Aguilar-Spinelli test?

Yes. The defendant personally participating in the crime meets the basis of belief prong. The information provided is not rumor because he had personal knowledge of all the facts of the crime and details of how he acquired them. Also, the defendant's statements are against his penal interest since he admitted to participation in the crime, therefore he is presumed to be credible. Because the hearsay is trustworthy under the Aguilar-Spinelli test, it can provide probable cause to search the storage garage and arrest the man who hired him to transport the stolen property.

Corroboration

Hearsay that fails either part of the Aguilar-Spinelli test cannot be relied upon by itself to establish probable cause, because it simply is not trustworthy. However, hearsay can be used to establish probable cause when it is supported by independent corroboration that makes the hearsay more trustworthy. For example, an anonymous tip, coupled with corroboration can sometimes provide probable cause.

Corroboration can be found in three forms:

1. Police verify the facts given by the informant through surveillance and further investigation.
2. Another source verifies the facts, usually from another disinterested informant.
3. The anonymous tip is consistent with police investigators' knowledge.

These three forms of corroboration can be used to bolster a tip that fails either one of the two prongs of the Aguilar-Spinelli test. The more defective the anonymous tip, the more corroboration that will be required to establish probable cause. Only the strongest corroboration of suspicious activity can bolster a tip that fails both prongs of the test.

For example, a reliable informant who has provided police with information leading to the seizure of drugs and stolen property on ten different occasions within the last year, informs a police investigator that Manny, Moe, and Jack are in town to purchase marijuana that they intend to transport to another state. The informant says he does not have time to explain how he received this information, but says that he has seen these three men in town on a previous occasion when they bought marijuana and that they are using the same modus operandi as in previous occasions. According to the informant, the men always rent two cars, one to be used locally to set up the marijuana transaction, and the other to make the trip to the other state. A police investigator initiates an investigation and locates the three men. He also confirms that Manny has rented a car he intends to return in the other state, and Moe has rented a car he intends to return to the original rental site. While conducting surveillance of the men's hotel, investigators observe Manny, Moe, and Jack load suitcases and bulky duffle bags into the car destined for out of state, and luggage into the car rented for local use. Manny leaves with the car containing the duffle bags, and heads out of town on the interstate highway. Moe and Jack drive their car in the opposite direction to the commercial airport. Do the police investigators have probable cause to search Manny's car for marijuana?

Yes. Probable cause can be based upon hearsay, provided the hearsay is trustworthy. Hearsay is trustworthy if the police can show the informant's basis of belief and credibility. In this example, the informant is clearly credible, based on his past performance. Unfortunately, the police do not know the informant's basis of belief. The police also do not know how the informant received his information. However, it is so detailed that it is reasonable to conclude the information is not based upon rumor. The tip alone, even from an established informant who has provided credible information in the past, fails to meet one of the two part Aguilar-Spinelli test, and cannot be used alone to establish probable cause.

However, to compensate for this, the police corroborate the informant's information through investigation and surveillance. They verify that Manny, Moe, and Jack were in town, and that they have rented the vehicle, just as the informant stated. Furthermore, surveillance teams witness them loading duffle bags, which are commonly used to transport drugs, into one of the vehicles which headed out of town. This corroboration of the facts provided by the informant makes his hearsay information more trustworthy. A defective tip, coupled with corroboration through investigation, can provide probable cause necessary for a search warrant.

In another example, police investigators receive an anonymous telephone tip from a caller who says that a silver-colored Cadillac with a specific license plate, is traveling from Los Angeles to their city where the driver will be dropping off a quantity of drugs that afternoon. The caller does not know where the drop off will take place, but can say specifically the route of travel that the driver will use. Police investigators set up surveillance on the road that the Cadillac will be traveling along, and within a short period of time spot the vehicle, positively identifying it based on the provided license number. Do the police have probable cause to stop and search the vehicle?

No. The anonymous tip fails both prongs of the Aguilar-Spinelli test. The police cannot show that the informant is credible, as they do not know his identity or his basis of belief. They do not know how the caller obtained the information, which is not extremely detailed. There is a good possibility that the information came from a rumor the caller overheard. Although hearsay failing both prongs of the test can be cured through corroboration, it must be strong and include corroboration of suspicious activity, not just innocent conduct, such as driving on a particular road. The police have merely corroborated the innocent details of a tip.

Reality Check!

Under the given set of circumstances, experienced police officers will realize they have no basis for a search warrant of the vehicle. However, independent probable cause can be sought. A uniformed patrol officer could follow the vehicle until a traffic violation occurs. Once stopped, the officer can look for signs of criminality, or ask permission to search the vehicle. Absent sufficient probable cause to search the vehicle renders the police powerless in stopping and investigating further.

Another possibility would be for police investigators to follow the Cadillac to its destination. When it arrives, the history of the occupants can be queried through police intelligence files, and further investigation may be warranted that could lead to establishing probable cause to search.

The information provided by the anonymous tipster can serve as "raw intelligence." This information may later be useful to provide the additional information needed to secure a search warrant for the vehicle or the location where it parks in the future. Investigators could also request a patrol officer to stop the vehicle after a traffic violation occurs, solely for the purpose of fully identifying the driver, checking for the existence of outstanding arrest warrents, and later determining if this person is the subject of any other criminal investigations by other police departments.

Hearsay on Hearsay

When an informant provides information to the police that he says was obtained from a third party, a hearsay on hearsay problem is created. If the third party received the information from a fourth party, then a hearsay on hearsay on hearsay problem exists.

The ultimate source of the information is the person who actually has first-hand knowledge of the facts, at the other end of a chain of informants. Often, one or more of these persons are unwittingly providing information that a police informant overhears. The trustworthiness of information coming from such a chain depends upon the trustworthiness of every link within the chain. To be trustworthy, every link in a hearsay chain must meet both prongs of the Aguilar-Spinelli test. Police must show that the basis of belief test and the credibility test are satisfied every time the information changes hands.

For example, a police investigator receives a phone call from a uniformed police officer of his department. He tells the investigator that one of his informants contacted him today. The informant told the officer that he was at Billy Bob's home today and bought a small amount of cocaine from him. During the transaction, Billy Bob told the informant that he was a runner for Joe Doe, and that Doe would be receiving several kilograms of cocaine within the week, so there would be a good supply on hand to sell. Is this information trustworthy?

Yes. The uniformed police officer meets both prongs of the test. His basis of belief is that he obtained the information from his informant. Furthermore, the officer's credibility is presumed because he is a law enforcement official. The informant meets both prongs of the test because his basis of belief stems from his being told personally about the cocaine by Billy Bob. The informant's credibility is established when he admitted he received the information while purchasing cocaine from Billy Bob. This information is against the informant's penal interests. Also, Billy Bob meets both prongs of the test because he is a runner and distributor of cocaine for Joe Doe, thus he had personal knowledge of Doe's drug operation, including when deliveries can be expected. Like the informant, Billy Bob's credibility is established because his statements are also against his penal interests. He admitted being a participant in a conspiracy.

Since every link in this chain of information satisfied the Aguilar-Spinelli test, this hearsay is trustworthy and can be used in most cases to establish probable cause.

Keep in mind that judges and magistrates are the ultimate decision makers if probable cause exists or not. Not all judicial officers will agree after hearing the identical set of circumstances. The local prosecutor is the best person to gauge if a particular judge will sign a search warrant or not. Based upon his or her experience in working with a particular judge, the prosecutor may suggest or require more facts be obtained, or more investigation be conducted, before seeking a search warrant from a particular judicial officer.

Reality Check!

In larger judicial districts, several judges, at various levels, may be available to grant search warrants. Prosecutors know which judicial officers may be more willing to grant authority to search than others. Due to time restraints, vacation schedules, holiday periods, etc., a more stringent judge may be the only judicial officer available at a given moment. Often, judges create a "duty judge" roster that designates a particular judge to review search warrant applications for a particular time period, such as a week's time. Prosecutors may wait until a particular judge is not "on duty" before seeking a search warrant, because of the judge's reputation for requiring information beyond what the law may require. If time permits, prosecutors will often seek out judges for search warrant applications that are more receptive to the law enforcement mission.

CONSTITUTIONAL REQUIREMENTS

Once probable cause has been established police may then seek a search warrant from a judicial officer. Subject to a few, very narrowly defined exceptions, every search and seizure must be conducted under the authority of a valid search warrant. The Fourth Amendment to the U.S. Constitution specifies "no warrants shall issue, but upon probable cause, supported by oath or affirmation, and particularly describing the place to be searched, and the persons or things to be seized."

A search conducted under a warrant is presumed by the courts to be lawful, especially since the U.S. Supreme Court decision in *United States* v. *Leon*.[11] The defense has the burden to demonstrate a search warrant was blatantly invalid, in order to have the evidence seized suppressed at trial. In the absence of clear exigent circumstances, police officers should always seek a valid search warrant before conducting searches.

Neutral and Detached Judicial Officers

Only neutral and detached judicial officers, sitting in the district where the property is located, can issue search warrants. Law enforcement officers, federal investigative agencies, and prosecutors cannot issue warrants. In federal matters, both magistrate-judges, whom the Chief Judge of the federal judicial district hires, and presidential appointed federal judges may issue search warrants. Since only a judicial officer can issue a search warrant, only he or she can change it or correct it.

Particularly Describing the Place to be Searched

A search warrant must particularly describe the place to be searched, and the persons or things to be seized. Describing in detail the area to be searched and things to be seized insures that the search will be as limited in scope as possible. The Fourth Amendment forbids "fishing expeditions."

By mandating that government agents (the police) particularly describe in the warrant the area to be searched, the Fourth Amendment prevents officers from conducting overly broad searches. By forcing the police to identify the objects to be seized, the Amendment prevents officers from "rummaging" in a person's belongings in the hopes of finding something incriminating.

For example, a warrant to search "Joe's Bar, 1234 5th Street, Any Town, California, and all persons on said premises for cocaine, heroin, and all other controlled substances in their possession in violation of the law" is overly broad and general in nature, therefore making it an invalid warrant.

Police officers must identify the place in as much detail as possible within reasonable efforts, so that the searching officers are able to easily locate the property, thereby eliminating the chance of confusion or mistake. A mere street address is insufficient. There could be a 1234 E. 5th Street, as well as a 1234 W. 5th Street, in the same city.

Police investigators routinely drive by or conduct surveillance on a location in order to obtain as complete a description of the property as possible. They also look for potential dangers they may encounter when they execute the warrant. High fences, dogs, existing lighting, etc. will be noted while planning how to safely access the property and gain entry.

Minor errors in description will not render a search warrant invalid, so long as the description as a whole enables the officers to identify the intended location. For example, police investigators provide a dedicated team of officers with a search warrant for them to execute. The warrant describes the apartment to be searched in great detail, including the fact it is "located on the second floor, third door on the north side of the stairway. The apartment door is painted red, and has the number 11 affixed to it. The apartment is under the custody and control of Joe Blow." The search team goes to the apartment building, walk up the stairway, turn north, and walk up to the third door, which is painted red. All of the apartments in the complex have doors that are painted different colors. However, the number affixed to the red door is "10" instead of "11." The officers find the manager of the apartment complex and determine that the renter's name to apartment "10" is Joe Blow, and that there is no apartment "11" in the complex. Is the description of Joe Blow's apartment sufficient, even though the apartment number is incorrect on the search warrant?

Yes. There is enough detail in the description to enable the officers to locate the property with reasonable effort, and there is little chance that there is a mistake in the location. The incorrect number is most probably a minor clerical error.

The Persons or Things to be Seized

The same accuracy that goes into describing places to be searched, also applies to persons and things. Persons should always be identified by name, physical description, and last known address whenever possible. The more description, the better, but no single identifier is indispensable. Because most suspects can be legally searched incidental to an arrest, search warrants for specific individuals are not usually sought.

Some "things" lend themselves to a detailed description more than others. A motor vehicle, for example, can be described in much detail such as make, model year, color, number of doors, registered owner, license plate, and

FIGURE 7.1 DEA Special Agents enter residence to execute a federal search warrant. *Courtesy Drug Enforcement Administration.*

vehicle identification number. All descriptive information should be included in the affidavit. For example, in describing a stolen bicycle, officers should not rely on the serial number alone, but also include its color make and model.

The description of drugs and other contraband may be difficult in that the officers have not normally seen the packing of the drugs before they are seized. However, if during an undercover operation or surveillance, the packaging description is obtained, it should also be included in an affidavit. Even if at the time the warrant is executed, and the contraband is now in different packaging, this fact will not preclude the items from being seized.

In describing items such as scales used to weigh drugs for sales, cutting agents, packaging items such as envelopes, condoms, balloons, etc. can, many times, be summarized as drug paraphernalia. This term has been recognized to include all these items, and is usually sufficient detail in a search warrant application. Many reviewing prosecutors, however, may still require the affiant to be more specific in the description of what drug paraphernalia is.

When seeking evidence of constructive possession, such as when drugs or stolen property is found stored in a home or business, it is advisable to describe these items in the warrant. Descriptions such as "items of identification to show constructive possession of the above contraband such as rent receipts, utility bills, personal letters and other personal identification" are particular enough and should be sufficient.

Supported By Sworn Affidavit

The Fourth Amendment requires the facts and circumstances that the police relied upon to establish probable cause, together with the other necessary elements of a warrant, to be presented to a judicial officer in a "sworn" format. The swearing or affirmation of the affiant is performed by the judicial officer and is documented in the affidavit.

In telephonic search warrant applications, the judicial officer can swear the affiant orally, provided the permission to conduct the search was electronically recorded and later reduced to writing. (See below for more details on telephonic search warrants.)

Probable Cause to Search

The information police officers provided to the judicial officer must contain sufficient facts and circumstances that would lead a reasonable person to conclude that the particular items sought are crime connected and can be found in a particular place.

Police are not required to provide the judicial officer with every fact and detail that has been learned about the case under investigation. They need only give the judicial officer enough information, so that an independent finding of probable cause can be made. The information provided, however, must establish probable cause on its face value. Only the information that the police provide to the magistrate will be considered in determining if probable cause exists or not. Other facts known by the police, but not the judicial officer, cannot later be used to establish probable cause for the issuance of the search warrant unless it is included in the affidavit.

Timeliness

Probable cause to search must exist at the time that the warrant is issued and also at the time that the search is conducted. To help in this regard, the facts contained in an affidavit must be referenced by the times they occurred. Terms such as "recently," or "lately," should be avoided in the affidavit.

Misstatement of Facts

Officers should be extremely careful not to misstate facts in an affidavit or testimony. Many courts will immediately invalidate search warrants that were issued based wholly or partially on misstatements, no matter how innocent or well intended, if the misstatement was intentional. Furthermore, if the misstatement is material to the matter at hand, and is intentionally precluded from the affidavit, the warrant is likely to be invalided also.

For example, a police investigator writes an affidavit in such a manner as to protect the true identity of the actual informant who provided him or her with the information to establish probable cause. The affidavit may imply the information came from informant A, when in fact it came from informant B. If it is later learned that the information stemmed from another source, even if it is absolutely true, the search warrant will most likely be rendered invalid and will certainly invoke many questions about the integrity of the affiant.

An example of another misstatement of fact would be when an express delivery security investigator discovers a package smelling of marijuana, but the affiant instead states in the affidavit that the security investigator "inspected" the package. Most readers of the affidavit would interpret the word "inspected" as a visual examination. Using these words would mislead the judicial officer into believing the package had been opened and the marijuana observed. Will this misrepresentation invalidate the warrant?

Yes. Although the affiant did not intentionally mislead the judicial officer, this misrepresentation is material. Without it, the affidavit possibly does not contain probable cause. Furthermore, the affiant did not include the fact that the inspectors had smelled marijuana, therefore that fact cannot be considered.

Police officers should never jeopardize their credibility with a judicial officer, or those who may review the results of their investigation. The following is a quote from a 9th Circuit Court of Appeals ruling on a 1991 case: "We agree with the district court that [Officer ***] included inaccurate statements in his [search warrant] affidavit and that he arguably did so with reckless disregard for their truth.[12]"

Also consider that if this police officer is so readily impeachable, whenever he or she testifies, the above statement of the court will haunt him or her in every future court appearance. Even routine matters such as chain-of-custody issues or the witnessing of the waiver of a Miranda warning, or the granting of a consent to search, will be in question. Such misstatements of facts will jeopardize an officer's ability to obtain future search warrants, and might be used as good reason to terminate his or her employment in law enforcement because they cannot fully function as a police officer. There is no search warrant worth losing credibility over. Misstatements are never a substitute for further investigation.

Another example of a misstatement of fact is when a drug investigator, seeking a search warrant for a residence where a confidential informant made a purchase of narcotics, knowingly or mistakenly states something happened when it did not. The affiant states in his affidavit that the informant was thoroughly searched to determine if he had any contraband, before being watched entering the dwelling where the purchase was made. In reality, the informant is a female, the officer is a male, and there were no female officers available to "thoroughly" search her. All the officer did was have her empty her pockets. This misstatement of fact could seriously jeopardize the prosecution later at trial.

Officers sometimes "cut and paste" excerpts of prior affidavits written on a word processing program, and insert it into a new affidavit. They should always be careful not to mistakenly paste the facts of one case into another.

Telephonic Search Warrants

When circumstances require immediate action, but are short of being exigent, police officers may seek a *telephonic search warrant* from a judicial officer. The officer must record the conversation between him or herself and the judicial officer, and later complete an affidavit for a search warrant using the identical probable cause and facts presented earlier in the telephone conversation.

All other requirements for a formal, written search warrant must be met for telephonic search warrants.

For example, a police investigator has arrested a burglary suspect, who after waiving his rights, admits to the crime and claims that his coconspirators intend to remove a stash of stolen high definition televisions from a rented storage garage in the city. The suspect knows the televisions are there because he helped move them there from another location. The other burglars further informed him that they intend to remove the televisions within the hour and take them to another city to be sold. Under this set of circumstances, a telephonic search warrant would be justified. However, exigent circumstances probably would not exist.

Anticipatory Search Warrants

Although rare, a valid search warrant can be issued to search property, even though at the time of its issue, the police and the judicial officer know that there are no items subject to seizure located at the specified location, but that there will be evidence there within a sort period of time.

For example, highway patrol officers arrest a man driving a panel truck that contained several hundred pounds of marijuana. The man cooperates with police investigators and reveals where he was going to deliver the drugs. The man agrees to drive the vehicle to the location to make the delivery to the recipient in order for the police to identify and arrest him. Even though the police have no reason to believe that the address now has drugs at the premises, they know it will once the cooperating defendant delivers the drugs there. Anticipatory search warrants cannot be executed unless the police have probable cause at the time of the search, for example, when the panel truck arrives at the address, and another person takes possession of it.

Both state and federal courts have upheld anticipatory search warrants.

WARRANTLESS SEARCHES AND EXIGENT CIRCUMSTANCES

During the course of a law enforcement career, police officers may find themselves in situations that require immediate, direct action that might include the searching of a vehicle, dwelling, or business without benefit of a search warrant. When there is a compelling reason for official police action and there is no time to secure a search warrant, officers are excused from compliance with the warrant requirement.

Warrantless searches are allowed incidental to an arrest, when vehicles and vessels are involved, when evidence is in plain view, when an inventory of a vehicle is conducted, leading to the discovery of evidence, when property is abandoned, during a stop and frisk of a suspect, during a border search, when consent is given to the officers, or when exigent circumstances exist. Some of the leading cases on Fourth Amendment exceptions, and a thumbnail description of each, are included below for further reserch and review:

Carroll v. *U.S.*, 267 U.S. 132 (1925). The Court held that a warrantless search of a vehicle is not a violation of the Fourth Amendment.

Henry v. *United States*, 361 U.S. 98 (1959). Despite the relaxation of the search warrant requirement in cases of automobile searches, it did not relax the probable cause requirement.

Lewis v. *United States*, 385 U.S. 206 (1966). The Court rejected the petitioner's motion to suppress the purchased narcotics by an undercover agent as illegally seized without warrant.

Schmerber v. *California*, 384 U.S. 757 (1966). The court upheld the taking of a blood sample from a person without a warrant under acceptable medical standards because there were exigent circumstances. In this case, if police officers waited for a warrant, alcohol in the suspect's blood would have dissipated.

Terry v. *Ohio*, 392 U.S. 1 (1968). "Where a reasonably prudent officer is warranted in the circumstances of a given case in believing that his safety or that of others is endangered, he may make a reasonable search for weapons of the person believed by him to be armed and dangerous regardless of whether he has probable cause to arrest that individual for crime or the absolute certainty that the individual is armed."

Bumper v. *North Carolina*, 391 U.S. 543 (1968). "A search cannot be justified as lawful on the basis of consent when that 'consent' has been given only after the official conducting the search has asserted that he possesses a warrant; there is no consent under such circumstances."

Chimel v. *California*, 395 U.S. 752 (1969). "An arresting officer may search the arrestee's person to discover and remove weapons and to seize evidence to prevent its concealment or destruction, and may search the area 'within the immediate control' of the person arrested, meaning the area from which he might gain possession of a weapon or destructible evidence."

Colonnade Corp. v. *United States*, 397 U.S. 72 (1970). The court held that health and other administrative exceptions, although different than searches for criminal evidence, still had to comply with the requirements of the Fourth Amendment.

United States v. *Biswell*, 406 U.S. 311 (1972). The Supreme Court upheld airport searches using metal detectors and X-ray devices.

Schneckloth v. *Bustamonte*, 412 U.S. 218 (1973). "When the subject of a search is not in custody and the State would justify a search on the basis of his consent, the Fourth and Fourteenth Amendments require that it demonstrate that the consent was in fact voluntary. Voluntariness is to be determined from the totality of the surrounding circumstances. While knowledge of a right to refuse consent is a factor to be taken into account, the State need not prove that the one giving permission to search knew that he had a right to withhold his consent."

Almeida-Sanchez v. *United States*, 413 U.S. 266 (1973). The Court ruled that searches without reasonable suspicion at checkpoints located away from the border are not permissible.

United States v. *Matlock*, 415 U.S. 164 (1974). "When the prosecution seeks to justify a warrantless search by proof of voluntary consent it is not limited to proof that consent was given by the defendant, but may show that permission to search was obtained from a third party who possessed common authority over or other sufficient relationship to the premises or effects sought to be inspected."

United States v. *Brignoni-Ponce*, 422 U.S. 873 (1975). "The Fourth Amendment held not to allow a roving patrol of the Border Patrol to stop a vehicle near the Mexican border and question its occupants about their citizenship and immigration status, when the only ground for suspicion is that the occupants appear to be of Mexican ancestry."

United States v. *Martinez-Fuerte*, 428 U.S. 543 (1976). "The Border Patrol's routine stopping of a vehicle at a permanent checkpoint located on a major highway away from the Mexican border for brief questioning of the vehicle's occupants is consistent with the Fourth Amendment."

Pennsylvania v. *Mimms*, 434 U.S. 106 (1977). "The order to get out of the car, issued after the respondent was lawfully detained, was reasonable and thus permissible under the Fourth Amendment. The State's proffered justification for such order – the officer's safety – is both legitimate and weighty, and the intrusion into respondent's personal liberty occasioned by the order, being at most a mere inconvenience, cannot prevail when balanced against legitimate concerns for the officer's safety."

Rakas v. *Illinois*, 439 U.S. 128 (1978). " . . . a person aggrieved by an illegal search and seizure only through the introduction of damaging evidence secured by a search of a third person's premises or property has not had any of his Fourth Amendment rights infringed."

Rawlings v. *Kentucky*, 448 U.S. 98 (1980). The Court ruled that Rawlings did not have standing to object to the search of a friend's purse in which he had placed drugs belonging to him.

New York v. *Belton*, 453 U.S. 454 (1981). "Not only may the police search the passenger compartment of the car in such circumstances, they may also examine the contents of any containers found in the passenger compartment. And such a container may be searched whether it is open or closed, since the justification for the search is not that the arrestee has no privacy interest in the container but that the lawful custodial arrest justifies the infringement of any privacy interest the arrestee may have."

Oliver v. *United States*, 466 U.S. 170 (1984). This decision discusses the open fields exception to the Fourth Amendment search warrant requirement.

Hudson v. *Palmer*, 468 U.S. 517 (1984). "A prisoner has no reasonable expectation of privacy in his prison cell entitling him to the protection of the Fourth Amendment against unreasonable searches."

United States v. *Karo*, 468 U.S. 705 (1984). "The monitoring of a beeper in a private residence, a location not opened to visual surveillance, violates the Fourth Amendment rights of those who have a justifiable interest in the privacy of the residence."

Winston v. *Lee*, 470 U.S. 753 (1985). "A compelled surgical intrusion into an individual's body for evidence implicates expectations of privacy and security of such magnitude that the intrusion may be 'unreasonable' even if likely to produce evidence of a crime."

New Jersey v. *T.L.O.*, 469 U.S. 325 (1985). "The Fourth Amendment's prohibition on unreasonable searches and seizures applies to searches conducted by public school officials and is not limited to searches carried out by law enforcement officers."

California v. *Carney*, 471 U.S. 386 (1985). The Court ruled that the warrantless search of respondent's motor home did not violate the Fourth Amendment.

United States v. *Sharpe*, 470 U.S. 675 (1985). "In assessing whether a detention is too long in duration to be justified as an investigative stop, it is appropriate to examine whether the police diligently pursued a means of investigation that was likely to confirm or dispel their suspicions quickly, during which time it was necessary to detain the defendant."

Arizona v. *Hicks*, 480 U.S. 321 (1987). Under the plain view doctrine, the incriminating character of the evidence must be immediately apparent to the police officer.

United States v. *Dunn*, 480 U.S. 294 (1987). Using drug dogs to detect narcotics in luggage is not a search because it exposes only contraband.

Skinner v. *Railway Labor Executives' Assn.*, 489 U.S. 602 (1989). Mandating submission of biological samples to be tested for drugs without suspicion or warrant, was upheld by the Court when the company requiring the samples was already heavily regulated by the government.

Florida v. *Riley*, 488 U.S. 445 (1989). The court decided that a law enforcement officer did not need a warrant to circle twice over a defendant's property in a helicopter at the height of 400 feet and make naked-eye observations through openings in the greenhouse roof and its open sides, to determine if there were marijuana plants inside.

Michigan Dept. of State Police v. *Sitz*, 496 U.S. 444 (1990). The Court ruled that the police may briefly detain all cars on a public road to check for intoxication.

Illinois v. *Rodriguez*, 497 U.S. 177 (1990). "A warrantless entry is valid when based upon the consent of a third party whom the police, at the time of the entry, reasonably believe to possess common authority over the premises, but who in fact does not."

Minnesota v. *Olson*, 495 U.S. 91 (1990). "Olson's status as an overnight guest is alone sufficient to show that he had an expectation of privacy in the home that society is prepared to recognize as reasonable."

Maryland v. *Buie*, 494 U.S. 325 (1990). "Here, the police had an analogous interest in taking steps to assure themselves that Buie's house was not harboring other persons who were dangerous and who could unexpectedly launch an attack, and the fact that Buie had an expectation of privacy in rooms that were not examined by the police prior to the arrest does not mean that such rooms were immune from entry. No warrant was required, and as an incident to the arrest the officers could, as a precautionary matter and without probable cause or reasonable suspicion, look in closets and other spaces immediately adjoining the place of arrest from which an attack could be launched."

Minnesota v. *Dickerson*, 508 U.S. 366 (1993). This decision discusses when a seizure is permissible without a warrant under the plain view doctrine.

Vernonia School Dist. 47J v. *Acton*, 515 U.S. 646 (1995). The Petitioner school district's Student Athlete Drug Policy authorizing random urinalysis drug testing of students who participate in its athletics programs, was held to be consistent with the Fourth Amendment.

City Of Indianapolis et al. v. *Edmond et al.* (2000). Unlike Sitz, because a narcotics checkpoint program's primary purpose is indistinguishable from the general interest in crime control, the checkpoints violate the Fourth Amendment.

Georgia v. *Randolph*, 04-1067 (2006). The Supreme Court held that a police search of a couple's home where one resident gave permission for the search but the other "unequivocally refused to give consent," is unconstitutional as to the resident who refused consent.

Exigent circumstances may include any circumstances that require immediate action to prevent imminent danger to life, serious damage to property, escape of a suspect, or the destruction of evidence.

FIGURE 7.2   DEA Special Agents making an arrest after drugs were found during the execution of a federal search warrant. *Courtesy Drug Enforcement Administration.*

U.S. Supreme Court Justice Warren Burger summarized this exception to a valid search warrant requirement:

"A myriad of circumstances could fall within the terms 'exigent circumstances' . . . smoke coming out of a window or under a door, the sound of gunfire in a house, threats from the inside to shoot through the door at police, reasonable grounds to believe an injured or seriously ill person is being held within" (and so forth).[13]

For example, police investigators arrest a suspected terrorist in their city, who claims during his interrogation to have a bomb at his residence that is set to explode within the hour. The investigators know that it will be impossible to get a formal search warrant, and attempts to locate a judicial officer to seek a telephonic search warrant have failed. Do the investigators have the legal ability to go to the suspect's residence to dismantle the bomb before a search warrant can be secured?

Yes. Police officers must be able to articulate the circumstances that led them to their actions, especially when they are contrary to law or the U.S. Constitution. Bear in mind that what might pass as exigent circumstances in one judicial district may not meet the threshold in another. Every case will be different, and the officer is required to exercise sound judgment before conducting a search without a warrant. In all cases, when exigent circumstances present themselves, a prosecutor should be consulted to seek his or her opinion as to the viability of conducting a search without a warrant. In almost every situation where the police can demonstrate there was a significant threat to public safety or someone's imminent death, the search will be judged as valid.

In such a case, the police should always document their actions, and if appropriate, seek a written search warrant once the crisis is over. For example, the police arrive at the suspected terrorist's residence and successfully dismantle the bomb they find in the garage. Would they be justified to further search the residence for other evidence or weapons?

No. Once the crisis has dissipated, the police can no longer shield themselves under exigent circumstances, and a search warrant would be required to further search the residence, except to conduct a "protective sweep" to look for other suspects or explosives that may be in the home. Any other contraband observed in plain view while conducting protective sweeps could be seized without a warrant.

In another example, a uniformed police officer is dispatched to a residence to check the welfare of an elderly person who has not been seen for several days. The officer receives no answer at the door, and decides to look through an adjacent window where he sees the elderly woman laying on the floor. The officer kicks in the door, renders aid to the woman, and calls an ambulance. While in the residence, the officer sees in plain view, an opened suitcase with a plastic bag containing drugs. The suitcase has a name tag of the old woman's son attached to it. The officer seizes the drugs. Would the seizure of the drugs be ruled inadmissible against the son because the officer lacked a valid search warrant?

No. The exigent circumstances created a valid, lawful reason for the officer's presence. Any contraband he observes in plain view would be admissible. However, searching further would require a search warrant.

EXECUTION OF THE SEARCH WARRANT

The actual execution of a search warrant requires adequate manpower, preplanning, specialized equipment, and training in officer safety techniques. Search warrant executions can be one of the most dangerous aspects of law enforcement. Some "high risk" warrants require extraordinary means to carry it out safely, for both the officers as well as occupants of the residence or building intended to be searched. No two search warrant executions are ever the same.

Officers Present

The Fourth Amendment does not require that a warrant name a specific officer to execute it. However, federal and state statutes generally specify classes of officers who are authorized to execute warrants and require that a warrant be directed to one of these officers within these classes.

As a general rule, persons not authorized to execute warrants can be present and can assist in the search when asked to by an authorized officer, but there are some caveats. For example, local police ask federal drug agents for their assistance in executing a search warrant at a residence suspected of containing explosive material. The police and federal agents enter the residence and find the explosives named in the warrant. However, the federal drug agents also find cocaine hidden inside a sugar container in the kitchen. Will the cocaine be admissible later in court?

No. The warrant authorized the local officer to enter and search only for explosives, not drugs. Under the guise of asking federal agents for help in searching for explosives, the officer was using his hunch and the drug agent's expertise to look for drugs, thereby going beyond the authority of the warrant.

Life of a Warrant

Once issued, another otherwise valid search warrant "dies" and cannot be executed when:

1. Probable cause vanishes
2. Period fixed by statue expires
3. Period fixed by warrant expires or
4. There is an unreasonable delay

As soon as any one of the above occurs, the warrant is considered dead. Obviously, once a warrant has been executed it is terminated. A second search later cannot be based upon the same warrant.

Probable cause to search must exist both at the time the warrant is issued and at the time the search is conducted. If the probable cause upon which the warrant was based vanishes before the warrant can be executed, the warrant is no longer valid.

Federal and state statutes control the maximum lifetime of a search warrant. In most cases, search warrants expire in 10 days after being signed by a judicial officeer.

Time of Day

Most state search warrants, and non-drug federal warrants, direct that they shall be served only in the daytime, unless the judicial officer finds reasonable cause for searching at night and inserts permission to search at night in the warrant.

Federal law defines "daytime" as the hours between 6 a.m. and 10 p.m. local time, regardless if there is no daylight at the time the warrant is served.

By contrast, since drug search warrants are inherently dangerous and evidence can easily be destroyed, federal warrants can authorize a nighttime search, without any special showing that a nighttime search is absoluted necessary.

Knock and Notice

During the actual execution of a search warrant, police are required by statute or court decision to announce their presence and purpose. The reason is to protect the owner's privacy and to prevent unnecessary violence. For example, State Police officers appear at the front door of a residence they have a search warrant for. An agent pounds heavily on the door and states, "Police Officers; we have a search warrant." A refusal by the occupant to permit the officers to enter can either be expressed or implied. The occupant expressly refusing or when he looks out a window and then runs to another part of the dwelling, both constitute refusal. Once a reasonable time has elapsed, the police may then forcibly enter the dwelling to conduct the search. Reasonable time has been defined as the amount of time it would take someone to walk from the rear of the building to the front door. The police have the burden to show the time interval between when they knocked and announced, and when they forcibly entered the dwelling was reasonable. Factors such as the physical condition of the occupant, time of day, and environmental conditions must be taken into account before forcible entry can be made.

As with almost everything, there are exceptions. Police do not need to give "knock and notice" if they are virtually certain it is a useless gesture or exigent circumstances require quick entry. It would be a useless gesture to knock and announce when the police are virtually certain the premises are unoccupied. It is equally a useless gesture when the police are virtually certain that the occupants already know their purpose and authority.

For example, police investigators wearing identifying clothing with "Police" on their caps and jackets, carrying firearms and wearing badges, approach a home with a valid warrant to search for stolen property. As the officers walk up to the residence, they recognize a recently arrested burglar who is out on bail, looking out of a window and then suddenly darts back further into the interior of the house, out of their view. From his shocked expression, the police are virtually certain the man recognizes them as police officers and knows their purpose. Under this set of circumstances, providing knock and notice would be a useless gesture.

In another example, Bureau of Immigration and Customs Enforcement (ICE) agents seize a large wooden box at a port of entry and they determine it contains about 50-pounds of hashish. The ICE agents conduct a "controlled delivery", in which they allow the container to be delivered to the international delivery company's warehouse where they wait for someone to claim it. A 35-year-old woman arrives and takes possession of the container. She is followed to her home where she takes the container inside. There does not appear to be anyone else inside the residence. The ICE agents have a warrant for the home and go to the door to execute it. They "knock and announce" their authority and intentions, wait ten seconds, and then burst through the front door. Have the ICE agents complied with the "knock and announce" requirement?

No. Although the ICE agents have property announced, they are not justified in concluding that the woman has expressly refused to allow them entry. Ten seconds is not a reasonable amount of time for someone to answer the door in this case since there is no reason to suspect violence, the likelihood of escape is low, and she could not possibly dismantle a container and dispose of the 50-pounds of hashish in ten seconds.

Manner of Entry

The Fourth Amendment does not require officers to exhibit, read, or provide anyone with a copy of a search warrant before executing it. State statutes may require it, but federal law does not.

Neither the Fourth Amendment nor federal law requires that the property be occupied at the time it is searched. From a strategic standpoint, "high risk" warrants are sometimes executed when the police believe the residence or building to be searched is unoccupied.

Use of Force

Reasonable force can be used to gain entry into a dwelling or business in order to execute a search warrant. A search warrant is an order issued by a judicial officer in the name of the government, commanding a police officer to conduct a search for specified objects.

Persons do not have the right to forcibly resist the execution of a search warrant, even though the warrant may later be held to be invalid.

Extent of the Search

The extent to which the police can search an area depends entirely upon the objects for which they are searching. If the police lawfully search a home for a stolen piano, they may not look in dresser drawers or kitchen cabinets.

Drugs, however, can virtually be hidden anywhere. The police are authorized to search any area where they feel drug evidence may be hidden.

Search Time

Police officers may remain on the premises for as long as they deem necessary, to conduct a thorough search for the objects named in the warrant. However, they must stop once all the objects named in the warrant are seized.

Things to be Seized

The activity of the police officers executing the warrant must be limited to searching for those items named in the warrant and no others.

The only exception to this restriction is a seizure made under the "plain view" theory. Plain view only applies to items that are immediately apparent and are inadvertently found within the scope of the originally limited search for those items named in the warrant.

Receipt for Seized Property

Although police officers are not required to display a search warrant before conducting the search, they are required by statue to leave a copy of the warrant and a receipt for property taken with the occupant. If the building or dwelling is found unoccupied, a copy of the warrant and a receipt must be left at the premises.

Returning the Warrant to the Court

Although the Fourth Amendment does not set any specific requirements regarding the return of a search warrant, many statutes often set out the mechanics for returning the warrant to the issuing judicial officer.

SUMMARY

A significant source of criminal evidence originates from the execution of search warrants. The Fourth Amendment of the U.S. Constitution specifies what steps the police must take in order to obtain such warrants.

The Fourth Amendment is intended to protect individuals from *unreasonable* search and seizures by the government, not private parties.

Things that the police can see, hear, or smell without invading a reasonable expectation of privacy are considered to be in plain view. Things that are in plain or open view have been exposed to the public and are not protected by the Fourth Amendment. Abandoned property is also not protected by the Fourth Amendment.

If the government is to conduct a search, it must be reasonable under the provisions of the Fourth Amendment. The courts have held that a search is presumed to be reasonable if a judicial officer issues a valid search warrant based upon probable cause.

There are two elements of probable cause. First, there must be probable cause to believe certain property or contraband is crime connected, therefore subject to seizure. Second, there must be probable cause to believe this property or contraband can be located in a particular place. Probable cause cannot be based upon a police officer's mere suspicions or upon his educated guess. These conclusions cannot be used to establish probable cause. It must be based on specific, articulable, facts and circumstances. Probable cause determination is based upon logic and common sense. The facts and circumstances must logically make it probable, not possible, that property or contraband subject to seizure is located in a particular place.

External factors, such as timeliness of the information, misstatements, and the circumstances establishing probable cause changing, all will have an effect on the validity of a search warrant.

Once probable cause has been established, police may then seek a search warrant from a neutral and detached judicial officer. Subject to a few, very narrowly defined exceptions, every search and seizure must be conducted under the authority of a valid search warrant.

The second prong measures the reliability of the information, usually provided by an informant. Police officers need to be prepared to answer questions on how they obtained the information.

Search warrants can be obtained telephonically when time is limited.

Exigent circumstances allow police officers to conduct searches under emergency conditions without benefit of a search warrant.

Search warrants can also be obtained in anticipation that a location will later contain items subject to seizure.

As a rule of thumb, most states have statutes that require police to only execute search warrants during "daytime," which is defined as between the hours of 6 a.m. and 10 p.m. There are exceptions, usually when drugs are involved, in order to lessen the chances of violence and the destruction of evidence.

Although police are not required to display a search warrant to the occupants of the place to be searched before entering the building or dwelling, they must leave a copy of the warrant once their search is conducted. They must also leave a receipt for the items seized during the execution of the search warrant.

NOTES

1. *Katz* v. *United States*, 389 U.S. 347 (1967).
2. See *U.S.* v. *McMillion*, 350 F. Supp. 593 (1972).
3. *Abel* v. *U.S.*, 80 S.Ct. 683 (1960) and *Hester* v. *U.S.*, 44 S.Ct. 445 (1924).
4. 267 U.S. 132 (1925).
5. 358 F.2d 833 (1966).
6. 254 F.2d 82 D.C. Cir. (1958).

7. *Smith* v. *U.S.* 358 F.2d 833 DC Circuit (1966).

8. 84 S.Ct. 1509 (1964).

9. 89 S.Ct. 584 (1969).

10. *U.S.* v. *Harris,* 91 S.Ct. 2075 (1971).

11. 468 U.S. 897 (1984).

12. *United States* v. Bertrand, 926 F.2d 838, 842 (9th Cir. 1991).

13. *Wayne* v. *U.S.,* 318 F2d 205 at 212, DC Cir. (1963).

8

The Crime Scene

Law enforcement agencies respond to thousands of crime scenes every day. Unfortunately, very few police agencies have specially trained crime scene investigators whose sole job is to respond to and process all crime scenes. Most departments must rely on their uniformed patrol officers to gather physical evidence and collect the facts that need to be written in an initial crime report. Reported crime, for example, burglary, robbery, murder, etc. usually results in a crime scene, where the evidence gathered can significantly contribute to identifying a suspect and obtaining a conviction.

Proactive criminal investigations, such as activities involving drugs, almost always lack a crime scene, but may lead investigators to a working clandestine laboratory or storage area where money and drugs might be found. These locations must also be handled as any other crime scene, in order to gather evidence that might lead to the identification of other conspirators. Some of these scenes, such as a methamphetamine laboratory, are dangerous and require specialized experience to tackle them.

No matter what type of crime scene is encountered, police officers must have a basic understanding on how to safely and effectively gather evidence.

CRIME SCENE SAFETY

Police supervisors and crime scene investigators have the ultimate responsibility of recognizing chemical, biological, and physical hazards when processing a crime scene. However, it is the responsibility of each agency, responding to and providing support at the crime scene, to develop policies, programs, and training on health and safety practices. Law enforcement agencies should consult with local, state, and federal environmental and occupational health and safety agencies when working with potential hazard forensic evidence.

Because many agencies do not have their own crime laboratories, they need to transport evidence to a state or federal laboratory for examination purposes. When shipping forensic evidence, agencies must comply with U.S. Department of Transportation and International Air Transport Association regulations. The following provides a familiarity of the hazards, safety precautions, safe work practices, and personal protective equipment recommended for personnel processing routine crime scenes. This section also describes the importance of compliance with waste-disposal regulations.

Routes of Exposure

Personnel operating in or around contaminated environments, such as a clandestine methamphetamine laboratory, must be aware of the various ways in which hazards may enter and harm the body.[1] Police officers who discover such laboratories should immediately seek the assistance of the Drug Enforcement Administration or state agency that has specially trained personnel to handle such matters.

Inhalation

Inhalation is the introduction of a toxic substance into the respiratory system. Airborne contaminants may be in the form of dust, aerosol, smoke, vapor, gas, or fume. Materials may be in a solid or liquid form and still represent an inhalation hazard because they produce vapors, mists, and fumes. Proper work practices and adequate ventilation can minimize the risk of airborne contaminant inhalation. When working in areas that may have airborne contaminants, respiratory protection must be worn. Only certified personnel should be allowed to enter hazardous crime scenes and they must wear respiratory protection.

Skin Contact

Contamination through the skin can result from direct contact or by absorption. The severity of the injury can depend on the concentration of the contaminant and the amount of exposure time. Systemic effects, such as dizziness, tremors, nausea, blurred vision, liver and kidney damage, shock, or collapse, can occur when the substances are absorbed through the skin and circulated

FIGURE 8.1   FBI Evidence Response Team members are reminded to attend a safety briefing before gathering evidence at the massive crime scene created by the crash of a hijacked airliner at the Pentagon by terrorists on September 11, 2001. *Courtesy FBI.*

throughout the body. Using personal protective equipment (e.g., gloves, safety glasses, goggles, face shields, and protective clothing) can prevent exposure.

Ingestion

Ingestion involves introducing contaminants into the body through the mouth, which can cause severe damage to the mouth, throat, and digestive tract. To prevent entry of contaminants into the mouth, safe work practices, such as washing hands before eating, smoking, or applying cosmetics, must always be used. Police officers should never bring food, drink, or cigarettes into areas where contamination can occur.

Injection

The direct injection of contaminants into the body, either by accidental needle punctures or mechanical injuries from contaminated glass, metal, or other sharp objects can cause severe complications. Contaminants enter directly into the bloodstream and can spread rapidly. Extreme caution should be exercised when handling objects with sharp or jagged edges. Work gloves must be worn at all times.

Bloodborne-Patheogen Safety

On December 6, 1991, the Occupational Safety and Health Administration issued Title 29, Section 1910.1030 of the Code of Federal Regulations (CFR), Bloodborne Pathogens.[2]

Occupations at risk from exposure to bloodborne pathogens include law enforcement, emergency response, and forensic laboratory personnel. Fundamental to the bloodborne pathogens standard is the concept of Universal Precautions. This concept is the primary mechanism for infection control. It requires employees to treat all blood, body fluids, or other potentially infectious materials as if infected with bloodborne diseases, such as hepatitis B virus (HBV), hepatitis C virus (HCV), and human immunodeficiency virus (HIV). The following protective measures should be taken to avoid direct contact with potentially infectious materials:

- Use barrier protection, such as disposable gloves, coveralls, and shoe covers, if contact may occur with potentially infectious materials. Change gloves when torn, punctured, or when their ability to function as a barrier is compromised. Wear appropriate eye and face protection to protect against splashes, sprays, and spatters of potentially infectious materials.
- Wash hands after removing gloves or other personal protective equipment. Remove gloves and other personal protective equipment

in a manner that will not result in contaminating unprotected skin or clothing.

- Prohibit eating, drinking, smoking, or applying cosmetics where human blood, body fluids, or other potentially infectious materials are present, regardless of personal protection that may be worn.
- Place contaminated sharp objects in appropriate closable, leak-proof, puncture-resistant containers, when transported or discarded. Label the containers with a BIOHAZARD warning label.
- Do not bend, recap, remove, or otherwise handle contaminated needles or other sharp objects.
- Decontaminate equipment after use with a daily-prepared solution of household bleach diluted 1:10 or 70 percent isopropyl alcohol or other appropriate disinfectant. Non-corrosive disinfectants are commercially available. It is important to allow sufficient contact time for complete disinfection.
- In addition to Universal Precautions, engineering controls and prudent work practices can reduce or eliminate exposure to potentially infectious materials. Some examples of engineering controls include puncture-resistant containers used for storage and disposal of sharp objects and paint stirrers and long-handled mirrors for use in locating and retrieving evidence in confined or hidden spaces.

Chemical Safety

Depending on the type of material encountered, a variety of health and safety hazards can exist. Some of those chemical safety hazards are identified by the following categories:[3]

- Flammable or combustible materials, such as gasoline, acetone, and ether, ignite easily when exposed to air and an ignition source, such as a spark or flame.
- Over time, some explosive materials, such as nitroglycerine and nitroglycerine-based dynamite, deteriorate to become chemically unstable. In particular, ether will form peroxides around the mouth of the vessel in which it is stored. All explosive materials are sensitive to heat, shock, and friction.
- Pyrophoric materials, such as phosphorus, sodium, and barium, can be liquid or solid and can ignite in air temperatures less than 130°F (540°C) without an external ignition source.
- Oxidizers, such as nitrates, hydrogen peroxide, and concentrated sulfuric acid, are a class of chemical compounds that readily yield oxygen to promote combustion. Avoid storage with flammable and combustible materials or substances that could rapidly accelerate its decomposition.

- Corrosive materials can cause destruction to living tissue or objects, such as wood and steel. The amount of damage is dependent upon the concentration and duration of contact.
- When working with chemicals, be aware of hazardous properties, disposal techniques, personal protection, packaging and shipping procedures, and emergency preparedness. This awareness comes from the information in a Material Safety Data Sheet and appropriate training. The Material Safety Data Sheet provides information on the hazards of a particular material so that personnel can work safely and responsibly with hazardous materials.

Light-Source Safety

When using ultraviolet lights, lasers, and other light sources, the eyes must be protected from direct and indirect exposure.[4]

Not all laser beams are visible, and irreversible eye damage can result from exposure to direct or indirect light from reflected beams. Prolonged exposure to the skin should also be avoided. All personnel in the vicinity of the light source should wear protective eyewear appropriate for the light source. Goggles must have sufficient protective material that fit snugly to prevent

FIGURE 8.2   FBI Evidence Response Team members go through decontamination at American Media, Inc. in Boca Raton, Florida, on October 10, 2001. An employee of the publishing company, which produces various tabloid newspapers, died from exposure to anthrax. Federal investigators say the strain was manmade. *Reuters/Corbis/Colin Braley.*

light from entering at any angle. The goggles must display the American National Standards Institute's (ANSI) mark denoting eye-protection compliance. Laser protective eyewear must be made of the appropriate optical density to protect against the maximum operating wavelength of the laser source.

Confined-Space Safety

A confined space is an enclosed area large enough for personnel to enter and work, but has limited or restricted means for entry and exit. Confined spaces are not designed for continuous occupancy (e.g., sewers, open pits, tank cars, and vats). Confined spaces can expose personnel to hazards, including toxic gases, explosive or oxygen-deficient atmospheres, electrical dangers, or materials that can engulf personnel entering the space.[5]

Conditions in a confined space must be considered dangerous and may not be entered until a confined-space permit has been issued. The atmosphere must be continuously monitored with a calibrated, direct-reading instrument for oxygen, carbon monoxide, flammable gases and vapors, and toxic air contaminants. Periodic readings from these monitors should be documented. Only certified confined-space personnel may operate in confined spaces. Rescue services must be immediately available to the site. The following practices must be followed when working in a confined space:

Never enter before all atmospheric, engulfment, mechanical, and electrical hazards have been identified and documented. Isolating hazards must be performed in accordance with Occupational Safety and Health Administration (OSHA) Title 29 CFR 1910.147, *Control of Hazardous Energy (Lockout/Tagout)*.[6]

Ensure that ventilation equipment does not interfere with entry, exit, or rescue procedures.

- Provide barriers to warn unauthorized personnel and to keep entrants safe from external hazards.
- Provide constant communication between personnel entering the confined space and attendants.
- Back-up communication must be in place prior to entry.
- Wear appropriate personal protective equipment, such as self-contained breathing apparatus (SCBA), full-body harness, head protection, and other necessary equipment.
- Never attempt a rescue unless part of a designated rescue team.
- Personnel certified in first aid and cardiopulmonary resuscitation (CPR) must be on-site.
- For additional information, refer to the Occupational Safety and Health Administration standard for *Permit Required Confined Spaces*, 29 CFR Section 1910.146.7.[7]

X-Ray Safety

Portable, handheld X-ray machines, often used to identify the contents of unknown packages, pose a risk for exposure to X-ray radiation at crime scenes. Keep X-ray exposure as low as reasonably achievable by adhering to the following:

- Shield the X-ray device, the questionable object, and the operator.
- Remove all non-essential personnel from the X-ray field.
- Limit the time that personnel must be in the area of operation.
- Always wear assigned monitoring devices appropriate for X-ray radiation.
- Ensure that standard X-ray operating procedures are in place and followed and that adequate training has been provided in accordance with federal and state regulations.

PERSONAL PROTECTIVE EQUIPMENT

At all crime scenes, the selection of personal protective equipment must be made in coordination with a hazard-risk assessment completed by trained and qualified personnel.

The hazard-risk assessment should identify the possible contaminants as well as the hazards associated with each product.

Hand Protection

Hand protection should be selected on the basis of the type of material being handled and the hazard(s) associated with the material.[8] Detailed information can be obtained from the manufacturer.[9] The following list provides information about glove material types and functions:

- Nitrile provides protection from acids, alkaline solutions, hydraulic fluid, photographic solutions, fuels, lubricants, aromatics, petroleum, and chlorinated solvents. It also offers some resistance to cuts and snags.
- Neoprene offers resistance to oil, grease, acids, solvents, alkalis, bases, and most refrigerants.
- Polyvinyl chloride (PVC) is resistant to alkali oils, and limited concentrations of nitric and chromic acids.
- Latex (natural rubber) resists mild acids, caustics, detergents, germicides, and ketonic solutions. Latex will swell and degrade if exposed to gasoline or kerosene. When exposed to prolonged, excessive heat or direct sunlight, latex gloves can degrade, causing the glove materials to lose their integrity.
- Powder-free gloves with reduced protein content will lower the risk of developing latex allergies. Personnel allergic to latex can usually wear nitrile or neoprene.

Guidelines for glove use include:

- Prior to donning, inspect the gloves for holes, punctures, and tears. Remove rings or other sharp objects that can cause punctures.
- When working with heavily contaminated materials, wear a double layer of gloves.
- Change gloves when torn or punctured or when their ability to function as a barrier is compromised.
- To avoid contaminating unprotected skin or clothing, remove disposable gloves by grasping the cuffs and pulling them off inside out. Discard disposable gloves in designated containers. Do not reuse.

Eye Protection

Appropriate eye protection, such as safety glasses and goggles, should be worn when handling biological, chemical, and radioactive materials.[10] Face shields offer better protection when there is a potential for splashing or flying debris. Face shields must be worn in combination with safety glasses or goggles, because face shields alone are not considered appropriate eye protection. Contact lens users must wear safety glasses or goggles to protect the eyes. In the event of a chemical splash into the eye, it can be difficult to remove the contact lens to irrigate the eye, and contaminants can be trapped behind the contact lens. Protective eyewear should be worn over prescription glasses. Safety glasses may be made to the wearer's eyeglass prescription.

Foot Protection

Shoes that completely cover and protect the foot are essential.[11] Protective footwear should be used at crime scenes when there is a danger of foot injuries from falling or rolling objects, from objects piercing the sole, and when feet are exposed to electrical hazards. The standard recognized by the Occupational Safety and Health Administration for protective footwear is the American National Standard for Personal Protection-Protective Footwear, ANSI Z41-1991. In some situations, non-permeable shoe covers can provide barrier protection to shoes and prevent the transfer of contamination outside of the crime scene.

Respiratory Protection

Certain crime scenes, such as bombings and clandestine laboratories, can produce noxious fumes and other airborne contaminants in which responders must use respiratory protection.[12] Compliance with Title 29 CFR 1910.134, *Respiratory Protection*,[13] is mandatory whenever respirators are used. Critical elements for the safe use of respirators include a written program, training, medical evaluation, fit testing, and a respirator-maintenance program. Without these elements, the wearer is not guaranteed protection.

Head Protection

In certain crime scenes, where structural damage has or can occur, protective helmets should be worn. The standard recognized by the Occupational Safety and Health Administration for protective helmets is ANSI's Requirements for Industrial Head Protection, Z89.1-1997.[14]

CRIME SCENE SEARCH

All crime scenes must be thoroughly searched to gather all available evidence and to deprive the suspect(s) or someone else from removing something later. Whatever method of search is chosen, it should be thorough and systematic, which usually means it will probably be time-consuming and difficult.

The Approach

Uniformed police officers are almost always the first responders to crime scenes. Their job is to recognize the location of the crime scene(s) where potential evidence is located, and to notify the appropriate investigators, if available, about the situation. In my jurisdictions, the uniformed officer who responded to the call for service handles all evidence collection, and in many cases is equipped with an evidence kit to help in its retrieval.

At the scene of a possible dead body, officers should ascertain if the person is alive, render care, and ensure the person is taken to an appropriate facility for treatment. If at all possible, efforts should be made to obtain an *integrity photograph* of the scene before any action so as to have a record of the area prior to it being disturbed by emergency medical personnel and other public officials.

Efforts must also be made to keep the public out of the area, to avoid contamination of evidence and to keep rubberneckers, souvenir hunters, and the media away until the scene has been thoroughly processed.

There are basically two approaches to searching a scene: a cautious search of visible areas, avoiding the loss or contamination of evidence, and a more vigorous approach of concealed areas in which buildings, cars, etc. may

FIGURE 8.3   FBI Evidence Response Team investigators process evidence gathered at American Media Inc. in Boca Raton, Florida, October 11, 2001. The publishing company's building was officially classified as a crime scene following the announcement that a female employee's test results showed her to have been infected with anthrax. REUTERS/Corbis/Colin Braley

be dismantled in the process. The officer in charge of the scene will make the determination as to the approach and methods to be used.

Preparation

Crime scenes range from simple to extraordinarily complex. For example, compare the crime scenes of a residential burglary to the 1995 bombing of Alfred P. Murrah Federal Building in Oklahoma City, Oklahoma, in which 168 people were killed. The latter would require a command post to facilitate communication and decision-making. As in any major event, a person in charge must be present to make decisions and resolve conflicts. The FBI recommends that the following activities should take place before and during prolonged, complicated crime scene searches:

- Discuss the search with involved personnel before arriving at the scene, if possible.
- Ensure that personnel are aware of the types of evidence usually encountered and the proper handling of the evidence.

- Make preliminary personnel assignments before arriving at the scene, if possible.
- Ensure that assignments are in keeping with the attitude, aptitude, training, and experience of search personnel. Personnel may be assigned two or more responsibilities.

Person in Charge Responsibilities include:

- Ensure scene security.
- Prepare administrative log.
- Conduct preliminary survey (initial walk-through).
- Prepare narrative description.
- Resolve problems.
- Make final decisions.
- Establish communication among the medical examiner, laboratory personnel, and prosecuting attorneys, so that questions arising during the crime scene search can be resolved.
- Coordinate agreements with all agencies in multi-jurisdictional crime scene searches.
- Accumulate evidence collection and packaging materials and equipment.
- Prepare the paperwork to document the search.
- Provide protective clothing, communication, lighting, shelter, transportation, equipment, food, water, medical assistance, and security for search personnel.
- In prolonged searches, use shifts of two or more teams. Transfer paperwork and responsibility in a preplanned manner from one team to the next.
- Secure and protect the scene.
- Take control of the scene immediately.
- Determine the extent to which the scene has been protected. Obtain information from personnel who have knowledge of the original condition.
- Determine personnel and equipment needs. Make specific assignments.

The Initial Approach

Personnel at the scene should:

- Be alert for evidence.
- Take extensive notes.
- Consider the safety of all personnel.
- Record who enters and leaves.
- Select a narrative technique (written, audio, or video).
- Continue to take extensive notes.

Preliminary Survey

The preliminary survey is an organizational stage to plan for the search. The person in charge will designate a case investigator who will:

- Cautiously walk through the scene.
- Maintain administrative and emotional control.
- Delineate the extent of the search area. Usually expand the initial perimeter.
- Organize methods and procedures.
- Recognize special problem areas.
- Identify and protect transient physical evidence.
- Develop a general theory of the crime.
- Take extensive notes to document the scene, physical and environmental conditions, and personnel movements.

Evaluate Physical Evidence Possibilities

This evaluation begins upon arriving at the scene and becomes detailed in the preliminary survey stage. This evaluation includes:

- Ensure that the collection and packaging materials and equipment are sufficient.
- Focus first on evidence that could be lost. Leave the least transient evidence last.
- Ensure all personnel consider the variety of possible evidence, not only evidence within their specialties.
- Search the easily accessible areas and progress to out-of-view locations. Look for hidden items.
- Evaluate whether evidence appears to have been moved inadvertently.
- Evaluate whether the scene appears contrived.

The Narrative

The narrative is a running description of the crime scene:

- Use a systematic approach in the narrative.
- Nothing is insignificant to record if it catches one's attention.
- Under most circumstances, do not collect evidence during the narrative.
- Use photographs and sketches to supplement, not substitute for, the narrative.

The narrative should include:

- Case number or other identifier.
- Date, time, and location.
- Weather and lighting conditions.
- Identity and assignments of personnel.
- Condition and position of evidence.

Photography

- Take preliminary photographs.
- Photograph and log evidence and scene. Note: there is no such thing as taking too many photographs of a crime scene.
- Photograph the crime scene as soon as possible.
- Prepare a photographic log that records all photographs and a description and location of evidence.
- Establish a progression of overall, medium, and close-up views of the crime scene.
- Photograph from eye level to represent the normal view.
- Photograph the most fragile areas of the crime scene first.
- Photograph all stages of the crime scene investigation, including discoveries.
- Photograph the condition of evidence before recovery.
- Photograph the evidence in detail and include a scale, the photographer's name, and the date.
- Take all photographs intended for examination purposes with a scale. When a scale is used, first take a photograph without the scale.
- Photograph the interior crime scene in an overlapping series using a normal lens, if possible. Overall photographs may be taken using a wide-angle lens.
- Photograph the exterior crime scene, establishing the location of the scene by a series of overall photographs, including a landmark. Photographs should have 360° of coverage. Consider using aerial photography, when possible.
- Photograph entrances and exits from the inside and the outside.
- Photograph important evidence at least twice.
- A medium-distance photograph that shows the evidence and its position to other evidence.
- A close-up photograph that includes a scale and fills the frame.
- Prior to entering the scene, acquire, if possible, prior photographs, blueprints, or maps of the scene.

FIGURE 8.4   FBI Evidence Response Team Investigators photographing evidence at a crime scene. *Corbis.*

Crime Scene Sketch

The sketch establishes a permanent record of items, conditions, and distance and size relationships. Sketch Preparer Responsibilities include:

- Sketch and log scene.
- Sketches supplement photographs.
- Sketch number designations should coordinate with the evidence log number designations.
- Sketches are normally not drawn to scale. However, the sketch should have measurements and details for a drawn-to-scale diagram, if necessary.
- The sketch should include:
    - Case identifier
    - Date
    - Time
    - Location
    - Weather and lighting conditions
    - Identities and assignments of personnel
    - Dimensions of rooms, furniture, doors, and windows
    - Distances among objects, persons, bodies, entrances, and exits

        – Measurements showing the location of evidence. Each object should be located by two measurements from non-movable items (e.g., doors or walls)
        – Key, legend, compass orientation, scale, scale disclaimer, or a combination of these features

Physical Evidence Collection and Recording

The designated Evidence Recorder responsibilities Include:

- Assuming the role as evidence custodian and logging evidence.
- Deciding what search pattern (grid, strip or lane, or spiral) will be used.
- Search from the general to the specific for evidence.
- Be alert for all evidence.
- Search entrances and exits.
- Ensures that photographs will be taken of all items before collection and notate the photographic log.
- Mark evidence locations on the sketch.
- Complete the evidence log with notations for each item of evidence. If possible, have one person serve as evidence custodian.
- Two persons should observe evidence in place, during recovery, and being marked for identification. Mark directly on the evidence when necessary, but first attempt to place identifying marks on evidence containers.
- Wear latex or cotton gloves to avoid leaving fingerprints.
- Do not excessively handle the evidence after recovery.
- Seal all evidence packages at the crime scene.
- Obtain known standards (e.g., fiber samples from a known carpet).
- Make a complete evaluation of the crime scene.
- Constantly check paperwork, packaging, and other information for errors.

Final Survey

The final survey is a review of all aspects of the search. The person in charge should:

- Discuss the search with all personnel.
- Ensure all documentation is correct and complete.
- Ensure there is a photograph the scene showing the final condition.
- Ensure all evidence is secured.
- Ensure all equipment is retrieved.
- Ensure hiding places or difficult access areas have not been overlooked.

Release of the Crime Scene

Release of the crime scene takes place:

- After the final survey.
- Crime scene release documentation is completed. It should include the time and date of release, to whom released, and by whom released.
- After ensuring that the evidence is collected according to legal requirements, documented, and marked for identification.
- After considering the need for specialists (e.g., a blood-pattern analyst or a medical examiner) to observe the scene before it is released.
- Once the scene has been released, re-entry may require a search warrant.
- The scene should be released only when all personnel are satisfied that the scene was searched correctly and completely.
- Only the person in charge should release the scene.

CHAIN OF CUSTODY

Whether evidence is located at a crime scene, or seized in some other manner, a *chain of custody* must be established. Chain of custody is the documentation of who located, possessed, and examined physical evidence from its discovery up to its admission at trial and eventual final disposition.

Chain of custody establishes exactly when and how an item of physical evidence was located, who found it, and what was done with it. These issues surrounding the custody of physical evidence may be important at trial if its integrity is questioned. Defense attorneys have been known to question the custody of every piece of physical evidence, in the hope of showing that the police acted incompetently or unprofessionally while it was in their possession. Lapses in evidence accountability will raise questions about it being tampered with, misplaced, or even replaced with a like item.

The Evidence Custodian

An important person responsible for the storage, security, and disposition of collected evidence for a law enforcement agency is known as an *evidence custodian*. Most evidence custodians are non-sworn, civilian employees of a law enforcement agency. He or she will document the receipt of evidence, when it was sent to a laboratory for scientific examination, and when it was released to officers for transportation to court for trial. They are also responsible for the destruction of contraband, and the returning of items of value to their owners when all court procedures have been exhausted.

FIGURE 8.5   Some crime scenes attract hordes of media. Members of the press should be kept away from crime scenes until all the evidence is collected and the area has been rendered safe. *Corbis.*

Many times, evidence includes items of value, such as watches, money, and other items, such as recovered stolen property. Evidence custodians are responsible for the accountability of these and other items of evidence. Often, unannounced inventories of items stored in evidence depositories are made in order to maintain the integrity of the system and to further illustrate the safety and accountability of evidence stored there.

SUMMARY

Most departments must rely on their uniformed patrol officers to gather physical evidence and collect the facts to write an initial crime report. Reported crime, for example, burglary, robbery, murder, etc. usually generates a crime scene, where the evidence gathered can significantly contribute to identifying a suspect and obtaining a conviction.

Proactive criminal investigations, such as in a drug, almost always lack a crime scene, but may lead investigators to a working clandestine laboratory or storage area where money and drugs might be found. These locations must also be handled as a crime scene, in order to gather evidence that might lead to the identification of other conspirators.

Police supervisors and crime scene investigators have the ultimate responsibility to recognize chemical, biological, and physical hazards when processing a crime scene.

Personnel operating in or around contaminated environments, such as a clandestine methamphetamine laboratory, must be aware of the various ways in which hazards may enter and harm the body. Inhalation is the introduction of a toxic substance into the respiratory system. Contamination through the skin can result from direct contact or by absorption. Ingestion involves introducing contaminants into the body through the mouth and can cause severe damage to the mouth, throat, and digestive tract. The direct injection of contaminants into the body, either by accidental needle sticks or mechanical injuries from contaminated glass, metal, or other sharp objects can cause severe complications. Occupations at risk for exposure to bloodborne pathogens include law enforcement, emergency response, and forensic laboratory personnel.

In addition to the hazards of some crime scenes, law enforcement officers need to have an understanding of how to actually collect and record physical evidence they locate.

All crime scenes must be thoroughly searched to gather all available evidence and to deprive the suspect(s) or someone else from removing something later. Whatever method of search is chosen, it should be thorough and systematic, which usually means it will probably be time-consuming and difficult.

Crime scenes should be photographed and sketched. The collection of physical evidence must be documented and a chain of custody established.

A law enforcement agency's evidence custodian is responsible for the storage, security, and disposition of physical evidence used at trial.

NOTES

1. National Research Council. Committee on Hazardous Substances in the Laboratory. *Prudent Practices for Handling Hazardous Chemicals in Laboratories*. National Academy Press, Washington, DC, 1981.
2. *Bloodborne Pathogens*, Title 29 CFR Section 1910.1030, U.S. Department of Labor, Occupational Safety and Health Administration, Washington, DC.
3. Upfal, M. J. *Pocket Guide to First Aid for Chemical Injuries*. Genium, Schenectady, New York, 1991.
4. American National Standards Institute. *Safe Use of Lasers* (ANSI Z136.1-1993). American National Standards Institute, New York, 1993.

5. Conforti, J. V. *Confined Space Pocket Guide*. Genium, Schenectady, New York, 1993.

6. *Control of Hazardous Energy (Lockout/Tagout)*, Title 29 CFR Section 1910.147, U.S. Department of Labor, Occupational Safety and Health Administration, Washington, DC.

7. *Permit-Required Confined Spaces*, Title 29 CFR Section 1910.146, U.S. Department of Labor, Occupational Safety and Health Administration, Washington, DC.

8. Environmental Health and Safety Office. *Laboratory Survival Manual*. University of Virginia, Charlottesville, Virginia, 1998.

9. Choose the proper gloves for chemical handling. In: *Best's Safety Directory*. 30th ed., A. M. Best, Oldwick, New Jersey, 1990.

10. American National Standards Institute. *Practices for Occupational and Educational Eye and Face Protection* (ANSI Z87.1-1989). American National Standards Institute, New York, 1989.

11. *Occupational Foot Protection*, Title 29 CFR Section 1910.136, U.S. Department of Labor, Occupational Safety and Health Administration, Washington, DC.

12. Gorman, C. *Hazardous Waste Handling Pocket Guide*. Genium, Schenectady, New York, 1991.

13. *Respiratory Protection*, Title 29 CFR Section 1910.134, U.S. Department of Labor, Occupational Safety and Health Administration, Washington, DC.

14. American National Standards Institute. *American National Standard for Personnel Protection: Protective Headwear for Industrial Workers: Requirements* (ANSI Z89.1-1997). American National Standards Institute, New York, 1997.

9

Physical Evidence

INTRODUCTION

In addition to circumstantial and testimonial evidence, **Physical evidence** is a term long used by police to describe any item of evidence that can be seen, heard, or scientifically examined. Often at crime scenes, evidence only exists in *trace* amounts, but it is still categorized as physical evidence. Carpet fibers found under the fingernails of a mudered victim would be considered trace evidence.

Also referred to as **real**, **tangible**, or **demonstrative** evidence, physical evidence is anything that speaks for itself and requires no explanation, merely its identification through testimony. It can be a firearm, a bullet fragment, a dead body, an ounce of cocaine, a photograph, or a recorded telephone conversation.

Most physical evidence is located at crime scenes where it is identified, and collected by investigators and police officers. Few law enforcement agencies have the luxury of full-time crime scene investigators who are specially trained to handle such matters.

Through the years, very sophisticated methods of collection of physical evidence have been developed, enhancing law enforcement's ability to determine the culprit who committed the crime under investigation.

TYPES OF PHYSICAL EVIDENCE

Physical evidence comes in many forms. It is anything tangible that is found at a crime scene which may lead to the identity of the perpetrator. It is evidence that will later stand the scrutiny of a defense attorney who will attempt to play down its significance or otherwise strive to render it inadmissible at trial.

The most frequently encountered physical evidence for police officers and crime scene investigators is fingerprints, foot and tire prints, tool markings, and blood, to name just a few.

Body intrusions to collect physical evidence, such as blood samples, fingerprints, saliva, or handwriting exemplars have been approved by the courts. A landmark case in 1957,[1] affirmed the Court's approval of police reasonably intruding into someone's body to secure evidence that he or she was intoxicated by alcohol or drugs. In *Breithaupt*, he was involved in an automobile accident in which the driver of the other vehicle expired. While unconscious at a local hospital, the police requested that the attending physician draw blood from him in order to determine his blood-alcohol content. The physician complied. The crime laboratory determined that he had a blood-alcohol content of 0.17% at the time. This evidence was used at trial and he was convicted. Breithaupt appealed on the grounds that he did not waive his privilege against self-incrimination and that the taking of his blood without his permission was a violation of his right to due process. The U.S. Supreme Court disagreed.

The Court further accepted the intrusion of the body to obtain blood samples to determine intoxication in another case, *Schmerber* v. *California*,[2] in which Schmerber had been arrested for driving under the influence of alcohol and was asked to give a blood sample for analysis. Schmerber refused upon the advice of his attorney, but the police obtained the sample regardless. He was later convicted and appealed on the Constitutional grounds of self-incrimination, right to counsel, and search and seizure violations.

The Supreme Court concluded that there was probable cause to arrest Schmerber for driving under the influence, and that the bodily intrusion for blood evidence could not be delayed while the police applied for a search warrant (the body metabolizes alcohol at the rate of .025% per hour). Furthermore, Schmerber did not make any objections based upon fear of the procedure, his health, or on religious grounds. The Court also concluded that the search was conducted in a reasonable manner, in that a physician performed the procedure.

In addition to understanding what physical evidence is, and how it can be legally obtained, police officers should also know how to collect such evidence. They should also be knowledgeable about what information a crime laboratory can furnish them with about the evidence, to assist them in identifying or developing a suspect.

Reality Check!

Defense attorneys have access to criminal justice textbooks and respected law enforcement training publications concerning crime scene forensic science applications. They may also employ expert witnesses who might challenge the techniques used by police officers to gather and collect evidence in an attempt to portray the police as being incompetent, untrained, or lazy. An officer who deviates from standard methods of collection, or did not subject physical evidence to certain examinations because he or she was unfamiliar with these techniques, can expect to be quizzed about why. Defense attorneys will always scrutinize reports generated as a result of scientific examinations. Police officers should have a good working knowledge of those scientific examinations that can be conducted to identify and enhance tangible items as physical evidence for trial.

According to a U.S. News and World Report article, "Defense attorneys, predictably, are capitalizing on the popularity of shows like CSI (*CSI: Crime Scene Investigation*), seizing on an absence of forensic evidence, even in cases where there's no apparent reason for its use. In another . . . case, jurors acquitted a man accused of stabbing his estranged girlfriend because police did not test her bloody bed sheets for DNA. The man went back to prison on a parole violation and stabbed his ex again when he got out – this time fatally.[3]"

Fingerprints

Arguably, the most useful of tool for law enforcement, fingerprints have probably been responsible for the identification and apprehension of more criminals than any other form of physical evidence collected by the police. So long as the latent fingerprint collected contains enough identifiable markings to distinguish it from other fingerprints, its admissibility at trial is hard to dispute. Juries understand that fingerprints are unique to each individual on the planet, and that there have never been two fingerprints found to be identical. The lack of identifiable fingerprints serves the defense well in that the defendant cannot be placed at the crime scene through this means.

Fingerprints are used for comparison and identification purposes. Automatic fingerprint systems can now narrow down millions of sets of fingerprints to a few, for an examiner to determine if there is a match.

Fingerprints reveal many characteristics that are unique to a particular individual. The Supreme Court in *Davis* v. *Mississippi*[4] held that where the police detain someone solely for the purpose of obtaining their fingerprints, this rendered the evidence invalid because it was an unreasonable search. However, the Court implied that the police might request a court order to obtain a suspect's fingerprints for comparison purposes. Obtaining fingerprints from a defendant at the time he is booked is not a violation of the defendant's rights and is normal police procedure.

The crime laboratory is the best place to develop latent prints found at a crime scene. However, because of environmental and other considerations, fingerprints are usually developed at crime scenes. Caution should always be taken to prevent destroying latent prints. The Federal Bureau of Investigation[5] recommends the following measures to ensure that crime scene latent prints are protected:

- Photograph latent prints prior to any processing.
- Examine all evidence visually and with a laser or an alternate light source before using any other latent print development process.
- When using latent print development processes, refer to the manufacturer's instructions and the Material Safety Data Sheets. Use personal protective equipment (e.g., safety glasses, masks, gloves, smocks).

When photographing latent fingerprints, the following precautions should be used:

- Use a tripod and cable release when photographing latent prints.
- Use a 35 mm or medium-format camera with a macro lens capable of half-size to full-size reproduction.
- Photograph latent prints at each step in the processing sequence before moving to the next process.
- Photograph latent prints developed with fingerprint powders before lifting them.
- Use T-Max 400 film. Set the f-stop to f/11. Adjust the shutter speed setting to correspond with the f-stop setting by using the camera's metering system.

Take three exposures of each latent print by bracketing:

- Original exposure.
- One-stop underexposed image.
- One-stop overexposed image.
- Photograph latent prints individually. This ensures that the target latent print is in focus.
- For reference purposes, photograph latent prints close to each other in one frame, if possible.
- Fill the frame completely.
- Photograph latent prints with an identification label that includes a scale, reference number, date, collector's initials, and location of the

latent prints. The identification label should be placed on the same plane as the latent prints.

- Maintain a photographic log that records each shot, reference number, date, collector's initials, location of prints, and other pertinent information.

Lifting Latent Prints:

- Photograph latent prints developed with fingerprint powders before lifting them.
- Apply black, gray, or white powder to the surface with a long hairbrush. The color of the powder should contrast with the color of the surface (e.g., black for light surfaces or gray or white for dark surfaces).
- Use a short hairbrush to remove excess powder. Use caution when powdering. Avoid over brushing a latent print and losing clarity.
- Use transparent tape or black-and-white rubber lifts to lift latent prints.
- When transparent tape is used, the color of the backing card should contrast with the color of the powders (e.g., white backing card for black powder).

FIGURE 9.1 Prince Williams County police officers in Manassas, Virginia search for evidence left behind by a sniper in the Washington, DC area. Two men were later convicted for their murder spree. *Corbis.*

Firearms Examinations

Firearms are frequently used in murders, suicides, robberies, and other crimes of violence. Firearms examinations can determine the general condition of a recovered firearm and whether the firearm is mechanically functional or in a condition that could contribute to an unintentional discharge. Trigger-pull examinations can determine the amount of pressure necessary to release the hammer of a revolver or firing pin of a semi-automatic firearm. Firearms examiners can determine whether a rifle or pistol was altered to fire in the full-automatic mode. Obliterated and/or altered firearm serial numbers can sometimes be restored. Firearms can be test-fired to obtain known specimens for comparison to evidence ammunition components, such as bullets, cartridge cases, and shotshell casings.

Comparisons of suspect firearms can be made with firearms depicted in surveillance images. Photogrammetry can determine the length of the weapon(s) used by the subject(s) depicted in the surveillance films.

Fired bullets can be examined to determine the general rifling characteristics, such as caliber and physical features of the rifling impressions and the manufacturer of the bullets. The microscopic characteristics on evidence bullets can be compared to test-fired bullets from a suspect firearm, to determine whether the evidence bullet was fired from that particular firearm.

Cartridge cases or shotshell casings examinations can determine the caliber or gauge, the manufacturer, and whether there are marks of value for comparison. The images of questioned cartridge cases and shotshell casings can be scanned into the National Integrated Ballistics Information Network to compare with evidence from other shooting incidents. The microscopic characteristics of evidence cartridge cases and shotshell casings can be examined to determine whether they were fired from a specific firearm.

Examinations of shot pellets, buckshot, or slugs can determine the size of the shot, the gauge of the slug, and the manufacturer.

Examinations of wadding components can determine the gauge and the manufacturer.

Examinations of unfired cartridges or shotshells can determine the caliber or gauge and whether there are marks of value for comparison. Examinations can also determine whether the ammunition was loaded in and extracted from a specific firearm. Unfired and fired cartridges or shotshells can be associated through manufacturing marks.

The deposition of gunshot residue on evidence, such as clothing, varies with the distance from the muzzle of the firearm to the target. Patterns of gunshot residue can be duplicated using a questioned firearm and ammunition combination fired into test materials at known distances. These patterns serve as a basis for estimating muzzle-to-garment distances.

Gun parts examinations can determine the caliber and model of gun from which the parts originated. Muzzle attachments, also known as silencers, can reduce the noise of a firearm by suppressing the sound during firing. Testing can determine whether a muzzle attachment can be classified as a silencer based on a measurable sound-reduction capability. Mere possessions of silences carry heavy federal criminal penalties.

DNA Examinations

Deoxyribonucleic acid (DNA) is analyzed in body fluids, stains, and other biological tissues recovered from evidence, including fingerprints. The results of DNA analysis of questioned biological samples are compared with the results of DNA analysis of known samples. This analysis can associate victim(s) and/or suspect(s) with each other or with a crime scene. There are two sources of DNA used in forensic analyses. Nuclear DNA (nDNA) is typically analyzed in evidence containing blood, semen, saliva, body tissues, and hairs that have tissue at their root ends. Mitochondrial DNA (mtDNA) is typically analyzed in evidence containing naturally shed hairs, hair fragments, bones, and teeth.

If DNA evidence is not properly documented, collected, packaged, and preserved, it will not meet the legal and scientific requirements for admissibility at trial. If DNA evidence is not properly documented, its origin can be questioned. If it is not properly collected, biological activity can be lost. If it is not properly packaged, contamination can occur. If it is not properly preserved, decomposition and deterioration can occur. When DNA evidence is transferred by direct or secondary (indirect) means, it remains on surfaces by absorption or adherence. In general, liquid biological evidence is absorbed into surfaces, and solid biological evidence adheres to surfaces. Collecting, packaging, and preserving DNA evidence depends on the liquid or solid state and the condition of the evidence. The more that evidence retains its original integrity until it reaches the laboratory, the greater the possibility of conducting useful examinations. It may be necessary to use a variety of techniques to collect suspected body fluid evidence.

Blood examinations can determine the presence or absence of blood in stains. Examinations can also determine whether blood is human or not. Blood examinations cannot determine the age or the race of a person. Conventional serological techniques are not adequately informative to positively identify a person as the source of a stain.

The FBI recommends that only qualified medical personnel should collect blood samples from a person. At least two 5-mL tubes of blood in purple-top tubes should be collected with EDTA as an anticoagulant for DNA analysis. Collect drug-or alcohol-testing samples in gray-top tubes with NaF (sodium fluoride). Identify each tube with the date, time, subject's name,

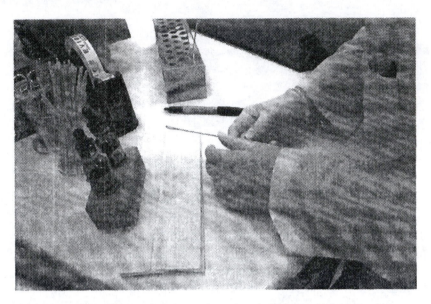

FIGURE 9.2   FBI DNA analysis is conducted at their national laboratory in Boston, Mass. *Corbis.*

location, collector's name, case number, and evidence number. Refrigerate, do not freeze, blood samples. Use cold packs, not dry ice, during shipping. Submit to the laboratory as soon as possible.

When collecting blood on a person, absorb the suspected liquid blood on to a clean cotton cloth or swab. Leave a portion of the cloth or swab unstained as a control. Air-dry the cloth or swab and pack in clean paper or an envelope with sealed corners. Do not use plastic containers. Absorb suspected dried blood on to a clean cotton cloth or swab moistened with distilled water. Leave a portion of the cloth or swab unstained as a control. Air-dry the cloth or swab and pack in clean paper or an envelope with sealed corners. Do not use plastic containers.

To collect blood on surfaces or in snow or water, the police officer should absorb suspected liquid blood or blood clots on to a clean cotton cloth or swab. Leave a portion of the cloth or swab unstained as a control. Air-dry the cloth or swab and pack in clean paper or an envelope with sealed corners. Do not use plastic containers. Collect suspected blood in snow or water immediately to avoid further dilution. Eliminate as much snow as possible. Place in a clean airtight container. Freeze the evidence and submit as soon as possible to the laboratory.

Wet bloodstains on garments should be air-dried. Once dried, the garments should be wrapped in clean paper. Do not place wet or dried garments in plastic or airtight containers. Place all debris or residue from the garments in clean paper or an envelope with sealed corners. Air-dry small suspected wet bloodstained objects and submit the objects to the laboratory.

To preserve bloodstain patterns, avoid creating additional stain patterns during drying and packaging. Pack to prevent stain removal by abrasive action during shipping. Pack in clean paper. Do not use plastic containers.

Whenever possible, cut a large sample of suspected bloodstains from immovable objects with a clean, sharp instrument. Collect an unstained control sample. Pack to prevent stain removal by abrasive action during shipping. Pack in clean paper. Do not use plastic containers.

Absorb suspected dried bloodstains on immovable objects on to a clean cotton cloth or swab moistened with distilled water. Leave a portion of the cloth or swab unstained as a control. Air-dry the cloth or swab and pack in clean paper or an envelope with sealed corners. Do not use plastic containers.

When absorbing suspected liquid semen on to a clean cotton cloth or swab, leave a portion of the cloth or swab unstained as a control. Air-dry the cloth or swab and pack in clean paper or an envelope with sealed corners. Do not use plastic containers. Submit small suspected dry semen-stained objects to the laboratory. Pack to prevent stain removal by abrasive action during shipping. Pack in clean paper. Do not use plastic containers. When possible, cut a large sample of suspected semen stains from immovable objects with a clean, sharp instrument. Collect an unstained control sample.

Officers can absorb suspected dried semen stains on immovable objects on to a clean cotton cloth or swab moistened with distilled water. Leave a portion of the cloth or swab unstained as a control. Air-dry the swab or cloth and place in clean paper or an envelope with sealed corners. Do not use plastic containers.

Sexual assault victim(s) must be medically examined in a hospital or a physician's office for semen, using a standard sexual assault evidence kit to collect vaginal, oral, and anal evidence. Refrigerate and submit the evidence as soon as possible to the laboratory.

Officers should use clean cotton buccal (oral) swabs to collect buccal (oral) samples. Rub the inside surfaces of the cheeks thoroughly. Air-dry the swabs and place in clean paper or an envelope with sealed corners. Do not use plastic containers. Identify each sample with the date, time, subject's name, location, collector's name, case number, and evidence number. Buccal samples do not need to be refrigerated.

Suspected saliva and urine should be absorbed on to a clean cotton cloth or swab. Leave a portion of the cloth unstained as a control. Air-dry the cloth or swab and pack in clean paper or an envelope with sealed corners. Do not use plastic containers. Submit suspected small, dry saliva, or urine-stained objects to the laboratory. Pack to prevent stain removal by abrasive action during shipping. Pack in clean paper or an envelope with sealed corners. Do not use plastic containers. When possible, cut a large sample of suspected saliva or urine stains from immovable objects with a clean, sharp instrument. Collect an unstained control sample. Pack to prevent stain removal by abrasive action during shipping. Pack in clean paper. Do not use plastic containers.

For saliva on cigarette butts, pick them up with gloved hands or clean forceps. Do not submit ashes. Air-dry and place the cigarette butts from the same location (e.g., ashtray) in clean paper or an envelope with sealed corners. Do not submit the ashtray unless a latent print examination is requested. Package the ashtray separately. Do not use plastic containers.

Pick up chewing gum with gloved hands or clean forceps. Air-dry and place in clean paper or an envelope with sealed corners. Do not use plastic containers.

Pick up envelopes and stamps with gloved hands or clean forceps and place in a clean envelope. Do not use plastic containers.

Pick up hair carefully with clean forceps to prevent damaging the root tissue. Air-dry hair mixed with suspected body fluids. Package each group of hair separately in clean paper or an envelope with sealed corners. Do not use plastic containers. Refrigerate and submit as soon as possible to the crime laboratory.

Pick up suspected tissues, bones, and teeth with gloved hands or clean forceps. Place tissue samples in a clean, airtight plastic container without formalin or formaldehyde. Place teeth and bone samples in clean paper or an envelope with sealed corners. Freeze the evidence, place in Styrofoam containers, and ship overnight on dry ice.

Hairs and Fibers Examinations

Hair examinations can determine whether hairs are animal or human. Race, body area, method of removal, damage, and alteration (e.g., bleaching or dyeing) can be determined from human hair analysis. Examinations can associate a hair to a person on the basis of microscopic characteristics in the hair but cannot provide absolute personal identification. Hairs that are associated can be submitted for mitochondrial DNA analysis. The animal species and family can be determined from hair analysis.

Fiber examinations can identify the type of fiber, such as animal (wool), vegetable (cotton), mineral (glass), and synthetic (manufactured). Questioned fibers can be compared to fibers from victim(s)' and suspect(s)' clothing, carpeting, and other textiles. A questioned piece of fabric can be physically matched to known fabric. Fabric composition, construction, and color can be compared, and impressions on fabric and from fabric can be examined. Clothing manufacturers' information can be determined by label searches.

Collect at least 25 known hairs from different parts of the head and/or pubic region. Comb and pull out the hairs. Submit hairs in clean paper or an envelope with sealed corners. When possible, submit the entire garment or textile. Submit fibers in clean paper or an envelope with sealed corners.

Computer Examinations

Terrorists, drug traffickers, and other criminals have long used computers to store information and communicate with each other:

- Examinations can determine the type of data files that are in a computer and compare data files to known documents and data files.
- Transaction examinations can determine the time and sequence that data files were created. Extraction data files can be extracted from the computer or computer storage media.
- Deleted data files can be recovered from the computer or computer storage media.
- Format conversion data files can be converted from one format to another.
- Keyword searching data files can be searched for a word or phrase and all occurrences recorded.
- Passwords can be recovered and used to decrypt encoded files.
- Limited source code can be analyzed and compared.

For most computer examinations, officers should submit only the central processing units and the internal and external storage media.

Questioned Documents Examinations

Handwriting exemplars can be obtained from defendants by court order. For comparison purposes, examiners will require known standards of the defendant's handwriting. These standards can be obtained from employment records, school records, loan documents, etc. Unless the possessor of these documents cooperates with the police, a search warrant or grand jury subpoena may be required to obtain them. Many banks, educational institutions, and other businesses are reluctant to cooperate with the police until presented with a subpoena or court order. This documentation is then used by the business establishment as a method of proving they were compelled to produce the documents to law enforcement.

Although not all handwriting is identifiable to a specific writer, the examination of handwriting characteristics can sometimes determine the origin or authenticity of questioned writing. Traits such as age, sex, personality, or intent cannot be determined from handwriting examinations.

Some reasons for inconclusive results include:

- Limited questioned and/or known writing.
- Lack of contemporaneous writing or lapse of time between execution of questioned and known writing.
- Distortion or disguise in the questioned and/or known writing.

- Lack of sufficient identifying characteristics.
- Submission of photocopied evidence instead of original evidence.

To obtain known handwriting exemplars, the FBI recommends:

- The text, size of paper, space available for writing, writing instrument, and writing style (handwriting or hand printing) must be as close to the original writing as possible. Give verbal or typewritten instructions concerning the text to be written. Do not give instructions in spelling, punctuation, or arrangement of writing.
- All exemplars must be on separate pieces of paper.
- The writer and witness must initial and date each page of writing.
- Do not allow the writer to see the previous exemplars or the questioned writing. Remove exemplars from the writer's sight as soon as completed.
- Obtain exemplars from dictation until normal writing has been produced. Normal handwriting is assessed by determining whether the writing is too quickly or slowly executed and whether the handwriting is consistent.
- Obtain exemplars from the right and left hands.
- Obtain hand-printing exemplars in upper- and lower-case letters.
- Obtain exemplars written rapidly, slowly, and at varied slants.
- Obtain a sufficient quantity of exemplars to account for natural variation in the writing.
- Obtain undictated writing such as business records, personal correspondence, and canceled checks.

FIGURE 9.3 Questioned document evidence can take many forms. Pictured is the letter sent to Senator Thomas Daschle shortly after the events of September 11, 2001, that was later found to contain anthrax. *Corbis.*

The presence of altered or obliterated writing can sometimes be determined, and the writing can sometimes be deciphered. The most common types of non-genuine signatures include traced signatures, which are prepared by using a genuine signature as a template or pattern. Simulated signatures are prepared by copying or drawing a genuine signature, and freehand signatures are written in the forger's normal handwriting with no attempt to copy another's writing style.

Despite the heavy use of computer word-processing programs, typewriters are still used on occasion to fashion ransom notes and other writings in which the writer's handwriting is not used. Questioned typewriting can occasionally be identified with the typewriter that produced it. This is most common when the typewriter is a typebar machine. The identification can sometimes be based on individual characteristics that develop during the manufacturing process and through use and abuse of the typewriter.

Typewriters with interchangeable elements (e.g., ball, printwheel, or thimble) are less likely to be associated with questioned typewriting. However, these elements and carbon film or correction ribbons can sometimes be associated with specific texts by examining individual characteristics of the elements and by correlating the text and ribbons. Comparison of questioned typewriting with reference standards can sometimes determine a possible make and model of the typewriter and/or the typewriter elements. Carbon film typewriter ribbons can sometimes be read for content or specific wording of questioned material. Carbon film ribbons can sometimes be identified with questioned typewritten impressions. Fabric ribbons cannot be read.

When obtaining known typewriter exemplars:

- Remove the carbon film ribbon if the typewriter has one, and submit it to the crime laboratory. Also submit the correction tape. Insert a new ribbon in the typewriter prior to obtaining exemplars.
- If the typewriter has a fabric ribbon, remove it from the typewriter and put the typewriter in the stencil position. Place a sheet of carbon paper over a sheet of blank paper and insert both into the typewriter. Allow the typeface to strike the carbon paper. Submit the fabric ribbon strike and the carbon paper strike exemplars to the laboratory.
- Obtain two full word-for-word texts of the questioned text and type the entire keyboard (all symbols, numbers, and upper- and lower-case letters) two times.
- Record the make, model, and serial number of the typewriter on the exemplars. Also record the date the exemplars were obtained and the name of the person who directed the exemplars.
- Obtain the typewriter service and/or repair history.

- It is not normally necessary to send the typewriter to the laboratory. However, in some cases, the examiner will request the typewriter. It must be packed securely to prevent damage during shipment. Typewriter elements (e.g., ball, printwheel, or thimble) must also be submitted to the laboratory.

Photocopies can sometimes be identified with the machine producing them, if the exemplars and questioned copies are relatively contemporaneous. The possible make and model of the photocopy machine can sometimes be determined by comparison with the Office Equipment File.

When obtaining known photocopy exemplars, officers should:

- Obtain at least ten exemplars with no document on the glass plate, with the cover down.
- Obtain at least ten exemplars with no document on the glass plate, with the cover up.
- Obtain at least ten exemplars with a document on the glass plate, with the cover down.
- Record on each exemplar the date the exemplars were obtained, the name of the person who directed the exemplars, and the conditions under which the exemplars were made.
- Record the make, model, and serial number of the photocopy machine, information about the toner supplies and components, whether the paper supply is sheet or roll fed, and options such as color, reduction, enlargement, zoom, mask, trim, or editor board.
- Do not store or ship photocopies in plastic envelopes.

Graphic arts and printed documents can sometimes be associated as originating from a common source or identified with known printing paraphernalia, such as artwork, negatives, and plates. Paper torn edges can sometimes be positively matched. The manufacturer can sometimes be determined if a watermark is present. Paper can be examined for indented writing.

Officers should not rub the indentations with a pencil. Do not add indentations by writing on top of the evidence.

Information on burned or charred documents can sometimes be deciphered. The document must be minimally handled. The document must be transported to the questioned document examiner in the container in which it was burned, in polyester film encapsulation, or between layers of cotton in a rigid container.

Examiners can possibly determined the earliest date that a document could have been prepared, by examining watermarks, indented writing, printing, and typewriting.

Examination of used carbon paper or carbon film ribbon can sometimes disclose the content of the text. A checkwriter impression can sometimes be identified with the checkwriter that produced it. Examining a checkwriter impression can sometimes determine the brand of the checkwriter.

An embossed or seal impression can sometimes be identified with the instrument that produced it.

A rubber stamp impression can sometimes be identified with the rubber stamp that produced it.

Plastic bags (e.g., sandwich and garbage bags) can sometimes be identified with a roll or a box from which it originated.

The FBI maintains what is called The Bank Robbery Note File, which contains images of notes used in bank robberies. This file can be searched in an attempt to associate by text a note from one bank robbery to others.

The FBI also maintains The Anonymous Letter File, which contains images of anonymous letters submitted to their Questioned Documents Unit for examination. This file can be searched in an attempt to associate by text a letter from one case to letters from others.

Documentary evidence must be preserved in the condition in which it was found. It must not be folded, torn, marked, soiled, stamped, written on, or handled unnecessarily. Protect the evidence from inadvertent indented writing. Mark documents unobtrusively by writing the collector's initials, date, and other information with a pencil. Whenever possible, officers should submit the original evidence to the laboratory. The lack of detail in photocopies makes examinations difficult. Copies are sufficient for reference file searches. Do not store or ship photocopies in plastic envelopes.

Paint Examinations

A painted object will transfer a portion of the paint to an item that it makes contact with. Examiners can possibly determine the source of paint found on the clothing and vehicles of hit and run victims. A comparison of the layer structure of a questioned paint sample can be compared with known sources. The sequence, relative thickness, color, texture, number, and chemical composition of each of the layers can be compared. The color, manufacturer, model, and model year of an automobile can be determined from a paint chip. Sourcing automotive paints is limited to factory-applied, original automotive paint. Paint on safes, vaults, windowsills, and doorframes can be transferred to and from tools. A comparison can be made between the paint from an object and the paint on a tool.

When conducting a hit and run accident, officers should search the accident or crime scene and the victim(s)' personal effects to locate paint fragments. Paint fragments are often found in the clothing of a hit-and-run victim(s).

Paints can be transferred from one car to another, from car to object, or from object to car during an accident or a crime. Control paint chips must be collected from the suspected source of the evidentiary paint. Controls must be taken from an area close to, but not in, any damaged area. If no damage is obvious, controls should be taken from several areas of the suspect substrate.

Each layer can be a point of comparison. Controls must have all of the layers of paint to the substrate to facilitate the examination.

Ropes and Cords Examinations

Suspects sometimes tie their victims or strangle them using rope or cord. A piece of rope or cord can be compared with a questioned rope or cord. The composition, construction, color, and diameter can be determined. If a tracer is present, the manufacturer can be determined.

The entire rope or cord should be submitted to the crime laboratory. If the rope or cord must be cut, it must be specified which end was cut during evidence collection. Label the known and questioned samples. Handle the sections of rope or cord carefully to prevent loss of trace material or contamination. Submit the questioned samples to the crime laboratory in a heat-sealed or resealable plastic or paper bag.

DRUG EVIDENCE

Much drug evidence comes from controlled purchases from defendants that were made by undercover police investigators. All evidence obtained through controlled purchases should be immediately returned to the office where it can be weighed and sealed in sturdy transparent plastic bags. The weight should not include any container that the drugs were held in, such as a box or suitcase. These items would be considered ***non-drug evidence***.

Unlike many forms of other physical evidence, controlled substances can pose a threat to police officers and investigators who handle them. Controlled substances, such as marijuana, cocaine, and heroin may be contaminated with caustic chemicals that are designed specifically to kill or injure drug investigators. These controlled substances, when handled, can seep through the pours of the skin and cause an adverse reaction to the handler. Latex gloves should be worn when handling such evidence. Gloves also help preserve any ***latent fingerprint evidence*** that may be present. Unlike as is often depicted in movies and television shows, police officers do not taste drugs to identify them or to determine their purity. To do so invites health problems. Even smelling a substance can create undesirable side effects and should be avoided.

Tablets seized as drug evidence should be counted as well as weighed. MDMA, or Ecstasy tablets are sometimes found in large, sealed plastic bags that can contain several hundred or up to a thousand in number. This type of evidence should always remain sealed and weighed only. The crime laboratory will determine the exact number.

When recording the drug weight of evidence seized, most police departments, as well as the Drug Enforcement Administration, include the weight of the plastic evidence container as the "gross" weight of the drugs seized. The laboratory, during its analysis, will determine the "net" weight.

Powdered drugs, such as cocaine and heroin, should remain in their original containers and placed inside transparent plastic evidence bags that are heat-sealed.

Crime laboratories have the ability to conduct both *quantitative* and *qualitative analysis* of controlled substances submitted for examination.

FIGURE 9.4 An Immigration and Customs Enforcement special agent shows an X-ray of a drug smuggler's stomach, who was arrested entering the United States at an international airport. The agent also displays the drugs recovered from the smuggler's stomach. *Corbis.*

Quantitative analysis deals with the purity of the drug submitted to the crime laboratory for analysis. Qualitative analysis addresses the weight of the drug submitted for analysis. From these figures, the amount of pure drug can be determined.

In drug investigations, the purity of the drug is an important measurement. When working undercover operations, a drug agent might conduct a controlled purchase of a drug from a suspected drug dealer. The undercover agent may pose as either a user, or a drug dealer himself, who is purchasing the drugs for later resale. After the drug agent purchases the purported drug, he or she must know the quantitative analysis of the drug, to determine if he has purchased a "good" drug, or if it is a counterfeit. Since the drug agent cannot rely on his own experience, or the experience of others in taking the drug, like many drug dealers do, the crime laboratory analysis is critical before an additional undercover meeting takes place.

Once the quantitative analysis results are known, the drug agent can talk intelligently with the drug dealer during future negotiations for additional purchases.

Testing seized drug evidence using a *field testing kit* can make a presumptive determination that a controlled substance is what it is purported to be or thought to be; however, they are not fool-proof. Field-testing seized

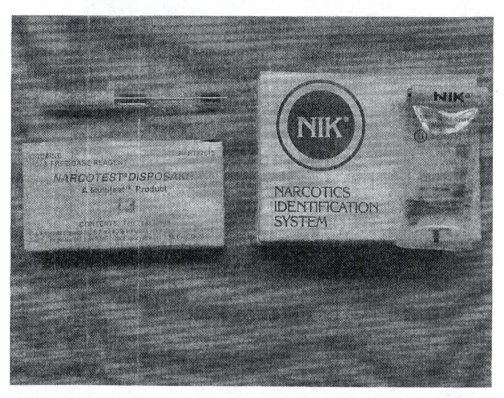

FIGURE 9.5   Drug Field Testing Kit. *Courtesy Drug Enforcement Administration.*

drugs is generally unnecessary, but may bolster a prosecutor's argument to hold the defendant on a substantial bail. The results of field-testing are not admissible at trial; only the findings of a scientific examination conducted by a forensic chemist can be used.

Clandestine Laboratories

The vast majority of the thousands of clandestine laboratories discovered every year in the United States manufacture methamphetmine. This trend of discovering thousands of laboratories, known as *clan labs,* is likely to continue so long as the drug remains popular among drug users. The vast majority of these labs were found in California, far more than any other state but, however, this trend appears to be shifting. A clandestine lab can literally be found anywhere in the United States. Most are capable of producing less than 10 pounds of methamphetamine at one time but, according to the Drug Enforcement Administration (DEA), 10% are *Super Labs,* as DEA refers to them, and are capable of producing well beyond 10 pounds, possibly up to 100 pounds or more per manufacturing session.

The investigation of clandestine laboratories is a specialty within drug law enforcement. Police officers are not normally trained and certified in the dismantling of such labs to collect physical evidence. Many labs are discovered accidentally, and officers not wearing special breathing apparatus and protective clothing should not enter any dwelling or building where a suspected laboratory may be. Many chemicals that are found in these laboratories are corrosive or flammable

FIGURE 9.6 The collection of physical evidence at clandestine laboratories should only be handled by specially trained and equipped investigators. Pictured is a typical methamphetamine laboratory. *Courtesy Drug Enforcement Administration.*

and can easily cause injury and even death. Vapors from laboratory equipment and chemical containers can create chemical reactions that attack mucous membranes, eyes, skin, and the respiratory tract. Other chemicals can react with water or other chemicals, which will most probably cause a fire or explosion.

The collection of physical evidence at clandestine labs must be conducted by specially trained investigators, who are properly trained and equipped for such an event.

Non-Drug Evidence

Other evidence that is developed over the course of a proactive drug investigation must be accounted for. Audiotapes of telephone conversations between informants and defendants, and videotapes made during surveillances, are other examples of non-drug evidence.

During drug investigations, it is not uncommon to seize other non-drug evidence, including:

- laboratory equipment, chemical containers, or hydroponics equipment indicative of manufacturing or growing controlled substances
- airline tickets
- hotel registration cards
- phone records
- firearms
- cell phones
- weigh scales, balloons, plastic bags, and other items indicative of drug sales
- cash

Bulk Drug Evidence

Drug investigators may find themselves with extremely large amounts of controlled substances, especially marijuana, that is categorized as *bulk evidence*. Law enforcement agencies that encounter large amounts of drugs that may exceed their evidence locker's capacity, should photograph and videotape the evidence and ask permission from their prosecutor and court to dispose of the majority of the evidence. Having large amounts of evidence serves no purpose and creates security problems for law enforcement and the courts alike.

When a marijuana field is located and the stalks are cut down and processed as evidence, most courts will accept each marijuana plant as weighing an average of one kilogram (2.2 pounds) each. This amount is multiplied by the total number of plants to determine an approximate weight.

Harvested marijuana plants lose a substantial amount of weight while in storage, due to dehydration and exposure to heat. The amount of marijuana seized may have an impact on the sentence a convicted defendant receives.

SUMMARY

Physical evidence is a term long used by police to describe any item of evidence that can be seen, heard, or scientifically examined. Also referred to as *real*, *tangible*, or *demonstrative* evidence, physical evidence is anything that speaks for itself and requires no explanation, merely its identification through testimony. It can be a firearm, a bullet fragment, a dead body, an ounce of cocaine, a photograph, or a recorded telephone conversation. The most frequently encountered physical evidence for police officers and crime scene investigators is fingerprints, foot and tire prints, tool markings, and blood to name just a few.

Body intrusions to collect physical evidence, such as blood samples, fingerprints, saliva, or handwriting exemplars can be obtained either under exigent circumstances without a warrant or court order for the purpose of determining the blood-alcohol content of a defendant. Fingerprints, saliva, and handwriting exemplars can be obtained through a routine court order commanding the defendant to comply.

In addition to understanding what physical evidence is, and how it can be legally obtained, police officers should also know how to collect such evidence, and be knowledgeable in what information a crime laboratory can furnish them to assist them in identifying or developing a suspect.

Drug evidence requires special handling and should not be touched without benefit of latex gloves. Bulk drug evidence poses special problems with storage and security, and should always be photographed and videotaped before being destroyed with the permission of the prosecutor and court.

SUGGESTED READING

Lee, Gregory D. *Global Drug Enforcement: Practical Investigative Techniques*, Boca Raton, FL; CRC Press, 2004.

Handbook of Forensic Services, U.S. Department of Justice, Federal Bureau of Investigation Laboratory Division.

NOTES

1. *Breithaupt* v. *Abram*, 352 U.S. 432 (1957).
2. 384 U.S. 737 (1966).
3. "The CSI Effect," by Kim. R. Roane, *U.S. News and World Report*, April 25, 2005.
4. 394 U.S. 721 (1969).
5. *Handbook of Forensic Services*, U.S. Department of Justice, Federal Bureau of Investigation Laboratory Division.

10

Audio, Video, Photographic and Computer Evidence

Police departments have routinely taken photographs of crime scenes, victims, and suspects during surveillance operations. With the advent of technology, and the cost of cameras plummeting through time, modern police agencies routinely use a variety of audio, video, and photographic equipment during the course of a criminal investigation. Recognizing the many advantages of recording crime as it occurs, within the last dozen or so years, police departments have even equipped their patrol vehicles with fixed video cameras trained on what the front seat officers are viewing while looking directly forward through their windshield. This videotape equipment has proved especially useful in the prosecution of drunk driving cases and police pursuits.

Capturing criminal activity on videotape, audiotape, and DVDs has become the norm, even for smaller departments. This is thanks, in part, to generous federal and state grants assisting in their purchase. In fact, juries have become so accustomed to seeing on television a videotape of a defendant committing a crime that they sometimes question why a videotape of the actual crime being tried is not available. Defense attorneys sometimes imply that if the police had recorded a particular criminal event, it would be contrary to the testimony given by the officers involved. The implication is that the officers and investigators cannot be trusted to tell the truth, and must be lying since they elected not to record their every move.

Reality Check!

Some juries expect to see hi-tech, digitized photographs and video of surveillance operations, undercover drug purchases, and even crimes in progress. Investigators, who testify that their departments did not possess the necessary equipment, or that it was in repair, run the risk of nullifying the jury. These jurors believe that every law enforcement agency has this equipment, at a minimum, and in a federal trial, think that satellite photographs should be made available also! Juror's exposure to popular television programming, such as "CSI: Crime Scene Investigation," don't understand how the process actually works, or the limitation that skilled personnel, equipment, and budgetary restraints has on its purchase and use. Those investigators who have access to the equipment should use it at every opportunity, as it often provides evidence that is hard to refute.

These devices can also be problematic with juries. Through television and movies, they receive some knowledge of forensic and technical investigative techniques, just enough to "make them dangerous." According to an article published in U.S. News and World Reports, "Stoked by technical

wizardry they see on the tube, many Americans find themselves disappointed when they encounter the real world of law and order. Jurors increasingly expect forensic evidence in every case, and they expect it to be conclusive."[1] Once used in an investigation, jurors will naturally wonder why all opportunities to record telephone calls, video surveillances, and photograph pertinent parts of the investigation was not done. Gaps in this equipment's use may raise questions, and provide a good defense attorney with the opportunity to claim a particular event was not recorded because it would have shown the defendant to be innocent of the crime.

No matter what is conveyed by the media, to be admissible, the activity captured by one of these devices must be relevant, accurate, and portray a correct depiction of the subject matter.

AUDIO TAPE RECORDINGS

Audio tape recordings have been used by law enforcement agencies for many years. With the advent of digital voice recording, where a memory chip is used in lieu of magnetic tape, police agencies have embraced the new technology because of the compact size of the recorders, making them easily concealable on undercover agents and informants. They also offer almost no chance of a mechanical malfunction, and there is no magnetic tape to break or be accidentally erased or otherwise affected by magnets. These recorders also offer virtually silent operation, because motors to drive the magnetic tape over recording heads is eliminated, which enhances the safety of undercover investigators and confidential informants who use them to capture conversation with suspects.

The capturing of a suspect talking, in his own words, about planning or committing a crime is hard to dispute. Undercover drug investigators routinely use such devices, as well as older style magnetic recorders, to gather evidence using the suspect as a virtual witness against himself.

Most states, and the federal government allow for one party consent in recording conversations. This means that so long as the police receive the permission of one of the parties to the conversation, a recording of that conversation can be legally made.[2] One party consent however does have limitations. For example, if an undercover agent has a meeting with two suspects inside a hotel room, and leaves his jacket containing the hidden recording device on the bed while visiting the bathroom, any conversations captured between the two suspects while he is absent cannot be used at trial.

In the absence of one party consent, many state and local police have the option of obtaining a court order to record conversations during the course of the investigation of specific crimes.

As a rule of thumb, police investigators who pose undercover or confidential informants who have meetings with suspects should always have their conversations recorded. No one is infallible, and the recording, if nothing else, fully documents what was said, as well as the reflection of their voices at the time it was uttered. Police should furnish a recording device to any confidential informant to use when he makes or receives telephone calls from a suspect. He should be instructed to record *all* conversations outside the presence of a sworn law enforcement officer for a variety of good reasons. Confidential informants are inherently trustworthy, and the recordings enhance his credibility with the jury. Furthermore, for example, the one telephone call that is not recorded could be challenged by the defense attorney who may imply that that particular phone call was made by the defendant to inform the confidential informant he wanted to call off the criminal activity. Recording all telephonic conversations will help eliminate any claim that the confidential informant threatened the defendant if he did not carry out the intended crime.

Many audio recordings are still made with cassette tape recorders. Whenever possible, police investigators should never use the same cassette tape more than once. The recording heads of the cassette tape recorder make microscopic markings on the tape, as do other parts when the tape is paused. These markings may be the basis for a scientific challenge by the defense to imply that the original recording was edited or erased in some way, when in fact it was not.

For example, a police investigator inserts a new, unused audiotape into a cassette tape recorder and attaches a microphone to a telephone receiver that a confidential informant will be using to call a suspected drug dealer. The investigator may record his own voice on to the tape to identify himself, the date and time, and the telephone number that will be called. The recorder is then stopped, and restarted when the informant dials the telephone number he intends to call. Someone other than the drug dealer answers the telephone and says the man is not there at the moment. The informant hangs up, and the investigator rewinds the tape in preparation to make another telephone. Should the investigator use a different tape for the next telephone call?

Yes. As wasteful as it may seem, cost of a fresh audiotape is nothing compared to the future costs of having to prove that the eventually recorded conversation was genuine and edit-free. Defense attorneys sometimes hire experts to examine the cassette or videotape in question to render an opinion as to authenticity. The markings made on the cassette audio or videotape may be misinterpreted as erasure marks, and call into question the authenticity of the recording. Using fresh audio and videotapes to record different events eliminates all of these potential problems.

Another unique quality of audiotapes is that there is a plastic leader at the beginning of the cassette that cannot be recorded on. If the investigator does not ensure that the leader is forwarded enough so the recording heads will rest on the magnetic tape, he runs the risk of missing part of the conversation he intended to record. Furthermore, any future examination of the tape will not reveal a "start" mark on the tape, since the recording heads began on the plastic leader strip. The absence of this marking may also call into question the authenticity of the recording.

Although videotapes do not have such plastic leaders, they should never be used more than once during the recording of any event.

Body Wires

Body wire transmitters are useful devices in overhearing conversations as they occur. The receiver for the transmitting device can be joined with a tape recorder to record the transmissions, thereby eliminating the need for both a body wire and a separate recording device being worn by an undercover investigator of confidential informant. As a rule of thumb, because these devices have limited capabilities, and often do not work at the most critical moments, police officers and confidential informants will often wear both during meetings with suspects.

Body wire transmitters can easily be concealed in clothing, hats, backpacks, etc. They have no mechanical or moving parts and are totally silent. They do, however, have certain limitations.

Body wire transmitters have a very limited range. When in the outer limits of the transmitter's range, or if there is not a clear line of sight with the receiver, the reception can become distorted or otherwise unintelligible. Because of their inherent unreliability, undercover agents cannot rely solely on a verbal signal over the transmitter to indicate he is in trouble, or when the suspect should be arrested. Undercover agents and informants should always have a secondary visual signal to alert their surveillance team there is a problem.

An additional problem with body wire transmitters is the use of detection devices by cautious suspects. These devices are sold as "spy equipment" at novelty shops and can easily be found on the Internet. Many suspects are paranoid about being arrested, and knowing police routinely use body wire transmitters, will spare no expense to ensure he is not dealing with an undercover agent or confidential informant working with the police.

Some devices that are no larger than a coin, can detect a transmitter in either a room or on a person. Being discovered wearing a body wire transmitter can cause tremendous safety problems for the wearer. Because of this, an initial meeting between an undercover agent or confidential informant with a suspect may not be recorded, if there is a reasonable belief that the suspect may either physically search the person he is about to talk with, or may use a device to detect transmissions. One way to counter this would be to record a subsequent telephone conversation, in which the topics of the original discussion are recapped or mentioned again.

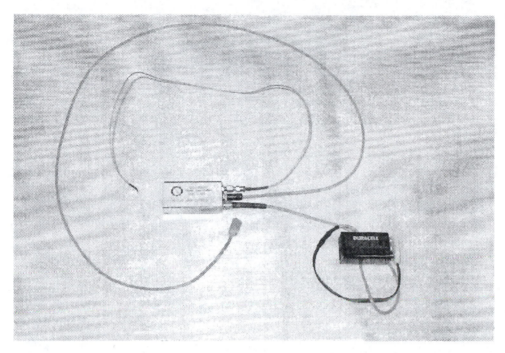

FIGURE 10.1   Body wire transmitter used by many law enforcement agencies around the world. *Photo by Gregory D. Lee.*

Most jurors will understand the reluctance of the police to use a body wire transmitter if the police had reason to believe the suspect would have used such a device, or intended to search them for a body wire transmitter.

Concealed Microphones

When the police have information that a suspect has a reputation for either physically searching people before discussing illegal activities, or carries a transmitter detector, a concealed room microphone may be a viable solution.

Assuming an undercover meeting is conducted in a hotel room or residence controlled by the police, concealed microphones can be placed inside to gather anticipated conversations. Microphones can be easily concealed in any item commonly found in a hotel room or home. These items may include a television, alarm clock, or lamp. They can be designed to route the sounds gathered by the microphone through existing electrical wires in the building to a receiver where it is heard while being recorded. No external wiring is required to accomplish this, and a transmitter detection device cannot detect these microphones, because the electronic impulses it generates is transmitted through hard wire.

These devices are inherently more reliable than body wire transmitters, since they do not rely on batteries or line of sight with the receiver. They do,

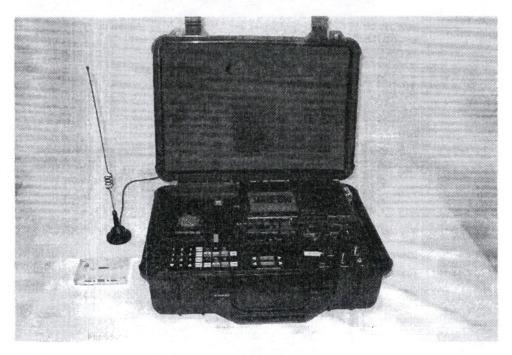

FIGURE 10.2 Body wire receiver and recorder with its carrying case. *Photo by Gregory D. Lee.*

however, have the limitation of not being portable. Police will often couple them to a digital or magnetic recording device that will serve as the basis for documenting what was said during the undercover meeting.

Again, these hidden microphones can be used without a warrant in those jurisdictions that allow for one party consent.

Wiretaps

For many years, federal agencies have relied on wiretaps, or the interception of verbal communication from telephones, to enhance their criminal investigations, particularly in drug and organized crime cases. Recently, large state and local departments have obtained the equipment and expertise to conduct such investigations. Modern technology has eliminated the need for the wiretap equipment to be in the proximity of the targeted telephone, and most telephonic intercepts are conducted at the local office of the federal agency or police department.

Regardless of who is conducting the wiretap, a specific court order has to be obtained before non-consenual wire communications are intercepted, and there are severe limitations on law enforcement agencies that use this investigative technique. For example, having authorization to listen to and record telephone conversations conducted on a particular telephone number does not mean every conversation can be overheard. Only conversations that are germane to the investigation may be intercepted. If the subject of the investigation is not actually talking on the phone, and law enforcement determines that the conversation is unrelated to a crime, they must conduct what is called "minimization." Operators of the wiretap must literally shut off the recording devices during these innocent conversations, and then after a reasonable time, monitor the conversation again to determine if the subject matter has changed before activating the recorders again. The subject's wife talking to an appointment receptionist to make a dental appointment would be an unauthorized interception, assuming the dentist or the receptionist is not a party to the subject's criminal enterprise.

Wiretap investigations are expensive, manpower intensive, and arduous. The equipment is expensive and must be manned by specially trained personnel. Interpreters may need to be screened and hired. Additional office space may be needed to house the equipment. Transcriptions of all conversations must be made, and copies of all recorded conversations must be created for pre-trial discovery. Monitors must be available on a 24-hour basis, including weekends and holidays. Surveillance agents must be standing by to follow the subject of the investigation, if he makes mention he is going to meet someone to conduct illegal activity.

All people intercepted during the course of the wiretap, which could be months long, must later be contacted and informed that their conversations on specific dates were intercepted.

The court authorizing the electronic intercept, either through wiretaps or hidden microphones in homes or businesses, usually requires updates on the progress of the investigation at least weekly. This way the judge can constantly reassess the need for the use of such an intrusive technique to continue. If there has been no directly related telephone calls for a certain time period, the judge can order the wiretap to cease at his discretion.

Many subjects of wiretaps assume that the government has unlimited budgets, resources, and manpower to conduct wiretap investigations, and that their home, business, and cellular telephones are all being listened to by the police or federal agents. This is definitely not the case. Because of the lofty requirements to conduct such an investigative technique, wiretaps are usually limited to investigations that have the potential of rendering the most criminal intelligence and evidence as possible, when other investigative techniques have failed.

Persons who assume they are being recorded often attempt to substitute words to make them appear to be engaged in innocent conversation. For example, if A calls B to order two kilograms of cocaine, A may say, "I need two white shirts." Or if A wants two kilograms of marijuana instead, may ask for "two green shirts," instead. Some subjects of wiretaps have been known to receive calls asking for "one half shirt," or "two and a half tires." When conversations like these are intercepted, it becomes clear to a jury that something illegal was being discussed. Many sophisticated criminals can be very clever in disguising their conversations from the police.

Most, but not all, investigations using wiretaps never go to trial. Once the government overcomes any challenge to the probable cause to conduct such an investigative technique, the defendant(s) will usually plead guilty.

Wiretaps often produce substantial evidence of guilt, and often leave the defendants with little choice but to plead guilty or enter into a plea-bargain agreement with the prosecutor.

Videotape Evidence

With the invention of videotape, law enforcement and prosecutors immediately recognized its tremendous potential to prove guilt. It can also be used to prove innocence as well, but overwhelmingly it provides evidence of guilt that is hard to dispute.

Videotape has been used extensively in criminal trials to provide juries with a first-hand account of criminal activity, and sometimes crimes as they occur. Videotaping a drug transaction, or the intoxicated state of a motorist, provides members of a jury an accurate account of exactly what happened. No longer do law enforcement officers or confidential informants have to rely solely on their memories to recount what transpired.

Over the years, video cameras have been transformed from large, bulky, intrusive analog machines to highly concealable, easy to operate digital models, some hardly larger than a deck of playing cards. The quality of the cameras has also increased; rendering almost television broadcast quality pictures of an event.

As stated, videotape and digital video recorders has shrunk in size to the point where police surveillance personnel can easily conceal them. They can also be incorporated inside items commonly found inside hotel and motel rooms to record the exchange of drugs or money, or other items. Many video cameras are separated from the actual recorder to further miniaturize their size.

In reality, only a small pinhole is needed for some camera lenses to capture an approximately 45° angle of view. A camera alone can be easily concealed within a lamp and receive power from the lamp's power cord. Coupled with a microwave transmitter, the pictures can be transmitted to a receiver in an adjacent room, where it is recorded on videotape. The recorder may have the ability to electronically etch the time and date that the recording is made.

Videotape and digital camera lenses can be incorporated into many other everyday items that would never be suspected by someone being recorded, including thermostats, room ceiling water sprinkler heads, air vents, televisions, and radios. When hooked up to a series of large batteries concealed cameras can operate within the trunk of a parked vehicle. Time-lapse video cameras can cover an area for an extended period of time, without the need to constantly change cassette tapes. Time-lapse video photography is particularly useful in determining what vehicles have arrived or left a particular location.

Video cameras with microwave transmitters can be concealed into an empty telephone pole transformer box or tube, with the camera lens trained on a home or business through slots designed to look like lettering. Even a close examination of these "pole cams" either in person or with the aid of binoculars, would not reveal the true nature of their use. The microwave transmitter sends the pictures to a nearby receiver, where it is recorded on videotape or DVD.

Videotapes have been highly successful in showing defendants personally engaging in criminal activity.

Police investigators are advised use videotape whenever possible. Juries have come to expect major events to be recorded, and may not understand why the police elected not to use this equipment if it was available. When a uniformed police officer knows a camera is videotaping him during an encounter with a traffic violator or suspected drunk driver, the officer will almost always display courteous, professional behavior.

DIGITAL PHOTOGRAPHS

With the advent of digital photography, photographs taken by police agencies using film have declined rapidly for both cost and storage reasons. Digital photographs cost nothing to develop and can be stored electronically. Scores of crime scene and other photographs can be stored on a compact disc, and rapidly distributed to other law enforcement agencies, prosecutors, and defense attorneys, as part of discovery material.

Many digital cameras now have interchangeable lenses for long-distance surveillance photography. Other digital cameras are compact enough to covertly obtain photographs of suspects, vehicles, and locations. Prices for these cameras are declining and more are being purchased by police agencies for use in most, if not all criminal investigations.

Digital photography does allow for cropping, editing, and additions of other images not originally captured by the camera's memory. This digitization may be challenged by defense attorneys as being manipulated by the police to portray the defendant in a different light. The attorney's goal is to create a reasonable doubt in the mind of at least one juror. The integrity of all digital photographs must be maintained to counter any such claims.

Despite sometimes being gruesome, crime scene photographs are routinely admitted at trial. Trial judges who feel that the need of a graphic photograph to illustrate a particular point, such as the manner in which a murder victim was killed, will allow such a photograph despite its possible prejudicial effect on the jury.

Juries are seldom allowed by the trial judge to personally view a crime scene. Photographs, diagrams, and videotapes made of the crime scene generally are adequate to satisfy the jury's questions about the scene of the crime and the location where evidence was seized. If a juror was to independently visit the crime scene, it could become the basis for a mistrial.

COMPUTER EVIDENCE

Criminals are increasingly using computers to assist them in their crimes. Terrorists have been using computers for years to communicate with each other, as well as to maintain files of their plans for future terrorism events. Files with communiqués can be e-mailed to other members of a criminal conspiracy that are disguised within a simple photograph. Drug dealers use computers to also communicate and keep records of past drug transactions. If a computer is included as evidence to be seized during a search warrant execution, then it is important for the officers to know how to properly unplug and transport it to a laboratory, where data from its hard drive can be safely obtained.

Electronic evidence is by its very nature fragile. For this reason special precautions should be taken to document, collect, preserve, and examine this type of evidence. Computers contain electrical components that, if not handled properly, may destroy the evidence or injure investigators who do not take property safety precautions. Improper handling can render the evidence unusable or might lead to an inaccurate conclusion. The investigator's primary job is to preserve the computer evidence and to transport the computer to a safe location, where a complete forensic image of all stored data areas can be made. The seizing officer's responsibility is to ensure that the computer system can be later reconfigured to match the configuration when it was found.

Before handling a computer, the investigator should first remove all of his jewelry, including watches, rings, bracelets, and necklaces. These objects, frequently made of gold, conduct electricity and cause static charges to the computer components.

In ordinary circumstances, static electricity is merely a nuisance. However, in an increasingly technological age, a simple static electricity shock one might receive while walking across carpeting can be very costly or dangerous to computer components and personnel alike. To avoid electrostatic discharge, the person handling the computer should ground himself by periodically touching unpainted metal on the computer case chassis.

Never open a recently used power supply or monitor or one that still has the power cable connected to an electrical outlet. Extremely high voltages can remain within the power supply's capacitors for a long period after the power has been turned off. The power cord plugged into the back of the computer should be removed instead of pulling the plug from the wall socket.

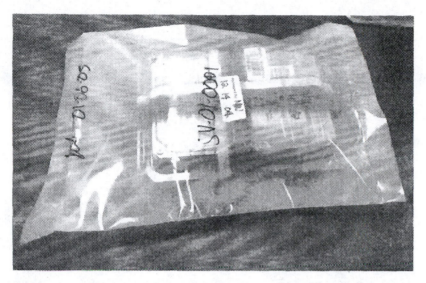

FIGURE 10.3 Photo of a hard drive taken in as evidence at the Silicon Valley Regional Computer Forensics Lab on January 7, 2005, in Menlo Park, California. Officials with the FBI and local law enforcement unveiled and gave a behind-the-scenes look at their new multi-million dollar facility in the heart of Silicon Valley. The lab recovers digital evidence in a way that is legally acceptable to the courts. A recent case of a Missouri woman accused of cutting a fetus from her victim was solved by a digital forensics team tracking down Internet messages on a computer. *Corbis.*

Because monitors do not store data, it is not necessary to remove them from the seized computer. However, printers should also be seized because they have memories that may contain vital data. If the computer is found to be on at the time of the search warrant execution, and an image is displayed on the monitor, a photograph of the screen should be made. If the computer is displaying a website, then the web address should be noted. If the computer is on, and the screen is displaying a screen saver or the computer is in sleep mode, moving the mouse will trigger the screen display to reappear. Investigators should not strike any keys to put the computer back into operation.

All original programs found at the time should also be seized as evidence for later use by forensic computer analysts, in the event that it is necessary to compare them to the programs maintained on the hard drive.

The keyboard should also be seized for later fingerprint analysis.

In the event that a suspect is operating the computer at the time investigators execute the search warrant, he should immediately be removed from the area to prevent him from performing keystrokes that could disable a website or destroy the data being processed, as well as any evidence that may be in the hard drive.

Once forensic examiners remove the hard drive(s) from the computer, they can replicate them for a thorough examination to uncover files, email messages, and other data that might prove useful in proving a crime, and identifying other members of a criminal conspiracy.

SUMMARY

Modern police agencies routinely use a variety of analog and digital audio, video, and photographic equipment during the course of criminal investigations. Recognizing the many advantages of recording crime as it occurs, within the last dozen or so years, police departments have even equipped their patrol vehicles with fixed video cameras. This videotape equipment has proved especially useful in the prosecution of drunk driving cases and police pursuits.

No matter what the media might convey, to be admissible, the activity captured by any of these devices must be relevant, accurate, and portray a correct depiction of the subject matter.

Audio tape recordings have been used by law enforcement agencies for many years. With the advent of digital voice recording, where a memory chip is used in lieu of magnetic tape, police agencies have embraced the new technology because of the compact size of the recorders, making them easily concealable on undercover agents and informants.

Body wire transmitters can easily be concealed in clothing, hats, backpacks, etc. They have no mechanical or moving parts and are totally silent. They do, however, have certain limitations.

When the police have information that a suspect has a reputation for either physically searching people before discussing illegal activities, or carries a transmitter detector, a concealed room microphone may be a viable solution. Microphones can be easily concealed in any item commonly found in a hotel room or home. These items may include a television, alarm clock, or lamp.

Federal law, and many states allow for the recording of conversations with one party consent. This means so long as one party to the conversation grants permission for the conversation to be recorded, it is admissible at trial. State and local police investigators should always check with their local prosecutor before attempting such an investigative technique.

For many years, federal agencies have relied on wiretaps, or the interception of verbal communication from telephones, to enhance their criminal investigations, particularly in drug and organized crime cases. A specific court order has to be obtained before wire communications are intercepted, and there are severe limitations on law enforcement agencies that use this investigative technique.

Wiretaps often produce substantial evidence of guilty, and often leave the defendants with little choice but to plead guilty or enter into a plea-bargain agreement with the prosecutor, once challenges to the probable cause leading to the granting of a wiretap are overcome.

With the invention of videotape, law enforcement and prosecutors immediately recognized its tremendous potential to prove guilt. It can also be used to prove innocence as well, but overwhelmingly it provides evidence of guilt that is hard to dispute.

Videotape has been used extensively in criminal trials to provide juries with a first-hand account of criminal activity. Videotaping a drug transaction, or the intoxicated state of a motorist provides members of a jury with an accurate account of exactly what happened. No longer do law enforcement officers or confidential informants have to rely solely on their memories to recount what transpired.

With the advent of digital photography, photographs taken by police agencies using film have declined rapidly, for both cost and storage reasons. Digital photographs cost nothing to develop and can be stored electronically. Scores of crime scene and other photographs can be stored on a compact disc, and rapidly distributed to other law enforcement agencies, prosecutors, and defense attorneys as part of discovery material.

Criminals are increasingly using computers to assist them in their crimes. If a computer is included as evidence to be seized during a search warrant execution, then it is important for the officers to know how to properly unplug and transport it to a laboratory, where data from its hard drive can be safely obtained.

Because monitors do not store data, it is not necessary to remove them from the seized computer. However, printers should also be seized, because they have memories that may contain vital data.

NOTES

1. "The CSI Effect," by Kit R. Roane, *U.S. News and World Report*, April 25, 2005.
2. Police should always check with their local prosecutor about the legality of such an investigative technique before it is employed.

11

Confessions and Admissions

Part of the investigative process is to confront suspects of crime, including interviewing and interrogating them in an effort to have them admit fully or partially to their participation in a crime. When a confession cannot be obtained, an admission is the next best thing that could make the difference between confirming the identity of the culprit, or closing the case as "unsolved." Obtaining a confession generally increases the possibility that the defendant will plead guilty rather than seek a jury trial.

A *confession* is an expressed and complete acknowledgement of guilt as to the commission of a crime; where as an *admission* is something less then a confession, but implies guilt. For example, a suspect being questioned admits to being at the crime scene during the event, but denies participation.

A suspect's confession can be made as either a verbal or written statement while being interrogated by the police. Many interviews quickly turn into interrogations when the investigator feels the suspect is holding back information and is reluctant to reveal his or others involvement in the crime. An interview is either conducted formally or informally, when the police are seeking general information from a person who is not necessarily a suspect in the crime.

196

Contrasting this, an *interrogation* is an intense, direct, and systematic questioning process in which the goal of the police interrogator is to have the suspect admit, if not confess, to his or someone else's involvement in the crime. The goal of the police in obtaining a confession is elicit the truth about the circumstances surrounding the crime, to obtain evidence, identify the method of operation used during the commission of the crime, and to identify other conspirators involved.

Often a series of well-thought out techniques are used to prompt the suspect to confess. Some of these techniques include using a room specially designed for interrogations and evaluating the suspect's "body language" during the interrogation.

All the training, techniques, and preparation are of no use if the confession is later ruled inadmissible in a court of law.

VOLUNTARINESS

When a confession is obtained, the question will always arise as to whether or not the confession was obtained voluntarily without any threats, promises, or coercion being used by the police. The question is a logical one, since many people find it hard to understand why someone would confess to engaging in criminal activity, knowing they are providing the police with damning evidence that will be used against them, unless they were somehow tricked, threatened, or coerced into providing it.

The roots of the test of voluntariness developed in common law in the eighteenth century, as the courts of England and then the United States recognized that coerced confessions are inherently untrustworthy.[1]

Generally, confessions are deemed admissible if they were obtained freely without the use or threat of violence, and the defendant was not promised a reward or other benefit, such as a reduced sentence, in return for confessing.

The standard of proof that the confession was voluntary rests with the prosecution. The trial judge will ultimately decide if the confession is voluntary and if it will be admitted as evidence at trial. When a confession is admitted as evidence, the jury can either accept it, or reject it entirely as they see fit.

In determining the voluntariness of any confession, the court will consider the totality of the circumstances in which it was obtained. The trial judge will evaluate if the defendant was deprived of any due process of law, such as the right not to be compelled to incriminate himself, and the physical and mental condition of the defendant. These factors do not in themselves render a confession inadmissible, but may make the confession involuntary.

For example, a defendant is arrested after being involved in a robbery, in which he shoots and kills a convenience storeowner after being shot himself.

He flees in his vehicle and due to the physical trauma he has experienced, passes out and crashes. Police investigators arrive at the hospital and interrogate the man, who is in intense pain, has lost a significant amount of blood, and is slowly becoming under the influence of pain medication. The emergency room doctors are ready to take the defendant into surgery. The defendant confesses that he shot and killed the storeowner just before he is rolled into the operating room. Will the defendant's confession be admitted as evidence at trial?

Maybe. The trial judge, in determining if the confession was conducted freely, will evaluate the circumstances carefully. A defense attorney surely would argue that the defendant was in pain, felt he may be allowed to die if he did not confess, and only confessed because the police either said or implied that he would not receive the necessary surgery until he confessed to shooting the storeowner. The defense may probe the professional reputations of the police investigators to search for past complaints of them being heavy-handed or prone to abusing prisoners. Whether these things in reality happened or not, the judge will have to make a finding. The more factors that exist leaning towards involuntariness will usually, but not always, render the confession inadmissible. The judge essentially has to crawl into the mind of the defendant to make such determinations. When in doubt, judges tend to err on the side of the defendant in order to insure a fair trial for him.

Reality Check!

Police can counter many claims of threats or coercion by electronically recording interrogation sessions. Juries now come to expect to see a videotape of crucial phases of an investigation, and question why one was not made. Jurors may think that lack of a videotape of a confession is evidence it was obtained through threats or coercion. When police departments possess such equipment, but did not use it because it was under repair or otherwise unavailable, many judges and jurors may believe that this is further evidence that illegal tactics were used in order to get the defendant to confess. Videotaping an interrogation session has almost become standard practice for many law enforcement agencies, and many others are going in that direction in order to remove any doubt about the voluntariness of any confession they receive.

RIGHT TO AN ATTORNEY

In the first of two landmark U.S. Supreme Court decisions involving the voluntariness of confessions obtained by police, *Escobedo* v. *Illinois*[2] established what is now the routine advisement by the police of the defendant's right to be represented by counsel before being questioned by police. Law enforcement officials took Escobedo into custody and interrogated him in a police station for the purpose of obtaining a confession. The police did not effectively advise him of his right to remain silent or of his right to consult with his attorney. Instead, they confronted him with an alleged accomplice who accused him of having perpetrated a murder. When Escobedo denied the accusation and said, "I didn't shoot Manuel, you did it," they handcuffed him and took him to an interrogation room. There, while handcuffed and standing, he was questioned for four hours until he confessed. During this interrogation, the police denied his request to speak to his attorney and they prevented his retained attorney, who had come to the police station, from consulting with him. At his trial, the prosecution, over his objection, introduced the confession against him. The Supreme Court held that the statements made were constitutionally inadmissible.

RIGHT TO REMAIN SILENT

In the second landmark decision two years later in *Miranda* v. *Arizona*,[3] the U.S. Supreme Court ruling effectively created the so-called "Miranda Warning," in which the police are compelled to warn a defendant that he has the right to remain silent and is not obligated to answer any incriminating questions.

On March 13, 1963, Ernesto Miranda, was arrested at his home and taken to a Phoenix police station. He was taken into custody after being identified by the complaining witness. The police then took him to "Interrogation Room No. 2" of the detective bureau. There he was questioned by two police officers. The officers admitted at trial that Miranda was not advised that he had a right to have an attorney present. Two hours later, the officers emerged from the interrogation room with a written confession signed by Miranda. At the top of the statement was a typed paragraph stating that the confession was made voluntarily, without threats or promises of immunity and "with full knowledge of my legal rights, understanding any statement I make may be used against me."

At his trial before a jury, the written confession was admitted into evidence over the objection of defense counsel, and the officers testified to the prior oral confession made by Miranda during the interrogation. Miranda was found guilty of kidnapping and rape. He was sentenced to 20 to 30 years' imprisonment on each count, the sentences to run concurrently. On appeal, the Supreme Court of Arizona held that Miranda's constitutional rights were not violated in obtaining the confession and affirmed the conviction.[4] In reaching its decision, the court emphasized heavily the fact that Miranda did not specifically request counsel.

The U.S. Supreme Court however ruled that there could be no doubt that the Fifth Amendment privilege is available outside the courtroom and serves to protect persons in all settings in which their freedom of action is curtailed in any significant way from being compelled to incriminate themselves. The Court concluded that without proper safeguards, the process of in-custody interrogation of persons suspected of crime contains inherently compelling pressures, which work to undermine the individual's will to resist and to compel him to speak where he would not otherwise do so freely. In order to combat these pressures and to permit a full opportunity to exercise the privilege against self-incrimination, the Court dictated that an accused "must be adequately and effectively apprised of his rights and the exercise of those rights must be fully honored."[5]

The Court went on to say, "At the outset, if a person in custody is to be subjected to interrogation, he must first be informed in clear and unequivocal terms that he has the right to remain silent. For those unaware of the privilege, the warning is needed simply to make them aware of it – the threshold requirement for an intelligent decision as to its exercise. More important, such a warning is an absolute prerequisite in overcoming the inherent pressures of the interrogation atmosphere. It is not just the subnormal or woefully ignorant who succumb to an interrogator's imprecations, whether implied or expressly stated, that the interrogation will continue until a confession is obtained or that silence in the face of accusation is itself damning and will bode ill when presented to a jury. Further, the warning will show the individual that his interrogators are prepared to recognize his privilege should he choose to exercise it."[6]

The Court also laid out the requirement that a defendant had a right to counsel, regardless of his ability to pay for such service. "If an individual indicates that he wishes the assistance of counsel before any interrogation occurs, the authorities cannot rationally ignore or deny his request on the basis that the individual does not have or cannot afford a retained attorney. The financial ability of the individual has no relationship to the scope of the rights involved here. The privilege against self-incrimination secured by the Constitution applies to all individuals. The need for counsel in order to protect the privilege exists for the indigent as well as the affluent. In fact, were we to limit these constitutional rights to those who can retain an attorney, our decisions today would be of little significance."[7]

The Court also made other observations and comments. "Once warnings have been given, the subsequent procedure is clear. If the individual indicates in any manner, at any time prior to or during questioning, that he wishes to remain silent, the interrogation must cease. At this point he has shown that he intends to exercise his Fifth Amendment privilege; any statement taken after the person invokes his privilege cannot be other than the product of compulsion, subtle or otherwise. Without the right to cut off questioning, the setting of in-custody interrogation operates on the individual to overcome free choice in producing a statement after the privilege has been once invoked. If the individual states that he wants an attorney, the interrogation must cease until an attorney is present. At that time, the individual must have an opportunity to confer with the attorney and to have him present during any subsequent questioning. If the individual cannot obtain an attorney and he indicates that he wants one before speaking to police, they must respect his decision to remain silent.

This does not mean, as some have suggested, that each police station must have a "station house lawyer" present at all times to advise prisoners. It does mean, however, that if police propose to interrogate a person they must make known to him that he is entitled to a lawyer and that if he cannot afford one, a lawyer will be provided for him prior to any interrogation. If authorities conclude that they will not provide counsel during a reasonable period of time in which investigation in the field is carried out, they may refrain from doing so without violating the person's Fifth Amendment privilege so long as they do not question him during that time.

FIGURE 11.1 A Chicago police officer makes an arrest. When uniform police officers arrest a wanted person, investigators strive to interrogate him as soon as possible. *Corbis.*

If the interrogation continues without the presence of an attorney and a statement is taken, a heavy burden rests on the government to demonstrate that the defendant knowingly and intelligently waived his privilege against self-incrimination and his right to retained or appointed counsel."[8]

MIRANDA WARNINGS

In order to not violate a suspect's Fifth Amendment rights, police officers need to know that before questioning a defendant in a *custodial* setting, they must first advise the defendant of his so-called **Miranda rights**. Advising defendants of these rights is so important that virtually all police departments issue printed cards with the Miranda warning to their officers and require them to recite the rights advisement verbatim. The simple rule is that if the police intend to interrogate a suspect who is in custody, they *must* advise him of his Miranda rights before any questioning begins. The suspect/defendant must be in custody and about to be subject to an interrogation before the police are compelled to advise him of these rights. Casual conversation with a witness or potential suspect on the street does not require a Miranda warning.

Furthermore, a defendant must be advised of their Miranda rights when he is in custody and about to be interrogated, regardless of their educational level, profession, or life experience. This includes attorneys, lawyers, judges, or others who probably do or should understand their rights. Anyone in a custodial situation who is about to be interrogated must be advised of his or her Miranda rights.

Most state statutes require juvenile suspects in custody be advised of their Miranda rights before formal police questioning.

For the purposes of *Miranda*, custody is defined as the defendant being aware that his freedom of movement has been restricted, or that he has been formally arrested and booked at a police facility. The police officer must ask him or herself: If this person wanted to leave, would I let him go? If the answer is no, then for all practical purposes, he is in custody, and must be advised of his Miranda rights before any questioning concerning the incident under investigation. Some state courts have voiced that someone placed in handcuffs and seated in the back of a police car is in custody for all practical purposes, and should be advised of his Miranda rights before being questioned.

Reality Check!

Advising a defendant of his Miranda rights is so important, that when confronted with a situation where the police officer does not know if he or she has an obligation to advise someone of their rights, the officer should always err on the side of caution and make the advisement. Not advising a defendant before questioning can bring serious damage to the prosecution, and may even prevent the filing of criminal charges because important evidence was lost.

Non-Custodial Settings

An example of a suspect not in custody, is when the police telephone a suspect at his residence and ask him to come to their police station for an "interview." The suspect arrives, is escorted to an interrogation room with no windows, very little furniture, and no paintings or photographs attached to the walls. The suspect is advised that he is not under arrest and free to leave at any time. The questioning becomes accusatory, and the police officers attempt to trick the suspect into believing his DNA was found at the scene of the crime.

In another example, police at a crime scene ask a witness to accompany them to their station for further questioning. The officer advises the witness that he is not under arrest, and will be taken to his home or place of business afterwards.

In a third example, police investigators interview a suspect who provides his own transportation to the police station. He is told he does not have to answer any of their questions and is free to go at any time. The questions are very specific about the crime and the suspect's alibi.

During the investigative process, an undercover agent meets with a suspect about purchasing drugs. The undercover agent is not required to give a Miranda advisement to the suspect before he elicits incriminating statements from him during the undercover phase of the investigation. It is impossible to meet the standards for the admonishment of the Miranda warning, because the suspect did not realize he was talking with a police officer, and his locomotion was not restricted.

In each of these examples, the police are not required to *Mirandize*, or advise the person of their right to remain silent, or have an attorney present during questioning. However, there may be some courts that will find these conditions as being "in custody." The judge has to weigh the totality of circumstances of how the suspect came to the attention of the police, what the police response and reaction was when contact was first made, and if the suspect knew, or should have known, he was not in custody. Sometimes the circumstances of the police-suspect encounter may sway a judge to rule that the suspect was in custody for the purpose of Miranda. For example, a police SWAT team breaks down the door to the suspect's apartment, temporarily handcuffs the suspect, and place him in the back of a police car equipped with a cage. He is shortly thereafter removed from the police car, the handcuffs are removed, and he is questioned while in the parking lot of his apartment. Some courts may rule that the manner in which the police came upon the suspect made it clear to him that he was in custody, despite never being arrested.

In another example of someone being in custody, despite never being arrested, is when a suspect volunteers to come to a police facility to be interviewed by investigators. He is then subject to an intense, two-hour interview in which he is told, "you're not goin' anywhere until you tell the truth!" The suspect is never told he was free to leave at any time.

It is even possible to not be "in custody" for the purposes of Miranda, despite being lodged at a jail facility. If a prison inmate telephones a police department and makes incriminating statements to a police investigator, no Miranda warning would be required.

In some states, police are also permitted to introduce an undercover agent in a jail facility to pose as a fellow inmate for the purpose of eliciting incriminating statements from the suspect. In this situation, a Miranda warning would not be necessary.

Police should never tell a suspect that he is not going to be arrested. This could be interpreted as a promise of leniency, making the subsequent statements involuntary, and therefore inadmissible at trial.

Detention Settings

Police officers frequently make contact with citizens during the course of their duties. Officers do not need to Mirandize someone during a consensual encounter when the person is freely and willingly talking. A *consensual encounter* is police contact with an individual that is voluntary. There is no exercise of police authority over the person who is free to leave as he or she chooses.

Police officers do not need to advise suspects of their Miranda rights if they are merely being detained, even if he is not free to go at the moment. A detention is the step above a consensual encounter, but below an arrest. The police may detain several people while conducting an initial investigation to gather facts, and those persons detained for the purpose of investigation should not be Mirandized until other facts surface. If a person being detained is determined to be responsible for the incident the police are investigating, the police may arrest the person and place them into custody.

At a subsequent evidentiary hearing, the defense may question the intention of the police officer making the arrest. The defense may ask if the defendant was free to leave the area, implying he had been arrested, thereby required to be Mirandized before asking incriminating questions.

Police officers should focus on the terminology and be careful not to use the term arrest, when in reality a detention was taking place. Miranda warnings do not have to be given to everyone the police encounter while conducting a preliminary investigation.

A common example of a police detention is a police officer making a traffic stop of a suspected drunk driver. The officer may ask if the driver has been drinking, and how much. This is all done during the police officer's preliminary investigation. If the officer feels there is enough probable cause to arrest the driver for being under the influence, he will be placed into custody and advised of his Miranda rights before being questioned further.

When the police arrest someone, advise him of his Miranda rights, and he elects to retain them, can subsequent incriminating statements he makes be used against him?

Yes, even if the statements the defendant makes was prompted by an overheard conversation between two police officers. For example, shortly after a taxicab driver, who had been robbed by a man wielding a sawed-off shotgun, identified a picture of a suspect, a Providence, R. I., patrolman spotted the suspect, who was unarmed, on the street, arrested him, and advised him of his Miranda rights. When other police officers arrived at the arrest scene, the suspect was twice again advised of his Miranda rights, and he stated that he understood his rights and wanted to speak with a lawyer. The suspect was then placed in a police car to be driven to the police station in the company of three officers who were instructed by superiors not to question him or intimidate him in any way. While en route to the station, two of the officers engaged in a conversation between themselves concerning the missing shotgun used in the robbery. One of the officers stated that there were "a lot of handicapped children running around in this area" because a school for such children was located nearby, and "God forbid one of them might find a weapon with shells and they might hurt themselves." The suspect interrupted the officers' conversation, stating that they should turn the car around so he could show them where the weapon was located. Upon returning to the scene of the arrest where a search for the shotgun was in progress, the suspect was again advised of his Miranda rights, replied that he understood those rights but that he "wanted to get the gun out of the way because of the kids in the area in the school," and then led the police to the shotgun.

Before trial on charges of kidnapping, robbery, and murder of another taxi-cab driver, the trial court denied the defendant's motion to suppress the shotgun and the statements he had made to the police regarding its discovery, ruling that the defendant had waived his Miranda rights. The Rhode Island Supreme Court set aside the conviction and held that respondent was entitled to a new trial, concluding that defendant had invoked his Miranda right to counsel and that, contrary to Miranda's mandate that, in the absence of counsel, all custodial interrogation then cease, the police officers in the vehicle had "interrogated" the respondent without a valid waiver of his right to counsel.

The U.S. Supreme Court in *Rhode Island* v. *Innis*,[9] held that the defendant was not "interrogated" in violation of his right under Miranda to remain silent until he had consulted with a lawyer. Justice J. Stewart wrote that Miranda safeguards come into play whenever a person in custody is subjected to either express questioning or its functional equivalent. That is to say, the term "interrogation" under Miranda refers not only to express questioning, but also to any words or actions on the part of the police (other than those normally attendant to arrest and custody) that the police should know are reasonably likely to elicit an incriminating response from the suspect. The latter portion of this definition focuses primarily upon the perceptions of the suspect, rather than the intent of the police.

Justice Stewart continued, "Here, there was no express questioning of respondent; the conversation between the two officers was, at least in form, nothing more than a dialogue between them to which no response from respondent was invited. Moreover, respondent was not subjected to the 'functional equivalent' of questioning, since it cannot be said that the officers should have known that their conversation was reasonably likely to elicit an incriminating response from respondent. There is nothing in the record to suggest that the officers were aware that respondent was peculiarly susceptible to an appeal to his conscience concerning the safety of handicapped children, or that the police knew that respondent was unusually disoriented or upset at the time of his arrest. Nor does the record indicate that, in the context of a brief conversation, the officers should have known that respondent would suddenly be moved to make a self-incriminating response. While it may be said that respondent was subjected to 'subtle compulsion,' it must also be established that a suspect's incriminating response was the product of words or actions on the part of the police that they should have known were reasonably likely to elicit an incriminating response, which was not established here."

Can the police directly question a defendant about the location of a weapon or other items that may be a hindrance to public safety?

Yes. In another U.S. Supreme Court ruling, *New York* v. *Quarles*,[10] Mr Quarles was charged in a New York state court with criminal possession of a weapon. The record showed that a woman approached two uniformed police officers and told them that she had just been raped, described her assailant, and told them that the man had just entered a nearby supermarket and was carrying a gun. While one of the officers radioed for assistance, the other entered the store and spotted Mr Quarles, who matched the description given by the woman. Mr Quarles ran toward the rear of the store, and the officer pursued him with a drawn gun but lost sight of him for several seconds. Upon regaining sight of Mr Quarles, the officer ordered him to stop and put his hands over his head; frisked him and discovered that he was wearing an empty shoulder holster. After handcuffing him, he asked him where the gun was. Mr Quarles nodded toward some empty cartons and responded, "The gun is over there." The officer then retrieved the gun from one of the cartons, formally arrested him and read him his rights per Miranda. Mr Quarles indicated that he would answer questions without an attorney being present and admitted that he owned the gun and had purchased it in Florida. The trial court excluded Mr Quarles' initial statement and the gun because he had not yet been given the Miranda warnings, and also excluded his other statements as evidence tainted by the Miranda violation. Both the Appellate Division of the New York Supreme Court and the New York Court of Appeals affirmed.

The U.S. Supreme Court, however, had a different opinion. The Court wrote: "The Court of Appeals erred in affirming the exclusion of respondent's initial statement and the gun because [the officer's] failure to read respondent his Miranda rights before attempting to locate the weapon. Accordingly, it also erred in affirming the exclusion of respondent's subsequent statements as illegal fruits of the Miranda violation. This case presents a situation where concern for public safety must be paramount to adherence to the literal language of the prophylactic rules enunciated in Miranda.

(a) Although respondent was in police custody when he made his statements and the facts come within the ambit of Miranda, nevertheless on these facts there is a 'public safety' exception to the requirement that Miranda warnings be given before a suspect's answers may be admitted into evidence, and the availability of that exception does not depend upon the motivation of the individual officers involved. The doctrinal underpinnings of Miranda do not require that it be applied in its entire rigor to a situation in which police officers ask questions reasonably prompted by a concern for the public safety. In this case, so long as the gun was concealed somewhere in the supermarket, it posed more than one danger to the public safety: an accomplice might make use of it, or a customer or employee might later come upon it."

Spontaneous Outbursts

A spontaneous outburst is a voluntary incriminating statement made by a defendant that was not in response to a question. Because spontaneous outbursts are not in direct response to an interrogator's questioning, they are admissible as evidence, even if the suspect is in custody and has not yet been advised of his Miranda rights, or even if he has evoked his right to remain silent and demands an attorney. Such statements must always be spontaneous and voluntary.

For example, police homicide detectives locate the wife of a shooting victim at a friend's home. The police place the woman into custody because eyewitnesses saw her shoot her husband. After being placed in handcuffs, and being led to the police car, the woman blurts, "Yeah, I shot the SOB, and I hope he dies." This would be an admissible statement since it was not solicited through questioning, and was brought on by the heat of the moment when she was arrested.

Spontaneous outbursts often occur when a defendant is initially arrested or otherwise detained. Police officers should be conscious that in the heat of the moment, there is a good chance that the defendant may say something admitting to guilt or knowledge of the crime.

In another example, a man walks into a police station and confesses to the desk officer that he is responsible for the murder of a child earlier that day. The police are not obligated to advise the defendant of his Miranda rights if they do not know what the man is likely to confess to.

Does the mental capacity of a defendant who utters a spontaneous outburst, and then waives his Miranda rights, affect the validity of the statement?

No. In the mid-1980s, the U.S. Supreme Court settled the issue in *Colorado* v. *Connelly*,[11] after a defendant approached a Denver police officer and stated that he had murdered someone and wanted to talk about it. The officer advised the defendant of his Miranda rights, and he said that he understood those rights but still wanted to talk about the murder. Shortly thereafter, a detective arrived and again advised the defendant of his rights. After he answered that he had come all the way from Boston to confess to the murder, he was taken to police headquarters. He then openly detailed his story to the police and subsequently pointed out the exact location of the murder.

He was held overnight and the next day he became visibly disoriented during an interview in the public defender's office and was sent to a state hospital for evaluation. Interviews with a psychiatrist revealed that the defendant was following the "voice of God" in confessing to the murder. The psychiatrist's testimony confirmed that the defendant suffered from a psychosis that interfered with his ability to make free and rational choices. Although not preventing him from understanding his rights, this motivated his confession. Therefore, the trial court suppressed the defendant's initial statements and custodial confession because they were "involuntary," notwithstanding the fact that the police had done nothing wrong or coercive in securing the confession. The court also found that the defendant's mental state vitiated his attempted waiver of the right to counsel and the privilege against self-incrimination. The Colorado Supreme Court affirmed, holding that the Federal Constitution requires a court to suppress a confession when the defendant's mental state, at the time he confessed, interfered with his "rational intellect" and his "free will," the very admission of the evidence in a court of law being sufficient state action to implicate the Due Process Clause of the Fourteenth Amendment. The court further held that the defendant's mental condition precluded his ability to make a valid waiver of his Miranda rights and that the State had not met its burden of proving a waiver by "clear and convincing evidence."

The Supreme Court reversed the lower court when it held:

1. "Coercive police activity is a necessary predicate to finding that a confession is not 'voluntary' within the meaning of the Due Process

Clause. Here, the taking of the respondent's statements and their admission into evidence constituted no violation of that Clause. While a defendant's mental condition may be a 'significant' factor in the 'voluntariness' calculus, this does not justify a conclusion that his mental condition, by itself and apart from its relation to official coercion, should ever dispose of the inquiry into constitutional 'voluntariness.'

2. Whenever the State bears the burden of proof in a motion to suppress a statement allegedly obtained in violation of the Miranda doctrine, the State needs to prove waiver only by a preponderance of the evidence. Thus, the Colorado Supreme Court erred in applying a 'clear and convincing evidence' standard. That court also erred in its analysis of the question whether the respondent had waived his Miranda rights. Notions of 'free will' have no place in this area of constitutional law. Respondent's perception of coercion flowing from the 'voice of God' is a matter to which the Federal Constitution does not speak."

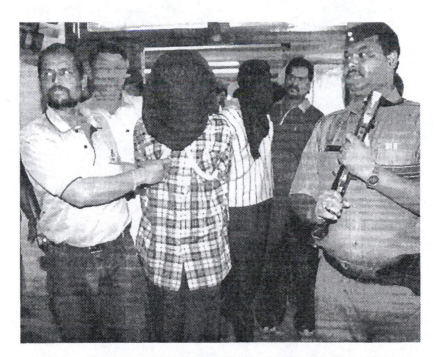

FIGURE 11.2   Policemen escort alleged Pakistani militants (with hoods) belonging to the Lashkar-e-Taiba terrorist group to a police station in Thane, a suburb around 6 miles outside Bombay, India. Interrogation techniques vary widely in different nations, and torture of suspects is not uncommon. The torture, or even the threat of torture of suspects in the United States will automatically render any confession obtained inadmissible as evidence. *Corbis.*

Evidence Confrontation

When police detectives confront a defendant who is in custody, with evidence of the crime that tends to show the defendant is responsible, the courts will probably rule that an interrogation was taking place because the action was designed to elicit a response.

This method used in interrogation is completely proper if the defendant has already waived his Miranda rights, or he is not in custody. Responses based on a defendant being confronted with evidence of guilt, will be ruled inadmissible at trial if they were obtained before the defendant was advised of his Miranda rights, or if he has asserted his right to remain silent.

Non-Interrogation Questions

Police officers may ask suspects questions that are not intended to elicit an incriminating response. For example, after a foot pursuit of a drug dealer, the police investigator observes the suspect swallow several pieces of crack cocaine. The investigator asks the suspect if he wants to go to the hospital to have his stomach pumped. The suspect responds, "Forget it. Let me die."

The question is an innocent one in that the investigator was looking out for the safety of the suspect. The answer, which implies he did swallow something dangerous, would be admissible at trial.

In another example, police may ask a suspect during a line-up to say or utter certain words to help in the identification process, even if he has already asserted his Miranda rights. Police officers may also ask a defendant who has evoked his Miranda rights, for consent to search his home, vehicle, or other items under his control.

During the booking process, a defendant may be asked questions to determine identification, medical needs, employment, next of kin and the like, which are allowed and admissible despite no Miranda warning being given. These questions are not intended to elicit an incriminating response. In fact, in many states it is a crime for someone to refuse to verbally identify himself or otherwise cooperate during the booking process.

A Miranda warning would only be necessary during the booking process, if an investigator or police officer intends to elicit incriminating statements from the defendant at that time.

In-Custody Interrogation Settings

Neglecting to advise a defendant of his rights before an interrogation in a formal, in-custody situation could have serious consequences on the outcome of any prosecution. If the police received a full, written confession from a defendant who was not advised of, nor waived his rights to remain silent and have an attorney present, that written confession will surely become inadmissible at trial. Furthermore, if the police find any evidence as a result of the outcome of the defendant's interrogation, that evidence is also in jeopardy of being inadmissible as well. Prosecutors would then be forced to rely on completely different evidence not connected to the confession of the defendant.

Remember that when the police solicit answers to questions that are not incriminating, no Miranda warning is necessary. In general, courts will find that an interview took place for only preliminary questioning.

For example, police officers arrest a man at his resident after executing a search warrant for drugs. The officers arrest the man, informing him that he is going to be charged with possession of marijuana with the intent to distribute. Upon hearing this, the man blurts out that the marijuana was for his and his girlfriend's personal use, and not for sale. This type of statement would be admissible in that it was not received as a direct result of a question, but merely from advising the suspect about the charges against him.

In another example, while at the police station, a defendant overhears two detectives discussing whether or not to arrest another man for the same crimes as the original defendant. The defendant who overhears the conversation exclaims, "Hey, it wasn't him; I'm the only one who did it." This statement would be admissible in that it also was not solicited by the investigators, but came as a result of overhearing the detectives discuss his matter.

ELEMENTS OF THE MIRANDA WARNING

Advising a suspect of his so-called Miranda rights is a serious matter. Forgetting to give a specific element, or wording a particular right in a way other than intended, can render the subsequent interrogation useless if the incriminating answers are inadmissible at trial.

There are only four elements that police are required to advise an in-custody defendant:

1. You have the right to remain silent.
2. Anything you say may be used against you in court.
3. You have the right to the presence of an attorney before and during any questioning.
4. If you cannot afford an attorney, one will be appointed for you, free of charge, before any questioning, if you want.

Nothing else is required. Police officers are not required to inform the defendant that he can stop answering questions at any time to seek an attorney.

Officers should read the advisement verbatim as opposed to reciting it from memory, no matter how many times they have done it in the past. If the rights are given to the suspect from memory, the defense may later ask the officer to recite the rights advisement while on the witness stand. If the officer becomes nervous and stutters, or stammers, or worse yet, forgets an element, this mistake will weigh heavily on the judge and jury.

Police officers are not required to remind the defendant about his right to remain silent or right to an attorney, once he has waived those rights and begins to incriminate himself. Doing so could seriously jeopardize the investigation at hand, and limit the government's ability to gather more evidence.

From a strategic standpoint, defendants should only be advised of their Miranda rights just prior to their interrogation. Long gaps of time between the defendant's arrest and interrogation could harm the investigation if the defendant has an inordinate amount of time to mull over his rights.

For example, a bank robbery occurs and thanks to good police work and superior patrol procedures, uniformed police officers arrest a suspect. The officers know that this suspect may be responsible for several other robberies that have occurred in the area over the past several months. Immediately upon arresting the suspect, the officer advises him of his Miranda rights. On the heels of the heat of the arrest, the defendant evokes his right to remain silent and requests an attorney. The officer then transports the defendant to the police station where a detective, who is assigned to the bank robbery task force investigating the series of robberies, meets the officer at the booking facility so that he and other knowledgeable investigators can conduct a methodical interrogation of the suspect. Since the defendant evoked his rights, the investigators no longer have the opportunity to question the suspect in an effort to clear the other bank robberies that are still under investigation.

Remember, a suspect need only be advised of his rights when he is in custody, and the police intend to ask him incriminating questions. The uniformed police officer may have hoped that the suspect would confess to the other bank robberies while in his custody, but in that the officer did not know any of the details about the other robberies, he could not have asked meaningful questions.

In this situation, when investigators are standing by to interview a suspect, uniform police officers should not advise the suspect of his Miranda rights because they do not intend to ask him any questions. Conducting an interrogation is part art and part science. Police officers not trained in conducting interrogations should leave that task to those investigators who are. Prematurely advising a suspect of his Miranda rights could easily jeopardize an interrogator's ability or solicit incriminating statements from the defendant; an opportunity that will probably not come along again.

Waiver of the Miranda Rights

Before police begin to ask incriminating questions of the defendant, they must ensure that they meet the requirement that the defendant's waiver was knowing, intelligent, and voluntary.

The waiver of rights can be either expressed or implied, but it must be voluntary, knowing, and intelligent. An expressed waiver stems from the defendant being asked if he understands his rights and is willing to waive them. If the defendant answers "yes" then he has expressly waived his rights. He only needs to be asked once, preferably in the presence of another police officer, followed by the defendant signing a written waiver, however this is not required.

The question concerning the defendant being willing to waive his Miranda rights does not have to be formal in nature. Instead of asking, "Having these rights in mind, are you now willing to answer my questions?" the police officer can merely ask, "Are you willing to tell me what happened?" Or, he can ask, "Do you want to tell me what happened?" The answer to any one of these types of questions will be considered a valid expressed waiver.

After being advised of his Miranda rights, a defendant may waive his rights with an implied waiver. This occurs when the defendant's actions indicate that he understands his rights and he intends to waive them. For example, even though the defendant did not specifically state he would waive his Miranda rights, after saying he understood them, willingly answers incriminating questions. His actions would be construed as an implied waiver of his Miranda rights.

Obviously an expressed waiver is better than an implied one. The burden is on the government to show that the waiver was made. An implied waiver may later have to be argued in court, or may become the basis for an appeal in the future, but it is still an acceptable means for a defendant to waive his Miranda rights, and has been upheld by numerous courts throughout the last three decades.

A valid waiver of Miranda rights, whether expressed or implied, must be voluntary, for example, given freely, not forced or coerced. The waiver must also be given knowing and intelligent, for example, the defendant was fully aware and understood what he or she was doing. If a police officer uses threats, promises, trickery, or deceitfulness in obtaining a waiver, it will be considered involuntary. Involuntary or coerced waivers are worse than not receiving a waiver, since any evidence developed as a result of the defendant's statements, even if voluntary, may also be suppressed at trial.

Once waived, the suspect can limit or qualify his invocation of his rights. For example, once a suspect waives his rights, he tells his interrogators, "I'll talk about the robbery, but I ain't sayin' nothin' about no murder." Such a statement qualifies his waiver, and any incriminating statements obtained about a murder would most probably be inadmissible.

Also, if the same suspect requested an attorney to talk about a murder investigation, but says he does not need or want an attorney for the original robbery investigation, the police are permitted to continue their line of questioning regarding the robbery, but must not explore the murder. This amounts to a limited invocation, and questioning him about the original crime may continue.

If after a suspect waives his rights and agrees to be questioned by the police, he refuses to demonstrate how an assault took place, or refuses to have a polygraph examination administered, he has not invoked his general right to remain silent.

If after a suspect is advised of his Miranda rights, and states that he may eventually want an attorney to be present, and will tell the officers when he thinks he needs one, the police may continue their interrogation. Incriminating statements may be taken because the language used by the suspect clearly indicates he did not want an attorney at that time.

Ambiguous Responses

Ambiguous invocations or responses must be clarified before the police can in good faith initiate or continue with their interrogation. The police are allowed to continue questioning in order to clear up any ambiguities, but if it is determined that the suspect has invoked his Miranda rights, the questioning must cease immediately. If a suspect should say something to the effect, "Maybe I should get myself a lawyer," during questioning, this sort of statement is generally thought to be ambiguous and does not amount to a clear and unambiguous invocation of his right to counsel, but neither is it a clear waiver.

Police officers who say or imply that it is better for the suspect to talk to them without an attorney being present, or that his lack of cooperation will be brought up later in court, are ensured of having the waiver invalidated by the court. Such statements will almost always be viewed as coercion and render any waiver invalid.

In addition to being voluntary, waivers must also be knowing and intelligent, for example, the suspect must fully understood the advisement and the nature of the rights being given up and the consequences of waiving them.

In determining whether a defendant voluntarily, knowing and intelligently waived his Miranda rights, the court will look at the totality of the circumstances surrounding the waiver to make this determination. Factors that will be considered include the suspect's background and involvement in the criminal justice arena. Has he been arrested before? Has he previously waived his Miranda rights? How old is he? Does he have any mental conditions that might make his understanding less than full?

A waiver can be knowing even though the police did not fully disclose the full nature of the offenses that the suspect is believed to have committed. If a valid waiver is made, the police are free to ask the suspect questions about different offenses that he may be involved in, even if he was not arrested for those specific offenses. In this situation, the police are not required to advise the suspect again of his Miranda rights for every separate crime under discussion.

Once a valid waiver has been obtained and the interrogation session has begun, under federal law, the police are under no obligation to inform the suspect that his attorney is attempting to meet with him. Some states, however, have statutes that attorneys must be allowed to see their clients.

The interrogation must stop immediately if the suspect invokes his right to counsel. The police are also forbidden to go back to the suspect later in an attempt to get him to change his mind about requesting an attorney.

If a police investigator encounters someone who insists that he knows his Miranda rights, the investigator is still compelled to go through the legal ritual and informed the defendant of these rights. It does not matter if the defendant understood his Miranda rights or not. The police are still obligated to advise the defendant regardless of his prior understanding of them. This way there will be no question that the police office made every attempt to ensure the defendant knew his Miranda rights, and he or she did everything in their power to make those rights clear to the defendant.[12]

The bottom line is that once an in-custody suspect requests an attorney, the police are obligated to provide him with one. All future contact must cease unless the suspect later initiates another contact or the suspect's lawyer is present during any subsequent interview or interrogation. Police officers are prohibited from initiating contact with the suspect so long as he remains in custody. A break in custody dissolves the prior invocation to request an attorney and remain silent. Once released from custody, the police may initiate contact with the suspect again.

Trickery and Deceit

Police interrogators are allowed to use forms of trickery and deceit as part of their interrogation bag of tricks to lawfully induce defendants to confess. The use of trickery became a Constitutional issue in *Frazier* v. *Cupp*.[13] Police arrested Cupp and his partner for a 1965 murder. Upon questioning Cupp, his interrogators told him that his partner had confessed to the murder, when he had not. Believing that his partner had implicated him in the crime, Cupp confessed in writing, and the written confession was used at his trial.

The U.S. Supreme Court ruled that the use of verbal trickery was acceptable and did not violate any rights afforded to the defendant. In another case, the Florida Court of Appeal ruled that the use of trickery must be kept at the verbal level. For example, in *State* v. *Cayward*,[14] police investigators produced a fabricated DNA report and showed it to the defendant. The investigators told the defendant that a laboratory report concluded that his DNA was found in the sperm found in the victim. The Justices said that they wanted to ensure that fabricated police reports were not mingled with genuine documents in order to ensure the integrity of the review process.

In Cayward, the District Court of Appeals stated: "We think . . . that both the suspect's and the public's expectations concerning the built-in adversariness of police interrogations do not encompass the notion that the police will knowingly fabricate tangible documentation or physical evidence against an individual . . . [T]he manufacturing of false documents by police officials offends our traditional notions of due process. . . . [M]anufactured documents have the potential of indefinite life and the facial appearance of authenticity."

Courts have generally ruled that the use of police interrogation tactics that would "shock the conscious of the community" during an interrogation session will not be allowed. A police investigator posing as a priest to hear the defendant's confession, or posing as an attorney to hear what the defendant had to say, are examples of types of forbidden trickery.

In general, the police use of deception is an acceptable interrogation technique that will not render the suspect's statements inadmissible.

For example, during a burglary investigation, the police have identified a suspect and begin to question him after he waives his Miranda rights. During the interrogation, one of the investigators asks the suspect how his finger-prints got on to the windowsill where the point of entry into the residence was made. The suspect responds, "Well, I guess you got me." He then gives a full confession to committing the burglary, and only later learns that no finger-prints were found at the crime scene. This technique would not render the suspect's statements inadmissible.

In another example, police interrogators tell a robbery suspect that his "partner" not only confessed, but also said he was the one who shot the shopowner. The suspect denies shooting anyone, and implicates his partner in the crime as the triggerman. Even though the other suspect made no such admission or confession, this deception technique should not create any legal exclusion in most states.

One potential problem using the technique of deception is jury nullification. Lying to the suspect may make jurors wonder if the police investigator is now lying about not coercing the suspect into confessing. The courts, how-ever, will weigh the totality of circumstances during the interrogation when deciding admissibility.

Suspect's Physical Condition

Before beginning any police interrogation, the interrogators must evaluate the suspect's physical condition, including his level of sophistication and mental capacity.

The fact that the suspect is intoxicated, is injured, is an unsophisticated juvenile, has a low IQ, or has an inferior education, should not in and of themselves, render any statement or confession inadmissible. However, a combination of these factors, as well as external factors, such as time of day, lack of sleep, etc. may sway a judge to make any statements made inadmissible. If any of these conditions are coupled with police misconduct, the statements of the suspect will most certainly be suppressed.

For example, a police interrogator obtains a Miranda warning waiver from a suspect who is obviously intoxicated. The man readily confesses to assaulting another man at a bar, and signs a written statement to that effect. The fact that the man gave the statement voluntarily will usually make it admissible in court. However, if the police refused to allow the man to go to the men's room during the two-hour interrogation period, until he signed the confession, the entire statement is in jeopardy of being inadmissible due to police misconduct.

Even if the suspect did not request to visit the men's room during the interrogation, the investigators should ask an obviously intoxicated individual frequently if he wants to. After sobering up and obtaining an attorney, he may later allege the police would not allow him to go to the men's room. This allegation, coupled with the interrogator's admitting the man was intoxicated, may convince a judge that possible police misconduct took place.

In almost every case in which the court finds that police misconduct took place, the interrogators run the risk of having any suspect's statements inadmissible.

SUMMARY

A *confession* is an expressed and complete acknowledgement of guilt as to the commission of a crime, whereas an *admission* is something less then a confession, but implies guilt. For example, a suspect being questioned admits to being at the crime scene during the event, but denies participation.

When a confession is obtained, the question will always arise as to whether or not the confession was obtained voluntarily without any threats, promises, or coercion being used by the police.

The roots of the test of voluntariness developed in common law in the eighteenth century, as the courts of England and then the United States recognized that coerced confessions are inherently untrustworthy.

In determining the voluntariness of any confession, the court will consider the totality of the circumstances in which it was obtained. The trial judge will evaluate if the defendant was deprived of any due process of law, such as the right not to be compelled to incriminate himself, and the physical and mental condition of the suspect. These factors do not themselves render any confession inadmissible, but may make the confession involuntary.

Generally, confessions are deemed admissible if they were obtained freely without the use or threat of violence, and the defendant was not promised a reward or other benefit, such as a reduced sentence, in return for confessing.

Landmark U.S. Supreme Court decisions in the 1960s created what is now commonly referred to as the Miranda rights warning. This warning, written by the Justices, is now given to any defendant who is in custody, and before any incriminating questions are asked during an interrogation. The key is that the defendant must be in custody. Mere suspects who are not in custody do not need to be given a Miranda rights warning, and doing so may hinder police investigations. The Miranda rights warning must include, at a minimum:

- The defendant has a right to remain silent
- anything said will be used against them in court
- the defendant has the right to talk to an attorney before any questioning; and
- if the defendant cannot afford an attorney, one will be appointed before any questioning.

Police are not obligated to elaborate any further, and if the arresting officer has no intention of questioning the defendant, there is no reason to advise the defendant of these rights. The police are compelled to advise the defendant of these rights only when an in custody interrogation is about to take place. If after being advised of his rights, the defendant elects to retain an attorney, no incriminating questioning can take place until the defendant has had the opportunity to consult with his counsel.

The defendant must not be ambiguous. He must definitely decide whether or not to consult an attorney. An ambiguous answer to the question of whether or not the defendant wants to consult with an attorney is not an invocation of his rights, but neither is it a clear waiver.

The use of trickery by the police in an attempt to elicit a confession or admission is authorized only if they do not resort to creating deceptive documents.

NOTES

1. See, *e.g.*, *King* v. *Rudd*, 1 Leach 115, 117–118, 122–123, 168 Eng. Rep. 160, 161, 164 (K. B. 1783) (Lord Mansfield, C. J.) (stating that the English courts excluded confessions obtained by threats and promises).
2. 378 U.S. 478 (1964).
3. 384 U.S. 436 (1966).
4. 98 Ariz. 18, 401 P.2d 721.
5. Ibid, Section III.
6. Ibid.

7. Ibid.
8. Ibid.
9. 446 U.S. 291 (1980).
10. 467 U.S. 649 (1984).
11. 479 U.S. 157 (1986).
12. *U.S.* v. *Patane*, No. 02-1183. Certiorari to the United States Court of Appeals for the Tenth Circuit. Argued December 9, 2003–Decided June 28, 2004.
13. 394 U.S. 731 (1969).
14. 552 So. 2d 971, 974 (Fla. App. 1989).

12

Lay and Police Witnesses

The testimony of witnesses, both police and lay, is the primary means used to introduce evidence at trial. A prosecutor or defense attorney's witness list might include victims, police officers, experts who possess knowledge in specialized fields, and possibly the defendant himself. Some witnesses may have personally seen the event in question, while others may provide circumstantial evidence that ties the defendant to the crime. An accomplice to the crime may be a key prosecution witness who testifies in return for favorable consideration in his own legal dilemma.

A witness may not testify to a matter unless evidence is introduced that is sufficient to support a finding that he or she has personal knowledge of the matter. Evidence to prove personal knowledge may, but need not, consist of the witness's own testimony.[1]

Either side may call witnesses. Many are impartial, but some may have a personal interest in the outcome of the case. Lay eyewitnesses are often sincere, but often unreliable. They are not trained observers, and sometimes their personal prejudices obscure what they actually saw. Others may become traumatized by what they have just seen and do not want to be reminded of it later when questioned by police officers. Laypersons, like police officers, are not infallible. Witnesses, who saw a robber wearing a "red shirt" as he fled the bank, may be surprised to later learn that the suspect actually wore an orange shirt instead. Not everyone can accurately identify every make and model of automobiles sold in the United States. A "small, compact Japanese car" may very well turn out to be a mid-sized Chevrolet.

Witnesses, be they lay or police, are generally called in a logical order to set out a story for the jury, so that it makes sense.

COMPETENCY

Before testifying, every witness is required to declare that he or she will testify truthfully, by oath or affirmation administered in a form calculated to awaken the witness's conscience and impress the witness's mind with the duty to do so.[2] Every person is competent to be a witness, except as otherwise provided in the rules of evidence. Competency deals with the witness's understanding that he has an obligation to tell the truth, and that he possesses personal knowledge related to the matter. After being sworn, the witness will be subjected to direct examination by one of the attorneys, followed by cross-examination by the other attorney if warranted.

CREDIBILITY

Jurors determine if a witness is credible or not. No matter what category the witness falls under, lay, police, informant, or expert, the jury will judge their credibility.

The witness's ability to communicate clearly, recall facts, and body language are factored into the witness's credibility. The jury will often discount even a witness possessing the most damning or exculpatory information if they do not appear credible. Attorneys will interview their witnesses ahead of time to determine for themselves the credibility the witness will display, and in many cases not use a particular witness if they give the impression they are either not telling the truth, or the testimony they are offering seems incredible. Attorneys do not want to be surprised by what their witness says. They carefully go over their questions with witnesses, to ascertain the exact contact of their testimony before they are called to the stand to testify.

Attorneys are not allowed to knowingly call witnesses they believe will commit *perjury*. Perjury is the intentional lying by a sworn witness on a relevant matter to the case at hand. Making a mistake about one's observations is one thing, but knowing lying about what they were told or observed is quite another.

Some witnesses, by their status, are perceived as incredible until proven otherwise. Jailhouse snitches, government informants, accomplices, or other persons who has something to gain by the defendant being convicted, all fall within this category.

For example, a jury may totally discount the testimony of an informant, because he has a history of child molestation. His criminal past may overcome any eyewitness testimony he may have to offer, even if it is totally unrelated to his criminal past.

IMPEACHMENT

If the prosecution or defense possesses derogatory information about a witness who has already testified, usually in support of the other's case, they have the option of attacking the credibility of the witness in an effort to impeach their testimony, including the attorney calling the witness.[3] This is because attorneys often cannot be selective in choosing their witnesses. The credibility of a witness may be attacked or supported by evidence in the form of opinion or reputation, but subject to these limitations:

1. the evidence may refer only to character for truthfulness or untruthfulness, and
2. evidence of truthful character is admissible only after the character of the witness for truthfulness has been attacked by opinion or reputation evidence or otherwise.[4]

A witness's criminal history will often weigh heavily on the jury's determination of credibility. Some states limit this examination to felony crimes involving honesty. In federal cases, if the criminal history of the witness includes a felony conviction, the evidence of the conviction shall be admitted if the court determines that the probative value of admitting this evidence outweighs its prejudicial effect to the accused.[5]

PRIOR INCONSISTENT STATEMENTS

Using prior inconsistent statements made by a witness that are relevant or material to the issues at hand, is a proven way to impeach them. Attorneys will cross-examine witnesses on their ability to accurately recollect what transpired, their sincerity, any biases or motives that may exist, and the witness's relationship to the defendant in an attempt to come to the truth. Juries usually carefully evaluate the answers to these probing questions to determine the witness's credibility.

For example, police respond to a sports bar where an aggravated assault has just occurred, and arrest the assailant. An officer locates a potential witness and interviews him about what he saw. The witness claims ignorance, telling the officer that he did not see the assault, and has no idea what led up to the incident.

Later at trial, the defense calls the witness who initially claimed ignorance, and he testifies that the defendant was acting in self-defense after being assaulted by the victim.

In this situation, the prosecutor will call the officer who originally interviewed the witness, and his testimony that the defense witness claimed ignorance can be used to impeach his testimony. This is why it is important for officers to always interview witnesses, whether or not they may be hostile to the efforts of the police. The results of the interviews must always be well documented in police reports, to give the prosecutor all the available information there is about potential witnesses that may be faced during trial.

LAY WITNESSES

Police officers, crime scene investigators, criminalists, and other criminal justice professionals spend a good portion of their careers preparing for and actually testifying as witnesses in court. It is a necessary part of the job. They are the professionals who juries expect to be impartial, honest, and free of prejudice.

Citizen lay witnesses are compelled to testify when served a subpoena to appear in court and the defendant, as their right under the Sixth and Fourteenth Amendments to the U.S. Constitution, can confront them during cross-examination. When served with a subpoena *duces tecum*, a witness must bring with them specified documents, records, or business records to court. Witnesses residing outside a court's jurisdiction, such as in another state, are still compelled to appear. Under the federal system, flight to avoid testifying is a felony offense.[6] Both the prosecutor and defense attorney have power of subpoena. Failure to appear in court after receiving a subpoena will subject the witness to punishment for contempt of court. Witnesses who appear, but refuse to answer questions or be sworn before testimony are also subject to punishment for contempt of court.

Lay witnesses come from all walks of life. Few have any experience in testifying, and none probably ever anticipated being a witness to a crime that would require their appearance in a court of law. Most are apprehensive about testifying, and some lose income from being away from work. Others have childcare problems to resolve or have to change their vacation dates in order to appear in court. Most become disillusioned by a system that seems to rarely begin on time, goes on longer than anticipated, and may require them to sit in a waiting room for hours, only to be told to come back the next day.

These witnesses are an important part of the criminal justice system and need to be treated with dignity and respect. Prosecutors will do whatever they can to accommodate lay witnesses, however many sudden, unexpected problems arise that make their continued cooperation difficult at times.

FIGURE 12.1   A woman sits in the witness stand in a courtroom being questioned by a lawyer. *Getty Images.*

None of these witnesses are trained observers who can recall with absolute certainty what they saw or heard. They are only expected to be truthful in their testimony. Some witnesses may have physical limitations that hinder their ability to see distant object clearly, or have a hearing impairment that prevents them from understanding entirely what has been said. The only requirements for a lay witness to testify is that they are competent and have relevant information to the trial at hand.

Some witnesses in high profile cases may express a desire to testify for the notoriety or to feel important. They voice disappointment if the information they have to offer to the prosecutor or defense is discounted as irrelevant. Such is the case when a witness's observations are proven false by means of physical evidence or other witnesses to the event, but he or she insists that what they saw is correct. For example, an elderly woman hears about the disappearance of a young pregnant woman who lives a few blocks away. The woman is later found dead, the victim of a homicide. The witness insists she saw the murder victim walking her dog in the neighborhood on the day of the murder, despite a confession by the killer that he had murdered the woman the day before. These witnesses are well-meaning, but the expectation of being a star witness sometimes shapes their perceptions.

CHILD WITNESSES

Children are sometimes called to testify when they become a witness or victim to a crime. Although there is no minimum age for a child to testify, they must demonstrate they have the ability to communicate, recall what he or she knows, and realize the difference between right and wrong.

Testifying as an adult can be an unpleasant experience, and this especially holds true for children. Being in an unfamiliar room, away from their parents and support groups, and subjected to unpleasant questions by serious minded adults can cause trauma for child witnesses, especially when the child is the victim of the crime being heard in court. The courtroom experience can only be an extension of the child's unpleasant experiences when the police initially interviewed him or her.

To counter the trauma child witnesses may face, over half of the states have instituted the use of either videotaped testimony, or closed circuit television, to shield the child-victim from the defendant.

In a 1990 Supreme Court decision, *Maryland* v. *Craig*,[7] the court upheld the use of closed-circuit television during the testimony of child abuse victims, ruling that a defendant's face-to-face confrontation with the child is not necessary.

Under the federal system, as a direct result of *Craig*, Congress passed legislation allowing the court to order the testimony of a child-victim by closed-circuit television if it finds the child will experience emotional trauma or cannot otherwise do so because of the presence or conduct of the defendant.[8]

Fortunately, police investigators have developed ways to interview child-victims to uncover the specific acts of sexual deviates. The use of an anatomically correct doll helps in this regard. Only specially trained investigators should engage in interviewing sexually exploited child-victims in order to ensure the child is forthcoming and not withholding information because of fear or intimidation.

POLICE WITNESSES

Juries generally view police officers and investigators as biased against the defendant. They realize it was the efforts of the police that brought the defendant to trial, and the officers and investigators testifying in court have a professional stake in the matter.

Police witnesses are considered credible until proven otherwise. Many defense attorneys have attempted to attack police witnesses by implying the defendant was arrested only to achieve "big promotions and big headlines." Putting the emphasis on the way the police conducted their investigation rather than on the evidence they collected, is one way in which defense attorneys attempt to destroy an investigator's assumed credibility with the jury. Investigators should not drop their professional demeanor when confronted by hostile defense attorneys. Giving the appearance of being annoyed or otherwise uncomfortable with the line of questioning, will surely make an impact on the jury.

Reality Check!

Although the majority of jurors hold the police in high regard, some jurors may have hidden bias against the police. They, or their family members, may have recently had an unpleasant experience with the police, or recently received a traffic ticket that resulted in a car insurance rate hike. Others who have never had any interaction with police officers may view them as unprofessional, uneducated, or thrill seekers who were primarily attracted to the job to exercise authority over others. Most police-citizen encounters are unpleasant, sometimes under the worst of circumstances. The memories of these negative encounters can stay with jurors when they have to decide whether or not the testifying police officers are being honest, truthful, and have performed their duties honorably.

Any biases a juror may have against the police may be overcome by testifying in a professional manner. Professionalism is part of the entire package the police witnesses project to the jury, not just the testimony itself.

1. **Be prepared**. Review all investigative reports for important details and dates of the incident. Sometimes a year or more could pass before the matter finally goes to trial. Memories fade, and police witnesses should be thoroughly familiar with what they wrote in their reports of investigation, and the circumstances leading to the defendant's arrest. Fortunately, police witnesses are allowed to refer to their notes and reports to refresh them memories while on the stand.

2. **Professional appearance**. Dress appropriately for court. Male police witnesses should either dress in a long-sleeve white shirt, dark, conservative suit and tie, with hard shoes, or wear their uniforms. This is not the time or place to make a fashion statement by wearing bold colors, inappropriate footwear, or excess jewelry. Ties should never be loosened, and always wear the suit coat while on the stand. Women officers should wear a business suit or skirt. Flashy colors and flowing dresses, as well as tight or low-cut blouses, are not appropriate for the courtroom. Too much make-up also gives false impressions to the jurors.

3. **Be well groomed**. A neat haircut and trimmed mustache is a reflection on the personal grooming habits of the male police witness. Someone who has unkempt, windblown hair, or is unshaven, speaks volumes to the jury. If the male police witness is in the process of growing a beard, he should shave and start to grow it again after his testimony in an important case has concluded. Otherwise, a trimmed beard is perfectly acceptable. Fingernails should be clean and trimmed. Male police witnesses who have since been transferred to a surveillance team or perform undercover drug investigations should be as neat as possible. Being assigned to a drug unit is no excuse for wearing a tee shirt, blue jeans, and tennis shoes to court. The jury will not understand. In extreme cases, the prosecutor may lead off with a question to the investigator concerning his appearance, to satisfy the jury that the witness looks unsavory because he has to look that way as part of his duties.

4. **To be on time is to be late**. Police witnesses should always strive to arrive in court at least 15 minutes prior to the start of the proceedings. Even when the police witness knows from his or her own personal experience that the court never seems to start on time, he or she should still arrive early so as to be available for the prosecutor for any final questions. Arriving late will throw the order of witnesses off, and could be construed as contemptuous behavior by the judge. Judges are inclined to forgive a lay witness who has never been in court before. Its almost unforgivable for the police witness to be late. The only acceptable excuse might be the officer was busy arresting someone breaking into the judge's car in the parking lot.

5. **Avoid distracting behavior**. Chewing gum, sucking on hard candy, using breath spray in the presence of the jury, slurping a soda or coffee and especially talking on a cell phone can cause an indelible negative impression. Police witnesses must ensure that their cell phones, and radios are turned off before entering the courtroom.

6. **Avoid police vernacular**. Using terms only another police officer understands while testifying will confuse and isolate the jury. Police witnesses should avoid all acronyms unless they are commonly known and understood.

7. **Discretely communicate with the prosecutor**. Writing a short note to the prosecutor is much more preferred to than talking or whispering to him or her during the proceedings.

8. **Show respect**. Police witnesses should always stand when the judge or jury enters and leave the courtroom. They should

always address the prosecutor and defense attorney as Sir or Ma'am. That salutation should not be reserved exclusively for the prosecutor.

9. **Be conscious of body language**. Police witnesses should keep their hands on their thighs while testifying to avoid unconscious body language that might be misinterpreted by the jury. Talking while constantly gesturing or shrugging the shoulders might give the wrong impression to the jury. Glaring at the defense attorney while he attacks your credibility or investigative technique is unacceptable. Displaying annoyance with repetitive questions from the defense should also be avoided.

10. **Look at the jury**. After being asked a question, the police witness should shift slightly in his or her chair and answer the question while looking at different jurors in the eye. Not ever looking at the jury could give the impression that the witness is unsure of himself, or has something to hide.

Following these simple, commonsense rules will avoid embarrassment and enhance his or her performance as a police witness. It will also save them personal embarrassment that could take years to overcome.

DEFENDANT WITNESSES

Although it is a rarity, defendants will sometimes testify in their own defense. The ultimate decision lays with the defendant, although most defense attorneys will caution their clients not to do so. Once the decision is made, the defendant is subject to a vigorous cross-examination by the prosecutor, who will surely ask probing questions that may solicit an unintended response. Even though defendants are never compelled to testify in their own defense, jurors might wonder why he did not take the stand to either deny the charges against him or provide an adequate explanation for his conduct.

If a defendant elects to testify, his attorney will most likely prepare him with anticipated questions by the prosecutor. The attorney may also ask another attorney to play the role of the prosecutor in a moot court setting to give him some experience in cross-examination. The defense attorney will criticize him on his demeanor, body language, and method of answering questions in an effort to discourage him from testifying, if appropriate.

The defense attorney will ask his client questions in court that will present him to the jury in the best light possible. However, the cross-examination that will follow will be as probing and extensive as any other witness, and in many cases more so.

CHARACTER WITNESSES

Character witnesses may be called to testify about the defendant's reputation within the community. The same applies to the character of other witnesses called in the trial in an effort to either bolster or impeach their previous testimony. The character witness is allowed to testify about what he either knows or has heard about the individual's reputation, but in most states, not the witness's personal knowledge or opinion. The source of this knowledge may be asked in either direct or cross-examination. In all cases, the information the witness has must be recent and timely.

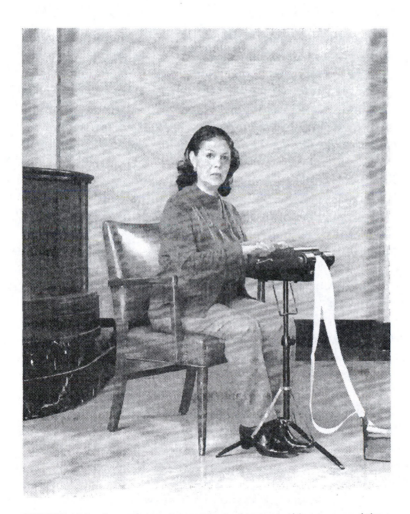

FIGURE 12.2   A court reporter uses a stenotype machine to record the testimony of witnesses, statements made by judges, and oral arguments of attorneys during criminal trials. Tape recorders, cameras, and other recording devices are not allowed in federal court, but are often used in many state courtrooms. *Getty Images.*

A technique to rebut the witness's truthfulness is to question his honesty and integrity during cross-examination. Evidence of the witnesses's good reputation may be introduced to counter this if he has been impeached.

A prosecutor may not produce witnesses who can testify about the defendant's bad character or reputation for the purpose of establishing his guilt. This evidence may be relevant, but it is now allowed since it might create prejudice towards the defendant.

In self-defense cases, the prosecution may produce witnesses that have knowledge of the defendant's reputation for violence to counter this claim.

INFORMANT WITNESSES

Government authorities have used informants to gather intelligence for thousands of years. Modern-day police departments and federal investigative agencies rely heavily on these individuals to provide intelligence that otherwise would not be available; provide specific information about the responsible parties of committed crimes; infiltrate criminal organizations; and introduce undercover agents to individual and organized criminals.

The overwhelming reason why someone becomes an informant is to receive a lesser sentence for a crime that he has committed. These informants are recruited after their arrest for a crime they are involved in, and the possibility of receiving a reduced sentence is a powerful motivator. Often, as a condition of his full cooperation, the informant must agree to testify at trial for the prosecution against accomplices and coconspirators.

Another motivational factor includes payment for information and assistance that the informant provides during an ongoing criminal investigation. These are professional informants who are paid for expenses and results. Most of these informants realize they will have to testify against the criminals that they have informed on, in order to justify his fee.

Other motivators include revenge, repentance, elimination of the criminal competition, altruism, and egotism.

Revenge is a powerful motivator. A woman whose husband has beaten her may extract revenge by informing the police her husband is a drug dealer and where his stash of drugs is hidden.

Although often given as a reason for becoming an informant, few informants are actually remorseful for past crimes as to why they are now informants. Usually there is a hidden motivational factor that police investigators must explore.

Drug informants have been known to provide information to the police in an effort to eliminate their competition in drug sales. Often, when the police suspect such a motive, they will target the informant with the suspects he has provided them with, after they are arrested.

Some informants are actually good citizens who by virtue of their professional positions, provide information to the police. This category of informant includes airline ticket counter persons, as well as employees of express delivery services. If these persons come across contraband or suspicious persons during the normal course of business, they will notify the police as part of their civic duty. These persons, however, understandably do not want to testify in a criminal trial if possible.

Still other informants provide information to the police who are known as "wannabes." These informants always wanted to be involved in police work, but for whatever reason, did not qualify to become police officers. Working with the police as an informant tends to satisfy their life-long desire to be police officers.

Many people have become informants to satisfy their ego. They want to play an important role in an otherwise uneventful life. The thought of infiltrating a criminal organization gives them a charge that is hard to replicate in legitimate business. Others become informants to receive praise from their police handlers for a job well done. Others want to play the role of a fictional spy who saves the world. There are probably as many motivators as there are people, and the police must recognize what is motivating their particular informant to provide them with information. If the police misjudge an informant's true motivation, it will cause tremendous control problems. Few informants completely comply with the instructions of their police handlers, and none should be totally trusted.

Juries view informants as being inherently unreliable and untruthful. Everyone has experienced a schoolmate "tattling" on them or someone else, and this type of person has always been considered untrustworthy by our society. The fact that their true intentions toward the defendant were to facilitate the defendant being arrested, may cause a juror to show sympathy towards the accused.

The vast majority of informants used by police have criminal backgrounds. This information is usually available to the defense and it will be used to impeach the credibility of the informant. This negative information also factors into a juror's decision as to whether to believe the informant's testimony or not, even if substantial evidence corroborating his information has been admitted at trial. An informant, who has a criminal background as a child molester, peeping tom, murderer, or rapist, creates tremendous credibility problems for prosecutors. Often credibility issues cannot be overcome. Most prosecutors who use an informant-witness with such a background, initiate their questioning by bringing out all of his past bad acts in an effort to "steal the thunder" from the defense. Once all known criminal history is revealed to the jury, the prosecutor will move on with the informant's testimony about the case in hand.

Defense attorneys have been known to hire private investigators to delve into the backgrounds of informants who will testify at trial. Any negative information will be used to impeach the informant. If the informant denies being involved in a specific indiscretion, and the defense can prove he was to the satisfaction of the jury, the informant's credibility will be entirely destroyed, and it could jeopardize the prosecutor's case. The jury will conclude that if the informant lied about his background, they will be sure that he lied about what the defendant did. For example, an informant has just testified that he purchased drugs from the defendant while working for the police. During cross-examination, the defense attorney asks the informant if he is required by a divorce settlement to provide alimony and child support payments to his ex-wife. After receiving an affirmative answer, the defense attorney asks the informant if he has ever failed to pay child support for his son. The informant denies missing any payments. Later the ex-wife testifies that she has not received child support payments from her ex-husband for over a year, and produces papers filed by her attorney to the divorce court documenting the informant's lack of payments. She also has certified copies of transcripts of the informant's testimony during another hearing that he did not make child support payments because he was fired from his job. This information, even though it has absolutely nothing to do with the criminal trial, will surely destroy the informant's credibility and most likely derail the prosecution against the defendant.

Despite the best efforts of the police and prosecutor, the informant in any criminal matter might be compelled to testify. Informants need to know that every effort will be made to shield them from the necessity to appear in court. However, it can never be guaranteed that they will not have to testify.

If an informant is required to testify, his police handlers and the prosecutor should ensure he is as prepared as any police officer would be, and that his conduct and appearance is similar to that of an officer testifying.

Informants are a necessary element of police investigations. However, there are inherent problems associated with their use. Police officers, investigators, and prosecutors need to be cognizant of these problems to avoid unexpected and embarrassing situations during trial.

JAILHOUSE WITNESSES

Jailhouse witnesses, a.k.a. jailhouse snitches, are almost always motivated to provide information in return for a reduction in sentence or the granting of privileges he may not otherwise be entitled to. Revenge against another inmate is a close second in motivators.

Juries will inevitably view these convicted criminals as unreliable, and many of them believe these witnesses are providing information simply to benefit themselves at the expense of the defendants. These are the most unreliable informants police will ever encounter, and their truthfulness should always be questioned. There have been many occasions when a jailhouse witness claims another inmate told him about a murder or other crime he committed, only to be discredited later.

These witnesses will be escorted to court by prison authorities and most likely will be in prison garb when they testify. The image of a serving convict will make an impression on the jury unlike any other witness that they encounter.

A *Los Angeles Times*[9] newspaper article illustrates the inherit unreliability and lack of credibility jailhouse witnesses have:

"In yet another challenge to the credibility of ex-Los Angeles Police Officer Rafael Perez, LAPD officials have belatedly turned over the statement

FIGURE 12.3 Ex-Los Angeles Police Detective Rafael Antonio Perez, 32, admitted to stealing at least 8 pounds of cocaine from police seizures as part of the Rampart Division corruption investigation. He later turned into a jailhouse witness and testified against fellow LAPD officers for a reduction in his sentence. *Corbis.*

of a jailhouse informant who told authorities that Perez once boasted of having the power to wreak havoc on the lives of those who crossed him, according to documents reviewed by *The Times*."

"If someone pisses me off, I'll throw their name into a hat and they'll get investigated – innocent or not," Perez allegedly told his cellmate as another prisoner listened in.

The allegation comes from Hank Rodriguez, another jailed ex-L.A. officer, according to the confidential documents that are the object of a court order forbidding their release. Rodriguez claims that he spent time in the cell next to Perez's after he was jailed on a parole violation stemming from a DUI conviction. Documents also show that Rodriguez was fired from the LAPD in 1974 after being accused of forgery.

Rodriguez alleged to Rampart task force investigators in March that, in the presence of fellow inmates, Perez adopted "a gang member type of attitude." According to the informant, he periodically broke into rap tunes and boasted of having a book and movie deal.

Winston Kevin McKesson, Perez's attorney, said his client has never met Rodriguez.

"This is pure folly," McKesson said. "Just more people coming out of the woodwork." He noted that there are several officers Perez does not like whom he has not implicated in the scandal.

It is not known whether authorities have confirmed that Rodriguez was in a cell next to Perez's. Nor is it known whether they have located or interviewed the cellmate to whom Rodriguez alleges Perez boasted of having the power to make problems for those who made him angry.

In general, information from jailhouse informants is viewed with skepticism. Often such informants trade fabricated information to win some benefit in their own cases, or to ingratiate themselves with authorities. In the late 1980s, the California Legislature passed a law requiring that jurors be warned to view informants' testimony with suspicion.

Perez, the central figure in the ongoing LAPD corruption scandal, has agreed to cooperate with authorities in exchange for a lighter prison sentence for stealing cocaine. He has implicated dozens of officers in crimes and misconduct. To date, nearly 100 convictions have been overturned largely as a result of his information.

While police officials contend that they have corroborated 70%–80% of Perez's allegations, his credibility has come under sharp attack from defense attorneys representing LAPD officers he has accused of crimes."

If necessary, police will offer the jailhouse witness the opportunity to be administered a polygraph examination to verify the truthfulness of his claims. Although the polygraph results cannot be admitted in trial, it serves to satisfy the police that the witness is probably telling the truth about his claims.

EXCLUSION OF WITNESSES IN THE COURTROOM

Under the Federal Rules of Evidence, at the request of one of the attorneys, the court shall order witnesses to be excluded so that they cannot hear the testimony of other witnesses, and it may make the order of its own motion. This rule does not authorize exclusion of:

1. a party who is a natural person
2. an officer or employee of a party, which is not a natural person designated as its representative by its attorney
3. a person whose presence is shown by a party to be essential to the presentation of the party's cause, or
4. a person authorized by statute to be present[10]

The primary police investigator or federal case agent who is the most knowledgeable about the details of the investigation leading to the defendant's arrest, may remain in the courtroom during the entire proceedings to sit at the prosecutor's table to assist in the government case. He or she most likely had a significant hand in the development of informants, locating of witnesses, and seizing of evidence. He or she is an important part of the prosecution team and assists in the pretrial preparation of the case. They will remain at the prosecutor's table throughout all phases of the trial.

They are readily available to round up witnesses to ensure their presence in the courtroom, and make last-minute phone calls and research matters as the trial progresses.

These investigators have a tremendous opportunity to witness all phases of the trial process, and can interact with the jury upon completion of the trial to ask their opinions about which witnesses were effective, and those that were not.

SUMMARY

The testimony of witnesses, both lay and police, is the primary means used to introduce evidence at trial. Police officers routinely testify as part of their duties.

Before any witness is allowed to testify, they must be determined to be both competent and credible. Competency deals with the witness's understanding that he has an obligation to tell the truth, and that he possesses personal knowledge related to the matter. The witness's ability to communicate clearly, recall facts, and body language are factored into the witness's credibility.

If the prosecution or defense possesses derogatory information about a witness who has already testified, usually in support of the other's case, they have the option of attacking the credibility of the witness in an effort to impeach their testimony, including the attorney calling the witness. Using prior inconsistent statements made by a witness that are relevant or material to the issues at hand, is a proven way to impeach them.

Citizen lay witnesses are compelled to testify when served a subpoena to appear in court and the defendant, as their right under the Sixth and Fourteenth Amendments to the U.S. Constitution, can confront them during cross-examination. Witnesses residing outside a court's jurisdiction, such as in another state, are still compelled to appear. Under the federal system, flight to avoid testifying is a felony offense.

Children are sometimes called to testify when they become a witness or victim of a crime. Although there is no minimum age for a child to testify, they must demonstrate they have the ability to communicate, recall what he or she knows, and realize the difference between right and wrong. In a 1990 Supreme Court decision, the court upheld the use of closed-circuit television during the testimony of child abuse victims, ruling that a defendant's face-to-face confrontation with the child is not necessary.

Many defense attorneys during cross-examination put emphasis on the way the police conducted their investigation rather than the evidence that they collected, as one way to destroy the investigator's assumed credibility with the jury. Investigators should not drop their professional demeanor when confronted by hostile defense attorneys. Giving the appearance of being annoyed or otherwise uncomfortable with the line of questioning will surely make an impact on the jury.

Although it is a rarity, defendants will sometimes testify in their own defense. The ultimate decision lays with the defendant, although most defense attorneys will caution their clients not to do so. Once the decision is made, the defendant is subject to a vigorous cross-examination by the prosecutor, who will surely ask probing questions that may solicit an unintended response.

Character witnesses may be called to testify about the defendant's reputation within the community. The same applies to the character of other witnesses called in the trial in an effort to either bolster or impeach their previous testimony.

The vast majority of informants used by police have criminal backgrounds. This information is usually available to the defense and will be used to impeach the credibility of the informant if he is called as a witness. This negative information also factors into a juror's decision, as to whether to believe the informant's testimony or not, even if substantial evidence corroborating his information has been admitted at trial. Informants who have criminal backgrounds as a child molester, peeping tom, murderer, or rapist create tremendous credibility problems for prosecutors. Often credibility issues cannot be overcome.

Jailhouse witnesses, a.k.a. jail house snitches, are almost always motivated to provide information in return for a reduction in sentence or the granting of privileges he may not otherwise be entitled to. Revenge against another inmate is a close second in motivators.

Juries will inevitably view these convicted criminals as unreliable, and many of them believe these witnesses are providing information simply to benefit themselves at the expense of the defendants.

In most cases, witnesses are excluded from the courtroom during the testimony of other witnesses. This is done to prevent them from hearing the previous testimony. Exceptions to this rule most often include the lead investigator in the case, who assists the prosecutor in preparation of the case, and is most knowledgeable of the evidence and facts.

NOTES

1. Rule 602, Federal Rules of Evidence.
2. Rule 603, Federal Rules of Evidence.
3. Rule 607, Federal Rules of Evidence.
4. Rule 608(a), Federal Rules of Evidence.
5. Rule 609(a), Federal Rules of Evidence.
6. Title 18, United States Code, Section 1073.
7. 497 U.S. 836, 845–847 (1990).
8. Title 18 United States Code Section 3509.
9. *Los Angeles Times,* by Matt Lait and Scott Glover, September 26, 2000.
10. Rule 615, Federal Rules of Evidence.

13

Expert Witnesses

Publications and Internet websites targeting attorneys are replete with advertisements and information detailing the specific areas of expertise and academic preparation for a growing number of *expert witnesses*. These experts are responsible for swaying numerous juries to see another side to a particular evidentiary issue that arises in court. They are most often employed by defense attorneys to attack a prosecutor's case on a point at issue.

Many expert witnesses, who are not government employees, are paid handsomely for their expertise. Many earn as much as $1500 a day or more when performing their services. These experts take on a variety of litigation around the country and often have extensive experience in testifying. Trial lawyers often use them to introduce scientific evidence in areas such as ballistics, handwriting analysis, and medicine. They are also often used to render opinions and draw conclusions about police investigate techniques, use of deadly force, and arrest procedures.

The fact that private expert witnesses are paid for their services sometimes leaves them vulnerable to attack by the opposite council. Jurors routinely accept testimony as being credible from experts that are full-time government employees. They recognize that these experts routinely work for the prosecution. Private experts, however, can sometimes have their credibility damaged when it is revealed in sworn testimony that they are being paid for their expertise by the defense, and/or they have never testified for the prosecution during their entire tenure a private expert witness. They are also vulnerable if their examination does not appear to be thorough, such as not ever having visited the crime scene or location of a particular event, or not having read all the police reports offered during discovery.

When an attorney hires an expert witness to render an opinion or conclusion, there is a risk involved. For example, a personal injury attorney hires an expert witness to review discovery material in a police-involved shooting incident, in which the person shot by the police is severely injured. The attorney requests the expert to review all documents, photographs, videotapes, news video, and police reports concerning the incident, in order to render an opinion as to whether the shooting was justified by standard police practice or policy. In some cases, if the expert provides the attorney with a written evaluation of the situation in which he or she feels the shooting was justified, and the report is subject to discovery, the opposing council can use the same expert to testify in the matter in support of the police. Some attorneys will ask the expert to not put his finding in writing until it is clear that the expert will be siding with the plaintiff.

Reality Check!

In many cases, both civil and criminal, attorneys will seek the advise of more than one expert, if necessary, until they find one that will provide expert testimony that will strengthen their case. Experts in the same field will possess various levels of expertise, and not all will come to the same conclusions given the identical facts to review. When two experts possess the same stellar qualifications, yet come to opposite opinions, their manner of testifying will sometimes sway a jury to their side of the argument.

Prosecutors also use expert witnesses when they feel the jury needs to hear from a disinterested party that the investigative procedures, methods of operation, or scientific examination conducted by the police were sound. For example, in a criminal court hearing, the prosecutor representing a police department might retain an outside expert in police tactics to explain that arresting officers used proper procedures and an appropriate amount of force to arrest a suspect who alleges that the police brutalized him. The defense might counter with their own expert, who will dispute the opinions of the government's expert. In any event, the jury has the option of either embracing or disregarding the opinions given by any expert.

Considering the vast number of expert witnesses available, it is possible to find someone qualified in a particular field that will disagree with other experts with the same credentials. For example, during the O. J. Simpson murder trial in 1995, DNA evidence collected by the Los Angeles Police

Department was vigorously attacked by a variety of credible expert witnesses, which helped in the jury reaching a decision to acquit.

EXPERT WITNESS CATEGORIES

Expert witnesses can be found in every imaginable field of endeavor, including the medical field, traffic accident reconstruction, and police procedures, to name just a few. They provide a useful service for both sides in civil and criminal trials, to help a jury to determine the truth about certain facts. The following are typical fields in which expert witnesses can be found.

Alcohol and Drug Intoxication

Many courts allow experienced police officers who are specially trained to testify as to alcohol impairment of the defendant's judgment, coordination, and reflexes based on the manner in which a vehicle was driven, coupled with personal observations and various field sobriety tests. These officers also offer opinions based on test results of Breathalyzer- or Intoxilyzer-type instruments.

Some of these officers are also qualified to render opinions concerning drug intoxication and are court-recognized experts in recognizing if someone is under the influence of drugs. These experts detect and measure pupil size, perform a Horizontal Gaze Nystagmus test that detects the defendant's inability to maintain visual fixation as they are turned to one side, certain odors, and other things indicative of drug intoxication.

Audio Tape Examinations

Authenticity examinations are conducted to determine whether audio recordings are original, continuous, unaltered, and consistent with the operation of the recording device used to make the recording.

These experts can also enhance the intelligibility of recording by selectively reducing interfering noise.

Bite Mark Analysis

These experts usually have academic credentials in the fields of forensic dentistry, and special training in the American Board of Forensic Odontology (ABFO) scale and other pathologist skills, such as saliva extraction. Their examination can determine if a defendant's teeth bit another person.

Blood Grouping and Spatter Analysis

Many courts allow competent analysts, other than serologists, to testify about the results of field tests on blood samples. Spatter analysis is more theoretical than scientific. Based largely on the laws of physics, a trail of blood droppings can often reveal its origin and the height and angle of impact on a floor or wall.

Criminal Profiling

Courts are increasing allowing experienced drug investigators to testify as experts in identifying actions indicative of drug dealers, as well as the meaning of certain drug terms, especially those captured during wiretap investigations.

DNA (Deoxyribonucleic Acid) Testing

Experts analyze DNA in body fluids, stains, and other biological tissues recovered from evidence. The results of DNA analysis of questioned biological samples are often compared with the results of DNA analysis of known samples, to associate victims and suspects with each other or with the crime scene.

Eyewitness Identification

Experts with backgrounds as social psychologists may enhance or impeach a witness's ability to perceive or recollect facts. They are usually retained when a witness viewing a line-up or show-up has identified a defendant.

Fingerprint Identification

One of the oldest technologies in American law enforcement, fingerprint identification, has proven to be a very effective tool in identifying suspects and convicting defendants. After a crime scene investigator collects latent fingerprints, they are examined by a specially-trained expert for comparison to known suspects. This expert testifies to the comparison of the recovered latent fingerprint and the defendant, and how he reached his conclusion.

Firearms Examiners

These firearms and ballistic experts can determine if a recovered bullet, and in many cases, fragments of a bullet, was fired from a specific firearm. These examiners reach their conclusions by studying breech face and/or firing-pin markings and striation patterns. They also will testify about gunpowder residue and can give opinions as to distance from the victim when the weapon was fired. Firearm examiners are also capable of examining spent cartridge cases to determine the exact or type of firearm it was fired from. Some firearms examiners also perform took mark analysis.

Forensic Anthropology

Forensic Anthropologists can determine if something is bone and, if so, whether it is human or animal in origin. Race, sex, approximate height and stature, and approximate age at death can be determined from human remains. Damage to bone, such as cuts, blunt-force trauma, and bullet holes may also be examined. Comparing X-rays of a known individual to skeletal remains can make personal identifications. Often these experts can reconstruct a facial appearance from skulls.

Forensic Biology

In addition to examinations of DNA, dried bloodstains, and other body fluids, some of these experts also compare botanical specimens. such as bark, wood, and plants.

Forensic Engineering

Forensic engineers are experts in the study of the causes of accidental and intentional structural failures. They are heavily involved in reconstructing accident scenes, and render opinions concerning responsibility or negligence.

Forensic Entomology

These experts deal with all aspects of insects and their relationship to criminal investigations. They often render opinions concerning the analysis of maggots as this related to determining the time of a person's death.

Forensic Odontology

Also known as forensic dentistry, these experts compare a corpse with known dental records, and even photographs of a victim's smile for identification purposes. Some of these experts can also perform bite mark analysis.

Forensic Pathology

These pathologists specialize in the investigation of sudden, violent, unexplained, or unnatural deaths.

Forensic Physical Science

Also known as criminalists, these experts are specially trained in crime scene examination, using their knowledge of chemistry, physics, and geology in identifying physical evidence.

Forensic Psychiatry

This is a psychiatrist who specializes in evaluating defendants for competency to stand trial, insanity issues, and sometimes deviate human behavior.

Hair and Fiber Analysis

These specialists in spectrography, the absorption of light by a substance, and chromotography, the chemical reactions of a substance, conduct examinations to render findings concerning hairs and fibers.

Hypnosis

These are experts who are used to refresh the memory of a victim for details of conversations and for the identification of suspects.

Microtrace Analysis

This is an expert in the field of the physical sciences and evidence collection, that is later subjected to microscopic examination.

Neutron Activation Analysis

These are experts who use a swabbing of nitric acid on the hands of a suspect to determine if he has recently fired a handgun.

Photography

Such experts expose and develop photographs at crime scenes, as well as render opinions pertaining to the authenticity of digital photographs.

Physical and Mental Condition

These experts render opinions regarding a defendant's mental state. They usually testify when there is an issue over the defendant's ability to formulate intent. Most are licensed psychiatrists. Psychologists have been limited in their areas of testimony by many courts.

Polygraphers

Also known as polygraph examiners, these specially trained experts measure the changes in involuntary body functions, when asked questions that are told to the examinee ahead of time. The results of polygraph examinations are inadmissible in American courts, expect with the consent of both the prosecutor and defense. The polygraph is most often used as an interrogation tool. Any admissions or confession given by the examinee is admissible in most cases.

Because of the wide range of polygraph training and standards that exists, courts have been reluctant to allow their findings at trial. The most respected polygraph school is operated by the Department of Defense, and trains all federal polygraph examiners for the U.S. government.

Questioned Document Examination

Although not all handwriting is identifiable to a specific person, the examination of handwriting characteristics can sometimes determine the origin or authenticity of questioned writing. Traits such as age, sex, personality, or intent cannot be determined from handwriting examinations.

Questioned document examiners rely on numerous exemplars and known writings of a suspect to render a conclusive opinion. Other experts focus on the analysis of ink, paper, and erasures. Many have the ability to restore charred documents.

Sketch Artists

Such experts base their sketches on the information provided to them by eyewitnesses. Sketches are drawn to give a visual description of a suspect as opposed to attempting to replicate his exact appearance.

Soil Sample Analysis

These experts usually have background and education in agricultural science, chemistry, geology, and a combination thereof. Their analysis is often used to determine the origin of soil as it pertains to the crime scene.

Speed Detection Devices

Many police officers are experts in the use of Radio Detection and Ranging (RADAR) and Visual Average Speed Computer and Recorder (VASCAR) devices. Both of these devices have been widely accepted in courts due to police departments demonstrating adequate training in their care and use. Other experts have successfully challenged these devices because of their lack of recent calibration.

Tool Mark Analysis

These are experts who have specialized knowledge in the manufacture of screwdrivers, hammers, pry bars and other tools used by burglars and other criminals. They render opinions about a particular tool making a specific mark or impression at a crime scene.

Toxicology

Chemists generally make up the bulk of these experts who make findings of drugs, poisons, and other toxins in human blood, other body fluids, and body tissue.

Traffic Accident Reconstruction

Many courts allow experts with significant experience in vehicular accident investigation to testify as to the approximate speed, stopping distance, point of impact, and other matters in an effort to determine primary and secondary collision factors.

Truth Serum Results

Also known as narcoanalysis, confessions given as a result of interrogations while the defendant was under the influence of truth serum is inadmissible. However, some courts allow the interpretations of statements by expert medical psychiatric witnesses if the substance used was a placebo.

Typewriter Comparison

Experts can occasionally identify questioned typewriting with the typewriter that produced it. This is most common when the typewriter is a typebar machine. The identification can sometimes be based on individual characteristics that develop during the manufacturing process and through use and abuse of the typewriter.

Experts often compare questioned typewriting with reference standards, to possibly determine the make and model of the typewriter.

Experts can sometimes read specific wording of questioned material on carbon film typewriter ribbons. Carbon film ribbons can sometimes be identified with questioned typewritten impressions. Fabric ribbons cannot be read.

Voice Comparisons

Spectrographic examinations experts compare an unknown recorded voice sample to a known verbatim voice exemplar produced on a similar transmission and recording device such as the telephone. Expert opinions regarding spectrographic voice comparisons are not conclusive. The results of voice comparisons are provided for investigative guidance only.

Expert witnesses are subject to cross-examination in the same way as other witnesses. He cannot, however, be cross-examined about the contrary findings contained in a scientific or professional journal, if the witness has not referred to it in his conclusions. Books and journals referred to by the expert witness can be admitted as evidence to either prove or contradict the opinion of the witness.

VOIR DIRE

Unlike laypersons who almost always are not allowed to testify about something they did not personally observe or hear, the rules of evidence allow a qualified expert witness to render opinions during their testimony, but they are limited to their particular area of expertise.

Before any expert testimony is admitted, the witness is sometimes subjected to a *voir dire* examination that will seek to bring out the expert's education, experience, background, publications, and formal training. If the judge deems that the witness possesses the qualifications that make him or her stand out from a layperson, and demonstrates that he is competent in the particular field of endeavor, the court will allow the witness to testify as an expert. Once the witness is deemed to be qualified, he or she can opine about observations that he or she has made.

Voir Dire, meaning "speak the truth," is the courtroom examination process, sometimes held outside the presence of the jury, in which a potential expert witness testifies about his qualifications to render an opinion about a particular fact at issue. Voir dire examinations are also used to establish the qualifications of an expert witness before he is allowed to offer direct testimony. After the direct examination by the attorney who wants the expert witness to testify, a cross-examination of the person's qualification is conducted in order to get the entire picture of the expert. The trial judge might also ask questions, and is the one who will ultimately determine if the person's testimony will be allowed. An "expert" with only a few years in a particular field might be found unqualified in one courtroom setting, but fully qualified in another. As a rule of thumb, an expert witness with an abundance of expertise, research, formal education in his field of endeavor, etc. is more likely to be found qualified than another person, who does not possess the breadth and experience level the court deems appropriate.

Most expert witnesses possess a combination of academic preparation and practical experience in their field.

FIGURE 13.1   A prosecutor questions a police forensic expert witness about DNA evidence at trial. *Getty Images.*

Reality Check!

The vast majority of professionals who make themselves available as expert witnesses for courtroom proceedings are credible, honest, and can be trusted to render an unbiased opinion based upon the information they have been provided. However, there are some so-called expert witnesses who lack the formal education, training, or experience in their field of endeavor to make opinions that could have a profound impact on a trial. Others may possess the appropriate credentials to render such opinions, but are biased for either the prosecution or the defense. Some of these "experts" have been known to embellish, or outright lie about their qualifications during voir dire examination in order to qualify as a court expert. These charla-tans often appear at the eleventh hour of trial and have the potential of completely derailing a prosecutor's case. Investigators should always do at least a cursory, if not a full background on these individuals in order to verify their work experience, for-mal education, and aca-demic credentials to ensure that they possess the particular expertise that they claim.

HIRED GUNS

There are a small number of expert witnesses who either are fully qualified, yet untruthful about their findings for the purpose of generating income, or who exaggerate about their qualifications for the purpose of being dubbed a court qualified expert witness.

For example, Drug Enforcement Administration special agents in Los Angeles had investigated a conspiracy whose members attempted to import 500 kilograms of cocaine into the United States from South America. All eight defendants were tried simultaneously, and most had "high-powered" criminal defense attorneys who attempted a variety of defense tactics while defending their clients.

Early in the government's case, one such attorney asked the Assistant U.S. Attorney (AUSA) if he could have an original recording of a particular telephone conversation between an informant and his client that was made during the investigation. The recording was significant, in that it captured the defendant talking, mostly in code, to the informant about his preparing the cocaine for delivery. This recording had been played for the jury. The defense attorney claimed his copy of the original tape that he had been given during discovery was hard to understand, and he wanted to compare it with the original. The AUSA agreed. The case agent heard the request, but offered no objection.[1]

Several weeks later, the government's case ended. The jury had heard weeks of damning evidence against all of the defendants. When the defense portion of the trial began, the DEA case agent was the first witness called by the defense attorney. The agent was only asked questions about his making the recording between the informant and the defendant, and truthfully stated that he had sole possession of the recording until the time of trial.

The second witness for the defense was a hired expert witness named Norman I. Perle.[2] Mr Perle needed a few minutes before he could testify, so he could assemble several cartloads of audio and other electronic equipment in the courtroom for demonstration purposes during his testimony. The AUSA and DEA case agent had no idea what Mr Perle was about to testify to, other than it had something to do with the tape recording in question.

Once set up, during his voir dire examination outside the presence of the jury, Mr Perle identified himself as an expert in audio and videotape authentication. He submitted his curriculum vitae that included an extensive listing of trials where he had previously testified. On the surface, based on Mr Perle's background, coupled with his professional demeanor and body language reflecting sincerity and thoughtfulness, he appeared to be a credible witness who possessed the training and experience necessary to render an expert opinion in such matters.

When the jury returned, Mr Perle explained in painful detail, the process in which he examined the original tape recording earlier furnished by the AUSA. He testified that part of his examination process included listening to the tape with a "critical ear," and then progressing to examining the tape electronically, with use of a computer and other equipment, as well as visually examining the tape for erasures, splices, and other tell-tale signs of tampering.

He explained that he had pulled out a portion of the tape from the cassette casing, and placed a hard-water solution on the side where the recording heads had pressed against it. Once dried, the solution revealed marks and scratches on the tape that Mr Perle said revealed that there had been numerous "stops and starts," and that this, along with other technical things, was indicative of edits and erasures. He placed the tape under a microscope and photographed the striations, and was given permission by the judge to post a series of photographs to the jury to view. He said there was also evidence of "micro-editing" and "sophisticated electronic splicing." He added that the techniques used in the splicing were so sophisticated, that they could only be done by someone who possessed expensive equipment, and implied the U.S. government possessed such equipment.

After over an hour of testimony in which the government, specifically the DEA case agent, appeared to be the one responsible for the doctoring of the tape recording, Mr Perle was asked to give his opinion as to whether or not the tape had been altered. Mr Perle testified, "It is beyond my opinion; it is in the real of scientific certainty that the tape has been altered."

The AUSA leaned over to the case agent at the prosecution table and said, "Don't show any emotion in front of the jury." He knew the agent was livid.

With that, the AUSA asked for a recess and to speak to the judge out of the presence of the jury. As the jury filed out of the courtroom, none would look at the case agent as they had in the past weeks of the trial. They were all convinced that the agent had altered the tape for the purpose of making the defendant appear guilty.

The AUSA said he needed time to prepare his cross-examination of Mr Perle, since it would require extensive preparation and needed to find a government expert to rebut Mr Perle's testimony. The judge gave the AUSA a week to prepare.

The case agent and co-case agent, ATF Special Agent Theresa Moreno-Fullerton, immediately began their search for a government expert to re-examine the tape. Although DEA had technical agents capable of such an examination, he opted to find someone outside of DEA in order to not give the appearance of a conflict of interest. The case agent succeeded in finding FBI Supervisory Special Agent Bruce Koenig,[3] who is a genuine magnetic tape expert in Washington, DC Mr Koenig directed that the original tape recordings, tape recorder, and all documents and examination findings of Mr Perle be express shipped to him. Five days later, the AUSA and case agent flew to Washington, DC and met with Mr Koenig and his staff over a weekend. Mr Koenig made himself and staff available to continue their examinations in light of the trial being already in progress.

During the conduct of the FBI's examination, the case agent and Special Agent Moreno-Fullerton examined Mr Perle's 50-page curriculum vitae and began to contact prosecutors in cases that he had testified in the past, as well as references he listed. In doing so, a different picture about Mr Perle's expertise began to emerge.

Mr Perle testified during direct voir dire examination that he was currently in negotiations with the Minnesota Mining and Manufacturing Company (3M), to become a consultant for the development of a tamper-free recording device that would be marketed to law enforcement agencies. When

FIGURE 13.2 U.S. forensic scientist and expert witness Henry Lee arrives to view evidence on the shooting of Taiwan president Chen Shui-bian in Taipei April 9, 2004. Lee, who has worked on high-profile cases such as the O. J. Simpson murder trial, arrived in Taipei after opposition parties raised suspicions that the March 19 shooting on the eve of Chen's re-election victory had been staged to win sympathy votes and demanded a probe by impartial foreign experts. *Corbis*

contacted, an executive at 3M said that it was Mr Perle who had contacted his company, and after he had sent a team of engineers to interview him about his theories of tamper-free recording, they concluded early on that he essentially did not know what he was talking about.

Mr Perle testified that he earned an Associate in Arts degree in criminal justice from a local community college. When the registrar of the college was contacted, he said that Mr Perle's official transcript reflected that he was never granted a degree and only possessed 35 semester hours of college education, almost an entire academic year less then he had claimed.

Mr Perle also testified that he helped train investigators for a California county sheriff's department. A check with the California Department of Motor Vehicles revealed that Mr Perle's driving record was flagged as "confidential" based on his claim of being a peace officer. When the Undersheriff of the department was contacted, he told the case agent that the previous sheriff of the county had appointed Mr Perle as a "special deputy," one who is called upon in times of an emergency or who can provide a special service on a voluntary basis. The Undersheriff said that the new sheriff had recalled all such positions, and that Mr Perle held no special status at the time he received confidential registration with DMV. The chief deputy speculated that Mr Perle used his special deputy badge to identify himself as a peace officer when he applied for confidential registration at DMV. The Undersheriff emphasized that Mr Perle was not, nor had he ever been, a sworn peace officer for his department, and that he was not entitled to such confidentiality.

The case agent contacted a Los Angeles County Deputy District Attorney who faced Mr Perle as a defense witness at a trial. According to the DDA, Mr Perle filed a declaration in his case stating his findings of an audiotape in question was "to a scientific certainty, rather than an opinion, that this recording has been tampered in that there is a section which shows that audio has been deliberately removed." As a result, the defense attorney filed a motion to dismiss the charges based on evidence tampering. When Mr Perle was confronted with the findings of the government experts, that it was impossible to erase a portion of this particular variety of tape, he retracted his declaration and said he had "made a mistake."

In Mr Perle's direct examination, he testified that he had spent an 11-month period as a student at a respected computer institute and became proficient in several complex computer languages. He also testified that he had a "degree" from the institution in "computer programming and systems analyses." When interviewed by the case agent, the director of the institution said that no such course of study existed at the time when Perle claimed to receive his degree, and that in checking his archives, revealed that he never graduated.

The case agent checked with an AUSA who handled a criminal matter in Ohio and learned that Mr Perle was withdrawn as a defense expert witness when, during voir dire examination, he failed to qualify as an expert witness.

According to the AUSA, the defense attorney wrote a letter to the legal publication that featured Mr Perle's ad, claiming it was false since he could not perform the services advertised. In this same case, Mr Perle had performed an electronic sweep of rooms occupied by defense attorneys and determined that their hotel room telephones had been tapped. This initiated an unwarranted FBI investigation into the matter that was later determined to be unfounded.

All of the prosecutor's contacted said that during their trials, Mr Perle's testimony was devastating to their case, and in some instances, he had succeeded in winning an acquittal for the defendant. All expressed their opinions that Mr Perle lacked any competence, and felt they had been blindsided by the impact of his testimony.

Based on a provided listing of cases Mr Perle furnished, the case agent contacted a detective for the Glendale, California police department. The detective said that not only was Mr Perle an alleged expert in tape authentication, but he also purported to have a "critical ear" that enable him to hear words on tape recordings no one else did. In a murder trial in Glendale, Mr Perle was given the opportunity to examine and listen to a tape recording of a confession made by a murder defendant, in which the defendant said, "I killed the man." Mr Perle testified that due to his experience and critical ear, he concluded that the defendant in actuality said, "I did not kill the man." The judge in the case dismissed Mr Perle's testimony as incredible, since it was obvious to any English-speaking listener what had been recorded, and instructed the jury to ignore Perle's testimony.

The case agent obtained copies of news footage of Mr Perle at his home "laboratory," as he examined a variety of audiotape and videotapes created during the investigation of John Delorean, a struggling automobile manufacturer. The government alleged that Delorean attempted to purchase 50 kilograms of cocaine from undercover FBI and DEA agents during a reverse-string operation, which he intended to sell and put the profits back into his fledgling company. The news videotapes depicted Mr Perle's laboratory resembling an electronics hobbyist's workshop. Mr Perle testified exclusively for the defense and opined that government tapes were fabricated, edited, and the like to make Delorean appear to be guilty. Delorean was eventually acquitted of all charges.

When Mr Koenig appeared as a rebuttal witness, he was also subjected to voir dire examination. Mr Koenig's graduate education in the field, coupled with experience of working on many high-profile cases left no doubt in the mind of the judge and jury that he was the foremost expert in the field of magnetic tape authentication in the world.

Mr Koenig explained the flaws in Mr Perle's methodology, and clearly communicated to the jury why his examination revealed that the tape recording question was in deed, authentic.

When the jury was polled after they had found the defendants guilty, they said that Mr Perle's initial testimony left them with no doubt that the government, and specifically the case agent, had tampered with the audiotape. They all agreed that they wanted to send a message to the government by acquitting not only the defendant who hired Mr Perle, but the others as well. They cited Mr Koenig's credentials and credibility as the reason they totally dismissed Mr Perle's findings. Several jurors said Mr Koenig's testimony re-established their faith in their government, and that they had been distressed at the idea of DEA fabricating evidence to win a conviction.

Despite the AUSA's efforts to seek an indictment for Mr Perle for perjury, he was overridden by his superiors who felt that he would claim he "thought" he possessed an Associate Degree, and other education as he claimed. The U.S. Attorney's Office knew that prosecuting Mr Perle would appear to be retaliatory in nature, and elected to move on instead. In the years following, the case agent was contacted by over a dozen prosecutors in the U.S. and Canada, who were facing Mr Perle in a criminal trial. All sought information about the federal case in Los Angeles to use to destroy his credibility.

Mr Perle was an exception to the rule for expert witnesses. Most are highly trained and well experienced in their chosen endeavor. Many Internet websites list expert witnesses in over 200 categories. Those involved in criminal litigation are usually retired law enforcement officials who possess an abundance of expertise and offer insights that most prosecutors and defense attorneys do not possess. Their opinions alone do not convict or acquit a defendant, but they can be very influential to a jury during both criminal and civil litigations. Their participation in both civil and criminal trials has become commonplace in the U.S. courts.

SUMMARY

Expert witnesses can be found in every imaginable field of endeavor, including the medical field, traffic accident reconstruction, and police procedures, to name just a few. There are literally hundreds of categories in which expert witnesses can be found. They provide a useful service for both sides in civil and criminal trials to help a jury determine the truth about certain facts. They are often retained in both civil and criminal trial matters.

Unlike laypersons, who almost always are not allowed to testify about something they did not personally observe or heard, a qualified expert witness may render opinions during their testimony. The rules of evidence allow qualified experts to assist the jury in understanding issues in complicated matters. Before the court will allow an expert witness to testify, he or she is sometimes subjected to voir dire examination. This testimony from the expert about his or her background, education, training and experience will be considered by the trial judge before granting the witness expert status. Upon being qualified as an expert, the witness may render opinions that will assist the jury in under-standing certain matters that come up in trial.

Although the vast majority of expert witnesses who make themselves available to testify for a fee are credible individuals, there are exceptions. Some expert witnesses either do not possess the amount of education, experience, and training they claim, and others who do possess the necessary qualifications to be an expert witness, will exaggerate or otherwise be untruthful about their findings in a particular matter in order to justify their fee.

Some experts have been known to exaggerate their qualifications and opinions in order to be retained by attorneys. These so-called experts can derail a prosecutor's case when fabricated evidence is offered by the defense. When an expert offers an opinion that is known to be incorrect, police investigators should immediately proceed in finding a credible witness who can counter these claims.

NOTES

1. The DEA Case Agent was the author.
2. Mr Perle is now deceased.
3. Mr Koenig has since retired from the FBI.

14

Hearsay Evidence

"Hearsay" is a statement, other than one made by the declarant while testifying at the trial or hearing, offered in evidence to prove the truth of the matter asserted.[1] These statements are made out of court and include expressions that are either verbal or written.

Hearsay evidence is testimony given by someone other than the person who made the original statement, and is excluded during trial with some notable exceptions. For example, if Officer Jones testifies that the victim of a residential burglary said she saw the defendant running away from her home on the day of the event, this statement would be excluded. The victim would have to personally testify about her observations.[2]

The reasons this type of testimony is not allowed is that the defense does not have the opportunity to cross-examine the declarant, or person who uttered the words, and the jury does not have the opportunity to observe and assess the credibility of the witness under oath. Furthermore, in this example, excluding hearsay eliminates the possibility that the officer misinterpreted what the victim said. Hearsay is essentially someone telling someone else's story. This second-hand information is objectionable because of its unreliability.

Conduct can also be considered a statement if the conduct in question is intended as a substitute for words, such as gesturing or pointing to identify a person or thing. The nodding of the head to signify agreement would also

255

apply as a gestured statement. Hearsay is limited to those statements that contain information, the truth of which is relevant to the case at hand. The need for hearsay evidence is often critical to a fair disposition of a case.

EXCEPTIONS TO THE HEARSAY RULE OF EVIDENCE

From a law enforcement standpoint, the most important exceptions to the hearsay rule of evidence are:

1. spontaneous outbursts
2. admissions
3. confessions
4. dying declarations
5. prior statements of witnesses
6. statements of coconspirators
7. former testimony
8. public and private records, including business records

Exceptions to the hearsay rule of evidence are allowed if circumstances warrant, and no other rule exists prohibiting it from being introduced as evidence. Exceptions are usually allowed when a witness is unable to be located, or cannot appear personally, such as in the case of his death. Other exceptions are made based upon the circumstances in which it was obtained, and when the probability of its truth is great.

Hearsay evidence is admitted when it meets established exceptions set forth in the rules of evidence. Law enforcement officers need to at least be familiar with these rules.

The following are not excluded by the hearsay rule, even though the declarant, or person who makes a statement, is available as a witness:

1. **Present sense impression**. A statement describing or explaining an event or condition made while the declarant was perceiving the event or condition, or immediately thereafter.
2. **Excited utterance**. A statement relating to a startling event or condition made while the declarant was under the stress of excitement caused by the event or condition.
3. **Then existing mental, emotional, or physical condition**. A statement of the declarant's then existing state of mind, emotion, sensation, or physical condition (such as intent, plan, motive, design, mental feeling, pain, and bodily health), but not including a statement of memory or belief to prove the fact remembered or believed unless it relates to the execution, revocation, identification, or terms of declarant's will.

4. **Statements for purposes of medical diagnosis or treatment.** Statements made for purposes of medical diagnosis or treatment and describing medical history, or past or present symptoms, pain, or sensations, or the inception or general character of the cause or external source thereof, insofar as reasonably pertinent to diagnosis or treatment.

5. **Recorded recollection.** A memorandum or record concerning a matter about which a witness once had knowledge but now has insufficient recollection to enable the witness to testify fully and accurately, shown to have been made or adopted by the witness when the matter was fresh in the witness' memory and to reflect that knowledge correctly. If admitted, the memorandum or record may be read into evidence but may not itself be received as an exhibit unless offered by an adverse party.

6. **Records of regularly conducted activity.** A memorandum, report, record, or data compilation, in any form, of acts, events, conditions, opinions, or diagnoses, made at or near the time by, or from information transmitted by, a person with knowledge, if kept in the course of a regularly conducted business activity, and if it was the regular practice of that business activity to make the memorandum, report, record, or data compilation, all as shown by the testimony of the custodian or other qualified witness, unless the source of information or the method or circumstances of preparation indicate lack of trustworthiness. The term "business," as used in this paragraph, includes business, institution, association, profession, occupation, and calling of every kind, whether or not conducted for profit.

7. **Absence of entry in records kept in accordance with the provisions of paragraph (6).** Evidence that a matter is not included in the memoranda reports, records, or data compilations, in any form, kept in accordance with the provisions of paragraph (6), to prove the non-occurrence or non-existence of the matter, if the matter was of a kind of which a memorandum, report, record, or data compilation was regularly made and preserved, unless the sources of information or other circumstances indicate lack of trustworthiness.

8. **Public records and reports.** Records, reports, statements, or data compilations, in any form, of public offices or agencies, setting forth:
   a. the activities of the office or agency,
   b. matters observed pursuant to duty imposed by law as to which matters there was a duty to report, excluding, however, in criminal cases matters observed by police officers and other law enforcement personnel, or

  c. in civil actions and proceedings and against the government in criminal cases, factual findings resulting from an investigation made pursuant to authority granted by law, unless the sources of information or other circumstances indicate lack of trustworthiness.

9. **Records of vital statistics**. Records or data compilations, in any form, of births, fetal deaths, deaths, or marriages, if the report thereof was made to a public office pursuant to requirements of law.

10. **Absence of public record or entry**. To prove the absence of a record, report, statement, or data compilation, in any form, or the non-occurrence or non-existence of a matter of which a record, report, statement, or data compilation, in any form, was regularly made and preserved by a public office or agency, evidence in the form of a certification in accordance with rule 902, or testimony, that diligent search failed to disclose the record, report, statement, or data compilation, or entry.

11. **Records of religious organizations**. Statements of births, marriages, divorces, deaths, legitimacy, ancestry, relationship by blood or marriage, or other similar facts of personal or family history, contained in a regularly kept record of a religious organization.

12. **Marriage, baptismal, and similar certificates**. Statements of fact contained in a certificate that the maker performed a marriage or other ceremony or administered a sacrament, made by a clergyman, public official, or other person authorized by the rules or practices of a religious organization or by law to perform the act certified, and purporting to have been issued at the time of the act or within a reasonable time thereafter.

13. **Family records**. Statements of fact concerning personal or family history contained in family Bibles, genealogies, charts, engravings on rings, inscriptions on family portraits, engravings on urns, crypts, or tombstones, or the like.

14. **Records of documents affecting an interest in property**. The record of a document purporting to establish or affect an interest in property, as proof of the content of the original recorded document and its execution and delivery by each person by whom it purports to have been executed, if the record is a record of a public office and an applicable statute authorizes the recording of documents of that kind in that office.

15. **Statements in documents affecting an interest in property**. A statement contained in a document purporting to establish or affect an interest in property if the matter stated was relevant to the

purpose of the document, unless dealings with the property since the document was made have been inconsistent with the truth of the statement or the purport of the document.

16. **Statements in ancient documents**. Statements in a document in existence 20 years or more the authenticity of which is established.

17. **Market reports, commercial publications**. Market quotations, tabulations, lists, directories, or other published compilations, generally used and relied upon by the public or by persons in particular occupations.

18. **Learned treatises**. To the extent called to the attention of an expert witness upon cross-examination or relied upon by the expert witness in direct examination, statements contained in published treatises, periodicals, or pamphlets on a subject of history, medicine, or other science or art, established as a reliable authority by the testimony or admission of the witness or by other expert testimony or by judicial notice. If admitted, the statements may be read into evidence but may not be received as exhibits.

19. **Reputation concerning personal or family history**. Reputation among members of a person's family by blood, adoption, or marriage, or among a person's associates, or in the community, concerning a person's birth, adoption, marriage, divorce, death, legitimacy, relationship by blood, adoption, or marriage, ancestry, or other similar fact of personal or family history.

20. **Reputation concerning boundaries or general history**. Reputation in a community, arising before the controversy, as to boundaries of or customs affecting lands in the community, and reputation as to events of general history important to the community or state or nation in which located.

21. **Reputation as to character**. Reputation of a person's character among associates or in the community.

22. **Judgment of previous conviction**. Evidence of a final judgment, entered after a trial or upon a plea of guilty (but not upon a plea of nolo contendere), adjudging a person guilty of a crime punishable by death or imprisonment in excess of one year, to prove any fact essential to sustain the judgment, but not including, when offered by the government in a criminal prosecution for purposes other than impeachment, judgments against persons other than the accused. The pendency of an appeal may be shown but does not affect admissibility.

23. **Judgments as proof of matters of personal, family or general history, or boundaries, essential to the judgment, if the same would be provable by evidence of reputation.**

24. **Other Exceptions**. This is sometimes called a "catch all" category that allow for other non-specific exemptions when circumstances warrant.[3]

The Federal Rules of Evidence also include six situations where exceptions are made when a declarant is unavailable to testify as a witness. The definition of unavailability include situations in which the declarant:

1. is exempted by ruling of the court on the ground of privilege from testifying, concerning the subject matter of the declarant's statement
2. persists in refusing to testify concerning the subject matter of the declarant's statement, despite an order of the court to do so
3. testifies to a lack of memory of the subject matter of the declarant's statement;
4. is unable to be present or to testify at the hearing because of death or then existing physical or mental illness or infirmity, or
5. is absent from the hearing and the proponent of a statement has been unable to procure the declarant's attendance (or in the case of a hearsay exception under subdivision (b)(2), (3), or (4), the declarant's attendance or testimony) by process or other reasonable means.

A declarant is not unavailable as a witness if exemption, refusal, claim of lack of memory, inability, or absence is due to the procurement or wrongdoing of the proponent of a statement, for the purpose of preventing the witness from attending or testifying.[4]

The following are not excluded by the hearsay rule, if the declarant is unavailable as a witness:

1. **Former testimony**. Testimony given as a witness at another hearing of the same or a different proceeding, or in a deposition taken in compliance with law in the course of the same or another proceeding, if the party against whom the testimony is now offered, or, in a civil action or proceeding, a predecessor in interest, had an opportunity and similar motive to develop the testimony by direct, cross, or redirect examination. Former testimony is considered hearsay, even though it was originally given under oath and subject to cross-examination, and the issues are the same. It is admissible hearsay when there is a retrial of a case and one of the witnesses who testified is not available to testify in the retrial. In criminal prosecutions, former testimony may be used when the witness is deceased, insane, out of the jurisdiction, or otherwise cannot be found. Many states allow the admissibility of former testimony that was given at a preliminary hearing where the witness is now out of the court's jurisdiction.

In this situation, the court reporter is called to the witness stand to read the testimony of the unavailable witness along with any cross-examination, re-direct, and recross-examination that may have taken place. The courts recognize that because of the stress for accuracy in transcribing courtroom testimony, there is a high probability that the record reflects the witness's testimony fully and accurately.

2. **Statement under belief of impending death**. In a prosecution for homicide or in a civil action or proceeding, a statement made by a declarant while believing that the declarant's death was imminent, concerning the cause or circumstances of what the declarant believed to be impending death.

3. **Statement against interest**. A statement which was at the time of its making so far contrary to the declarant's pecuniary or proprietary interest, or so far tended to subject the declarant to civil or criminal liability, or to render invalid a claim by the declarant against another, that a reasonable person in the declarant's position would not have made the statement unless believing it to be true. A statement tending to expose the declarant to criminal liability and offered to exculpate the accused is not admissible unless corroborating circumstances clearly indicate the trustworthiness of the statement.

4. **Statement of personal or family history**
   a. A statement concerning the declarant's own birth, adoption, marriage, divorce, legitimacy, relationship by blood, adoption, or marriage, ancestry, or other similar fact of personal or family history, even though declarant had no means of acquiring personal knowledge of the matter stated; or
   b. a statement concerning the foregoing matters, and death also, of another person, if the declarant was related to the other by blood, adoption, or marriage or was so intimately associated with the other's family as to be likely to have accurate information concerning the matter declared.

5. **Transferred to Rule 807**.

6. **Forfeiture by wrongdoing**. A statement offered against a party that has engaged or acquiesced in wrongdoing that was intended to, and did, procure the unavailability of the declarant as a witness.[5]

WRITTEN STATEMENTS

Many law enforcement agencies obtain written statements from victims and witnesses to crimes. Written statements taken within a short period after the event usually qualify for an exception to the hearsay rule of evidence when the witness verifies its contents. Stale written statements may not be allowed.

Fresh written statements are no substitute for personal testimony, but they serve as a means of preserving the original thoughts and observations of the interviewee.

Hostile Witnesses

It is crucial that police officers take written or oral statements from every witness, even if the witness may potentially be hostile to law enforcement efforts. Many witnesses perceive their testimony will hurt the defendant, and want to avoid contact with the police due to either not wanting to become involved in a police inquiry, or because they have a friendly relationship with the defendant. Many of these witnesses later become defense witnesses. Knowing what they might say before trial greatly helps prosecutors prepare their cases and can help them impeach such witnesses.

Reality Check!

Hostile witnesses should always be interviewed by police officers, even if they do not believe they will obtain any useful information in their case. These hostile witnesses are potential defense witnesses who can be impeached at trial. Even witnesses who claim they have no knowledge about an event under investigation should be interviewed, and his self-proclaimed ignorance should be documented in reports. If this type of witness later surfaces as a defense witness, he can possibly be impeached by the prosecutor later during trial.

Hostile witnesses can sometimes tie the suspect to a crime. They should always be encouraged to either tell the truth or remain with their statements. For example, police are investigating a burglary and have developed a suspect. Upon questioning the man, he says he was with a friend on the night in question, who can verify that they were somewhere else, making it impossible for him to have committed the burglary.

While the interrogation is still taking place, investigators locate the alibi witness who denies being with his friend, the suspect. If this alibi witness later changes his claim in support of the suspect, he can be impeached at trial for his prior inconsistent statements.

It is best for police officers and investigators to interview witnesses orally first, then reduce their statements in writing. Many people will talk more openly if their interviewer is not taking notes or has a tape recorder running. Once the witness has orally presented his thoughts, then a written statement should be taken.

Statements that have been reduced to writing should always be read to the witness for accuracy. A commitment from the witness that the statement is accurate should be received. The witness should also be allowed to read the statement before signing it. Even if the witness refuses to sign the statement, it should not pose an insurmountable problem for the prosecutor.

PRIOR STATEMENTS OF WITNESSES

A prior statement of a witness is hearsay if offered to prove that something happened. Prior statements of witnesses are used to impeach the witness by showing a self-contradiction that is inconsistent with his testimony. Under certain circumstances, prior statements can support the witness's credibility if the statement is consistent.

The witness's prior statement is admissible as proof of the matter asserted as substantive evidence, only when falling within one of the exceptions to the hearsay rule.

SPONTANEOUS OUTBURSTS

Oral statements uttered by suspects can often be damning. The trauma of an arrest sometimes produces incriminating statements that can be used against the defendant at trial. These statements are viewed as credible since the defendant did not have the opportunity to reflect on what to say to police officers before they were made. They are allowed as an exception to the hearsay rule of evidence.

For example, an armed robbery occurs at a local convenience store. The responding police officers obtain a description of the vehicle that the robber fled in from the female clerk. Another police officer spots the vehicle within 10 minutes and arrests the driver. Upon placing handcuffs on him, the man exclaims, "I should have shot the bitch." Can the arresting officer testify to what the man said at the time of his arrest?

Yes. Spontaneous outbursts have long been recognized as statements made under stress that have an inherent degree of truthfulness. These types of statements are not limited to those made by defendants. Witnesses's statements that narrate a particular upsetting event, observation, or are made in an attempt to explain an action, are also recognized as an exception to the hearsay rule of evidence.

A hostile witness who is a friend of a defendant may make a spontaneous outburst against the interests of the defendant. When informed by the police that his friend had been recently arrested for murder, the friend may say, "I can't believe he actually went ahead and did it." This statement implies the defendant had told the witness he intended to kill the victim. This statement could be used against the defendant at trial in the event that the friend recants or denies his statement after time to reflect on his relationship with the defendant and the damage such a statement may have.

Police officers need to recognize when spontaneous outbursts may occur in the heat of the moment, and should always document them in their reports.

HEARSAY WITHIN HEARSAY

Hearsay within hearsay is when a hearsay declaration contains another hearsay statement. Despite this, the hearsay within hearsay statement should be admissible if each part of the combined statements conforms to the hearsay exemption rules.

For example, a witness interviewed by the police said that his neighbor, John Smith, told him that he noticed that the bedroom lights of an unoccupied residence on their same street had been turned on for a few minutes in the night that the residence had been burglarized. If, for whatever reason the witness and John Smith are both unavailable to testify, the police investigator should be able to testify about what the witness had told him about John Smith's observation.

When a hearsay statement has been admitted in evidence, either the defense or prosecutor may attack the credibility of the declarant. Any evidence that would be admissible under the same conditions as if the declarant had testified as a witness may support the attack.

Evidence of a statement or conduct by the declarant at any time, inconsistent with the declarant's hearsay statement, is not subject to any requirement that the declarant may have been afforded an opportunity to deny or explain. If the party against whom a hearsay statement has been admitted calls the declarant as a witness, the party is entitled to examine the declarant on the statement as if under cross-examination.[6]

DYING DECLARATIONS

Dying declarations about who the responsible party is or the circumstances leading up to the declarant's death, can only be admitted if the deceased firmly held the belief that his or her death was imminent. There is a long held belief that a person who realizes that he or she is about to die has no reason to lie, and will tell the truth. This is the most important element of a dying declaration.

For example, police officers respond to a shooting in front of a tavern. Upon their arrival they contact the victim who has been shot several times. His injuries lead the officers to believe that the victim will die before an ambulance arrives to transport him to a hospital. One of the officers asks the victim who shot him. He responds by telling him the name of the person, and says that an argument over a sporting event led to the shooting. The man expires. Has the victim provided a dying declaration that can be introduced in court?

No. The police failed to inform the victim that his death appeared imminent, nor did the man state his belief he was about to die.

In another example, the police respond to a similar situation. However, this time the police inform the victim that his condition looks bad, and that he may not make it to the hospital in time to save his life. They ask the victim who shot him. The victim clearly tells the officers that he has been in situations like this before, and he has no intention of dying. He expresses his belief that he will be out of the hospital soon so he can "pay back" the shooter for what he did. He tells the police officers, "John Smith's gonna regret shooting me tonight." About that time, the victim expires from his wounds. Have all the elements of a dying declaration been met?

No. The victim expressed his opinion that he would like to see the day when he could bring revenge against John Smith. The fact he did not believe his death was immediate probably eliminates the use of such a statement as a dying declaration from being used. However, the knowledge that John Smith shot the victim is a monumental investigative lead the detectives can pursue in building a criminal case against Smith. Just because the dying declaration may not be used in trial does not restrict the detectives from gathering independent evidence against Smith.

In addition to a murder victim believing that his or her death is imminent, the prosecutor has to demonstrate that the victim had personal knowledge of who the culprit was. Speculation on the victim's part will not qualify as a dying declaration, but it will probably provide investigators with substantial leads.

STATEMENTS MADE BY CO-CONSPIRATORS

An agreement between two or more people to commit a crime constitutes a conspiracy. Reaching an agreement, in itself, is usually insufficient to commit the crime of conspiracy.[7] In most cases the prosecution must also prove a member of the conspiracy committed an **overt act** in furtherance of the conspiracy before the crime is consummated.[8] An overt act is anything done to further the goal of the conspiracy. Overt acts do not have to be criminal in nature.[9]

Because of the Pinkerton theory of vicarious liability,[10] the justices ruled that conspirators could be charged with substantive offenses committed by coconspirators throughout the life of the conspiracy, provided that they were in the conspiracy at the time the offense was committed. The offense must be committed in furtherance of the conspiracy, and was a foreseeable consequence of the conspiracy.

The Federal Rules of Evidence recognizes that a statement by a coconspirator, who is a party during the course and in furtherance of the conspiracy, is not hearsay.[11] This is a powerful tool for prosecutors to convict all the members of the criminal conspiracy and to dismantle their organization. Many conspirators offer to testify against other members of the conspiracy in return for consideration in their legal dilemma. Frequently these defendants are organizers, managers, or supervisors of others within the conspiracy, and they can provide the jury with damning testimony about the breadth and scope of the conspiracy.

FIGURE 14.1   The U.S. Supreme Court decided that hearsay is admissible at trial in conspiracy cases in *Pinkerton* v. *United States*, in 1946. *Corbis.*

Reality Check!

To the relief of many defense attorneys, police and prosecutors frequently overlook the crime of conspiracy when formulating criminal indictments. Conspiracies are hard to defend against, since the agreement is the essence of the crime. Police investigators should make the agreement the focus of their investigation when targeting organized criminal groups.

If a cooperating defendant in a conspiracy trial reneges on his agreement with the prosecutor to testify about coconspirators, any written statements he made concerning their involvement may be admissible in lieu of his testimony.

ADMISSIONS AND CONFESSIONS

Police investigators always strive to elicit admissions and confessions from suspects involved in a crime. A written, taped, or oral statement from a defendant who has waived his constitutional rights, per Miranda, is a powerful piece of evidence pointing to guilt.

An admission is a statement or conduct by a party to the action that is offered against him at trial. Admissions in criminal cases may be either expressed or implied and are merely acknowledgements of some facts that tend to prove or imply guilt.

An implied admission consists of conduct by a party to the action, introduced as circumstantial evidence to establish a consciousness of guilt. Implied admissions are not subject to the hearsay objection, and their admissibility is based upon relevancy. Examples of implied admissions include fleeing from a crime scene, attempted escape, attempted suicide, and attempts made to bribe witnesses or destroy evidence.

An example is when police investigators locate one of several suspects involved in the rape of a woman. He admits he was present while others committed the rape, but denies raping the woman himself. The fact he admitted to being present during the rape, coupled with the victim's testimony that he had raped her, may lead to his conviction. Such an admission is clearly hearsay, but is admitted into evidence as an exception to the hearsay rule of evidence. The rationale is that a person is not likely to make such a statement unless it is true.

A confession, on the other hand, is a complete acknowledgement of guilt as to the commission of a crime. In either instance, investigators should obtain written statements containing either. Even if the suspect refuses to sign the statement acknowledging it is his own, the statement should be taken.

According to the Federal Rules of Evidence, an admission is not hearsay when:

1. The statement is offered against a party and is the party's own statement, in either an individual or a representative capacity.
2. The statement of which the party has manifested an adoption or belief in its truth.
3. It is a statement by a person authorized by the party to make a statement concerning the subject.
4. It is a statement by the party's agent or servant concerning a matter within the scope of the agency or employment, made during the existence of the relationship.
5. It is a statement by a coconspirator of a party during the course and in furtherance of the conspiracy.[12]

Since admissions and confessions are against the penal interests of the person making the statement, they are generally considered to be reliable.

Criminals often brag about committing a crime to a friend or associate. If these people are located, a statement from them can be significant evidence at trial.

Miranda Warnings

Before interviewing anyone suspected of committing a crime, the police must advise them of their Miranda rights and obtain either an oral or written waiver. The interrogators should ascertain that the suspect understands English. If the suspect speaks Spanish or some other language, the police should have a fluent Spanish or other language speaker read the warning to the suspect.

Investigators should not merely hand a printed copy of the Miranda warning to the suspect, in any language, and assume he can read and fully comprehend what he is reading.

Voluntariness

After a suspect waives his rights and elects to be questioned by the police, the statements that follow must be voluntary. The suspect must voluntary waive his rights *and* voluntarily provide a statement before his statements will be admissible at trial.

During an interrogation, statements resulting from coercive police conduct, physical force, threats, or unlawful inducements are always going to be deemed involuntary and inadmissible for any purpose, since a violation of the "Due Process" clause of the Fourteenth Amendment occurred.

A defendant's statement will be deemed involuntary if the police used coercion or threats, either direct or implied. The mere mention of the defendant spending the rest of his life in prison, or being subject to the death penalty may be viewed as a threat or coercion. Stating that the police will seek immunity for the suspect can be construed as a promise of leniency.

Urging a suspect to clear his conscious by confessing would not meet the elements of coercion. Even promising the suspect that his cooperation will be made known to the prosecutor is an acceptable technique to gain his cooperation. Only false promises of leniency are viewed as inappropriate in most states. Investigators should always include in the closing of the written statement, or early on during a taped interrogation that they did not make any specific or implied promises to induce the suspect to give a statement.

During any interrogation, it is easy to cross the line into the arena of coercion. Investigators must discipline themselves to stay within the acceptable areas of police interrogation.

DECLARATIONS AGAINST PENAL INTERESTS

When a defendant makes statements that will possibly subject him to legal punishment, these statements are generally considered to be inherently trustworthy, and are usually admissible as an exception to the hearsay rule. The logic is that such statements would not have been made unless they were true. The same applies to statements made that tend to lessen the declarant's status in the community, or damages his reputation within his family.

Any declaration against one's self interest is usually admissible under an exception to the hearsay rule of evidence, when the declarant is unavailable to testify in court. However, every effort must be made by the prosecution or defense to present the declarant in court, where he can repeat his statements under oath before the jury.

PUBLIC AND PRIVATE RECORDS

An exception to the hearsay rule of evidence is usually made for public and private records, including business records, in criminal trials. To allow for the exception, business records must be made during the regular course of business, be created about the time of the event in question, the custodian or records testifies to the records authenticity, and sources of the records and the method used to prepare them tend to show trustworthiness.

Public records are also admissible under an exception to the hearsay rule of evidence, when they are offered as proof. Public records must have been made by a public employee acting within the scope of his employment and duty, created at or near the time in question and prepared by sources of information that are indicative of trustworthiness. Public records can include records of births and deaths, military service, driving records, and the like.

Law enforcement officers testifying are allowed to refresh their memories by reviewing reports, personal notes, photographs, or crime scene sketches, to aid in their testimony regarding the particulars of the crime.

Before any records of the event are reviewed, the officer must first receive the approval of the court and defense. The defense can demand to see the material being reviewed and may subject the officer to cross-examination.

BUSINESS RECORDS

Entries in business books or records may be offered in evidence if a party to the action made the entry. If someone other than a party made the entries, it may constitute a declaration against interest. If the person making the entry is available, it may be used to refresh his or her memory or recollection. In some circumstances, it may be necessary to resort to the business record exception to the hearsay rule. In general, business entries are admissible when someone with personal knowledge of the transaction made the entry during the regular course of business, or by one who has received his information from a regular report of a fellow employee who had personal knowledge. The entry has to have been made close to the time of the transaction.

If the percipient witness is unavailable, or if the business in question is so large as to make it extremely burdensome, a supervisor or custodian of records may authenticate the record by testifying as to its mode of preparation and the fact it was made in the regular course of business.

SUMMARY

"Hearsay" is a statement, other than one made by the declarant while testifying at the trial or hearing, offered in evidence to prove the truth of the matter asserted. Hearsay evidence is testimony given by someone other than the person who made the original statement. Hearsay evidence is excluded during trial with some notable exceptions.

Exceptions to the hearsay rule of evidence are allowed if circumstances warrant, and no other rule exists prohibiting it from being introduced as evidence. Exceptions are usually allowed when a witness is unable to be located, or cannot appear personally, such as in the case of his death. Other exceptions are made based upon the circumstances in which it was obtained, and when the probability of its truth is great.

Many law enforcement agencies take written statements from victims and witnesses to crimes. Written statements taken within a short period after the event usually qualify for an exception to the hearsay rule of evidence when the witness verifies its contents. Stale written statements may not be allowed.

Spontaneous statements uttered by suspects can often be damning. The trauma of an arrest sometimes produces incriminating statements that can be used against the defendant at trial. These statements are viewed as credible, since the defendant did not have the opportunity to reflect on what to say to police officers before they were made, and are an exception to the hearsay rule.

Hearsay within hearsay is when a hearsay declaration contains another hearsay statement. Despite this, the hearsay within hearsay statement should be admissible, if each part of the combined statements conforms to the hearsay exemption rules.

Dying declarations about who the responsible party is or the circumstances leading up to the declarant's death, can only be admitted if the deceased firmly held the belief that his or her death was imminent.

Another exception to the hearsay rule of evidence is statements made by coconspirators. If one member of a conspiracy elects to cooperate with the prosecution, he may testify against the others about their words, deeds, and actions.

Police investigators always strive to elicit admissions and confessions from suspects involved in a crime. A written, taped, or oral statement from a suspect who has voluntarily waived his constitutional rights, per Miranda, is a powerful piece of evidence pointing to guilt. An admission is when a suspect admits to having knowledge of material facts that do not amount to guilt. A confession is a complete acknowledgement of guilt.

Public and private records, including business records, can be introduced as evidence in court under certain circumstances. Custodians of these records must appear in court to attest to their authenticity and trustworthiness.

In general, business records are admissible when someone with personal knowledge of the transaction made the entry in a business record during the regular course of business, or by one who has received his information from a regular report of a fellow employee who had personal knowledge. The entry has to have been made close to the time of the transaction.

SUGGESTED READING

Lee, Gregory D. *Conspiracy Investigations: Terrorism, Drugs and Gangs*, Upper Saddle River, NJ; Pearson Education, Inc., 2005.

NOTES

1. Rule 801 (c), Federal Rules of Evidence.
2. California allows police officers to testify what victims told them during preliminary hearings, in order to preclude the necessity of the victim to presonally attend court. Readers should check the rules of evidence in their particular state to determine if this practice is allowed.
3. Rule 803, Federal Rules of Evidence.
4. Rule 804 (a), Federal Rules of Evidence.
5. Rule 804 (b), Federal Rules of Evidence.
6. Rule 806, Federal Rules of Evidence.
7. Gregory D. Lee, *Conspiracy Investigations: Terrorism, Drugs and Gangs* (Upper Saddle River, NJ; Pearson Education, Inc., 2005) p.3.
8. Ibid, p. 13.
9. Ibid, p. 13.
10. *Pinkerton v. United States*, 328 U.S. 640, 66 S. CT 1180, 90 L.Ed. 1489 (1946).
11. Rule 801 (d)(E), Federal Rules of Evidence.
12. Rule 801(d)(2), Federal Rules of Evidence.

15

Testimonial Privileges

Even though evidence may be relevant, and competent witnesses are prepared to testify concerning it, the evidence may be nonetheless excluded because of various Constitutional rules and public policies.

The law recognizes the sanctity of certain relationships and encourages freedom of communication between persons engaged in those relationships. Because free communication would be hampered if one of the parties is later required to divulge in court what was communicated, the law grants certain carefully limited privileges not to testify concerning confidential communications.

The vast majority of evidence in criminal trials is communicated to the jury through testimony. However, evidence that is completely relevant, material, and competent may still be excluded at trial, on the grounds that it is privileged. Certain interests and relationships are considered by law to be important enough to justify the exclusion of otherwise relevant evidence in order to protect those interests.

A witness will not be required to testify when a *testimonial privilege* is properly claimed. Most testimonial privileges are personal in nature, in that only the person protected can claim the privilege. Furthermore, the privilege is not automatically asserted. If the holder does not claim the privilege, then it is considered to have been waived. Only the holder of the privilege may later claim the trial judge erred if the court disallowed a claim of privilege.

Those interests and relationships that enjoy testimonial privilege include:

1. self-incrimination
2. immunity from prosecution
3. attorney–client
4. husband and wife
5. physician–patient and psychotherapist–patient
6. clergy–confessor
7. official information
8. confidential informant

Self-Incrimination

This testimonial privilege is based upon the Fifth Amendment to the U.S. Constitution, which provides that "no person ... shall be compelled in any criminal case to be a witness against himself." This privilege is twofold in that it protects the accused from testifying against himself and it also protects someone from being subject to criminal charges, as in the case where his testimony before Congress may result in his indictment.

The privilege not only extends to answers to questions that would in themselves support a conviction under a criminal statute, but likewise embraces those that would furnish a link in the chain of evidence that is needed to prosecute the claimant for a crime. However, the witness is not excused from answering only because he declared that in doing so he would incriminate himself. His say-so does not in itself establish the possibility of incrimination. The court decides whether the witness's refusal to testify is justified, and to require him to answer if it clearly appears to the court that he is mistaken.[1]

The witness may not assert the privilege in advance of questions that will be asked. In no event may an ordinary witness refuse to give sworn testimony.

Since the privilege against self-incrimination of a witness is a personal one, another person cannot claim it for him. An ordinary witness waives his privilege in any court proceeding when he or she fails to claim it.

An accused in a criminal trial cannot be compelled to testify, and his failure to do so may not be made the subject of adverse comment. He also cannot prescribe or impose limitations on his waiver of self-incrimination if he does not voluntary take the witness stand. When a defendant chooses to testify in his own defense, the Constitution does not require that he be permitted to selectively suppress other relevant facts that may be incriminating or inconsistent with his defense.

A defendant who elects to testify on his own behalf does not have the right to only tell the jury the facts that tend to favor him. He leaves himself open to cross-examination by the prosecutor. Most defendants do not testify on their own behalf, since their cross-examinations usually erases any good that their testimony provides.

Reality Check!

On those rare occasions when a defendant elects to testify in trial on his own behalf, a good defense counsel will usually rehearse the testimony beforehand. He will subject his client to questions that he anticipates will be asked by the prosecutor and evaluate his answers and body language before advising the defendant if he should risk testifying or not.

Immunity From Prosecution

In order to gain testimony that would not otherwise be obtained, federal and state legislative bodies have enacted legislation to grant immunity to certain witnesses. These statutes provide that if a witness claims Fifth Amendment protection, and the government still seeks his answers, the proper authorities can grant immunity and the person will then be required to testify. The theory is that if immunity is granted to such persons, then there is no longer any reason to claim the privilege. These statutes have been challenged on Constitutional grounds, however, if the statutes give complete immunity, the witness can be required to testify, thus eliminating any violation of any Constitutional provision.

Immunity is sometimes granted to key defendants involved in multi-defendant conspiracy trials in order to secure their testimony. These defendants are mostly in a position to divulge the criminal actions of the other defendants and to reveal the inner workings of the conspiracy. Immunity might also be given to one of two convenience store robbers to testify about the other defendant shooting the store clerk if no other witnesses are available. The granting of immunity is a decision that the prosecutor makes, not law enforcement.

There are limitations of the privilege. The privilege applies to specified *communication* only. It does not apply to the defendant appearing in a police line-up, submitting to a blood test to detect the presence of alcohol. Nor does it apply to obtaining a suspect's fingerprints, handwriting exemplars, modeling hats, other articles of clothing, or other actions not involving communication. It also does not apply to the obtaining of routine booking information at the time of the suspect's arrest, such as his full name, address, occupation, work place, next of kin, and the like.

Attorney-Client

In most states, the client of an attorney, whether or not he is a party to a criminal or civil action, has a privilege to refuse to disclose, and to prevent others from disclosing, a confidential communication between himself and his attorney during the course of the attorney-client relationship. A "client" is defined as any person who consults an attorney for the purpose of retaining him or securing legal advice from him in his professional capacity. It is based on the theory that a client should be encouraged to make a full disclosure to his attorney so that his attorney will be better able to represent him.

No actual employment has to result after the consultation, and the payment or agreement to pay a fee is not essential to claim the privilege. Even if the person consulted is not in fact an attorney, it has been held sufficient if the client had good faith and reasonable belief that he was such a person.

The subject matter of the privilege includes all oral communication made by a client to his attorney. If the client demonstrates an action, or reveals a scar or tattoo, or opens a drawer to reveal a weapon, these actions are privileged.

Most written communications between the attorney and client, including reports and documents prepared by the client for his attorney's use, are covered by the privilege. The privilege is limited to those communications that the client has expressly made confidential or those that he could reasonably, and in good faith, assume would be understood by the attorney to be so.

The known presence of a third party during these communications will not dilute their confidential nature if the persons are present to further the client's interests or are necessary to accomplish the purpose of consultant. These third parties include the attorney's secretary, law partners, and family members of the client.

Some states, such as California, take the position that the holder of the privilege may present testimony by eavesdroppers to confidential communications, but cannot prevent testimony by disinterred third parties who were knowingly present, or within hearing distance, at the time of the conversation. The privilege belongs solely to the client, and the client alone can waive it. The attorney is obligated to claim the privilege unless waived by the client. However, if it is waived, the attorney cannot refuse to testify. Attorneys may testify with the permission of the client.

The privilege is waived automatically if the client or his representative fails to object to testimony regarding the privileged communication when he has the opportunity to do so. Also, a voluntary disclosure of privileged information to a third party made by the client, or by this attorney with his consent, functions as a waiver, except where the disclosure is made by the attorney for the purpose of furthering the client's interest, or where the disclosure is itself privileged, as when the client tells his wife in confidence what he related to his attorney.

FIGURE 15.1   Attorney-client privilege includes all oral communication made by a client to his attorney. *Corbis.*

Confidential communications between an attorney and his client are privileged and most state laws cannot force either the client or the attorney to divulge those communications. There are many exceptions to this rule. For example, if the services of the lawyer were sought or obtained to enable or aid anyone to commit or plan to commit a crime or fraud, the communications are not protected.

Husband and Wife

A married person, including those persons married by common law, has the privilege not to take the stand to testify against his spouse in any criminal proceeding. Even if the spouse takes the stand, he or she may refuse to disclose a confidential communication and the defendant may prevent his spouse from doing so. The only exception in criminal proceedings is when one spouse is charged with a crime against the other, such as in domestic battery cases.

There are two husband and wife privileges that must be distinguished: the testimonial privilege and the confidential communications privilege.

The testimonial privilege relates to the question of whether one spouse can be compelled to testify for or against the other during the marriage. The confidential communications privilege deals with the question of whether one spouse may withhold testimony or prevent disclosure of confidential communications made to the other.

In early common law, a spouse was deemed to be an incompetent witness in any action to which the other spouse was a party. This privilege stems from efforts to protect the relationship of marriage. However, later a spouse was recognized as a competent witness, albeit subject to certain limitations. In most state evidence codes, the privilege to refuse to testify belongs solely to the witness spouse and not the defendant. The logic behind this is because the witness spouse is in a better position to evaluate the probable affect his or her testimony will have on the marital relationship.

The privilege to refuse to testify against a spouse may be claimed only if there is a valid marriage in existence at the time that the testimony is sought. The privilege terminates upon divorce or annulment. If the marriage is dissolved, either of the former spouses may testify freely and, in fact, may even be compelled to testify for or against each other without the other's consent.

The basic rule concerning husband and wife confidential communications privilege is that a spouse, whether or not a party to the action, has a privilege both during and after the marriage to refuse to disclose and to prevent another from disclosing a confidential communication between the two, while they were married. This privilege is considered necessary to promote domestic harmony through a free exchange of confidence between the spouses.

The privilege applies only to confidential communications made between the spouses while they were married. However, as long as such communication was made during the marriage, the privilege survives the marriage and can be asserted after it is terminated.

The privilege includes spoken words, writings from one spouse to another, or other conduct intended as communication. The known presence of a third person is likely to destroy the confidential nature of the communication, unless their presence is unavoidable and precautions have been taken by the spouses to insure their privacy.

If the communication was not originally confidential, it may be testified to freely by both spouses or by anyone hearing the communication. If the communication is originally confidential, many states allow a spouse to prevent someone from disclosing the communication. For example, the privilege would prevent a friend of the wife who read a letter between the spouses, from disclosing its contents.

Under many state evidence codes, the privilege belongs equally to both spouses, and either may assert it. In California, the evidence code provides that where one spouse is a defendant in a criminal proceeding and calls the other spouse to testify to a confidential communication, the witness spouse

FIGURE 15.2 Former President Bill Clinton whispers in the ear of his wife, now New York Senator Hillary Clinton, at an informal event at the White House. Husband and wife privilege includes spoken words, writings from one spouse to another, or other conduct intended as communication. *Corbis.*

cannot refuse to do so.[2] This is based upon the theory that the witness spouse should not be privileged to withhold information that the defendant spouse deems necessary to his or her defense.

A party spouse waives the privilege when he or she fails to object to disclosures of confidential communications made by the witness spouse on the stand. If one spouse makes a voluntary, out-of-court disclosure to a third person, that spouse is deemed to have waived the privilege. However, the other spouse has not waived the privilege and he or she can still prevent the testimony of the other spouse or third person about the confidential communication.

This privilege does not apply to civil actions between spouses or to criminal actions where one spouse is charged with a crime against the person or property of the other. Furthermore, the privilege does not apply to communications between the spouses that were made for the purpose of obtaining assistance in the commission of a crime or fraud.

Physician–Patient and Psychotherapist–Patient

In many states, including the military, there is no physician–patient privilege in criminal proceedings. The defendant may, however, prevent a psychotherapist from testifying against him or her, unless the court appointed the psychotherapist. A psychotherapist is defined as a person authorized to practice medicine in any state or nation who devotes, or is reasonably believed by the patient to devote, a substantial portion of his or her time to the practice of psychiatry. In many states, this privilege extends to school psychologists.

Other exceptions to the privilege include the patient being a juvenile under 16 years old or when the psychotherapist believes his juvenile patient is the victim of child abuse. In fact, in many states, persons holding professional licenses are required to report instances of child abuse to law enforcement.

Even when the services of the psychotherapist have terminated, the privilege remains.

Clergy–Confessor

In most states, clergymen may not be required to disclose penitential communications made to them. The term "clergyman" includes a minister, priest, rabbi, or other similar functionary of a religious organization. For example, a defendant who confesses to his priest about committing the murder he is currently being tried for could not have this confidential communication disclosed at his trial.

To qualify for the privilege, the privileged communication must have been communicated to the clergyman or priest in a confidential manner, properly entrusted to him in his professional capacity, wherein the person so communicating is seeking spiritual counsel and advice.

Although the privilege belongs to the confessor, the clergyman may claim the privilege on behalf of the person. The confessor is entitled to prevent disclosure not only by himself, but also by the clergyman.

While the privilege covers confessions for crime already committed, it does not protect actions amounting to a conspiracy between the confessor and clergyman. As with attorneys, the clergyman and confessor are subject to conspiracy prosecution and could not hide behind this privilege if such were the case. Furthermore, the clergyman cannot claim the privilege for himself, should he be the defendant.

Official Information Privilege

Many states have evidence code provisions that grant the government the privilege of refusing to disclose official information. For example, the California evidence code[3] provides:

1. a. As used in this section, "official information" means information acquired in confidence by a public employee in the course of his or her duty and not open, or officially disclosed, to the public prior to the time that the claim of privilege is made.
    b. A public entity has a privilege to refuse to disclose official information, and to prevent another from disclosing official

information, if the privilege is claimed by a person authorized by the public entity to do so, and

c. Disclosure is forbidden by an act of the Congress of the United States or a statute of this state; or

2. Disclosure of the information is against the public interest because there is a necessity for preserving the confidentiality of the information that outweighs the necessity for disclosure in the interest of justice, but no privilege may be claimed under this paragraph if any person authorized to do so has consented that the information be disclosed in the proceeding. In determining whether disclosure of the information is against the public interest, the interest of the public entity as a party in the outcome of the proceeding may not be considered.

Notwithstanding any other provision of law, the Employment Development Department shall disclose to law enforcement agencies, in accordance with the provisions of subdivision (k) of Section 1095 and subdivision (b) of Section 2714 of the Unemployment Insurance Code, information in its possession relating to any person if an arrest warrant has been issued for the person for commission of a felony.

In all cases, the burden on the government is to prove there is a necessity for preserving the confidentiality of the information that outweighs the necessity for disclosure in the interest of justice.

Confidential Informant Privilege

Police agencies rely heavily on information provided by confidential sources of information. Many of these informants are involved in drug investigations that lead to the seizures of huge amounts of controlled substances and the arrests of thousands of drug traffickers each year in the United States and elsewhere.

A dilemma for many drug investigators is keeping the identity of their sources confidential. Revealing an informant's identity runs a significant risk to not only his own personal safety, but that of his family as well. Furthermore, disclosing an informant's identity most probably will end his effectiveness in developing future criminal investigations.

The most prevalent motivational factor for someone to become a confidential informant for the police is the fear of receiving punishment for past criminal acts. In the vast majority of drug cases, police investigators will ask a person they have just arrested to cooperate in their investigation to expand it to its fullest potential. His or her cooperation may include introducing undercover police officers to drug traffickers, or revealing the location where quantities of drugs are stored, so they can be seized. Either way, there is a well-founded fear that if the source of such information were revealed, it would potentially bring retaliation against those responsible. In the light of this, many states have passed legislation to provide the government with a privilege to refuse disclosure of the identity of confidential sources of information.

Reality Check!

In the vast majority of drug investigations, the usefulness of informants is limited. If an informant introduces an undercover officer to drug traffickers for the purpose of making purchases of drug evidence, it is obvious to the traffickers who made the introduction. Often, the government cannot overcome the burden of demonstrating why the defendant should not be allowed to face his accusers, and the informant is compelled to testify.

An example of the government's privilege, as it relates to informants can be found in California's evidence code:[4]

a. Except as provided in this section, a public entity has a privilege to refuse to disclose the identity of a person who has furnished information as provided in subdivision (b) purporting to disclose a violation of a law of the United States or of this state or of a public entity in this state, and to prevent another from disclosing such identity, if the privilege is claimed by a person authorized by the public entity to do so and:
   1. Disclosure is forbidden by an act of the Congress of the United States or a statute of this state; or
   2. Disclosure of the identity of the informer is against the public interest, because there is a necessity for preserving the confidentiality of his identity that outweighs the necessity for disclosure in the interest of justice; but no privilege may be claimed under this paragraph if any person authorized to do so has consented that the identity of the informer be disclosed in the proceeding. In determining whether disclosure of the identity of the informer is against the public interest, the interest of the public entity as a party in the outcome of the proceeding may not be considered.
b. This section applies only if the information is furnished in confidence by the informer to:
   1. A law enforcement officer;
   2. A representative of an administrative agency charged with the administration or enforcement of the law alleged to be violated; or
   3. Any person for the purpose of transmittal to a person listed in paragraph (1) or (2).
c. There is no privilege under this section to prevent the informer from disclosing his identity.

As with official information maintained by federal and state governments, the burden is on the government to demonstrate that the necessity for preserving the confidentiality of the informant outweighs the necessity for disclosure in the interest of justice.

An informant's identity does not need to be disclosed when a judge finds there was probable cause to either arrest or search. If police made an arrest or conducted a search based upon the information provided by a reliable, trustworthy informant, there is no constitutional requirement to disclose the informant's identity during a preliminary hearing.[5] When the officers conducting the police action are questioned, and when their testimony, under oath, withstands probing cross-examination, the judge will most likely be satisfied that the officers are being truthful about the information they received from the informant, and this should eliminate the need for the informant to testify. At trial, however, other issues may arise that will require the informant to personally testify in the matter.

Skilled drug investigators have developed ways to reduce the likelihood of their informants having to testify in court. For example, an informant who discloses the sale of drugs at a particular residence can be shielded by the investigators initiating a surveillance of the residence to develop independent probably cause for a search warrant.

If at the direction of the police, an informant goes to the residence and personally purchases drugs there, the police can continue their surveillance of the residence over a several-day period, and observe others doing the same. This information may sway a magistrate to issue a search warrant for the residence. If the prosecutor agrees not to charge the defendant with the specific drug sales count involving the informant, the informant's identity should not be an issue. Furthermore, because of the potentially large number of persons who purchased drugs at the residence before the warrant is served, it would be almost impossible for the defendant to discern who told the police about his activity.

Another way of lessening the possibility of the informant testifying in trial is to limit his role in the investigation. Even if the informant introduces undercover investigators to drug traffickers for the purpose of purchasing drug evidence from them, the informant's identity can be concealed if he was not a percipient witness to the event. He can later claim to the drug trafficker that he too, was duped, and did not realize the purchaser was a police official.

If, despite the efforts of investigators to shield the identity of the informant during the course of their investigation, the prosecutor always has the option of dismissing charges if the circumstances warrant. Close coordination should always take place with the prosecutor in protecting the identity of the informant.

█████ **SUMMARY** █████ ████ █████

Even though evidence may be relevant, and competent witnesses are prepared to testify concerning it, the evidence may be nonetheless excluded because of various Constitutional rules and public policies.

A witness will not be required to testify when a testimonial privilege is properly claimed. Most testimonial privileges are personal in nature, in that only the person protected can claim the privilege.

Those interests and relationships that enjoy testimonial privilege include self-incrimination, immunity from prosecution, attorney–client, husband and wife, physician–patient and psychotherapist–patient, clergy–confessor, official information, and confidential informant privilege.

The privilege of self-incrimination is based upon the Fifth Amendment to the U.S. Constitution, which provides that "no person . . . shall be compelled in any criminal case to be a witness against himself." This privilege is twofold, in that it protects the accused from testifying against himself and it also protects someone from being subject to criminal charges, as in the case where his testimony before Congress may result in his indictment.

In order to gain testimony that would not otherwise be obtained, federal and state legislative bodies have enacted legislation to grant immunity to certain witnesses.

In some states, the client of an attorney, whether or not he is a party to a criminal or civil action, has a privilege to refuse to disclose, and to prevent others from disclosing, a confidential communication between himself and his attorney during the course of the attorney–client relationship.

A married person, including those persons married by common law, has the privilege not to take the stand to testify against his spouse in any criminal proceeding. Even if the spouse takes the stand, he or she may refuse to disclose a confidential communication and the defendant may prevent his spouse from doing so. The only exception in criminal proceedings is when one spouse is charged with a crime against the other, such as in domestic battery cases.

In many states, including the military, there is no physician–patient privilege in criminal proceedings. The defendant may, however, prevent a psychotherapist from testifying against him or her unless the court appointed the psychotherapist. A psychotherapist is defined as a person authorized to practice medicine in any state or nation who devotes, or is reasonably believed by the patient to devote, a substantial portion of his or her time to the practice of psychiatry.

In many instances, clergymen may not be required to disclose penitential communications made to them. The term "clergyman" includes a minister, priest, rabbi, or other similar functionary of a religious organization.

Many states have evidence code provisions that grant the government the privilege of refusing to disclose official information and identities of confidential informants that have assisted the police. The burden is on the government to demonstrate the necessity for preserving the confidentiality of the official information, or an informant's identity, and that it outweighs the necessity for disclosure in the interest of justice. The government always has the option of dropping their criminal case, if a judge should rule that the information or the informant's identity must be disclosed.

NOTES

1. *Hoffman* v. *United States*, 341 U.S. 479, 95 L.Ed.1118, 71 S. CT. 814 1951.
2. California Evidence Code, Section 987.
3. California Evidence Code, Section 1040.
4. California Evidence Code, Section 1041.
5. *McCray* v. *Illinois* 386 U.S. 300 (1967).

Appendix A

Federal Rules of Evidence

ARTICLE I

General Provisions

Article I – General Provisions

- Rule 101. Scope
- Rule 102. Purpose and Construction
- Rule 103. Rulings on Evidence
- Rule 104. Preliminary Questions
- Rule 105. Limited Admissibility
- Rule 106. Remainder of or Related Writings or Recorded Statements

Article II – Judicial Notice

- Rule 201. Judicial Notice of Adjudicative Facts

Article III – Presumptions in Civil Actions and Proceedings

- Rule 301. Presumptions in General Civil Actions and Proceedings
- Rule 302. Applicability of State Law in Civil Actions and Proceedings

Article IV – Relevancy and Its Limits

- Rule 401. Definition of "Relevant Evidence"
- Rule 402. Relevant Evidence Generally Admissible; Irrelevant Evidence Inadmissible

- Rule 403. Exclusion of Relevant Evidence on Grounds of Prejudice, Confusion, or Waste of Time
- Rule 404. Character Evidence Not Admissible To Prove Conduct; Exceptions; Other Crimes
- Rule 405. Methods of Proving Character
- Rule 406. Habit; Routine Practice
- Rule 407. Subsequent Remedial Measures
- Rule 408. Compromise and Offers to Compromise
- Rule 409. Payment of Medical and Similar Expenses
- Rule 410. Inadmissibility of Pleas, Plea Discussions, and Related Statements
- Rule 411. Liability Insurance
- Rule 412. Sex Offense Cases; Relevance of Victim's Past Behavior or Alleged Sexual Predisposition
- Rule 413. Evidence of Similar Crimes in Sexual Assault Cases
- Rule 414. Evidence of Similar Crimes in Child Molestation Cases
- Rule 415. Evidence of Similar Crimes in Civil Cases Concerning Sexual Assault and Child Molestation Cases

Article V – Privileges

- Rule 501. General Rule

Article VI – Witnesses

- Rule 601. General Rule of Competency
- Rule 602. Lack of Personal Knowledge
- Rule 603. Oath or Affirmation
- Rule 604. Interpreters
- Rule 605. Competency of Judge as Witness
- Rule 606. Competency of Juror as Witness
- Rule 607. Who May Impeach
- Rule 608. Evidence of Character and Conduct of Witness
- Rule 609. Impeachment by Evidence of Conviction of Crime
- Rule 610. Religious Beliefs or Opinions
- Rule 611. Mode and Order of Interrogation and Presentation
- Rule 612. Writing Used to Refresh Memory
- Rule 613. Prior Statements of Witnesses
- Rule 614. Calling and Interrogation of Witnesses by Court
- Rule 615. Exclusion of Witnesses

Article VII – Opinions and Expert Testimony

- Rule 701. Opinion Testimony by Lay Witnesses
- Rule 702. Testimony by Experts

- Rule 703. Bases of Opinion Testimony by Experts
- Rule 704. Opinion on Ultimate Issue
- Rule 705. Disclosure of Facts or Data Underlying Expert Opinion
- Rule 706. Court Appointed Experts

Article VIII – Hearsay

- Rule 801. Definitions
- Rule 802. Hearsay Rule
- Rule 803. Hearsay Exceptions; Availability of Declarant Immaterial
- Rule 804. Hearsay Exceptions; Declarant Unavailable
- Rule 805. Hearsay Within Hearsay
- Rule 806. Attacking and Supporting Credibility of Declarant
- Rule 807. Residual Exception

Article IX – Authentication and Identification

- Rule 901. Requirement of Authentication or Identification
- Rule 902. Self-authentication
- Rule 903. Subscribing Witness' Testimony Unnecessary

Article X – Contents of Writings, Recordings and Photographs

- Rule 1001. Definitions
- Rule 1002. Requirement of Original
- Rule 1003. Admissibility of Duplicates
- Rule 1004. Admissibility of Other Evidence of Contents
- Rule 1005. Public Records
- Rule 1006. Summaries
- Rule 1007. Testimony or Written Admission of Party
- Rule 1008. Functions of Court and Jury

Article XI – Miscellaneous Rules

- Rule 1101. Applicability of Rules
- Rule 1102. Amendments
- Rule 1103. Title

ARTICLE I

General Provisions

Rule 101. Scope

These rules govern proceedings in the courts of the United States and before United States bankruptcy judges and United States magistrate judges, to the extent and with the exceptions stated in rule 1101.

Rule 102. Purpose and Construction

These rules shall be construed to secure fairness in administration, elimination of unjustifiable expense and delay, and promotion of growth and development of the law of evidence to the end that the truth may be ascertained and proceedings justly determined.

Rule 103. Rulings on Evidence

(a) Effect of erroneous ruling Error may not be predicated upon a ruling which admits or excludes evidence unless a substantial right of the party is affected, and

1. **Objection.** In case the ruling is one admitting evidence, a timely objection or motion to strike appears of record, stating the specific ground of objection, if the specific ground was not apparent from the context; or
2. **Offer of proof.** In case the ruling is one excluding evidence, the substance of the evidence was made known to the court by offer or was apparent from the context within which questions were asked.

(b) Record of offer and ruling The court may add any other or further statement which shows the character of the evidence, the form in which it was offered, the objection made, and the ruling thereon. It may direct the making of an offer in question and answer form.

(c) Hearing of jury In jury cases, proceedings shall be conducted, to the extent practicable, so as to prevent inadmissible evidence from being suggested to the jury by any means, such as making statements or offers of proof or asking questions in the hearing of the jury.

(d) Plain error Nothing in this rule precludes taking notice of plain errors affecting substantial rights, although they were not brought to the attention of the court.

Rule 104. Preliminary Questions

(a) Questions of admissibility generally Preliminary questions concerning the qualification of a person to be a witness, the existence of a privilege, or the admissibility of evidence shall be determined by the court, subject to the provisions of subdivision (b). In making its determination it is not bound by the rules of evidence, except those with respect to privileges.

(b) Relevancy conditioned on fact. When the relevancy of evidence depends upon the fulfillment of a condition of fact, the court shall admit it upon, or

subject to, the introduction of evidence sufficient to support a finding of the fulfillment of the condition.

(c) Hearing of jury Hearings on the admissibility of confessions shall in all cases be conducted out of the hearing of the jury. Hearings on other preliminary matters shall be so conducted when the interests of justice require, or when an accused is a witness and so requests.

(d) Testimony by accused The accused does not, by testifying upon a preliminary matter, become subject to cross-examination as to other issues in the case.

(e) Weight and credibility This rule does not limit the right of a party to introduce before the jury evidence relevant to weight or credibility.

Rule 105. Limited Admissibility
When evidence that is admissible as to one party or for one purpose but not admissible as to another party or for another purpose is admitted, the court, upon request, shall restrict the evidence to its proper scope and instruct the jury accordingly.

Rule 106. Remainder of or Related Writings or Recorded Statements
When a writing or recorded statement or part thereof is introduced by a party, an adverse party may require the introduction at that time of any other part or any other writing or recorded statement, which ought in fairness to be considered contemporaneously with it.

ARTICLE II

Judicial Notice

Rule 201. Judicial Notice of Adjudicative Facts

(a) Scope of rule This rule governs only judicial notice of adjudicative facts.

(b) Kinds of facts A judicially noticed fact must be one not subject to reasonable dispute in that it is either (1) generally known within the territorial jurisdiction of the trial court or (2) capable of accurate and ready determination by resort to sources whose accuracy cannot reasonably be questioned.

(c) When discretionary A court may take judicial notice, whether requested or not.

(d) When mandatory A court shall take judicial notice if requested by a party and supplied with the necessary information.

(e) Opportunity to be heard A party is entitled upon timely request to an opportunity to be heard as to the propriety of taking judicial notice and the tenor of the matter noticed. In the absence of prior notification, the request may be made after judicial notice has been taken.

(f) Time of taking notice Judicial notice may be taken at any stage of the proceeding.

(g) Instructing jury In a civil action or proceeding, the court shall instruct the jury to accept as conclusive any fact judicially noticed. In a criminal case, the court shall instruct the jury that it may, but is not required to, accept as conclusive any fact judicially noticed.

ARTICLE III

Presumptions in Civil Actions and Proceedings

Rule 301. Presumptions in General Civil Actions and Proceedings
In all civil actions and proceedings not otherwise provided for by Act of Congress or by these rules, a presumption imposes on the party against whom it is directed the burden of going forward with evidence to rebut or meet the presumption, but does not shift to such party the burden of proof in the sense of the risk of nonpersuasion, which remains throughout the trial upon the party on whom it was originally cast.

Rule 302. Applicability of State Law in Civil Actions and Proceedings
In civil actions and proceedings, the effect of a presumption respecting a fact that is an element of a claim or defense as to which State law supplies the rule of decision is determined in accordance with State law.

ARTICLE IV

Relevancy and its Limits

Rule 401. Definition of "Relevant Evidence"
"Relevant evidence" means evidence having any tendency to make the existence of any fact that is of consequence to the determination of the action more probable or less probable than it would be without the evidence.

Rule 402. Relevant Evidence Generally Admissible; Irrelevant Evidence Inadmissible
All relevant evidence is admissible, except as otherwise provided by the Constitution of the United States, by Act of Congress, by these rules, or by other rules prescribed by the Supreme Court pursuant to statutory authority. Evidence that is not relevant is not admissible.

Rule 403. Exclusion of Relevant Evidence on Grounds of Prejudice, Confusion, or Waste of Time

Although relevant, evidence may be excluded if its probative value is substantially outweighed by the danger of unfair prejudice, confusion of the issues, or misleading the jury, or by considerations of undue delay, waste of time, or needless presentation of cumulative evidence.

Rule 404. Character Evidence Not Admissible To Prove Conduct; Exceptions; Other Crimes [Proposed Amendment]

(a) Character evidence generally Evidence of a person's character or a trait of character is not admissible for the purpose of proving action in conformity therewith on a particular occasion, except:

1. **Character of accused.** Evidence of a pertinent trait of character offered by an accused, or by the prosecution to rebut the same;
2. **Character of victim.** Evidence of a pertinent trait of character of the victim of the crime offered by an accused, or by the prosecution to rebut the same, or evidence of a character trait of peacefulness of the victim offered by the prosecution in a homicide case to rebut evidence that the victim was the first aggressor;
3. **Character of witness.** Evidence of the character of a witness, as provided in rules 607, 608, and 609

(b) Other crimes, wrongs, or acts Evidence of other crimes, wrongs, or acts is not admissible to prove the character of a person in order to show action in conformity therewith. It may, however, be admissible for other purposes, such as proof of motive, opportunity, intent, preparation, plan, knowledge, identify, or absence of mistake or accident, provided that upon request by the accused, the prosecution in a criminal case shall provide reasonable notice in advance of trial, or during trial if the court excuses pretrial notice on good cause shown, of the general nature of any such evidence it intends to introduce at trial.

Rule 405. Methods of Proving Character

(a) Reputation or opinion In all cases in which evidence of character or a trait of character of a person is admissible, proof may be made by testimony as to reputation or by testimony in the form of an opinion. On cross-examination, inquiry is allowable into relevant specific instances of conduct.

(b) Specific instances of conduct. In cases in which character or a trait of character of a person is an essential element of a charge, claim, or defense, proof may also be made of specific instances of that person's conduct.

Rule 406. Habit; Routine Practice

Evidence of the habit of a person or of the routine practice of an organization, whether corroborated or not and regardless of the presence of eyewitnesses, is relevant to prove that the conduct of the person or organization on a particular occasion was in conformity with the habit or routine practice.

Rule 407. Subsequent Remedial Measures

When, after an injury or harm allegedly caused by an event, measures are taken that, if taken previously, would have made the injury or harm less likely to occur, evidence of the subsequent measures is not admissible to prove negligence, culpable conduct, a defect in a product, a defect in a product's design, or a need for a warning or instruction. This rule does not require the exclusion of evidence of subsequent measures when offered for another purpose, such as proving ownership, control, or feasibility of precautionary measures, if controverted, or impeachment.

Rule 408. Compromise and Offers to Compromise

Evidence of (1) furnishing or offering or promising to furnish, or (2) accepting or offering or promising to accept, a valuable consideration in compromising or attempting to compromise a claim which was disputed as to either validity or amount, is not admissible to prove liability for or invalidity of the claim or its amount. Evidence of conduct or statements made in compromise negotiations is likewise not admissible. This rule does not require the exclusion of any evidence otherwise discoverable merely because it is presented in the course of compromise negotiations. This rule also does not require exclusion when the evidence is offered for another purpose, such as proving bias or prejudice of a witness, negativing a contention of undue delay, or proving an effort to obstruct a criminal investigation or prosecution.

Rule 409. Payment of Medical and Similar Expenses

Evidence of furnishing or offering or promising to pay medical, hospital, or similar expenses occasioned by an injury is not admissible to prove liability for the injury.

Rule 410. Inadmissibility of Pleas, Plea Discussions, and Related Statements

Except as otherwise provided in this rule, evidence of the following is not, in any civil or criminal proceeding, admissible against the defendant who made the plea or was a participant in the plea discussions:

1. a plea of guilty which was later withdrawn;
2. a plea of nolo contendere;

3. any statement made in the course of any proceedings under Rule 11 of the Federal Rules of Criminal Procedure or comparable state procedure regarding either of the foregoing pleas; or

4. any statement made in the course of plea discussions with an attorney for the prosecuting authority which do not result in a plea of guilty or which result in a plea of guilty later withdrawn.

However, such a statement is admissible:

1. in any proceeding wherein another statement made in the course of the same plea or plea discussions has been introduced and the statement ought in fairness be considered contemporaneously with it, or

2. in a criminal proceeding for perjury or false statement if the statement was made by the defendant under oath, on the record and in the presence of counsel.

Rule 411. Liability Insurance

Evidence that a person was or was not insured against liability is not admissible upon the issue whether the person acted negligently or otherwise wrongfully. This rule does not require the exclusion of evidence of insurance against liability when offered for another purpose, such as proof of agency, ownership, or control, or bias or prejudice of a witness.

Rule 412. Sex Offense Cases; Relevance of Victim's Past Sexual Behavior or Alleged Sexual Predisposition

(a) Evidence generally inadmissible The following evidence is not admissible in any civil or criminal proceeding involving alleged sexual misconduct except as provided in subdivisions (b) and (c):

1. Evidence offered to prove that any alleged victim engaged in other sexual behavior.

2. Evidence offered to prove any alleged victim's sexual predisposition.

(b) Exceptions
1. In a criminal case, the following evidence is admissible, if otherwise admissible under these rules:
   a. evidence of specific instances of sexual behavior by the alleged victim offered to prove that a person other than the accused was the source of semen, injury, or other physical evidence;
   b. evidence of specific instances of sexual behavior by the alleged victim with respect to the person accused of the sexual misconduct offered by the accused to prove consent or by the prosecution; and

      c. evidence the exclusion of which would violate the constitutional rights of the defendant.

2. In a civil case, evidence offered to prove the sexual behavior or sexual predisposition of any alleged victim is admissible if it is otherwise admissible under these rules and its probative value substantially outweighs the danger of harm to any victim and of unfair prejudice to any party. Evidence of an alleged victim's reputation is admissible only if it has been placed in controversy by the alleged victim.

(c) Procedure to determine admissibility

1. A party intending to offer evidence under subdivision (b) must:
    a. file a written motion at least 14 days before trial specifically describing the evidence and stating the purpose for which it is offered unless the court, for good cause requires a different time for filing or permits filing during trial; and
    b. serve the motion on all parties and notify the alleged victim or, when appropriate, the alleged victim's guardian or representative.
2. Before admitting evidence under this rule the court must conduct a hearing in camera and afford the victim and parties a right to attend and be heard. The motion, related papers, and the record of the hearing must be sealed and remain under seal unless the court orders otherwise.

Rule 413. Evidence of Similar Crimes in Sexual Assault Cases

a. In a criminal case in which the defendant is accused of an offense of sexual assault, evidence of the defendant's commission of another offense or offenses of sexual assault is admissible, and may be considered for its bearing on any matter to which it is relevant.

b. In a case in which the Government intends to offer evidence under this rule, the attorney for the Government shall disclose the evidence to the defendant, including statements of witnesses or a summary of the substance of any testimony that is expected to be offered, at least fifteen days before the scheduled date of trial or at such later time as the court may allow for good cause.

c. This rule shall not be construed to limit the admission or consideration of evidence under any other rule.

d. For purposes of this rule and Rule 415 "offense of sexual assault" means a crime under Federal law or the law of a State (as defined in section 513 of title 18, United States Code) that involved:

1. any conduct proscribed by chapter 109A of title 18, United States Code;
2. contact, without consent, between any part of the defendant's body or an object and the genitals or anus of another person;
3. contact, without consent, between the genitals or anus of the defendant and any part of another person's body;
4. deriving sexual pleasure or gratification from the infliction of death, bodily injury, or physical pain on another person; or
5. an attempt or conspiracy to engage in conduct described in paragraphs (1)–(4).

Rule 414. Evidence of Similar Crimes in Child Molestation Cases

a. In a criminal case in which the defendant is accused of an offense of child molestation, evidence of the defendant's commission of another offense or offenses of child molestation is admissible, and may be considered for its bearing on any matter to which it is relevant.

b. In a case in which the Government intends to offer evidence under this rule, the attorney for the Government shall disclose the evidence to the defendant, including statements of witnesses or a summary of the substance of any testimony that is expected to be offered, at least fifteen days before the scheduled date of trial or at such later time as the court may allow for good cause.

c. This rule shall not be construed to limit the admission or consideration of evidence under any other rule.

d. For purposes of this rule and Rule 415, "child" means a person below the age of 14, and "offense of child molestation" means a crime under Federal law or the law of a State (as defined in section 513 of title 18, United States Code) that involved:

   1. any conduct proscribed by chapter 109A of title 18, United States Code, that was committed in relation to a child;
   2. any conduct proscribed by chapter 110 of title 18, United States Code;
   3. contact between any part of the defendant's body or an object and the genitals or anus of a child;
   4. contact between the genitals or anus of the defendant and any part of the body of a child;
   5. deriving sexual pleasure or gratification from the infliction of death, bodily injury, or physical pain on a child; or
   6. an attempt or conspiracy to engage in conduct described in paragraphs (1)–(5).

Rule 415. Evidence of Similar Crimes in Civil Cases Concerning Sexual Assault and Child Molestation Cases

a. In a civil case in which a claim for damages or other relief is predicated on a party's alleged commission of conduct constituting an offense of sexual assault or child molestation, evidence of that party's commission of another offense or offenses of sexual assault or child molestation is admissible and may be considered as provided in Rule 413 and Rule 414 of these rules.

b. A party who intends to offer evidence under this Rule shall disclose the evidence to the party against whom it will be offered, including statements of witnesses or a summary of the substance of any testimony that is expected to be offered, at least fifteen days before the scheduled date of trial or at such later time as the court may allow for good cause.

c. This rule shall not be construed to limit the admission or consideration of evidence under any other rule.

ARTICLE V

Privileges

Rule 501. General Rule

Except as otherwise required by the Constitution of the United States or provided by Act of Congress or in rules prescribed by the Supreme Court pursuant to statutory authority, the privilege of a witness, person, government, State, or political subdivision thereof shall be governed by the principles of the common law as they may be interpreted by the courts of the United States in the light of reason and experience. However, in civil actions and proceedings, with respect to an element of a claim or defense as to which State law supplies the rule of decision, the privilege of a witness, person, government, State, or political subdivision thereof shall be determined in accordance with State law.

ARTICLE VI

Witnesses

Rule 601. General Rule of Competency

Every person is competent to be a witness except as otherwise provided in these rules. However, in civil actions and proceedings, with respect to an element of a claim or defense as to which State law supplies the rule of decision, the competency of a witness shall be determined in accordance with State law.

Rule 602. Lack of Personal Knowledge

A witness may not testify to a matter unless evidence is introduced sufficient to support a finding that the witness has personal knowledge of the matter. Evidence to prove personal knowledge may, but need not, consist of the witness' own testimony. This rule is subject to the provisions of rule 703, relating to opinion testimony by expert witnesses.

Rule 603. Oath or Affirmation

Before testifying, every witness shall be required to declare that the witness will testify truthfully, by oath or affirmation administered in a form calculated to awaken the witness' conscience and impress the witness' mind with the duty to do so.

Rule 604. Interpreters

An interpreter is subject to the provisions of these rules relating to qualification as an expert and the administration of an oath or affirmation to make a true translation.

Rule 605. Competency of Judge as Witness

The judge presiding at the trial may not testify in that trial as a witness. No objection need be made in order to preserve the point.

Rule 606. Competency of Juror as Witness

(a) At the trial A member of the jury may not testify as a witness before that jury in the trial of the case in which the juror is sitting. If the juror is called so to testify, the opposing party shall be afforded an opportunity to object out of the presence of the jury.

(b) Inquiry into validity of verdict or indictment Upon an inquiry into the validity of a verdict or indictment, a juror may not testify as to any matter or statement occurring during the course of the jury's deliberations or to the effect of anything upon that or any other juror's mind or emotions as influencing the juror to assent to or dissent from the verdict or indictment or concerning the juror's mental processes in connection therewith, except that a juror may testify on the question whether extraneous prejudicial information was improperly brought to the jury's attention or whether any outside influence was improperly brought to bear upon any juror. Nor may a juror's affidavit or evidence of any statement by the juror concerning a matter about which the juror would be precluded from testifying be received for these purposes.

Rule 607. Who May Impeach

The credibility of a witness may be attacked by any party, including the party calling the witness.

Rule 608. Evidence of Character and Conduct of Witness

(a) Opinion and reputation evidence of character The credibility of a witness may be attacked or supported by evidence in the form of opinion or reputation, but subject to these limitations:

1. the evidence may refer only to character for truthfulness or untruthfulness, and
2. evidence of truthful character is admissible only after the character of the witness for truthfulness has been attacked by opinion or reputation evidence or otherwise

(b) Specific instances of conduct Specific instances of the conduct of a witness, for the purpose of attacking or supporting the witness' credibility, other than conviction of crime as provided in rule 609, may not be proved by extrinsic evidence. They may, however, in the discretion of the court, if probative of truthfulness or untruthfulness, be inquired into on cross-examination of the witness (1) concerning the witness' character for truthfulness or untruthfulness, or (2) concerning the character for truthfulness or untruthfulness of another witness as to which character the witness being cross-examined has testified.

The giving of testimony, whether by an accused or by any other witness, does not operate as a waiver of the accused's or the witness' privilege against self-incrimination when examined with respect to matters which relate only to credibility.

Rule 609. Impeachment by Evidence of Conviction of Crime

(a) General rule. For the purpose of attacking the credibility of a witness:

1. evidence that a witness other than an accused has been convicted of a crime shall be admitted, subject to Rule 403, if the crime was punishable by death or imprisonment in excess of one year under the law under which the witness was convicted, and evidence that an accused has been convicted of such a crime shall be admitted if the court determines that the probative value of admitting this evidence outweighs its prejudicial effect to the accused; and
2. evidence that any witness has been convicted of a crime shall be admitted if it involved dishonesty or false statement, regardless of the punishment.

(b) Time limit Evidence of a conviction under this rule is not admissible if a period of more than ten years has elapsed since the date of the conviction or of the release of the witness from the confinement imposed for that conviction,

whichever is the later date, unless the court determines, in the interests of justice, that the probative value of the conviction supported by specific facts and circumstances substantially outweighs its prejudicial effect. However, evidence of a conviction more than 10 years old as calculated herein, is not admissible unless the proponent gives to the adverse party sufficient advance written notice of intent to use such evidence to provide the adverse party with a fair opportunity to contest the use of such evidence.

(c) Effect of pardon, annulment, or certificate of rehabilitation Evidence of a conviction is not admissible under this rule if:

1. the conviction has been the subject of a pardon, annulment, certificate of rehabilitation, or other equivalent procedure based on a finding of the rehabilitation of the person convicted, and that person has not been convicted of a subsequent crime which was punishable by death or imprisonment in excess of one year, or
2. the conviction has been the subject of a pardon, annulment, or other equivalent procedure based on a finding of innocence.

(d) Juvenile adjudications Evidence of juvenile adjudications is generally not admissible under this rule. The court may, however, in a criminal case allow evidence of a juvenile adjudication of a witness other than the accused if conviction of the offense would be admissible to attack the credibility of an adult and the court is satisfied that admission in evidence is necessary for a fair determination of the issue of guilt or innocence.

(e) Pendency of appeal The pendency of an appeal therefrom does not render evidence of a conviction inadmissible. Evidence of the pendency of an appeal is admissible.

Rule 610. Religious Beliefs or Opinions

Evidence of the beliefs or opinions of a witness on matters of religion is not admissible for the purpose of showing that by reason of their nature the witness' credibility is impaired or enhanced.

Rule 611. Mode and Order of Interrogation and Presentation

(a) Control by court The court shall exercise reasonable control over the mode and order of interrogating witnesses and presenting evidence so as to:

1. make the interrogation and presentation effective for the ascertainment of the truth,
2. avoid needless consumption of time, and
3. protect witnesses from harassment or undue embarrassment.

(b) Scope of cross-examination Cross-examination should be limited to the subject matter of the direct examination and matters affecting the credibility of the witness. The court may, in the exercise of discretion, permit inquiry into additional matters as if on direct examination.

(c) Leading questions. Leading questions should not be used on the direct examination of a witness except as may be necessary to develop the witness' testimony. Ordinarily leading questions should be permitted on cross-examination. When a party calls a hostile witness, an adverse party, or a witness identified with an adverse party, interrogation may be by leading questions.

Rule 612. Writing Used to Refresh Memory
Except as otherwise provided in criminal proceedings by section 3500 of title 18, United States Code, if a witness uses a writing to refresh memory for the purpose of testifying, either:

1. while testifying, or
2. before testifying, if the court in its discretion determines it is necessary in the interests of justice,

an adverse party is entitled to have the writing produced at the hearing, to inspect it, to cross-examine the witness thereon, and to introduce in evidence those portions which relate to the testimony of the witness. If it is claimed that the writing contains matters not related to the subject matter of the testimony the court shall examine the writing in camera, excise any portions not so related, and order delivery of the remainder to the party entitled thereto. Any portion withheld over objections shall be preserved and made available to the appellate court in the event of an appeal. If a writing is not produced or delivered pursuant to order under this rule, the court shall make any order justice requires, except that in criminal cases when the prosecution elects not to comply, the order shall be one striking the testimony or, if the court in its discretion determines that the interests of justice so require, declaring a mistrial.

Rule 613. Prior Statements of Witnesses

(a) Examining witness concerning prior statement In examining a witness concerning a prior statement made by the witness, whether written or not, the statement need not be shown nor its contents disclosed to the witness at that time, but on request the same shall be shown or disclosed to opposing counsel.

(b) Extrinsic evidence of prior inconsistent statement of witness Extrinsic evidence of a prior inconsistent statement by a witness is not admissible unless

the witness is afforded an opportunity to explain or deny the same and the opposite party is afforded an opportunity to interrogate the witness thereon, or the interests of justice otherwise require. This provision does not apply to admissions of a party-opponent as defined in rule 801(d)(2).

Rule 614. Calling and Interrogation of Witnesses by Court

(a) Calling by court The court may, on its own motion or at the suggestion of a party, call witnesses, and all parties are entitled to cross-examine witnesses thus called.

(b) Interrogation by court The court may interrogate witnesses, whether called by itself or by a party.

(c) Objections Objections to the calling of witnesses by the court or to interrogation by it may be made at the time or at the next available opportunity when the jury is not present.

Rule 615. Exclusion of Witnesses

At the request of a party the court shall order witnesses excluded so that they cannot hear the testimony of other witnesses, and it may make the order of its own motion. This rule does not authorize exclusion of:

1. a party who is a natural person, or
2. an officer or employee of a party which is not a natural person designated as its representative by its attorney, or
3. a person whose presence is shown by a party to be essential to the presentation of the party's cause, or
4. a person authorized by statute to be present.

ARTICLE VII

Opinions and Expert Testimony

Rule 701. Opinion Testimony by Lay Witnesses [Proposed Amendment]

If the witness is not testifying as an expert, the witness' testimony in the form of opinions or inferences is limited to those opinions or inferences which are (a) rationally based on the perception of the witness and (b) helpful to a clear understanding of the witness' testimony or the determination of a fact in issue.

Rule 702. Testimony by Experts [Proposed Amendment]

If scientific, technical, or other specialized knowledge will assist the trier of fact to understand the evidence or to determine a fact in issue, a witness qualified as an expert by knowledge, skill, experience, training, or education, may testify thereto in the form of an opinion or otherwise.

Rule 703. Bases of Opinion Testimony by Experts [Proposed Amendment]

The facts or data in the particular case upon which an expert bases an opinion or inference may be those perceived by or made known to the expert at or before the hearing. If of a type reasonably relied upon by experts in the particular field in forming opinions or inferences upon the subject, the facts or data need not be admissible in evidence.

Rule 704. Opinion on Ultimate Issue

    a. Except as provided in subdivision (b), testimony in the form of an opinion or inference otherwise admissible is not objectionable because it embraces an ultimate issue to be decided by the trier of fact.

    b. No expert witness testifying with respect to the mental state or condition of a defendant in a criminal case may state an opinion or inference as to whether the defendant did or did not have the mental state or condition constituting an element of the crime charged or of a defense thereto. Such ultimate issues are matters for the trier of fact alone.

Rule 705. Disclosure of Facts or Data Underlying Expert Opinion

The expert may testify in terms of opinion or inference and give reasons therefore without first testifying to the underlying facts or data, unless the court requires otherwise. The expert may in any event be required to disclose the underlying facts or data on cross-examination.

Rule 706. Court Appointed Experts

(a) Appointment The court may on its own motion or on the motion of any party enter an order to show cause why expert witnesses should not be appointed, and may request the parties to submit nominations. The court may appoint any expert witnesses agreed upon by the parties, and may appoint expert witnesses of its own selection. An expert witness shall not be appointed by the court unless the witness consents to act. A witness so appointed shall be informed of the witness' duties by the court in writing, a copy of which shall be filed with the clerk, or at a conference in which the parties shall have opportunity to participate. A witness so appointed shall advise the parties of the witness' findings, if any; the witness' deposition may be taken by any party; and the witness may be called to testify by the court or any party. The witness shall be subject to cross-examination by each party, including a party calling the witness.

(b) Compensation Expert witnesses so appointed are entitled to reasonable compensation in whatever sum the court may allow. The compensation thus fixed is payable from funds which may be provided by law in criminal cases and civil actions and proceedings involving just compensation under the Fifth Amendment. In other civil actions and proceedings the compensation shall be paid by the parties in such proportion and at such time as the court directs, and thereafter charged in like manner as other costs.

(c) Disclosure of appointment In the exercise of its discretion, the court may authorize disclosure to the jury of the fact that the court appointed the expert witness.

(d) Parties' experts of own selection Nothing in this rule limits the parties in calling expert witnesses of their own selection.

ARTICLE VIII

Hearsay

Rule 801. Definitions
The following definitions apply under this article:

(a) Statement

- A "statement" is
  1. an oral or written assertion or
  2. nonverbal conduct of a person, if it is intended by the person as an assertion.

(b) Declarant

- A "declarant" is a person who makes a statement.

(c) Hearsay

- "Hearsay" is a statement, other than one made by the declarant while testifying at the trial or hearing, offered in evidence to prove the truth of the matter asserted.

(d) Statements that are not hearsay

- A statement is not hearsay if:
  - (1) **Prior statement by witness.** The declarant testifies at the trial or hearing and is subject to cross-examination concerning the statement, and the statement is (A) inconsistent with the

declarant's testimony, and was given under oath subject to the penalty of perjury at a trial, hearing, or other proceeding, or in a deposition, or (B) consistent with the declarant's testimony and is offered to rebut an express or implied charge against the declarant of recent fabrication or improper influence or motive, or (C) one of identification of a person made after perceiving the person; or

- (2) **Admission by party-opponent.** The statement is offered against a party and is (A) the party's own statement, in either an individual or a representative capacity or (B) a statement of which the party has manifested an adoption or belief in its truth, or (C) a statement by a person authorized by the party to make a statement concerning the subject, or (D) a statement by the party's agent or servant concerning a matter within the scope of the agency or employment, made during the existence of the relationship, or (E) a statement by a coconspirator of a party during the course and in furtherance of the conspiracy.

The contents of the statement shall be considered but are not alone sufficient to establish the declarant's authority under subdivision (C), the agency or employment relationship and scope thereof under subdivision (D), or the existence of the conspiracy and the participation therein of the declarant and the party against whom the statement is offered under subdivision (E).

Rule 802. Hearsay Rule

Hearsay is not admissible except as provided by these rules or by other rules prescribed by the Supreme Court pursuant to statutory authority or by Act of Congress.

Rule 803. Hearsay Exceptions; Availability of Declarant Immaterial [Proposed Amendment]

The following are not excluded by the hearsay rule, even though the declarant is available as a witness:

1. Present sense impression. A statement describing or explaining an event or condition made while the declarant was perceiving the event or condition, or immediately thereafter.
2. Excited utterance. A statement relating to a startling event or condition made while the declarant was under the stress of excitement caused by the event or condition.

3. Then existing mental, emotional, or physical condition. A statement of the declarant's then existing state of mind, emotion, sensation, or physical condition (such as intent, plan, motive, design, mental feeling, pain, and bodily health), but not including a statement of memory or belief to prove the fact remembered or believed unless it relates to the execution, revocation, identification, or terms of declarant's will.

4. Statements for purposes of medical diagnosis or treatment. Statements made for purposes of medical diagnosis or treatment and describing medical history, or past or present symptoms, pain, or sensations, or the inception or general character of the cause or external source thereof insofar as reasonably pertinent to diagnosis or treatment.

5. Recorded recollection. A memorandum or record concerning a matter about which a witness once had knowledge but now has insufficient recollection to enable the witness to testify fully and accurately, shown to have been made or adopted by the witness when the matter was fresh in the witness' memory and to reflect that knowledge correctly. If admitted, the memorandum or record may be read into evidence but may not itself be received as an exhibit unless offered by an adverse party.

6. Records of regularly conducted activity. A memorandum, report, record, or data compilation, in any form, of acts, events, conditions, opinions, or diagnoses, made at or near the time by, or from information transmitted by, a person with knowledge, if kept in the course of a regularly conducted business activity, and if it was the regular practice of that business activity to make the memorandum, report, record, or data compilation, all as shown by the testimony of the custodian or other qualified witness, unless the source of information or the method or circumstances of preparation indicate lack of trustworthiness. The term "business" as used in this paragraph includes business, institution, association, profession, occupation, and calling of every kind, whether or not conducted for profit.

7. Absence of entry in records kept in accordance with the provisions of paragraph (6). Evidence that a matter is not included in the memoranda reports, records, or data compilations, in any form, kept in accordance with the provisions of paragraph (6), to prove the nonoccurrence or nonexistence of the matter, if the matter was of a kind of which a memorandum, report, record, or data compilation was regularly made and preserved, unless the sources of information or other circumstances indicate lack of trustworthiness.

8. Public records and reports. Records, reports, statements, or data compilations, in any form, of public offices or agencies, setting forth (A) the activities of the office or agency, or (B) matters observed pursuant to duty imposed by law as to which matters there was a duty to report, excluding, however, in criminal cases matters observed by police officers and other law enforcement personnel, or (C) in civil actions and proceedings and against the Government in criminal cases, factual findings resulting from an investigation made pursuant to authority granted by law, unless the sources of information or other circumstances indicate lack of trustworthiness.

9. Records of vital statistics. Records or data compilations, in any form, of births, fetal deaths, deaths, or marriages, if the report thereof was made to a public office pursuant to requirements of law.

10. Absence of public record or entry. To prove the absence of a record, report, statement, or data compilation, in any form, or the nonoccurrence or nonexistence of a matter of which a record, report, statement, or data compilation, in any form, was regularly made and preserved by a public office or agency, evidence in the form of a certification in accordance with rule 902, or testimony, that diligent search failed to disclose the record, report, statement, or data compilation, or entry.

11. Records of religious organizations. Statements of births, marriages, divorces, deaths, legitimacy, ancestry, relationship by blood or marriage, or other similar facts of personal or family history, contained in a regularly kept record of a religious organization.

12. Marriage, baptismal, and similar certificates. Statements of fact contained in a certificate that the maker performed a marriage or other ceremony or administered a sacrament, made by a clergyman, public official, or other person authorized by the rules or practices of a religious organization or by law to perform the act certified, and purporting to have been issued at the time of the act or within a reasonable time thereafter.

13. Family records. Statements of fact concerning personal or family history contained in family Bibles, genealogies, charts, engravings on rings, inscriptions on family portraits, engravings on urns, crypts, or tombstones, or the like.

14. Records of documents affecting an interest in property. The record of a document purporting to establish or affect an interest in property, as proof of the content of the original recorded document and its execution and delivery by each person by whom it purports to

have been executed, if the record is a record of a public office and an applicable statute authorizes the recording of documents of that kind in that office.

15. Statements in documents affecting an interest in property. A statement contained in a document purporting to establish or affect an interest in property if the matter stated was relevant to the purpose of the document, unless dealings with the property since the document was made have been inconsistent with the truth of the statement or the purport of the document.

16. Statements in ancient documents. Statements in a document in existence twenty years or more the authenticity of which is established.

17. Market reports, commercial publications. Market quotations, tabulations, lists, directories, or other published compilations, generally used and relied upon by the public or by persons in particular occupations.

18. Learned treatises. To the extent called to the attention of an expert witness upon cross-examination or relied upon by the expert witness in direct examination, statements contained in published treatises, periodicals, or pamphlets on a subject of history, medicine, or other science or art, established as a reliable authority by the testimony or admission of the witness or by other expert testimony or by judicial notice. If admitted, the statements may be read into evidence but may not be received as exhibits.

19. Reputation concerning personal or family history. Reputation among members of a person's family by blood, adoption, or marriage, or among a person's associates, or in the community, concerning a person's birth, adoption, marriage, divorce, death, legitimacy, relationship by blood, adoption, or marriage, ancestry, or other similar fact of personal or family history.

20. Reputation concerning boundaries or general history. Reputation in a community, arising before the controversy, as to boundaries of or customs affecting lands in the community, and reputation as to events of general history important to the community or State or nation in which located.

21. Reputation as to character. Reputation of a person's character among associates or in the community.

22. Judgment of previous conviction. Evidence of a final judgment, entered after a trial or upon a plea of guilty (but not upon a plea of nolo contendere), adjudging a person guilty of a crime punishable

by death or imprisonment in excess of one year, to prove any fact essential to sustain the judgment, but not including, when offered by the Government in a criminal prosecution for purposes other than impeachment, judgments against persons other than the accused. The pendency of an appeal may be shown but does not affect admissibility.

23. Judgments as proof of matters of personal, family or general history, or boundaries, essential to the judgment, if the same would be provable by evidence of reputation.

24. Transferred to Rule 807.

Rule 804. Hearsay Exceptions; Declarant Unavailable

(a) Definition of unavailability "Unavailability as a witness" includes situations in which the declarant:

1. is exempted by ruling of the court on the ground of privilege from testifying concerning the subject matter of the declarant's statement; or

2. persists in refusing to testify concerning the subject matter of the declarant's statement despite an order of the court to do so; or

3. testifies to a lack of memory of the subject matter of the declarant's statement; or

4. is unable to be present or to testify at the hearing because of death or then existing physical or mental illness or infirmity; or

5. is absent from the hearing and the proponent of a statement has been unable to procure the declarant's attendance (or in the case of a hearsay exception under subdivision (b)(2), (3), or (4), the declarant's attendance or testimony) by process or other reasonable means.

A declarant is not unavailable as a witness if exemption, refusal, claim of lack of memory, inability, or absence is due to the procurement or wrongdoing of the proponent of a statement for the purpose of preventing the witness from attending or testifying.

(b) Hearsay exceptions The following are not excluded by the hearsay rule if the declarant is unavailable as a witness:

1. Former testimony. Testimony given as a witness at another hearing of the same or a different proceeding, or in a deposition taken in compliance with law in the course of the same or another proceeding, if the party against whom the testimony is now offered, or, in a civil

action or proceeding, a predecessor in interest, had an opportunity
and similar motive to develop the testimony by direct, cross, or
redirect examination.

2. **Statement under belief of impending death.** In a prosecution for
homicide or in a civil action or proceeding, a statement made by a
declarant while believing that the declarant's death was imminent,
concerning the cause or circumstances of what the declarant
believed to be impending death.

3. **Statement against interest.** A statement which was at the time of its
making so far contrary to the declarant's pecuniary or proprietary
interest, or so far tended to subject the declarant to civil or
criminal liability, or to render invalid a claim by the declarant against
another, that a reasonable person in the declarant's position would not
have made the statement unless believing it to be true. A statement
tending to expose the declarant to criminal liability and offered to
exculpate the accused is not admissible unless corroborating
circumstances clearly indicate the trustworthiness of the statement.

4. **Statement of personal or family history:**
   a. A statement concerning the declarant's own birth, adoption,
   marriage, divorce, legitimacy, relationship by blood, adoption,
   or marriage, ancestry, or other similar fact of personal or
   family history, even though declarant had no means of
   acquiring personal knowledge of the matter stated; or
   b. a statement concerning the foregoing matters, and death
   also, of another person, if the declarant was related to the
   other by blood, adoption, or marriage or was so intimately
   associated with the other's family as to be likely to have
   accurate information concerning the matter declared.

5. **Transferred to Rule 807.**

6. **Forfeiture by wrongdoing.** A statement offered against a party that
has engaged or acquiesced in wrongdoing that was intended to, and
did, procure the unavailability of the declarant as a witness.

Rule 805. Hearsay Within Hearsay
Hearsay included within hearsay is not excluded under the hearsay rule if each
part of the combined statements conforms with an exception to the hearsay
rule provided in these rules.

Rule 806. Attacking and Supporting Credibility of Declarant
When a hearsay statement, or a statement defined in Rule 801(d)(2),(C),(D), or
(E), has been admitted in evidence, the credibility of the declarant may be
attacked, and if attacked may be supported, by any evidence which would be

admissible for those purposes if declarant had testified as a witness. Evidence of a statement or conduct by the declarant at any time, inconsistent with the declarant's hearsay statement, is not subject to any requirement that the declarant may have been afforded an opportunity to deny or explain. If the party against whom a hearsay statement has been admitted calls the declarant as a witness, the party is entitled to examine the declarant on the statement as if under cross-examination.

Rule 807. Residual Exception

A statement not specifically covered by Rule 803 or 804 but having equivalent circumstantial guarantees of trustworthiness, is not excluded by the hearsay rule, if the court determines that:

  a. the statement is offered as evidence of a material fact
  b. the statement is more probative on the point for which it is offered than any other evidence which the proponent can procure through reasonable efforts; and
  c. the general purposes of these rules and the interests of justice will best be served by admission of the statement into evidence.

However, a statement may not be admitted under this exception unless the proponent of it makes known to the adverse party sufficiently in advance of the trial or hearing to provide the adverse party with a fair opportunity to prepare to meet it, the proponents intention to offer the statement and the particulars of it, including the name and address of the declarant.

ARTICLE IX

Authentication and Identification

Rule 901. Requirement of Authentication or Identification

(a) General provision The requirement of authentication or identification as a condition precedent to admissibility is satisfied by evidence sufficient to support a finding that the matter in question is what its proponent claims.

(b) Illustrations By way of illustration only, and not by way of limitation, the following are examples of authentication or identification conforming with the requirements of this rule:

  1. Testimony of witness with knowledge. Testimony that a matter is what it is claimed to be.
  2. Nonexpert opinion on handwriting. Nonexpert opinion as to the genuineness of handwriting, based upon familiarity not acquired for purposes of the litigation.

3. Comparison by trier or expert witness. Comparison by the trier of fact or by expert witnesses with specimens, which have been authenticated.

4. Distinctive characteristics and the like. Appearance, contents, substance, internal patterns, or other distinctive characteristics, taken in conjunction with circumstances.

5. Voice identification. Identification of a voice, whether heard first-hand or through mechanical or electronic transmission or recording, by opinion based upon hearing the voice at any time under circumstances connecting it with the alleged speaker.

6. Telephone conversations. Telephone conversations, by evidence that a call was made to the number assigned at the time by the telephone company to a particular person or business, if (A) in the case of a person, circumstances, including self-identification, show the person answering to be the one called, or (B) in the case of a business, the call was made to a place of business and the conversation related to business reasonably transacted over the telephone.

7. Public records or reports. Evidence that a writing authorized by law to be recorded or filed and in fact recorded or filed in a public office, or a purported public record, report, statement, or data compilation, in any form, is from the public office where items of this nature are kept.

8. Ancient documents or data compilation. Evidence that a document or data compilation, in any form, (A) is in such condition as to create no suspicion concerning its authenticity, (B) was in a place where it, if authentic, would likely be, and (C) has been in existence 20 years or more at the time it is offered.

9. Process or system. Evidence describing a process or system used to produce a result and showing that the process or system produces an accurate result.

10. Methods provided by statute or rule. Any method of authentication or identification provided by Act of Congress or by other rules prescribed by the Supreme Court pursuant to statutory authority.

Rule 902. Self-authentication [Proposed Amendment]

Extrinsic evidence of authenticity as a condition precedent to admissibility is not required with respect to the following:

1. Domestic public documents under seal. A document bearing a seal purporting to be that of the United States, or of any State, district, Commonwealth, territory, or insular possession thereof, or the Panama Canal Zone, or the Trust Territory of the Pacific

Islands, or of a political subdivision, department, officer, or agency thereof, and a signature purporting to be an attestation or execution.

2. Domestic public documents not under seal. A document purporting to bear the signature in the official capacity of an officer or employee of any entity included in paragraph (1) hereof, having no seal, if a public officer having a seal and having official duties in the district or political subdivision of the officer or employee certifies under seal that the signer has the official capacity and that the signature is genuine.

3. Foreign public documents. A document purporting to be executed or attested in an official capacity by a person authorized by the laws of a foreign country to make the execution or attestation, and accompanied by a final certification as to the genuineness of the signature and official position (A) of the executing or attesting person, or (B) of any foreign official whose certificate of genuineness of signature and official position relates to the execution or attestation or is in a chain of certificates of genuineness of signature and official position relating to the execution or attestation. A final certification may be made by a secretary of an embassy or legation, consul general, consul, vice consul, or consular agent of the United States, or a diplomatic or consular official of the foreign country assigned or accredited to the United States. If reasonable opportunity has been given to all parties to investigate the authenticity and accuracy of official documents, the court may, for good cause shown, order that they be treated as presumptively authentic without final certification or permit them to be evidenced by an attested summary with or without final certification.

4. Certified copies of public records. A copy of an official record or report or entry therein, or of a document authorized by law to be recorded or filed and actually recorded or filed in a public office, including data compilations in any form, certified as correct by the custodian or other person authorized to make the certification, by certificate complying with paragraph (1), (2), or (3) of this rule or complying with any Act of Congress or rule prescribed by the Supreme Court pursuant to statutory authority.

5. Official publications. Books, pamphlets, or other publications purporting to be issued by public authority.

6. Newspapers and periodicals. Printed materials purporting to be newspapers or periodicals.

7. Trade inscriptions and the like. Inscriptions, signs, tags, or labels purporting to have been affixed in the course of business and indicating ownership, control, or origin.

8. Acknowledged documents. Documents accompanied by a certificate of acknowledgment executed in the manner provided by law by a notary public or other officer authorized by law to take acknowledgments.

9. Commercial paper and related documents. Commercial paper, signatures thereon, and documents relating thereto to the extent provided by general commercial law.

10. Presumptions under Acts of Congress. Any signature, document, or other matter declared by Act of Congress to be presumptively or prima facie genuine or authentic.

Rule 903. Subscribing Witness' Testimony Unnecessary

The testimony of a subscribing witness is not necessary to authenticate a writing unless required by the laws of the jurisdiction whose laws govern the validity of the writing.

ARTICLE X

Contents of Writings, Recordings and Photographs

Rule 1001. Definitions

For purposes of this article the following definitions are applicable:

- (1) Writings and recordings. "Writings" and "recordings" consist of letters, words, or numbers, or their equivalent, set down by handwriting, typewriting, printing, photostatting, photographing, magnetic impulse, mechanical or electronic recording, or other form of data compilation.

- (2) Photographs. "Photographs" include still photographs, X-ray films, videotapes, and motion pictures.

- (3) Original. An "original" of a writing or recording is the writing or recording itself or any counterpart intended to have the same effect by a person executing or issuing it. An "original" of a photograph includes the negative or any print therefrom. If data are stored in a computer or similar device, any printout or other output readable by sight, shown to reflect the data accurately, is an "original".

- (4) Duplicate. A "duplicate" is a counterpart produced by the same impression as the original, or from the same matrix, or by means of photography, including enlargements and miniatures, or by mechanical or electronic re-recording, or by chemical reproduction, or by other equivalent techniques, which accurately reproduces the original.

Rule 1002. Requirement of Original
To prove the content of a writing, recording, or photograph, the original writing, recording, or photograph is required, except as otherwise provided in these rules or by Act of Congress.

Rule 1003. Admissibility of Duplicates
A duplicate is admissible to the same extent as an original unless (1) a genuine question is raised as to the authenticity of the original or (2) in the circumstances it would be unfair to admit the duplicate in lieu of the original.

Rule 1004. Admissibility of Other Evidence of Contents
The original is not required, and other evidence of the contents of a writing, recording, or photograph is admissible if:

- (1) Originals lost or destroyed. All originals are lost or have been destroyed, unless the proponent lost or destroyed them in bad faith; or
- (2) Original not obtainable. No original can be obtained by any available judicial process or procedure; or
- (3) Original in possession of opponent. At a time when an original was under the control of the party against whom offered, that party was put on notice, by the pleadings or otherwise, that the contents would be a subject of proof at the hearing, and that party does not produce the original at the hearing; or
- (4) Collateral matters. The writing, recording, or photograph is not closely related to a controlling issue.

Rule 1005. Public Records
The contents of an official record, or of a document authorized to be recorded or filed and actually recorded or filed, including data compilations in any form, if otherwise admissible, may be proved by copy, certified as correct in accordance with rule 902 or testified to be correct by a witness who has compared it with the original. If a copy, which complies with the foregoing cannot be obtained by the exercise of reasonable diligence, then other evidence of the contents may be given.

Rule 1006. Summaries
The contents of voluminous writings, recordings, or photographs that cannot conveniently be examined in court may be presented in the form of a chart, summary, or calculation. The originals, or duplicates, shall be made available for examination or copying, or both, by other parties at reasonable time and place. The court may order that they be produced in court.

Rule 1007. Testimony or Written Admission of Party

Contents of writings, recordings, or photographs may be proved by the testimony or deposition of the party against whom offered or by that party's written admission, without accounting for the nonproduction of the original.

Rule 1008. Functions of Court and Jury

When the admissibility of other evidence of contents of writings, recordings, or photographs under these rules depends upon the fulfillment of a condition of fact, the question whether the condition has been fulfilled is ordinarily for the court to determine in accordance with the provisions of rule 104. However, when an issue is raised:

    a. whether the asserted writing ever existed

    b. whether another writing, recording, or photograph produced at the trial is the original, or

    c. whether other evidence of contents correctly reflects the contents, the issue is for the trier of fact to determine as in the case of other issues of fact.

ARTICLE XI

Miscellaneous Rules

Rule 1101. Applicability of Rules

(a) Courts and judges These rules apply to the United States district courts, the District Court of Guam, the District Court of the Virgin Islands, the District Court for the Northern Mariana Islands, the United States courts of appeals, the United States Claims Court, and to the United States bankruptcy judges and United States magistrate judges, in the actions, cases, and proceedings and to the extent hereinafter set forth. The terms "judge" and "court" in these rules include United States bankruptcy judges and United States magistrate judges.

(b) Proceedings generally These rules apply generally to civil actions and proceedings, including admiralty and maritime cases, to criminal cases and proceedings, to contempt proceedings except those in which the court may act summarily, and to proceedings and cases under title 11, United States Code [11 USCS §§ 1 et seq.].

(c) Rule of privilege The rule with respect to privileges applies at all stages of all actions, cases, and proceedings.

(d) Rules inapplicable The rules (other than with respect to privileges) do not apply in the following situations:

1. Preliminary questions of fact. The determination of questions of fact preliminary to admissibility of evidence when the issue is to be determined by the court under *rule 104*.
2. Grand jury. Proceedings before grand juries.
3. Miscellaneous proceedings. Proceedings for extradition or rendition; preliminary examinations in criminal cases; sentencing, or granting or revoking probation; issuance of warrants for arrest, criminal summonses, and search warrants; and proceedings with respect to release on bail or otherwise.

(e) Rules applicable in part In the following proceedings these rules apply to the extent that matters of evidence are not provided for in the statutes that govern procedure therein or in other rules prescribed by the Supreme Court pursuant to statutory authority:

- the trial of misdemeanors and other petty offenses before United States magistrate judge; review of agency actions when the facts are subject to trail de novo under section 107(2)(F) of title 5, United States Code;
- review of orders of the Secretary of Agriculture under section 2 of the Act entitled "An Act to authorize association of producers of agricultural products" approved February 18, 1922 (7 U.S.C. 292), and under section 6 and 7(c) of the Perishable Agricultural Commodities Act, 1930 (7 U.S.C. 499f, 499g(c));
- naturalization and revocation of naturalization under sections 310–318 of the Immigration and Nationality Act (8 U.S.C. 1421–1429);
- prize proceedings in admiralty under sections 7651–7681 of title 10, United States Code; review of orders of the Secretary of the Interior under section 2 of the Act entitled "An Act authorizing associations of producers of aquatic products" approved June 25, 1934 (15 U.S.C. 533);
- review of orders of petroleum control boards under section 5 of the Act entitled "An act to regulate interstate and foreign commerce in petroleum and its products by prohibiting the shipment in such commerce of petroleum and its products produced in violation of State law, and for other purposes", approved February 22, 1935 (15 U.S.C. 715d); actions for fines, penalties, or forfeitures under part V of title IV of the Tariff Act of 1930 (19 U.S.C. 1581–1624), or under the Anti-Smuggling Act (19 U.S.C. 1701–1711);

- criminal libel for condemnation, exclusion of imports, or other proceedings under the Federal Food, Drug, and Cosmetic Act (21 U.S.C. 301–392);
- disputes between seamen under sections 4079, 4080, and 4081 of the Revised Statutes (22 U.S.C. 256–258);
- habeas corpus under sections 2241–2254 of title 28, United States Code; motions to vacate, set aside or correct sentence under section 2255 of title 28, United States Code;
- actions for penalties for refusal to transport destitute seamen under section 4578 of the Revised Statutes (46 U.S.C. 679);
- actions against the United States under the Act entitled "An Act authorizing suits against the United States in admiralty for damage caused by and salvage service rendered to public vessels belonging to the United States, and for other purposes", approved March 3, 1925 (46 U.S.C. 781–790), as implemented by section 7730 of title 10, United States Code.

Rule 1102. Amendments
Amendments to the Federal Rules of Evidence may be made as provided in section 2072 of title 28 of the United States Code.

Rule 1103. Title
These rules may be known and cited as the Federal Rules of Evidence.

Appendix B

SAMPLE CRIMINAL INDICTMENT

UNITED STATES OF AMERICA,)	CR 06-<u>79</u>
)	
Plaintiff,)	I N D I C T M E N T
)	
vs.)	
)	[21 U.S.C. § 846:
JOSEPH CHARLES SMITH)	Conspiracy; 21 U.S.C. §
aka Joey,)	841 (a) (1): Distribution
JOHN WILLIAM JONES,)	of and Possession with
RICHARD EUGENE RICCO)	Intent to Distribute
aka Ricky,)	Cocaine; 18 U.S.C. § 2:
STEVEN ROBERT STOKES)	Aiding and Abetting]
aka Stevie,)	
)	
Defendants.)	
)	

The Grand Jury charges:

COUNT ONE

[21 U.S.C. § 846]

A. <u>OBJECTS OF THE CONSPIRACY</u>

Beginning on a date unknown to the Grand Jury and continuing to on or about January 4, 2006, in Los Angeles

County, within the Central District of California, and elsewhere, defendants JOSEPH SMITH, aka Joey ("SMITH"), JOHN JONES ("JONES"), RICHARD RICCO, aka Ricky ("RICO"), STEVEN ROBERT STOKES, aka Stevie ("STOKES"), and others known and unknown to the Grand Jury, knowingly and intentionally conspired and agreed with each other to commit the following offenses:

1. To distribute at least 5 kilograms of a mixture or substance containing a detectable amount of cocaine, a schedule II narcotic drug controlled substance, in violation of Title 21, United States Code, Section 841(a) (1).

2. To possess with the intent to distribute at least 5 kilograms of a mixture or substance containing a detectable amount of cocaine, a schedule II narcotic drug controlled substance, in violation of Title 21 United States Code, Section 841(a) (1).

B. MEANS BY WHICH THE OBJECTS OF THE CONSPIRACY WERE TO BE ACCOMPLISHED

The objects of the conspiracy were to be accomplished in substance as follows:

1. Defendant SMITH would arrange for the importation of narcotics into the United States for the purpose of distribution.

2. Defendant RICCO would distribute narcotics for SMITH in the New York City, New York area.

3. Defendant STOKES would transport narcotics from Los Angeles, California to New York City, New York for defendants SMITH and RICCO.

4. Defendant JONES would create a hidden storage compartment in a vehicle for defendants SMITH and JONES for the purpose of hiding narcotics.

C. OVERT ACTS

In furtherance of the conspiracy and to accomplish the objectives of the conspiracy, on or about the following dates, defendants SMITH, JONES, RICCO, STOKES, and other co-conspirators known and unknown to the Grand Jury, committed various overt acts within the Central District of California and elsewhere, including but not limited to the following:

1. On January 4, 2006, by telephone, defendant SMITH and an unindicted co-conspirator agreed to have defendant RICCO distribute cocaine in New York City, New York.

2. On January 4, 2006, in person, defendant RICCO agreed to distribute 5 kilograms of cocaine for defendant SMITH and an unindicted co-conspirator.

3. On January 6, 2006, by telephone, defendant SMITH offered to pay defendant STOKES $3000 to transport cocaine from Los Angeles, California to New York City, New York.

4. On January 6, 2006, by telephone, defendant STOKES agreed to transport cocaine for defendant SMITH and an unindicted co-conspirator from Los Angeles, California to New York City, New York for $3,000.

5. On January 6, 2006, by telephone, defendant SMITH agreed to wire money to defendant JONES to create a hidden storage compartment within a vehicle to be used by STOKES to transport cocaine from Los Angeles, California to New York City, New York.

6. On January 6, 2006, by telephone, defendant STOKES told defendant SMITH that he would arrive in Los Angeles, California on January 10, 2006.

7. On January 10, 2006, defendant RICCO arrived in Los Angeles, California and met with defendant JONES to pay him for creating a hidden storage compartment within a vehicle.

8. On January 11, 2006, STOKES received $3,000 by wire from defendant SMITH for payment to transport cocaine from Los Angeles, California to New York City, New York.

9. Sometime after January 6, 2006, defendant JONES created a hidden storage compartment in a gray 1999 Chrysler LHS ("LHS").

10. On January 12, 2006, by telephone, defendants JONES and STOKES discussed the hidden storage compartment in the LHS.

11. On January 15, 2006, defendant JONES drove defendant STOKES to a location where the LHS, loaded with approximately 4,995 grams of cocaine, was parked, and provided him with the keys to the vehicle.

12. Between January 15, 2006, and January 21, 2006, defendant STOKES drove the LHS, which contained approximately 4,995 grams of cocaine, from Los Angeles, California to New York City, New York.

13. On January 22, 2006, defendant RICCO attempted to sell approximately 4,995 grams of cocaine to an undercover agent of the Drug Enforcement Administration.

COUNT TWO

[21 U.S.C. § 841 (a) (1); 18 U.S.C. § 2 (a)]

On or about January 15, 2006, in Los Angeles County, within the Central District of California, defendants SMITH, JONES, RICCO, and STOKES knowingly and intentionally distributed, and aided, abetted, counseled, commanded, induced, and procured the distribution of, with intent to distribute, more than 500 grams, that is approximately 4,995 grams, of a mixture or substance containing a detectable amount of cocaine, a schedule II narcotic drug controlled substance.

A TRUE BILL

Foreperson

ABRAHAM LINCOLN
United States Attorney

JOHN PAUL JONES
Assistant United States Attorney
Chief, Criminal Division

MICHAEL ANGELO
Assistant United States Attorney
Chief, Major Narcotics

Appendix C

Sample Search Warrant Affidavit

STATEMENT OF PROBABLE CAUSE

GARY EDGINGTON
Special Agent
California Department of Justice
Bureau of Investigations

Your affiant has been a Southern California peace officer for the last sixteen years. Since October of 1994 your affiant has been employed as a Special Agent (SA) with the California Department of Justice (DOJ). Since November of 1996 your affiant has been assigned to the Fraud Investigation Unit of DOJ's Bureau of Investigation in Los Angeles California. Prior to this assignment your affiant was a SA assigned to DOJ's Bureau of Narcotic Enforcement. During this time period your affiant was the lead investigator in several cases involving the fraudulent obtaining of controlled substances. During these investigations your affiant prepared and executed numerous search warrants, which resulted in the seizure of evidence. Much of this evidence was ultimately utilized during the prosecution of these defendants. Much of the evidence seized consisted of records, and other documentary evidence.

Your affiant was also personally involved in several major cocaine trafficking investigations. Each investigation involved multiple suspects who exhibited typical narcotics trafficker methods of operation, i.e. use of counter surveillance driving techniques, pagers and cellular telephones, car switches and multiple addresses. One of these investigations led to the seizure of over $450,000.00 in narcotics proceeds hidden in the tailgate of a typical "load" type vehicle. This case also resulted in the arrest of two suspects and the seizure of a money counting machine and hand written recordation's of sales/accounts receivable commonly called "pays and owes". Further, since becoming a Special Agent your affiant has made one purchase of cocaine while in an undercover capacity. This purchase resulted in the arrest on one suspect and the service of a search warrant prepared by your affiant.

Prior to October 1994, your affiant was employed for seven and a half years as an Investigator for the Los Angeles County District Attorney's Office, the last four years of which were spent in the Major Narcotics Investigations Section. During that time period your affiant was the case agent on numerous investigations involving the trafficking of Cocaine, Marijuana, Methaqualone and other controlled substances. As a case agent your affiant prepared and served in excess of thirty search warrants related to narcotics investigations and testified in open court on narcotics cases once.

Many of the cases your affiant investigated concerned large trafficking organizations involving multiple suspects. Most of these cases concluded in the service of search warrants, the seizure of large amounts contraband, assets and the successful prosecution of numerous defendants. Further, during this time your affiant was an active participant in excess of one hundred narcotics related surveillances. On over twenty occasions your affiant directed Confidential Informants, operating under his control, to purchase controlled substances such as Methaqualone, Cocaine and Marijuana. In most instances, these purchases led to criminal convictions for trafficking related offenses.

During this time period your affiant also conducted an investigation into a group of individuals involved in the cloning of cellular telephones. This investigation resulted in the arrest of two persons and the seizure of numerous cellular telephones, computers and related equipment. This investigation resulted in the conviction of both defendants.

Also during this time period, your affiant conducted dozens of in-depth interviews with narcotics traffickers and cell phone cloners. The subject matter of these interviews included trafficking and communication methods, counter surveillance techniques, "pays and owes" ledgers, methodology and effects of various narcotics/drugs.

While employed as a District Attorney Investigator, your affiant was assigned to the Welfare Fraud Unit for approximately sixteen months. During this time your affiant became familiar with various types of fraud investigation and common methods used by suspects such as the falsification of birth records and other official documents and the forgery of various official documents. During this time period your affiant was the case investigator on a fraud case wherein he was the co-affiant on a search warrant served in the State of Nevada. This investigation also resulted in the conviction of the defendant in a California court.

Prior to this your affiant was employed by the Beverly Hills Police Department as a Police Officer for a period of six years. Three of those six years were spent as a Detective assigned to work auto theft and in custody narcotics arrests, the remainder spent as a patrol officer. During the six years your affiant was a Beverly Hills Police Officer he interviewed about seventy narcotic abusers/arrestees, testified in open court on narcotics cases four times, and arrested approximately fifty people for narcotics offenses such as possession for sale of Cocaine, possession of Amphetamines, Barbiturates, Hallucinogens, Marijuana, Phencyclidine, Heroin and Drug Paraphernalia. Also during this time period he attended ten hours of in-service narcotics training sponsored by the Beverly Hills Police Department. Prior to this, your affiant was employed as a Police Officer by the City of Manhattan Beach for a period of two years and was assigned to the Patrol Division. While in that assignment your affiant arrested, or participated in the arrest of approximately thirty persons for narcotics violations. Your affiant also interviewed approximately fifty persons who were under the influence of narcotics and or drugs.

Your affiant attended basic Peace Officer training at the Los Angeles County Sheriff's Academy in 1979, for a period of nineteen weeks. Approximately twenty hours of this training was devoted to narcotics/drugs offenses and their investigation. In 1990 and 1991 your affiant attended five eight-hour training seminars sponsored by the California Narcotics Officers Association dealing with the following subjects: Marijuana Hydroponics and Cultivation; Origin and History of Cocaine and Manufacture of "Rock Cocaine"; Officer Safety, Tactical Response to Undercover Activities; Narcotics Trafficker Profiling and Investigation. In addition your affiant attended a twenty-four-hour class entitled "Drug Abuse Recognition" through the Glendale Police Department. He also attended an eighty-hour narcotics investigation course taught by the California State Department of Justice, Bureau of Narcotic Enforcement. Some of the subjects covered during the eighty-hour course included Heroin investigation; Marijuana cultivation, abuse and trafficking; Methamphetamine manufacturing abuse and trafficking methods; Anabolic Steroid abuse; major Cocaine trafficking investigations including common trafficking methods used by drug cartels. In June of 1991 he attended sixteen hours of narcotics training sponsored by the Western States Information Network. In October/November of 1994 your affiant successfully completed a four-week Special Agent Orientation Course presented by the California Department of Justice Bureau of Narcotic Enforcement. Some of the subjects covered in this course included Search and Seizure, Surveillance Operations including identifying counter surveillance techniques as practiced by drug traffickers, Current Trends in Heroin and Cocaine Trafficking, and Informant Handling. Additionally, in 1991, 1992, and 1993 your affiant attended three annual training conferences sponsored by the California Narcotics Officer Association. Each training conference consisted of over twenty-four hours of narcotics related training.

Your affiant's education includes an Associate of Arts Degree in Administration of Justice from West Los Angeles College and a Bachelor of Arts Degree from the University of Redlands.

In June of 1997 your affiant was assigned to investigate allegations that a male subject named Michael Low, Doing Business As (D.B.A.) Four Seasons Investing, had stolen $350,000.00 from members of the Pritzkau family who currently reside in the Plano, Texas area.

In June of 1997 your affiant interviewed Robert Pritzkau concerning the facts surrounding the investments that his family made with Michael Low, D.B.A. Four Seasons Investing. Pritzkau told your affiant that in late January of 1996 he was given proxy and control of all Pritzkau family communication and business matters related to Michael Low and Four Seasons Investing. Pritzkau told your affiant that this was done due to stress and the failing health of his father, Edward Pritzkau. Pritzkau told your affiant that until the moment he assumed control of the Pritzkau family investments, his father, Edward Pritzkau was acting as a proxy for the other involved family members.

Pritzkau told your affiant that in January 1994, Edward Pritzkau noticed an advertisement in the newspaper "The Spotlight." This advertisement was for investment opportunities with "Four Seasons Investing" located in Beverly Hills, California. The ad specified high profits with low risk. Edward Pritzkau subsequently contacted Four Seasons Investing and spoke with a male who identified himself as Michael Low. Low promised Edward Pritzkau superior growth and performance with low risk, by investing in his Standard & Poors (S&P) 100 options program. Edward Pritzkau told Low that he and his family were looking for a liquid, low risk investment. Low assured Edward Pritzkau that his (Low's) Option Trading program was very low risk. Edward Pritzkau, having Power of Attorney over Frieda Wesch and Gertrude Pritzkau's (family members) investments, as well as his own, slowly began investing in Low's option program. Robert Pritzkau said that his father Edward Pritzkau handled all of the initial contacts with Low and acted as a proxy for the other family members who ultimately invested funds with Four Seasons Investing.

The following persons are members of the Pritzkau family who invested money with Michael Low D.B.A. Four Seasons Investing:

Edward Pritzkau
Anneliese Pritzkau
Frieda Wesch
Gertrude Pieritz

Tom Pritzkau

Karen Pritzkau

Debbie Pritzkau

Robert Pritzkau

"Daniel's Trust" a trust fund set up for Robert Pritzkau.

During the time period of 2/94 to 7/95, there were occasions where withdrawals were requested by Pritzkau family members and these requests were honored by Low without difficulty or delay. The following is a listing of funds wired by Pritzkau family members to the account of Four Seasons Investing. These wire transfers were sent with the understanding that the funds would be invested by Low (Four Seasons Investing) in stock options investments.

Name	Start Date	Stop date	Total	Withdrawals
Total # of Trans.				
Frieda Wesch:	2/15/94	9/21/95	$59,000.00	$20,000 (7/20/94)
Total: 8				
Debbie Pritzkau:	12/27/96	12/27/96	$5,000.00	0
Total: 1				
Gertrude Pritzkau:	8/12/94	7/3/95	$61,000.00	0
Total: 4				
Anneliese Pritzkau:	11/7/94	11/7/94	$5,365.00	0
Total: 1				
Karen Pritzkau:	12/23/95	12/23/95	$25,000.00	$20,000 (3/95)
Total: 1				
Edward Pritzkau:	10/11/95	9/15/95	$113,000.00	$20,000 (5/22/95)
Total: 9				
Daniel's Trust:	2/8/95	9/15/95	$76,187.25	$5,000 (10/26/94)
Total: 4				
Robert Pritzkau:	6/10/95	9/20/95	$9,246.00	0
Total: 4				

Robert Pritzkau told your affiant that throughout the time period that the Pritzkau family did business with Low, i.e. Four Seasons Investing, they communicated through their proxy, Edward Pritzkau, that the funds in question should remain in low risk investments. It was also repeatedly stated to Low that the funds be available for quick access should the need arise.

In the summer of 1995, Low presented the possibility of investing Pritzkau family funds in an investment scheme called Prime Bank Guarantees. At first the Pritzkau family expressed interest in this type of investment. However, when they were told by Low that their funds would have to be invested for one year in an account whose location would only be known to Low and these funds would be inaccessible for one year, they advised Low that they would not be interested in the Prime Bank Guarantee investment. The Pritzkau's later learned that Prime Bank Guarantee investments are a very popular fraud scheme. Through his own investigation, your affiant verified this information.

According to professionals in the investment community that your affiant spoke with, Prime Bank Notes or Guarantees fraud schemes, typically involve having the victim investor deposit their funds in an offshore account. The victim is then told their funds will be used to purchase short-term notes from so-called "Prime" rated financial institutions. Apparently, the funds are then diverted to the perpetrator's hidden accounts and the victim loses their investment. It is your affiant's belief that the "Prime Bank Guarantee" investment opportunity was actually an attempt by Low to defraud the Pritzkau's out of more of their family funds and/or to cover prior losses or embezzled family funds not reported or discovered by the Pritzkau family.

Robert Pritzkau told your affiant, that in October of 1995, the Pritzkau family (through Edward Pritzkau) made a request to withdraw $100,000 to help run the family business. After several weeks of demanding the $100,000, Low finally disclosed to Edward Pritzkau that the funds were placed in an investment scheme that he called a "bond program" and the funds would not be accessible for one year. At one point, Low wanted the Pritzkau family to sign an agreement preventing them from reporting Low and Four Seasons Investing to law enforcement authorities. In your affiant's opinion Low's insistence on having the Pritzkau family sign an agreement to not establish contact with law enforcement is a further indication that Low was knowingly involved in unlawful activities and was fearful of detection by law enforcement authorities.

Robert Pritzkau told your affiant that throughout the time period of October 1995 to March 1996, repeated demands for a full return of funds, or at least a disclosure of the location of the funds and current balance were made to Low. Pritzkau told your affiant, Low's response consisted of constant delaying tactics and to date neither he or any other member of his family have received any information concerning the current status of their investments made with Four Seasons Investing, nor have they received any sort of return of funds from Low or Four Seasons Investing. Pritzkau told your affiant that as of this date the total amount of money invested by his family with Four Seasons Investing was $353,798.00, of which $65,000.00 was returned by Low when requested by family members. However, these returns of funds by Low, as the previous chart shows, all occurred prior to 6/95.

On 7/18/97, your affiant received a pager message to call Low at his home telephone number (310) 555–8682. Your affiant telephoned that number and spoke with Low for approximately 30 minutes. During that conversation, your affiant asked Low if he traded the Pritzkau's money with any other brokerage house besides Benjamin and Jerrold of Chicago Ill. Low replied that the only investments he made with the Pritzkau's money was through Benjamin and Jerrold. During the conversation, Low also told your affiant that the statements he sent to the Pritzkau family concerning their investments were true and accurate. Low also told your affiant he had no partners in Four Seasons Investing and worked by himself.

Your affiant asked Low if he had bank statements that pertain to the Pritzkau family investments. Low replied that they must have been "thrown out." In your affiant's opinion and experience, it is very unusual for a legitimate business dealing in investments of the size made by the Pritzkau family to misplace, loose, or destroy important records such as bank account statements/records and client statements. These records would be vital not only for business purposes, but also for tax reasons. In your affiant's opinion Low either destroyed these records or is withholding them in an effort to conceal his criminal activities from your affiant.

During his review of correspondence between Low and the Pritzkau family, your affiant noted that the business address for Four Seasons Investing is listed as 9601 Wilshire Blvd. suite 1700, Beverly Hills CA. On 8/1/97, your affiant went to that location in an attempt to locate the address listed. Your affiant was informed by a building security guard that suite 1700 is in fact Camden Cleaners, which in addition to dry cleaning, also operates a private post office box commonly called a "mail drop." Your affiant went to that location and spoke with a male white adult who was acting as the manager for the location. This subject confirmed that Michael Low rents a post office box at that location and has been receiving mail there for several years. However, he refused to give your affiant any other information concerning Low or other D.B.A.s that he may be receiving mail under, at that location.

In your affiant's experience it is common for persons involved in criminal activity to use a post office box as their address of record. This provides them with additional security and makes their location by law enforcement or other entities more difficult. Furthermore, it is not unusual for persons involved in schemes involving fraud to use a business address, i.e. mail drop locations such as the one described above, in a well-known seemingly affluent area such as Beverly Hills. This is done to add more credibility to their schemes by seeming to conduct business in a prosperous city.

Also during his review of copies of written communications between Low and the Pritzkau family, your affiant noted that Low stated that he had a business associate. Specifically, a fax sent to Edward Pritzkau dated 2/22/96, 11:31 PM, in which Low says he and his "partner" may be able to provide funding for a construction project. In a later telephone conversation between Low and Edward Pritzkau on 2/29/96, Low stated that his partner is R.W. Runis. Additionally, Robert Pritzkau provided your affiant with copies of documents obtained by the Pritzkau's Private Investigator Jack Crosby, in February, 1996. These documents list R. W. Runis, Michael Low and Jay L. Werelius as corporate officers in company called C.A.P.C.A. Corporation with offices in Kirkland, Washington. This document pertains to an investment opportunity in "Special Mining Ore" located in "Unknown Mining District, Washoe County Nevada." The Pritzkau's also provided your affiant with a document listing Michael Low as the Executive Managing Director C.A.P.C.A. Corporation. This document pertains to a supposed 704 Karat Sapphire offered as an asset. This document also bears the names of "U.S. Mandate Office", 9601 Wilshire Blvd suite 1700, Beverly Hills CA (the same location as Four Seasons Investing), and Robert Cohen, General Counsel, Amlin Capital Administration, Los Angeles CA. Pritzkau also provided your affiant with a copy of a document entitled "Escrow Agreement"; this document pertained to the Prime Bank Guarantee investment that Low was attempting to involve the Pritzkau's in. It lists Balanced Investment International LTD, a Bahamas Corporation, Prosperity Bank and Trust Corporation, P.O. Box 300, Nauru, Central Pacific and Signature Interests Inc. Plano Texas, as parties to the transaction.

Also in February of 1996 Crosby telephoned Robert Cohen at his office in Laguna Beach CA. Cohen told Crosby that he was very familiar with Low and "wanted nothing to do with him." He also told Crosby that Low thought he (Cohen) had lots of foreign contacts that could be useful to him (Low). Crosby next telephoned R. W. Runis at his residence in Denver Colorado, on the pretext of being a potential investor with Four Seasons. Runis said that he knew Low, but if he (Crosby) was going to do business with Low then he needed to speak with Low directly. Crosby said that Runis' tone was very sharp during their short conversation. Finally, Crosby called Jay L. Werelius in Kirkland Washington. Werelius admitted that he knew Low, but said nothing further and the conversation was terminated.

In your affiant's experience, it is quite common for persons involved in investment fraud to use bank accounts and business addresses outside the United States. It is also a common practice to market supposedly legitimate commodities such as mining ore or rare gems. However, these types of transactions are frequently used by persons involved in investment schemes as a method to fraudulently obtain funds. The reason why off-shore accounts and business addresses are used is to avoid US Government regulations, scrutiny by law enforcement and to make taking legal action against them very difficult. Additionally, marketing commodities such as "special mining ore" and gemstones are potentially very attractive to the victim investor. If legitimate, they could provide high profits. However, to determine the legitimacy of the commodities themselves requires specific knowledge, such as geology and expertise in gem stone evaluation. The would-be investor frequently does not posses this knowledge and has no way of verifying the transactions legitimacy. This is why these types of "investment opportunities" are offered by persons involved in fraudulent schemes. It is your affiant's opinion that this information is further evidence that Low is involved in a criminal conspiracy with other individuals. Furthermore, it indicates that Low may be involved in other fraudulent schemes.

On 7/20/97, your affiant interviewed Mr Jack Crosby by telephone concerning his investigation on behalf of the Pritzkau family. Crosby said that he is a former Special Agent with the Federal Bureau on Investigation now working in private practice as a Private Investigator. He traveled to Los Angeles in February of 1996 to conduct an investigation into Michael Low on behalf of the Pritzkau family. During that time period Crosby said that he conducted a surveillance at Low's residence on Sherbourne in Los Angeles and watched Low take trash from his apartment and dump it in a large dumpster in an alley at the rear of the complex. Crosby said he recovered several documents including the previously mentioned investment documents. Additionally, Crosby said he discovered correspondence addressed to Michael Lowenstein mixed with these other documents. As part of his investigation, Crosby said he conducted a search to attempt to locate bank accounts under the control of Low. Crosby located an account at Citibank in New York, New York, account number 4–0006346940 under the name Michael Scott Low, Artiste Corp, Balanced Investment International, Ltd. At the time of his inquiry, i.e. February 1996, the balance was $263,561.72. Your affiant noted that Balanced Investments appears to be a D.B.A. for Michael Low in that it appears as in the previously mentioned Prime Bank Guarantee "Escrow Instructions", and it's business address was listed as 9601 Wilshire Blvd suite 1700, Beverly Hills Ca (this is the same location as Four Seasons Investing). Additionally, your affiant noted that the Pritzkau's received a copy of a statement from Low purporting to be from Citibank, New York, in February 1996. Furthermore, this statement indicated a balance of $255,358.61. However, the date of the statement and the account number had been blocked out. Crosby told your affiant that when he rechecked the account several weeks later the balance had been reduced to zero.

Your affiant noted that during his review of documents provided by the Pritzkau family and Jack Crosby he saw a fax cover sheet from Michael Low, "Artiste Corp." to Jack Lubock. The fax was dated, however the subject area of the face sheet was blank.

Crosby also located the following other accounts for Low: Citibank, Rancho Park branch, account number 13324424400. Wells Fargo Bank, Beverly Hills branch (9354 Wilshire Blvd) account #6814171070.

Additionally the following account information was provided to the Pritzkau family by Low in order for them to wire funds to his accounts. Those accounts were:

Swiss Bank Corp. Zurich Switzerland, account# PO–146,726.0, Swift routing number# SBCO CIIZZ80A, account name Fidenas International Bank Ltd, Prosperity Bank and Trust Corp. It should be recalled that Prosperity Bank and Trust is listed in the previously mentioned "Escrow Instructions" for the Prime Bank Guarantee investment scheme offered by Low to the Pritzkau family.

First Interstate Bank, 9601 Wilshire Blvd., Beverly Hills Ca, Account number #156522941, account name "Four Seasons Investing." This is the account that the Pritzkau family wired their funds into.

Crosby also advised your affiant that he located information indicating that Low was also operating a business called Four Corners Investing, Beverly Hills CA. On 7/20/97 your affiant telephoned directory assistance requesting a telephone number for that company. Your affiant was advised that Four Corners Investing's telephone number is (310) 659–1838. Your affiant telephoned that number and spoke with an answering service for that company. They advised that Four Corners Investing begins answering their phones at 9:00 AM. The answering service could not confirm if Low was associated with the company because they did not have an employee list. However, your affiant noted that this telephone number is identical to one listed on a fictitious business name statement for Four Seasons Investing. This fictitious business statement was provided to your affiant by Crosby. Crosby also provided your affiant with other fictitious business name statements for Four Seasons Investing. The addresses listed included the Wilshire Blvd. location, as well as 1351 N. Crescent Heights Blvd. Los Angeles CA. 90046.

As part of his investigation your affiant obtained Los Angeles County Assessor's records for 2017/2011 South Sherbourne, Los Angeles. According to the Assessor's records 2011/2013 is owned by Marjorie Kahn, C/O the Trust of Frances Kahn, deceased; 2015/2017 also shows ownership under the name of Marjorie and lists a former owner of Frances Kahn Trust. Your affiant recalled that during his review of Fictitious Business Name (FBN) statements filed by Michael Low he noted that on 1/18/96, Low filed a FBN statement (file number 960096778) using the name "Frances Kahn Family Trust Co., 9601 Wilshire Blvd., suite 1700, Beverly Hills 90210." Furthermore, your affiant reviewed a photocopy of what appears to be a 3-day notice to the renter of 2015 South Sherbourne that they were in violation of their rental agreement. Your affiant noted that Michael Low was listed as the Plaintiff/Manager; it appeared to bear the signature of Michael Low and was dated 2/3/96. This document was submitted to your affiant by Jack Crosby and the Pritzkau family.

It should be noted that during his physical inspection of the exterior of Low's residence, he noted that 2017/2015 share a common two-story building, as does the adjacent address 2011/2013. Additionally, both buildings seem to share a common exterior design and share a common open walkway running between the buildings. Based on these facts and observations, it is your affiant's opinion that Michael Low occupies a position of control over both of the properties located at 2017/2015 and 2013/2011 South Sherbourne, Los Angeles, such as manager. It is therefore reasonable to assume that Low has total access to the garages and storage areas at both properties.

On 8/4/97 your affiant interviewed Daniel Updegraff. Updegraff told your affiant that he, along with his friends Lilly Vickson and Jean and George

Snyder, had invested money with Michael Low D.B.A. Four Seasons Investing and had later been told by Low that their investments had been lost. Updegraff told your affiant that he first met Low in March of 1995 during a meeting with he, the Snyders and Low. The meeting took place at the Snyder residence located in Van Nuys CA. Updegraff told your affiant that he has known Jean and George Snyder since 1991 and was actually living with them at the time of the meeting. Low explained his investment methods to Updegraff and the Snyders. Low said that funds invested with him were absolutely safe. In April 1995 Updegraff met with Low and gave him a cashier's check made out to Four Seasons Investing for $50,000.00. Updegraff said that the funds were to be invested in stock options as per his contract with Low. In May of 1995 Updegraff gave Low another $50,000 to invest in stock options. Updegraff told your affiant that these funds were proceeds from a medical retirement settlement and their safety was very important to him. Updegraff said that he had arranged with Low to receive monthly payments of $1000.00, which would be his share of the profits from his investment.

Updegraff told your affiant that he received monthly checks and account statements until December of 1995 when he called Low and left a message requesting a withdrawal of $1200.00. Updegraff said he never received a return call from Low. Updegraff said he finally spoke with Low in January of 1996. During that conversation, Low told him that he was having a problem with the FBI and all of the Four Seasons accounts had been frozen by them (the FBI). Updegraff said that Low assured him that "everything would work out soon." Updegraff said soon after that he received an account statement (his last) from Low. This statement indicated that he had an account balance of approximately $112,000.00. Updegraff said that he telephoned Low several times over the next few months in order to ascertain the status of his funds. Then in April of 1996, he received a telephone call from Jean Snyder. Snyder said that she had arranged a four-way conference call between she, Low, Updegraff, and Lilly Vickson. Snyder then told Updegraff that all of their investments were gone. Updegraff asked Low if this was true. Low replied, "The way it looks . . . yes." Low then explained that he had lost all of their money in bad stock investments. Updegraff asked Low if he (Low) could get the money back. Low replied he might be able to, but it would take time. Updegraff said that due to the shock of the bad news he had just received he failed to ask specifics about how the money was lost and why his statements had shown a profit until then. Updegraff said he last spoke with Low on 5/3/97. During that conversation Low said that the money was gone due to bad investments he (Low) made.

Your affiant asked Updegraff how much money the Snyders and Lilly Vickson had invested with Low. Updegraff replied that the Snyders had invested $30,000.00 and Lilly Vickson had invested $16,000.00. Updegraff also said that the Snyders also became suspicious in December of 1995, when they received two checks from Low, one was for $6000.00 and the other for $5000.00. Both checks were returned by the bank as "Non Sufficient Funds."

Based on the previously stated facts, it is your affiant's belief that Michael Low is involved with other persons, possibly R. W. Runis, Jay Werelius, and Robert Cohen, in a criminal conspiracy to defraud investors such as the Pritzkau family, Jean and George Snyder, Lilly Vickson, and Daniel Updegraff out of hundreds of thousands of dollars. It is your affiant's belief that Low may be using the name Michael Lowenstein as well as other unknown names as alias' to further his criminal activities. Furthermore, it is your affiant's belief that Low is probably involved in the following "businesses": US Mandate, Four Seasons Investing, Amlin Capital Administration, C.A.P.C.A., Balanced Investment International LTD, Signature Interests Inc, Prosperity Bank and Trust Corp and Artiste Corp. It is your affiant's opinion that Low and his associates are currently involved in other fraudulent schemes as yet undiscovered.

Based on your affiant's training and experience, your affiant is aware that criminal conspiracies frequently involve persons with close personal association. This is necessary because a high degree of trust is frequently necessary for a criminal conspiracy to be successful. Members of the conspiracy must be able to trust each other not to inform law enforcement or the intended victim. Therefore they would be expected to maintain close communication with each other via the telephone, fax machine, written and electronic mail.

In your affiant's experience it is common for persons involved in a criminal conspiracy to maintain lists of telephone numbers and addresses for the other conspirators, and they will also maintain payment records indicating how much money was paid each member of the conspiracy. Additionally, there may be letters, notes or other forms of communication between the conspirators. This type of documentation will enable your affiant to demonstrate the relationship that is believed to exist between all of the previously identified persons. Furthermore, it may serve to identify involved persons who are unknown at this time as well as previously unknown bank accounts and investments.

In your affiant's experience, records such as those previously listed could be located inside file cabinets, locked containers, such as safes, lock boxes and brief cases. Additionally, it is common for these records to stored in electronic storage devices such as computer hard drives, floppy disks, external disks, other removable data storage media such as CD ROM disks, tape drives and so called "Jazz" and "Zip Drives." It is your affiant's opinion that because Low has told your affiant that he is a computer software engineer, it is highly likely that records will be found in the previously mentioned computer storage devices.

In your affiant's experience, it is common for persons involved in criminal conduct to store items such as those listed above inside vehicles under their care and control, in storage lockers, garages, attics, outbuildings, and occasionally buried in the soil of their property. It should be noted that Low told your affiant that at one point in time he maintained a storage locker at an unidentified facility. He also told your affiant that he stored some his documentation related to Four Seasons at his mother's residence. Your affiant also recalled Low had said that during early 1996, he had resided with his parents. Your affiant conducted a computerized records inquiry on Michael Low. Your affiant noted that according to Low's California Driver's History, he listed a residence address of 2906 Overland Ave., Los Angeles CA in 1994. Your affiant noted that this location is in the Rancho Park area of West Los Angeles, the same area as the previously mentioned bank account that Low maintained. Your affiant next conducted a utility check through official law enforcement channels and learned that utilities for that location are paid by Charlotte Low. It is your affiant's belief that this location is the residence of Low's parents and Low may be storing bank records and other evidence that would be valuable to this investigation.

Despite the passage of time, in your affiant's experience it is very common for persons involved in criminal activity centering on fraudulent or stolen documents to maintain some or all of the documents in question even though the actual criminal activity occurred several years prior. In nearly every search warrant service location your affiant has been present at he has noted the presence of documentation/items of evidence that tends to establish the identity of persons who have control of the premises; this documentation/items could consist of utility company bills, rent receipts, mortgage payment receipts, addressed envelopes and keys.

It is your affiant's belief that members of this conspiracy communicate via the telephone and may even use pagers. Therefore your affiant requests to be allowed to answer and monitor all in-coming and out-going calls made from the locations listed in the attached Search Warrant. It is your affiant's belief based on the previously stated facts that if he is allowed to search the locations outlined in the attached Search Warrant for the items listed on said warrant he will find evidence of criminal activity.

Glossary

Acquittal – Result of a judge or jury's not guilty finding at trial.

Admission – Admission of material facts not amounting to guilt. They can be expressed or implied. Less than a confession that infers guilt.

Adversarial System – System used in the United States in which prosecutor verses defense in presenting their sides of the criminal case at trial. The most effective adversary usually convinces the jury that their position about the criminal matter is correct.

Aggravating Circumstances – Circumstances related to the commission of a crime that causes it gravity to be greater than that of an average instance of the given offense. Also see *mitigating circumstances.*

Alibi – The contention that the defendant could not have committed the crime, due to being at another location or involved in other activities at the time of the offense.

Appellate Court – A court whose function is to review the judgments of lower courts.

Arraignment – The appearance before a magistrate after a criminal complaint has been filed or an indictment is returned by a grand jury. The defendant is informed of the formal criminal charges against him, and is given the opportunity to make a plea of guilty or not guilty. If the defendant refuses to make a plea, the magistrate will enter a not guilty plea for him.

Arrest – The taking of a person, either an adult or juvenile, into custody for the purpose of charging them with a criminal offense.

Arrest Warrant – A warrant issued by a judicial officer for the arrest of an individual suspected of committing a crime. Arrest warrants are based upon probable cause as outlined by the affiant.

Attorney – Someone trained in the law and admitted to a state bar, who is authorized to advise, counsel, and represent others in criminal or civil matters. Also known as a lawyer.

Bail – Posting a specified amount of money or surety bond to an officer at the jail facility that is returned upon the suspect appearing in court.

Bail Bond – A formal document that pledges money or property to guarantee the appearance of a defendant. The money or property posted for the bond is forfeited if the defendant does not appear at trial.

Bailiff – A court officer, usually a peace officer, who maintains order in the court during trial proceedings. Bailiffs also provide security for juries during deliberations.

Bail Revocation – The decision of the court to revoke a defendant's posted bail and withdraw his status of release on bail.

Ballistics – Study of the motion of projectiles; firearms examination and identification; spent bullets, empty shell casings and cartridges.

Bench Warrant – An arrest warrant issued by a judicial officer directing any peace officer to take a particular defendant into custody. Bench warrants are usually issued when a defendant has failed to appear or when someone has defied a court order.

Best Evidence Rule – Pertains to documents. The original writing must be produced as evidence, unless there is an adequate explanation why it is not available.

Bind Over – See *held to answer*.

Blanket Immunity – Provides a defendant with immunity for all crimes committed during a specific time period. Seldom granted to defendants.

Blind Mule Defense – The blind mule defense is when someone denies any knowledge of being in possession of something illegal while transporting it.

Booking Process – The booking process is when the police obtain identifying data of the suspect, as well as his photograph and fingerprints.

Brady Material – Material consisting of all exculpatory evidence.

Bulk Evidence – Large amounts of material (i.e. drugs) that cannot be easily moved or stored. Required to be recorded by photograph and video after permission is granted from the prosecutor and court for disposal of the majority of the material.

Burden of Proof – In criminal cases, the government has the burden of proving "beyond a reasonable doubt" that a defendant committed a crime. A reasonable doubt is an honest and reasonable uncertainty about the guilt of the defendant.

In civil cases, the plaintiff has the burden of proving by a "preponderance of the evidence" that a defendant is liable for some tort or civil wrong. Only a simple majority of the jury is needed.

Capital Offense – A criminal offense in which the punishment can be death.

Capital Punishment – The death penalty.

Case Agent – Lead investigator in the criminal investigation that has been brought to trial. The case agent sits at the prosecutor's table in court to offer assistance, since he is most knowledgeable about the evidence. He or she usually has the opportunity to give input to the prosecutor during jury selection. Also see *Case Investigator.*

Case Investigator – Same as *Case Agent.*

Case Law – See *precedent.*

Case Load – The number of matters pending judicial action.

Chain of Custody – The documentation of who located, possessed, and examined physical evidence, from its discovery up to its admission at trial and disposal.

Charge – A written allegation that a particular person committed a specific criminal act. Also referred to as a *count.*

Circumstantial Evidence – Also known as indirect evidence, is evidence that relates to facts other than those in issue.

Citation – Also referred to as a *promise to appear.* A written order issued by a peace officer commanding an alleged misdemeanor offender to appear in a specific court at a given time to answer to the charge. Citations are only issued with the alleged offender's signature in which he promises to appear in court. Without the person's promise to appear, he is taken into custody and required to post bail.

Clan Lab – Clandestine laboratory.

Closing Arguments – An oral summation of a case by the prosecutor or defense attorney to the judge and jury.

Common Law – Laws derived from custom rather than written statutes. Many statutory laws have evolved from common law practices.

Complaint – A written statement of fact, constituting a public offense, made upon an oath or affirmation before a magistrate.

Concurrent Sentence – A term of prison for multiple convictions that is served simultaneously.

Confession – An expressed and complete acknowledgement of guilt as to the commission of a crime.

Consecutive Sentence – A term of prison for multiple convictions, in which one sentence is completed before another can commence.

Consensual Encounter – Police contact with an individual that is voluntary. There is no exercise of police authority over the person being contacted, and he or she is free to leave at anytime.

Conspiracy – An agreement between two or more people to commit a crime constitutes a conspiracy. Reaching an agreement, in itself, is usually insufficient to commit the crime of conspiracy. In most cases, the prosecution must also prove that a member of the conspiracy committed an overt act in furtherance of the conspiracy before the crime of conspiracy is consummated.

Contempt of Court – The intentional obstruction of a court in the administration of justice. Judges may hold someone in contempt for failing to obey a specific judicial order. Prosecutors, defense attorneys, witnesses, spectators, jurors and the defendant may be held in contempt if the judge so orders it.

Conviction – The judgment of the court, based upon a guilty verdict by the jury.

Corroborative Evidence – Additional evidence of a different character to the same point.

Count – See *charge*.

Court – Entity of the judicial branch of government that has the authority to decide criminal and civil cases, as well as disputed matters of fact.

Court Calendar – A court's schedule. Also called a *docket*.

Court of Record – A court where the permanent record of all proceedings is maintained.

Court Jurisdiction – Jurisdiction is the court's right to entertain a particular proceeding and to render a decision.

Court Order – A command or directive issued by a judicial officer while exercising his judicial authority.

Court Reporter – Sometimes referred to as a *court stenographer*, who is present during all courtroom proceedings and records all testimony and oral arguments made during the proceedings.

Corpus Delicti – Elements of a crime, also known as "the body of the crime."

Corroborative Evidence – Additional evidence of a different character to the same point. Anything that corroborates evidence already offered.

Crime – A violation of the criminal laws of a local, state, or the federal government.

Cross Examination – Follows *direct examination*. Questioning of a witness by opposing counsel after direct examination.

Cumulative Evidence – Evidence of the same character to the same point.

Custodian of Records – A person who can authenticate a particular record or document before it is introduced in evidence.

Criminalist – A skilled person who conducts crime scene examinations or laboratory analysis of physical evidence.

Criminalistics – The application of scientific examinations to the detection and evaluation of criminal evidence.

Criminal Evidence – Anything that is offered to prove or disprove a fact.

Criminal Intent – The intentional commission of an act prohibited by law, a determination of the mind.

Criminal Justice – The law of criminal procedure and the enforcement of criminal laws.

Criminal Justice System – The combined divisions of law enforcement, the courts, and corrections.

Criminal Law – Law that relates to violations against society, property, and social order. Also referred to as *penal law*.

Criminal Proceedings – The steps directed by statute or a court in determining whether an adult defendant is guilty or not guilty of a crime.

Custody – The legal physical control over a person or thing.

Declarant – Person making a statement.

Defendant – Someone who has been arrested or indicted, and formally accused of committing a crime.

Defense – Evidence and arguments showing the defendant is not guilty of a criminal act.

Defense Attorney – A hired or appointed licensed trial lawyer who provides the legal defense of a defendant. Also known as a *defense counsel*.

Defense Counsel – See *defense attorney*.

Demonstrative Evidence – See *Physical Evidence*.

Detention – The legally authorized confinement of someone subject to criminal court proceedings.

Diminished Capacity – A defense based upon the defendant's claims of a mental condition that may not absolve him of guilt, but may be relevant to specific mental elements of certain crimes or degrees of crimes.

Direct Evidence – Positive evidence that proves the fact in dispute directly. An example is when an eyewitness testifies that they saw the defendant commit the crime.

Direct Examination – Comes before *cross-examination*. The initial questioning of a witness by either the prosecutor or defense attorney.

Discovery Process – The discovery process is when the prosecutor and the defense disclose to each other certain evidence they intend to introduce at trial. With such disclosure, the parties can prepare in advance to test that evidence through cross-examination or expert testimony, ensuring that the judge or jury hears all sides of the case before they decide guilt.

Disposition – The action of a criminal justice agency signifying that all, or a portion, of the justice process has been completed.

Docket – See *court calendar*.

Double Jeopardy – The double jeopardy clause of the Fifth Amendment to the U.S. Constitution prevents a defendant from being tried twice for the same offense, regardless if the verdict was for conviction or acquittal.

Documentary Evidence – Evidence that can be a hotel registration card, rental car contract, lease agreement, or any other writings that tend to prove a fact.

Due Process – The Fifth, Sixth, and Fourteenth Amendment to the U.S. Constitution guarantees defendants *due process*, meaning the due course of legal proceedings when charged with a criminal offense.

Entrapment – A common defense ploy used in drug and prostitution cases. The entrapment defense is when the defense counsel submits that the defendant had no predisposition to commit the criminal offense until the idea was planted in his mind by law enforcement, solely for the purpose of arresting him.

Evidence Custodian – A law enforcement agency employee, usually a non-sworn civilian, who is responsible for the storage, security, and disposition of collected evidence.

Evidentiary Hearing – A court hearing to determine if evidence should be suppressed, or inadmissible, if it was seized in violation of the Fourth Amendment to the U.S. Constitution. Same as *suppression hearing*.

Exclusionary Rule of Evidence – Prohibits the admissibility of evidence that was illegally obtained by the police. It is a judicial invention conceived to serve as both a remedy and deterrent to police misconduct, and applies to both unlawfully seized evidence and confessions in violation of the U.S. Constitution.

Exculpatory Evidence – Evidence that tends to exonerate the defendant of the offense.

Expert Opinion – Opinion that may be given in sworn testimony about the scientific examination of physical evidence, or the particular investigative procedures used by the police, if the expert possesses the necessary expertise and qualifications to offer such opinions.

Expert Witness – A witness recognized by the court to possess special knowledge, training, and skills to render an opinion and draw conclusions.

Expungement – Upon petitioning the court, a defendant may have his criminal record of the specific charge erased.

Extradition Hearing – A hearing that a defendant is subject to, if arrested outside the jurisdiction where the arrest warrant was issued, to determine if the defendant should be returned to the original court jurisdiction to stand trial.

Field testing kit – A transportable kit used by drug investigators to determine if a substance is most likely a controlled substance.

Felony – A crime punishable by death or imprisonment in a state prison.

Filing – The initiation of a formal criminal case specifying particular charge(s) against a specific individual.

Fine – A monetary penalty imposed by the court upon a convicted defendant.

First Appearance – See *initial appearance*.

Forfeiture – The authorized seizure of money, securities, or property by the government.

Fruits of the Poisonous Tree Doctrine – U.S. Supreme Court decisions following *Mapp* v. *Ohio*, extending the exclusion of evidence located as a result of a Fourth Amendment violation. These cases spawned the doctrine known as *fruits of the poisonous tree*.

Grand Jury – A body of citizens the government presents evidence to when seeking an indictment of a defendant. Grand Juries return *true bills of indictments* when they find that there is sufficient evidence to formally charge a defendant with an offense. Defense attorneys are not allowed to represent a defendant during grand jury proceedings.

Guilty Plea – A defendant's formal acknowledgement of guilt to charge(s) contained in a complaint, information, or indictment.

Handwriting Exemplar – An example of someone's handwriting that will be used for comparison with a questioned document.

Hearsay – Testimony derived from sources other than personal knowledge; secondhand.

Hearsay Rule – Hearsay cannot be used in American courtrooms with some exceptions, as when the person with direct knowledge is either dead or otherwise unable to testify in person.

Held to Answer – If, at the conclusion of a preliminary hearing, the judge finds there is sufficient probably cause to bring the matter to trail, the defendant will be "held to answer" the accusation.

Hung Jury – A jury that fails to reach a verdict after deliberations.

Incompetent To Stand Trial – A finding by the court in criminal proceedings that, as a result of a mental illness, defect, or disability, the defendant is incapable of understanding the nature of the charges and cannot consult with his attorney or aid in his own defense.

Illegally Seized Evidence – Evidence seized by police as a result of violating the provisions of the Fouth Amendment to the U.S. Constitution.

Illegal Search and Seizure – Police conduct in violation of the Fourth Amendment to the U.S. Constitution.

Impeachment – When the credibility of either a prosecution or defense witness is directly challenged.

In Camera – A hearing before a judicial officer in chambers. Not in open court.

Indeterminate Sentence – A sentence in which the period of confinement, instead of being a specific length of time, is for a range of time, such as two to five years. See *Indeterminate Sentencing*.

Indeterminate Sentencing – Criminal punishment that encourages rehabilitation by the use of general and unspecific sentences.

Indictment – A grand jury's formal accusation of a crime. If the grand jury determines that a crime has occurred and there is reason to believe the defendant committed it, a true bill of indictment will be returned to the grand jury. If the defendant is not in custody, an arrest warrant is immediately issued for his arrest.

Indirect Evidence – See *Circumstantial Evidence*.

Information – A formal written accusation of a crime submitted to the court by a prosecutor alleging a particular person committed a specific criminal violation.

Initial Appearance – The judge informs the defendant of the specific charges against him, advises him of his rights, and appoints counsel if he is an indigent. Sometimes called a *first appearance*.

Interrogation – An intensive interview, in which police investigators ask direct questions to a person who is reluctant to tell the truth or provide the information sought.

Jail – A confinement facility operated by a local government, such as a city or county jail, designed to house persons convicted of misdemeanor violations. Also see *prison*.

Judge – An elected or appointed public official who presides over a criminal or civil court of law.

Judgment – A statement of the court's decision that a defendant is either acquitted or convicted of the charged offense(s).

Jurisdiction – The territory, subject matter, or group of people over which a court may exercise lawful authority.

Jurisprudence – The philosophy, study, and science of the law.

Juror – A person who is a member of a trial or grand jury, having been selected for duty.

Jury Consultant – An expert who conducts a scientific analysis of potential jurors to forecast if they will vote guilty or not guilty during deliberations.

Jury Panel – Group of people summoned to appear in court as potential jurors for a particular trial. Also, people selected from the group of potential jurors to be further considered by the prosecution and defense to serve as members of a particular jury.

Jury Selection – Process by which members of a particular jury are selected.

Justice – The principle of fairness and moral equity.

Justification – A legal defense where the defendant admits to committing the criminal act in question, but asserts it was necessary to avoid some greater evil. Self-defense is an example of justification.

Landmark Case – A precedent setting court decision that changes the understanding of due process requirements.

Latent Evidence – Evidence that is not readily seen by the unaided eye, such as a latent fingerprint.

Latent Fingerprint Evidence – Not ordinarily visible; must be searched for.

Law – A rule of conduct enacted by statute that mandates or prohibits certain forms of behavior.

Law Enforcement – A generic name given to agencies responsible for the enforcement of laws, investigation of crime, apprehension of criminals, and the maintaining of public order.

Law Enforcement Officer – A sworn employee of a law enforcement agency who is empowered to make arrests, collect evidence, and perform other duties required by law.

Lawyer – See *attorney*.

Lay Witness – A witness who is not considered to be an expert. Lay witnesses must confine their testimony to facts alone, and are not allowed to draw conclusions or express personal opinions.

Mandatory Sentence – A statutorily required sentence that must be carried out in all cases upon conviction of certain specified crimes.

Material Witness Warrant – Prosecutors can seek a material witness warrant in some venues for persons who are essentially unindicted co-conspirators, and their testimony is necessary for future court proceedings. These witnesses are required to post a bond, and in some cases are incarcerated to ensure their presence at trial.

Miranda rights – Before questioning a suspect beyond ascertaining identifying date, police must inform a suspect of his right to remain silent and to have counsel present during questioning. Also, that an attorney will be provided to him if he cannot afford to hire one. If a person requests an attorney, in most cases, all questioning must stop.

Misdemeanor – In most jurisdictions, a misdemeanor is a crime punishable for less than one year in a county jail facility.

Mistrial – A trial that has been terminated and declared by the trial judge as being invalid, due to some circumstance that created a substantial and uncorrectable prejudice to the conduct of a fair trial.

Mitigating Circumstances – Circumstances related to the commission of the crime that may be considered to reduce the culpability of the defendant. Also see *aggravating circumstances*.

Motive – The reason a person committed a crime.

Negative Evidence – When a witness states that he does not know anything about the event in question.

No Bond – Required when a defendant is accused of a capital offense when proof is evident or the presumption of guilt is great.

Non-Drug Evidence – Any items, such as boxes or suitcases, which contained drugs.

Nolo Contendere – Latin for *No Contest*; the legal equivalent of pleading guilty to a criminal offense that cannot be later used as an admission of guilt.

No Contest – See *nolo contendere*.

Not Guilty – A legal plea entered by the defendant to charges against him.

Not Guilty By Reason of Insanity – A defendant's plea or the verdict of a jury or judge in a criminal proceeding that the defendant is not guilty of the offense, due to him not having the mental capacity to be held criminally responsible for his actions.

Offense – Violation of criminal or traffic laws.

Opening Statement – The initial statement of the prosecutor or defense attorney to the jury.

Opinion – The judge's official announcement of a decision, together with the reasons for the decision.

Original Jurisdiction – The court's authority to hear or act upon a criminal case from its beginning and to pass judgment on the law and the facts.

Overt Act – Anything done to further the goal of a conspiracy. The act does not have to be criminal in nature.

Own Recognizance (O.R.) – The pretrial release of a defendant on his own written promise to appear in court to stand trial.

Parole – Early release from prison, usually based on the prisoner's good behavior and potential of not committing further crime. Many conditions may be placed on the convict before parole is granted.

Parole Board – A state's paroling authority. Most states convene parole boards that will decide when a confined inmate is worthy of conditional release.

Parolee – A person who has been released prior to the completion of his state sentence by a paroling authority. The federal government abolished parole for federal inmates in 1987.

Parole Revocation – The removing of a person from parole status in response to a violation of the conditions of parole.

Parole Violation – An act or omission by a parolee in violation of his conditions for parole.

Penal Code – The written form of criminal laws for a specific jurisdiction.

Penitentiary – See *prison*.

Penal Law – See *criminal law*.

Peremptory Challenges – The right of the prosecutor and defense attorney to challenge a potential juror without providing a reason for the challenge.

Perjury – The intentional lying by a sworn witness on a relevant matter to the case at hand.

Perpetrator – A person who directly commits a criminal act.

Petit Jury – Trial jury.

Physical Evidence – A term long used by police to describe any item of evidence that can be seen, heard, or scientifically examined. Also referred to as *real* or *demonstrative* evidence, it is anything that speaks for itself and requires no explanation, merely its identification through testimony. It can be a firearm, a bullet fragment, a dead body, an ounce of cocaine, a photograph, or a recorded telephone conversation.

Plain View – A legal term that describes readily visible evidence. Police may seize illegal items if they can justify their presence that led them to their observations.

Plea – The defendant's formal answer in court to the charge(s) against him. In most states, the defendant has the option of pleading guilty, not guilty, or no contest.

Plea-Agreement – An agreement between a prosecutor, criminal defense lawyer, and defendant that the defendant will plead guilty in exchange for a reduced sentence or to be charged with a less serious crime.

Plea-Bargain – The process by which a plea-agreement is made.

Positive Evidence – When a witness states that something did or not did not happen, occur, or exist.

Post-Trial Motions – A device to undo a conviction handed down to the defendant, submitted after conviction.

Precedent – Also referred to as case law. It is a principle within the law that ensures that previously judicial decisions are incorporated into future cases.

Pre-Sentence Investigation Report – A report, written by a probation officer, which details a convicted offender's background prior to sentencing by the trial judge.

Pre-Trial Intervention – A program offered to some defendants that diverts them from the criminal court system. A pre-trial intervention program allows some first-time offenders to perform community service in lieu of prosecution, resulting in the dismissal of all criminal charges. This program is used extensively for first-time, non-violent drug offenders.

Pre-Trial Motion – A petition requesting the court to make a specific finding or decision, presented by the defense before commencement of trial.

Pre-Trial Services – Arm of the court that interview a defendant and obtain his criminal history so they can advise the court of bail worthiness. A Pre-trial Service caseworker will gather facts so the court can determine if the defendant is a potential flight risk, a danger to the community, or should be released on his own recognizance. In some cases, they will determine if the defendant is entitled to free legal counsel at government expense.

Prima Facie Evidence – Evidence that stands alone and suffices for the proof of a particular fact until it is contradicted or overcome by other evidence.

Prison – A state or federal confinement facility designed to house convicted adult felons. Also called a penitentiary.

Prisoner – A person lodged into a federal, state, or local detention facility.

Probable Cause – Of a higher standard than mere suspicion. The facts and circumstances that would induce a reasonably intelligent person that a particular person has committed a specific criminal act. Also, the reasonable grounds to make an accusation.

Probable Cause Arrest – Police officers may arrest someone when the officer has reason to believe a crime occurred, and the person being arrested committed the crime.

Probation – A specified period of court supervision in lieu of jail time, in which the defendant may be ordered to not commit any other offenses, seek or maintain employment, not associate with known criminals, and or perform community service and appear before a probation officer who will track his progress and behavior.

Probationer – A person placed on probation status.

Probation Revocation – A court order revoking probation in response to a violation of the terms and conditions of probation.

Probation Violation – An act or omission by a probationer in violation of his probation.

Proffer – Formal offer of information and testimony revealing the involvement and knowledge of the defendant regarding the crime to the police and prosecutor.

Promise To Appear – Similar to a traffic citation in which the suspect signs a written promise to appear in court at a specific time and date, and is then released on his own recognizance.

Prosecutor – An attorney that is elected or appointed as the chief of a prosecuting agency and who has the duty to conduct criminal proceedings on behalf of the state or federal government.

Prosecutorial Discretion – The authority of a prosecutor to file criminal charges and conduct plea-bargaining sessions.

Public Defender -- An attorney employed by a government agency to provide legal defense services to indigent defendants. Also, the head of a public defender office.

Qualitative Analysis – The gross weight of a drug submitted for analysis to the crime laboratory.

Quantitative Analysis – Determination of the purity of a drug submitted to a crime laboratory for analysis.

Real Evidence – See *Physical Evidence*.

Reasonable Doubt – Not possible doubt. It is what jurors experience in their minds after considering the totality of evidence that leaves them unable to conclude the guilt of the defendant. The law does not require the prosecutor present proof to the degree that it eliminates any possibility of error. Only moral certainty is required. The defendant's failure to substantiate his defense does not relieve the prosecutor from his burden to prove guilt beyond a reasonable doubt.

Reasonable Suspicion – The level of suspicion that would justify a police officer in making further inquiries or to conduct a further investigation into a criminal matter. See *probable cause*.

Recidivism – The repetition of criminal behavior by a convicted person.

Recidivist – A convicted person who has committed further crime.

Relevant Evidence – Relates to the case at hand and is confided to the point at issue.

Residential Commitment – A sentence in which the offender is allowed to work during the day, but must reside at night at the confinement facility.

Restitution – A court ordered requirement that a convicted defendant pay money to provide services to the victim of the crime. Providing community services is sometimes considered restitution.

Restraining Order – This order prohibits the person suspected of committing violence against, or otherwise harassing someone from having any contact with the victim, under penalty of criminal charges. The court will schedule a hearing within ten days of issuing this temporary restraining order, for the purpose of determining whether to grant a permanent restraining order.

Revocation Hearing – A hearing held before a parole or probation board to determine if the parolee or probationer has violated the conditions of his parole or probation.

Rules of Evidence – Rules that govern the admissibility of evidence at criminal hearings and trials.

Search Incidental To An Arrest – A warrantless search of an arrested person for officer safety purposes. Courts have recognized that many arrested persons carry weapons on or around their person that may be used against law enforcement officials.

Search Warrant – An order issued by a judicial officer directing a law enforcement officer to conduct a search of a specified location for particular items related to a crime, and to seize the property if found.

Self-Defense – The justification that the person responsible for an act that would otherwise constitute a criminal offense, reasonably believed that his actions were necessary to protect himself or his property from immediate danger.

Sentence – The penalty imposed by a court upon conviction of a crime.

Sentencing Disposition – Disposition by the court after a defendant's conviction that is expressed as a penalty, such as payment of a fine or imprisonment.

Sentencing Hearing – A hearing where the court or jury considers relevant evidence and information, mitigating and aggravating circumstances, to determine a sentencing disposition for the convicted defendant.

Sequestered Jury – An isolated jury from the public during the course of a trial, including deliberation.

Sidebar – A conference between a judge and the attorneys during a case being tried, held outside of the jury's range of hearing.

Spontaneous Outburst – A voluntary incriminating statement made by a defendant that was not in response to a question.

Suppression Hearing – A court hearing to determine if evidence should be suppressed, or inadmissible, if it was seized in violation of the Fourth Amendment to the U.S. Constitution. Same as *evidentiary hearing*.

Stare Decisis – "Standing by decided matters." Legal principle that in subsequent cases on similar issues of law, courts are bound by their earlier decisions and by the decisions of higher courts over them.

State Action Doctrine – Long-standing principle that only government officials in the criminal justice process can be held accountable for violating someone's civil rights.

State Court System – Almost every state has three court levels: trial courts, appellate courts, and a state supreme court.

Status Offender – A person who commits a criminal act by virtue of being a juvenile. Examples of status offenses may include purchasing cigarettes, alcohol, or truancy.

Statutory Law – Codified law enacted by a government body having the authority to make laws.

Stay of Execution – The halting of the implementation of a judgment (sentence) by a court.

Stop and Frisk – Known also as an "investigative stop." A superficial examination of a suspect by an officer to discover weapons or other things related to criminal activity.

Subpoena – A grand jury or court's written order requiring an individual to either appear in court and give testimony or bring specified material. Other subpoenas, sometimes called "administrative subpoenas," are issued by government agencies requiring certain documents other than bank records.

Subpoena Duces Tecum – A subpoena compelling a witness to bring with them specified documents, records, or business records to court.

Super Labs – A clandestine laboratory capable of producing 10 or more pounds of methamphetamine.

Suspended Sentence – A court's decision to delay the imposition of a sentence for a specified or unspecified period of time.

Suppression Hearing – A court hearing to determine if evidence should be suppressed, or inadmissible, if it was seized in violation of the Fourth Amendment to the U.S. Constitution.

Statutes of Limitation – Limits the maximum time period in which a prosecutor can present formal charges.

Supervized O.R. Release – The pretrial release of a defendant on conditions set by the judge to avoid contact with an alleged victim, other defendants, reporting person, and other witnesses. The defendant may be required to report to a supervized realease program case office, while undergoing trail.

Suppression Motion – A motion made by the defense to suppress evidence. Suppression motions usually stem from police conduct, for example, searching a home without a valid search warrant.

Suspect – Someone thought to be responsible for the commission of a crime, but not yet arrested or indicted.

Tangible Evidence – See *Physical Evidence.*

Testimony – Oral evidence given by a sworn witness.

Testimonial Evidence – A witness, under oath, communicates through testimony to the jury what he or she has seen, heard, or done.

Testimonial Privilege – The law recognizes the sanctity of certain relationships and encourages freedom of communication between persons engaged in those relationships. Because free communication would be hampered if one of the parties is later required to divulge what was communicated in court, the law grants certain carefully limited privileges not to testify concerning confidential communications.

Third Party Custody – A third party, usually a relative, cosigns a release order guaranteeing that the defendant attends trail and that no conditions of the defendant's release are violated.

Thresholds – Minimum required, such as amount of drugs possessed, before indictment will be sought.

Trial – The examination in a court of the issues, facts, law, and evidence to reach a judgment of conviction or acquittal.

Trial Judge – The judicial officer who is authorized to conduct jury and nonjury trials, but does not hear appellate cases. A judicial officer who conducts the trial.

Trial Jury – A statutory defined number of people selected and sworn to determine the facts presented at trial and to render a verdict. Also called a petit jury.

Triers of Fact – Jurors.

True Bill of Indictment – See *Indictment*.

Unsecured Appearance Bond – An order signed by the defendant on release, stating that he will execute an appearance bond, binding him to pay the state a designated sum of money should he fail to appear at trial.

Unconditional Release – The final release of a prisoner from the control and jurisdiction of a correctional facility. Also, the final release from the jurisdiction of a specific court.

Use Immunity – The granting of immunity to a defendant for certain, specific crimes committed during a particular time period.

Venue – The locality where a crime is committed or political subdivision from which a jury is called and in which a trial is held.

Verdict – The decision of the jury or judge after deliberations.

Victim – The person who has suffered either death, physical, or mental anguish, or has lost property as a direct result of a criminal offense.

Victim-Impact Statement – Statement by a victim or survivor supplied to the court so as to make a better sentencing judgment.

Waiver of Search and Seizure – As a condition of parole, a parolee is usually required to waive his Fourth Amendment rights to search and seizure. Once signed, the parolee is subject to search at any time by parole agents or peace officers.

Warrant – An order issued by a judicial officer in criminal proceedings, directing a law enforcement officer to perform a specified act.

Witness – Someone who has knowledge of the circumstances of a particular criminal case. One who testifies about what they say, heard, or did, or is an expert in a particular field.

Writ of Certiorari – An order issued from an appellate court, demanding the record of a lower court's proceedings.

Writ of Habeas Corpus – A court directive directing a person or agency detaining a prisoner to bring him to the court to determine the lawfulness of the imprisonment.

Index

Abandoned property, 110–112
Acquittal, 10, 335
Admission, 8, 196, 217, 266–267, 335
Adversarial system, 10, 335
Affidavits (*see* Arrest warrant; Search warrant)
Aggravating circumstances, 36, 335
Aguilar-Spinelli test, 115–117, 119, 120
Alibi, 64, 335
American Bar Association, 49
Appeals, 57, 58
    appellate decision, 37
    review of Court of Appeals' decision,
      37–38
Appellate court, 37, 57, 335
Appointed counsel, 61
Arraignment, 32, 335
Arrest, 23–24, 40, 336
Arrest warrant, 81, 336
    sealed, 83
Assigned counsel, 61
Assistant U.S. Attorneys (AUSAs), 79
Attenuation, 95–96
Attorney, 49–50, 60, 336
Audiotape, 180, 182, 184–186

Bail, 24, 26, 27–28, 336
Bail bond, 336

Bail revocation, 336
Bailiff, 336
Ballistics, 336
Bench warrant, 32, 336
Best evidence rule, 4, 336
Bind over (*see* Held to answer)
Blanket immunity, 84, 336
Blind mule defense, 65–66, 336
Body intrusions, 162
Body wires, 186–187
Booking process, 23–24, 210, 336
Brady Material, 16–17, 336
Bulk evidence, 180, 336
Burden of proof, 10–11, 46, 336–337
Bureau of Alcohol, Tobacco, Firearms
    and Explosives, 16
Bureau of Immigration and Customs
    Enforcement (ICE), 136–137

Capital offense, 36, 65, 337
Capital punishment, 337
Case agent, 87, 337
Case investigator (*see* Case agent)
Case law (*see* Precedent)
Case load, 337
Chain of custody, 157, 337
Challenges for cause, 87

Challenges of array, 87
Change of plea, 46–47
Character witness, 229–230
Charge, 337
Child witness, 225
Circumstantial evidence, 2–3, 66, 337
Citation, 337
City attorney (*see* Prosecutor)
Clan lab (clandestine laboratory), 141,
     179–180, 337
Clerk of court, 37
Closing arguments, 337
Co-conspirator statements, 265–266
Code of Federal Regulations (CFR), 144
Common law, 337
Competent witness, 6, 221
Complaint, 22–23, 41, 337
Computer evidence, 171, 192–194
Concealed microphones, 187–188
Concurrent sentence, 36, 337
Confession, 8, 57, 196, 217–218, 266–267, 337
     coerced, 92
     voluntariness, 197–198
Consecutive sentence, 36, 337
Consensual encounter, 337
Consent, 63
Conspiracy, 71–73, 80, 337–338
Constitutional protections, 11–13
     Fifth Amendment, 12–13, 92, 199, 201
     Fourth Amendment, 9, 11–12, 90–92,
         94, 104, 109, 123, 126, 134,
         138–139
     Sixth Amendment, 13, 44, 58, 93
Constitutional requirements for search, 123
     anticipatory search warrants,
         128–129
     misstatement of facts, 126–128
     neutral/detached judicial officers, 123
     particularly describing place to be
         searched, 123–124
     persons/things to be seized, 124–126
     probable cause to search, 126
     supported by sworn affidavit, 126
     telephonic search warrants, 128
     timelines, 126
Contempt of court, 338
Control of Hazardous Energy (Lockout/Tagout), 147
Conviction, 11, 338
Corpus Delicti, 8, 338
Corroborative evidence, 4, 119–121, 338
Count (*see* Charge)
County attorney (*see* Prosecutor)
Court, 338
Court calendar, 338
Court jurisdiction, 24–25, 56, 338
Court of record, 338

Court order, 338
Court reporter, 338
Credibility, 7, 117–119, 221–222
     counsel is present, 117
     eyewitnesses, 118
     good citizen informant, 117
     law enforcement official, 118
     past reliability, 117
     statements against penal interest, 117
     victim of the crime, 118
Crime, 11, 12, 22, 25, 33, 49, 56, 80, 338
Crime scene, 141
     chain of custody, 157–158
     personal protective equipment,
         148–150
     summary, 158–159
Crime scene investigator, 3
Crime scene safety, 142
     bloodborne-pathogen, 144–145
     chemical, 145–146
     confined-space, 147
     ingestion, 144
     injection, 144
     light-source, 146–147
     routes of exposure, 142–144
     skin contact, 142, 144
     X-ray, 148
Crime scene search
     approach, 150–151
     evaluate physical evidence possibilities, 153
     final survey, 156
     initial approach, 152
     narrative, 153–154
     photography, 154
     physical evidence collection/recording, 156
     preliminary survey, 153
     preparation, 151–152
     release of crime scene, 157
     sketch, 155–156
Criminal evidence, 338
     definition, 1–2
     purpose, 2
     summary, 19–20
     types, 2–4
Criminal intent, 64–65, 338
Criminal justice, 338
Criminal justice system, 338
Criminal law, 339
Criminal proceedings, 339
Criminalist, 338
Criminalistics, 338
Cross examination, 18–19, 34, 232,
     269, 338
Cumulative evidence, 4, 338
Custodian records, 338
Custody, 35, 40, 52, 339

Declarant, 256, 260, 339
Defendant, 22, 56, 61, 339
    involved in different conspiracy, 71–73
    witness, 228
Defense, 339
Defense attorney, 34, 55–56, 339
    role, 60–62
    strategies, 62–75
    summary, 75–76
Defense counsel (*see* Defense attorney)
Demonstrative evidence (*see* Physical evidence)
Department of Justice (DOJ), 16
Detention, 26–30, 204–207, 339
Digital photographs, 191–192
Diminished capacity, 67, 339
Direct evidence, 2, 339
Direct examination, 18, 339
Disclosure of material, 18
Discovery process, 13–14, 32, 84, 339
Disposition, 339
District attorney (*see* Prosecutor)
Diversion programs, 78
DNA (deoxyribonucleic acid) examination,
    167–170
Docket (*see* Court calendar)
Documentary evidence, 4, 171–175, 339
Double jeopardy, 12, 25, 43, 339
Drug Enforcement Administration (DEA),
    7, 8, 16, 26, 179
Drug evidence, 62–63, 125, 176–179
    bulk, 180
    clandestine laboratories, 179–180
    field testing kit, 178–179
    informant witnesses, 230–231
    non-drug evidence, 180
    search warrants, 136–137
Due process, 14, 17, 208, 339
Duty judge, 122–123
Dying declarations, 264–265

Entrapment, 62–63, 339–340
Evidence custodian, 157–158, 340
Evidence materiality, 8
Evidentiary hearing, 9, 92, 340
Exclusionary rule of evidence, 8–10, 90–92, 340
    attenuation, 95–96
    collateral use of evidence seized in violation
        of Fourth Amendment, 104
    exceptions, 93–104
    fruit of the poisonous tree, 92–93
    good faith, 94–95
    independent source, 96–98
    inevitable discovery, 99–103
    principle of stare decisis, 105
    standing, 95–96
    summary, 105–106

Exculpatory evidence, 16, 340
Exigent circumstances, 129–134
Expert evidence, 4
Expert opinion, 340
Expert witness, 35, 61, 238–240, 340
    alcohol and drug intoxication, 240
    audio tape examinations, 240
    bit mark analysis, 240
    blood grouping/spatter analysis,
        240–241
    categories, 240–246
    criminal profiling, 241
    DNA, 241
    eyewitness identification, 241
    fingerprint identification, 241
    firearms examiners, 241
    forensic anthropology, 242
    forensic biology, 242
    forensic engineering, 242
    forensic entomology, 242
    forensic odontology, 242
    forensic pathology, 242
    forensic physical science, 242
    forensic psychiatry, 243
    hair and fiber analysis, 243
    hired guns, 248–253, 248–255
    hypnosis, 243
    microtrace analysis, 243
    neutron activation analysis, 243
    photography, 243
    physical and mental condition, 243
    polygraphers, 243–244
    questioned document examination, 244
    sketch artists, 244
    soil sample analysis, 244
    speed detection devices, 244
    summary, 253–254
    tool mark analysis, 244–245
    toxicology, 245
    traffic accident reconstruction, 245
    truth serum results, 245
    typewriter comparison, 245
    voice comparisons, 246
    voir dire, 246–247
Expungement, 340
Extradition hearing, 25, 340
Eyewitness, 118

Factors that may warrant departure
    from guidelines, 55
    addendum, 55
Federal Bureau of Investigation
    (FBI), 16
Federal Constitution, 9
Federal court, 9
Federal Rules of Criminal Procedure, 14

Federal Rules of Evidence, 14
    authentication, 310–313
    contents of writing, recordings,
        photographs, 313–315
    general provisions, 285–289
    hearsay, 303–310
    judicial notice, 289–290
    miscellaneous rules, 315–317
    opinions and expert testimony, 301–303
    presumptions in civil actions/proceedings, 290
    privileges, 296
    relevancy and its limits, 290–296
    witnesses, 296–301
Felony, 23, 340
Field testing kit, 178–179, 340
Filing, 340
Fine, 340
Firearms examiner, 3, 166, 241
First appearance (*see* Initial appearance)
Forensic experts, 242–243
Forfeiture, 340
Fruits of the poisonous tree doctrine, 9,
        92–93, 340
Fundamental fairness (*see* Due process)

Giglio issues, 18
Government conduct, 73–75
Grand jury, 30–31, 82, 340
Guilty plea, 41–42, 341

Hairs and fibers examinations, 170–171
Handwriting exemplar, 171–173, 341
Health and safety (*see* Crime scene safety;
        Personal protective equipment)
Hearsay evidence, 255–256
    conduct, 255–256
    exceptions, 256, 261–269
    summary, 269–270
Hearsay evidence admissions, 256
    absence of entry in records, 257
    absence of public record or entry, 258
    excited utterance, 256
    family records, 258
    forfeiture by wrongdoing, 261
    former testimony, 260–261
    judgment of previous conviction, 269
    judgments as proof of matters of personal,
        family, general history, boundaries, 269
    learned treatises, 269
    market reports, commercial
        publications, 269
    marriage, baptismal, similar certificates, 258
    other exceptions, 260
    present sense impression, 256
    public records and reports, 257–258
    recorded recollection, 257

records of documents affecting an interest
    in property, 258
records of regularly conducted
    activity, 257
records of religious organizations, 258
records of vital statistics, 258
reputation as to character, 269
reputation concerning boundaries/general
    history, 269
reputation concerning personal/family
    history, 269
statement against interest, 261
statement for purposes of medical
    diagnosis/treatment, 257
statement of personal/family history, 261
statement under belief of impending
    death, 261
statements in ancient documents, 269
statements in documents affecting
    an interest in property, 258–259
then existing mental, emotional, physical
    condition, 256
Hearsay evidence exceptions
    admissions and confessions, 266–267
    business records, 269
    declarations against penal interests, 268
    dying declarations, 264–265
    hostile witness, 262–263
    Miranda warnings, 267–268
    prior statements, 263
    public a private records, 269
    spontaneous outbursts, 263
    statements by co-conspirators,
        265–266
    written statements, 261–262
Hearsay rule, 10, 341
Hearsay within hearsay, 264
Held to answer, 31, 341
Henthorn issues, 15–16
Homeland Security, 16
Hostile witness, 262–263
Hung jury, 35, 341

Identity, 63–64
Illegal search and seizure, 341
Illegally seized evidence, 341
Immunity, 83–84, 274
Impeachment, 4, 16, 34, 222, 341
In camera, 15, 341
Incompetent to stand trial, 341
Independent source, 96–98
Indeterminate sentence, 341
Indeterminate sentencing, 341
Indictment, 30–31, 40, 41, 79, 82, 341
Indirect evidence (*see* Circumstantial evidence)
Inevitable discovery, 99–103

Informant, 73–74, 115–116, 230–232
    confidential privilege, 280–282
    credibility, 7–8
    good citizen, 117
Information, 14, 41, 55, 83, 115–116, 118,
        121–122, 162–163, 196, 341
Initial appearance, 26, 341
Insanity
    legal, 67–71
    not guilty by reason of insanity, 43, 343
    present sanity, 43, 85
Integrity photograph, 150
Interrogation, 197, 199–200, 210–211, 341

Jail, 23, 33, 36, 37, 342. (*see also* Prison)
Jailhouse witness, 221, 232–234
Jencks Material, 17
Judge, 10, 13, 27, 31, 32, 36, 122–123, 342
Judgment, 85–86, 342
Judicial officers, 123
Jurisdiction, 25, 63, 342
Jurisprudence, 342
Juror, 198, 342
Jury consultant, 87, 342
Jury panel, 342
Jury selection, 34, 86–88, 342
Justice, 342
Justification, 342

Landmark case, 109, 342
Latent evidence, 342
Latent fingerprint evidence, 164–165,
        176, 342
Law, 342
Lawyer (*see* Attorney)
Lay witness, 220–221, 223–225, 342
Legal insanity, 67–71
Legal justification, 66–67
Logical inferences, 112–113

Mandatory sentence, 342
Material witness warrant, 82, 343
Medical examiner, 3
Military attorney, 11
Miranda rights, 12–13, 92, 199, 202–203,
        212–214, 218, 343
Miranda warnings
    ambiguous responses, 214–215
    detention settings, 204–207
    elements, 211–217
    evidence confrontation, 210
    exception to hearsay evidence, 267–268
    in-custody interrogation settings,
        210–211
    non-custodial settings, 203–204
    non-interrogation questions, 210

spontaneous outbursts, 207–209
    suspect's physical condition, 216–217
    trickery and deceit, 215–216
    waiver of Miranda rights, 212–214
Miscarriage of justice, 57
Misdemeanor, 23, 37, 343
Misstatement of fact, 126–128
Mistrial, 35, 85, 343
Mitigating circumstances, 36, 48, 343
Motions, 32–33, 45–46
Motive, 64, 343
Multiple-defendant case, 11, 84
Municipal court, 25

National Integrated Ballistics Information
        Network, 166
National Labor Relations Act, 17
Negative evidence, 4, 343
No bond, 28, 343
No contest (*see* Nolo contendere)
Nolo contendere, 32, 42–43, 343
Non-drug evidence, 176, 180, 343
Not guilty, 11, 35, 41, 343
Not guilty by reason of insanity, 43, 343

Occupational Safety and Health
        Administration (OSHA), 147
Offense, 343
Opening statement, 343
Opinion, 10, 343
Original jurisdiction, 343
Overt act, 71, 80, 343
Own recognition (O.R.), 27, 344

Paint examinations, 175–176
Parole, 36, 48, 50, 344
Parole board, 344
Parole revocation, 9, 344
Parole violation, 344
Parolee, 36, 344
Penal code, 344
Penal law (*see* Criminal law)
Penitentiary (*see* Prison)
Peremptory challenges, 34, 87, 344
Perjury, 344
Perpetrator, 344
Personal protective equipment, 148
    eye protection, 149
    foot protection, 149
    hand protection, 148–149
    head protection, 150
    respiratory protection, 149–150
Petit jury, 344
Petition, 37–38
Photocopy exemplars, 174
Photographic equipment, 182, 191–192

Physical evidence, 3–4, 161, 344
    computer, 171
    DNA, 167–170
    drug evidence, 176–180
    fingerprints, 163–165
    firearms, 166–167
    hairs and fibers, 170
    paint, 175–176
    questioned documents, 171–175
    ropes and cords, 176
    summary, 181
    types, 162–176
Plain view, 109–110, 138, 344
Plea, 344
Plea-agreement, 344
Plea-bargain, 33, 37, 41, 49, 61, 78, 83, 344
Pleadings, 41, 58
Police, 22, 23, 32, 49, 62, 80, 83, 113, 115
Police credibility, 15–16, 127
Police witness, 225–226
    avoid distracting behavior, 227
    avoid police vernacular, 227
    be conscious of body language, 128
    be prepared, 226
    be well groomed, 227
    discretely communicate with
        prosecutor, 227
    look at the jury, 128
    professional appearance, 226
    show respect, 227–228
    to be on time is to be late, 227
Positive evidence, 4, 344
Post-conviction appeals, 37
Post-trial motions, 85, 344
    motion for a mistrial, 85
    motion for a new trial, 86
    motion for arrest of judgment, 85–86
Pre-sentence Investigation Report (PSI),
        36, 50, 345
    adjustment for acceptance
        of responsibility, 52
    adjustment for obstruction of justice, 52
    criminal convictions, 53
    criminal history computation, 53
    custody status, 52
    defendant's juvenile criminal history, 53
    face sheet, 51
    impact of plea agreement, 55
    impact on victim, 52
    offender characteristics, 54
    offense behavior not part of relevant
        conduct, 53
    offense, charges, conviction(s), 51
    offense conduct, 51–52
    offense level computation, 52–53
    other arrests, 54

    other criminal conduct, 54
    pending charges, 54
    sentencing options, 54
Pre-trial intervention, 345
Pre-trial motions, 84, 345
    motion for bill of particulars, 85
    motion for change of venue, 85
    motion for continuance, 85
    motion for discovery, 84
    motion for severance of defendants, 85
    motion for severance of offenses, 85
    motion to determine present sanity, 85
    motion to dismiss charges, 84
    motion to suppress evidence, 85
Pre-trial services, 25–26, 345
Precedent, 37, 345
Preliminary hearing, 31, 312
Pretrial Services, 25–26
Prima facie evidence, 4, 345
Prison, 33, 36, 37, 345. (*see also* Jail)
Prisoner, 345
Private criminal lawyers, 60
Probable cause, 12, 108, 345
    basis of belief, 115–117
    corroboration, 119–121
    credibility, 117–119
    establishing, 115–123
    hearsay on hearsay, 121–123
    logical inferences, 112–113
    professional inferences, 114–115
    time affects probability, 113–114
Probable cause arrest, 23, 345
Probation, 36, 48, 345
Probation officer, 50, 55
Probation revocation, 37, 48–49, 345
Probation violation, 37, 345
Probationer, 345
Professional inferences, 114–115
Proffer, 83, 345
Promise to appear, 24, 345
Prosecutor, 49, 346
    coordination with, 80–81
    grand jury proceedings, 82
    issuing of warrants, 81–82
    jury selection, 86–88
    offers of immunity, 83–84
    plea bargaining, 83
    post-trial motions, 85–86
    pre-trial motions, 84–85
    role, 77–88
    sealed indictments/arrest
        warrants, 83
    subpoenas, 82
    summary, 88–89
Prosecutorial discretion, 78–79, 346
Public defender, 60–61, 346

Qualitative analysis, 177, 346
Quantitative analysis, 177, 346

Real evidence (*see* Physical evidence)
Reasonable doubt, 11, 43, 346
Reasonable expectation of privacy test,
        109–111
Reasonable search
        abandoned property, 110–112
        plain view, 109–110
Recidivism, 346
Recidivist, 346
Relevant evidence, 6, 8, 346
Residential commitment, 346
Restitution, 36, 346
Restraining order, 346
Revocation hearing, 346
Right to an attorney, 198–199
Right to remain silent, 199–202
Rope and cord, 176
Rules of evidence, 5–8, 346
        material requests, 14–15

Sanity (*see* Insanity)
Sealed indictment, 31, 83
Search incidental to an arrest, 347
Search warrant, 81, 108–109, 118, 347
        anticipatory, 128–129
        Constitutional requirements, 123–129
        establishing probable cause, 115–123
        execution, 134–138
        exigent circumstances, 129–134
        extent of search, 137
        knock and notice, 136–137
        life of a warrant, 135
        manner of entry, 137
        officers present, 134–135
        probable cause, 112–115
        reasonableness, 109–112
        receipt for seized property, 138
        returning warrant to court, 138
        sample affidavit, 322–334
        search time, 138
        summary, 138–139
        telephonic, 128
        things to be seized, 138
        time of day, 135–136
        use of force, 137
        warrantless searches, 129–134
Secured Appearance Bond, 28
Self-defense, 66–67, 347
Self-incrimination, 273–274
Sentence, 36–37, 47–49, 347
Sentence Reform Act (1984), 50
Sentencing disposition, 347
Sentencing guidelines, 50–55

Sentencing hearing, 347
Sequestered jury, 347
Sexual crime, 56, 63
Sidebar, 347
Solicitor (*see* Prosecutor)
Speedy trial, 33–34, 44
Spontaneous outburst, 207–209, 263, 347
stare decisis, 105, 347
State action doctrine, 347
State court system, 25, 347
State's attorney (*see* Prosecutor)
Status offender, 347
Statutes of limitation, 44–45, 348
Statutory law, 347
Stay of execution, 347
Stop and frisk, 347
Subpoena, 82, 348
Subpoena duces tecum, 348
Summons, 23
Super labs, 179, 348
Superior court, 25, 37
Supervised O.R. Release, 27, 348
Suppression hearing, 9, 91–92, 94, 347, 348
Suppression motion, 46, 85, 348
Supreme Court, 26, 37–38, 90–91, 109, 162,
        205, 208–209
Suspect, 22, 348
Suspended sentence, 348

Tangible evidence (*see* Physical evidence)
Technology, 182–195
Testimonial privilege, 272–273, 348
        attorney–client, 275–276
        clergy–confessor, 279
        confidential informant privilege, 280–282
        husband–wife, 276–278
        immunity from prosecution, 274
        official information privilege, 279–280
        physician–patient, 278–279
        psychotherapist–patient, 278–279
        self-incrimination, 273–274
        summary, 283–284
Testimony, 4, 18, 19, 255, 260–261, 348
Third party custody, 27–28, 348
Thresholds, 78–79, 348
Trial, 31, 34–36, 348
Trial by surprise, 13–14
Trial judge, 197–198, 246, 348
Trial jury, 349
Trial process, 10, 22–23
        arraignment, 32
        arrest, 23–24
        change of plea, 33
        court jurisdiction, 24–25
        detention hearing, 26–30
        discovery, 32

grand jury, 30–31
  indigence determination, 25–26
  initial appearance hearing, 26
  motions, 32–33
  post-conviction appeals/pleadings, 37–38
  preliminary hearing, 31–32
  sentencing, 36–37
  speedy trial issues, 33–34
  summary, 38–39
  trial, 34–36
Triers of fact, 35, 349
True bill of indictment (*see* Indictment)
Typewriters, 173–174, 245

Unconditional release, 349
Unsecured appearance bond, 28, 349
U.S. Attorney (*see* Prosecutor)
U.S. Marshall Service, 16
U.S. Sentencing Commission, 50
Use immunity, 84, 349

Venue, 80, 349
Verdict, 35, 349

Vicarious liability, 265
Victim, 49, 56, 118, 349
Victim-impact statement, 349
Videotape, 182, 190–191
Voir Dire, 246–247
Voluntariness, 197–198, 217, 268

Waiver of search and seizure, 36, 349
Wannabe informants, 231
Warrant, 23, 92, 349. (*see also* Arrest warrant;
    Search warrant)
Wiretaps, 188–190
Witness, 220–221, 349
  competency, 221
  credibility, 7, 221–222
  exclusion in the courtroom, 235
  impeachment, 222
  prior inconsistent statements,
    222–223
  summary, 235–237
  types, 223–234
Writ of certiorari, 349
Writ of habeas corpus, 349